AMONG THE ELEVATORS.

From photograph by George Barker, Niagara Falls.

William J. Brown

American Colossus: The Grain Elevator, 1843 to 1943

Colossal Books
Cincinnati, Ohio

First published March 2009

Colossal Books
POB 20201
Cincinnati, OH 45220

www.american-colossus.com

ISBN 978-0-578-01261-2

Frontispiece: illustration accompanying article by Jane Meade Welch, "The City Of Buffalo," *Harper's Monthly*, July 1885, p. 197. Reproduced courtesy Maritime History of the Great Lakes.

Printed and bound in the USA.

"The New Colossus"

Not like the brazen giant of Greek fame
With conquering limbs astride from land to land;
Here at our sea-washed, sunset gates shall stand
A mighty woman with a torch, whose flame
Is the imprisoned lightning, and her name
Mother of Exiles. From her beacon-hand
Glows world-wide welcome; her mild eyes command
The air-bridged harbor that twin cities frame,
"Keep, ancient lands, your storied pomp!" cries she
With silent lips. "Give me your tired, your poor,
Your huddled masses yearning to breathe free,
The wretched refuse of your teeming shore,
Send these, the homeless, tempest-tossed to me,
I lift my lamp beside the golden door!"

– Emma Lazarus, New York City, 1883

"The American Colossus was fiercely intent on appropriating and exploiting the riches of all continents – grasping with both hands, reaping where he had not sown, wasting what he thought would last forever. New railroads were opening new territory. The exploiters were pushing farther and farther into the wilderness. The man who could get his hands on the biggest slice of natural resources was the best citizen. Wealth and virtue were supposed to trot in double harness."

– Gifford Pinchot, *Breaking New Ground*, 1946

Table of Contents

Preface

"The history of any passed era is obviously tied to the knowledge, experience and discoveries of the present. There is also a continual dialectic between one and the other of these terms, which often favors their reconsideration and enrichment. But, nevertheless, at certain moments of regression and brutalization, one can quite easily organize the forgetting of the past, its reductive re-writing, so as to obtain the cumulative augmentation – not of discoveries of the real facts – but, on the contrary, ridiculous legends that are useful to the dominant interests, deliberate ignorance, etc. Our society has made progress in decadence; and it re-reads all of its past with the eyes and techniques of its most recent progress." (Guy Debord to Pascal Dumontier, letter dated 24 October 1989.)

Despite their initially banal appearance, grain elevators have been great sources of aesthetic and technical interest across such specialized fields as modernist architecture, industrial archeology, agricultural history, and the business of industrial commodities. Though other books about grain elevators have been published in the last 25 years, none of them focuses as intently and productively on the circumstances and consequences of their invention as does this one by William Brown, which is an important contribution to the field and the best book on the subject in quite some time. Brown works hard to define not only the architectural and technological significance of these magnificent industrial artifacts, but also the blurry space in between those two poles. As a result, Brown's history of the American grain elevator will be welcomed in a number of disciplines and institutions. Written over the course of 15 years, Brown's history is built on in-depth research, buttressed by intensely personal experience and observation. Receiving his Ph.D. in American Literature from the State University of New York at Buffalo, Brown lived and worked in Buffalo for several years. While there, he developed an intimate knowledge of the city's spectacular collection of abandoned grain elevators by observing, climbing and exploring them.

A generalist both in spirit and by training, Brown reformulates the history of the grain elevator by consulting the broadest variety of voices and sources. Brown places the invention of the world's first mechanized grain elevator (the Dart) in the contexts of American history and geography with the construction of the Erie Canal and its connection to the Great Lakes; engineering and mechanical design with the construction of fireproofed warehouses; and the international grain trade, financial speculation and capitalism in general. But Brown also calls upon biblical mythology and modern poetry to explain why these buildings, which have apparently been seen as either monstrously ugly or sublimely beautiful, continue to fascinate so many in both Europe and the United States. This makes Brown's narrative voice unique, and his book a valuable resource.

Though it focuses upon Buffalo, the city in which the grain elevator was invented and perfected, Brown's history also examines the beginnings of the grain trade in several other key cities, including Minneapolis, Montreal, New York, Chicago and New Orleans. There are even discussions of grain elevators built in Argentina, France, Germany, Iraq and the Soviet Union. When necessary, Brown has translated documents from the original French, which allows us better access to information about grain elevators built in Montreal, and he has double-checked existing translations from the original German, which helps us re-evaluate the fantastic claims made about American *getreidespeicher* by European modernist architects in the 1910s and 1920s (many of these architects were German). Brown's scope and methodology perfectly suits a trade in which the local, national and international levels are closely linked.

Brown's other achievement in this book is that he challenges us to reconsider the myths and propaganda that surround the origins of modern architecture in both Europe and America. As a Harvard trained architect myself, I especially appreciate how Brown gives a thorough examination to the legacy of Walter Gropius, in a way that only someone outside the field of architecture could. The heart of Brown's book is the assertion that all of the developments and conditions that one associates with the 1880s and 1890s (the first skyscrapers and the birth of the modern city) were already present 50 years previously, when the first grain elevators were built. If he is right, then Brown's history has made an important contribution to our understanding of the origins of the American identity, the modern city, and architectural modern architecture itself, all of which may have been emerging much earlier than has previously been considered. And though it is primarily a work of historical research, Brown's book is highly relevant to our post-industrial culture, in which American grain remains one of the world's most important commodities and American grain elevators continue to be formidable monuments that function as critical links in the global food supply chain.

Marshall Brown
Urban Designer and Architect
Assistant Professor, Illinois Institute of Technology

iv

Acknowledgments

I would like to thank the Humanities Division of the Rhode Island School of Design for providing the funds that allowed me to travel to Buffalo, New York, in 1991 and 1992, and the Fulbright Scholar Program (U.S. Department of State, Bureau of Educational and Cultural Affairs), for providing me with the opportunity to live in and travel throughout Europe in 1992 and 1993. I would also like to thank the staffs of the Buffalo and Erie County Historical Society, the Robert A. Deshon and Karl J. Schlachter Library for Design, Architecture, Art, and Planning at the University of Cincinnati, and the Architecture & Planning Library at the University of Buffalo, State University of New York. Thanks go to the many scholars in the field who came before me, but especially Peter Reyner Banham, Henry H. Baxter, William Cronon, Robert M. Frame III, Francis R. Kowsky, Thomas E. Leary, and Elisabeth C. Sholes. My good friend, Orrin Bram Pava, accompanied me on all my explorations of Buffalo's grain elevators. To him I give special thanks.

Introduction

Some of my readers may already be familiar with grain elevators because they grew up on or near a farm, at which these simple mechanical devices – buckets attached to revolving, vertically arrayed conveyor belts that can be powered by horses or small engines – are widely used to scoop up piles of loose grain and bring them to the top of the structure to which the elevator is attached. Once at the top, the grain can, using the force of gravity, be sent down into a scale and weighed, and then sent into a waiting railcar, truck or barge, or, if need be, into a grain bin for temporary storage. (Gravity will once again be used to conduct the grain down through the bin's bottom and into a pit, from which the grain will be elevated once more, weighed once more, and then sent by chutes or spouts into a railcar, truck or barge). Such readers may wonder why grain elevators, or any other ubiquitous and apparently ordinary invention, for that matter, would merit an entire book.[1]

But to most of my readers, the subject of grain elevators will be an unfamiliar one. Indeed, some readers may even find the very phrase "grain elevator" – not to mention the machine/building hybrid to which it refers – to be obscure, even strange. "Why would *grain* need to be *elevated*?" they might ask. "Isn't grain shipped horizontally, along the surface of the earth, not raised above it?" Such readers might

---

[1] To date, with the exception of about a dozen books of *photographs* of grain elevators, no comprehensive work has ever been devoted to their invention and development.

also wonder why they hadn't heard about grain elevators before.[2]

And so, precisely because the grain elevator remains "the most important yet least acknowledged invention in the history of American agriculture,"[3] and because agriculture has been so important to America's growth and world-wide power,[4] I am aware of the need to write this history of the

---

[2] Lewis Mumford, for example, doesn't mention "grain elevator" in his long list of key technical inventions created between 1041 and 1933 C.E., and only mentions "the application of machines to sowing, reaping, threshing, instituted on a large scale with the multitude of new reapers invented at the beginning of the [twentieth] century" in the context of factors that "hastened the pace" of migration from the countryside to the cities. Lewis Mumford, *Technics and Civilization* (Harcourt, Brace & World, 1934), pp. 192, 437-446.

[3] William Cronon, *Nature's Metropolis: Chicago and the Great West* (W.W. Norton, 1992), p. 111.

[4] "The three decades following 1860 witnessed the rapid transformation of American agriculture from a primitive, pioneer, largely self-sufficient type of industry into a modern business organized on a scientific, capitalistic, commercial basis. The most significant result of this transformation was the rise of the United States to the leading place among the nations of the world in the production of grain and live stock [...] Grain was the most important American product and the leading item entering into the nation's domestic and foreign commerce. Its production and distribution therefore constitutes a subject of fundamental interest and significance in the study of American economic development." Louis Bernard Schmidt, "The Internal Grain Trade of the United States, 1860-1890," *Iowa Journal of*

American grain elevator from 1843 to 1943 with *two* groups of readers in mind. I would like to educate and inspire the first (the neophytes, if you will), but without frustrating or boring the second (the already-initiated). Conversely, I would like to delight and provoke the second group, but without confusing or "losing" the first.

Writing the same book for two groups of readers isn't easy. It is possible, even likely, that being an expert in one of the many highly specialized "fields" upon which grain elevators are built and operate – agricultural production and storage, transportation and exports, prices and markets, mathematics and mechanical engineering, architecture and fireproofing, urbanism and modern life, symbolism and myths, et. al – doesn't necessarily give someone the ability to write a good book. Indeed, despite or perhaps precisely because of his or her specialization, an expert might not be able to adequately cover those fields that *weren't* his or her specialty and would thus fail to capture a glimpse of "the big picture," which is precisely what one seeks in an instance such as this. Only an enthusiastic generalist such as myself, skilled in research and writing, could undertake a history of the grain elevator in which all of the specialized fields are called upon, but only when a detail in "the big picture" needs to be filled in and explained.

Depending on the source, there are at least two and as many as six different types of grain elevators. To one writer, "Elevators, as they are now constructed, belong to two classes: those which are simply for transferring and weighing grain ('elevating'), and may be fixed upon land or are more often floating, and elevators which store as well as transfer

---

History and Politics (State Historical Society of Iowa, 1922), pp. 196-197.

4

grain."[5] There would seem to be *three* classes here: floating elevators; land-based transfer towers; and land-based elevators that store as well as transfer grain. But, of course, this writer also neglected to mention "country elevators," which are storage-and-transfer elevators that are built in-land along railroad tracks,[6] and "receiving elevators," which store grain that will eventually be processed by an adjoining flourmill, feed mill, distillery, oil-extraction plant or malt-house.[7] Another source asserts that grain elevators "can be

---

[5] Cf. "Report on the Cereal Production of the United States," *The Tenth Census of the United States, 1880, Volume III*, quoted in Louis Bernard Schmidt, "The Grain Trade of the United States, 1860-1890," *Iowa Journal of History and Politics* (State Historical Society of Iowa, 1922), p. 435.

[6] According to Barbara Krupp Selyem, "The Legacy of Country Grain Elevators," *Kansas History*, the Kansas State Historical Society (Spring/Summer, 2000), p. 44, country elevators can be subdivided into those that are "cribbed, a technique whereby wood was stacked horizontally, with broad sides together, interlocking at the corners log-cabin style," and those that "were built using stud or frame, sometimes called, balloon, construction," in which "horizontal wood bands placed every four feet vertically secured the perimeter."

[7] Note well that in the pages and chapters that follow, the word "house" will have many different meanings and resonances. First and foremost, it will be a place in which a commercial or industrial function is executed: and so one speaks of malt-houses, warehouses, storehouses, etc. Second, it will be a structure that encloses a machine: and so I will say, for example, that the elevating mechanism is *housed* in a long narrow box or that the box is the *housing* for the elevator. Third, "house" will be a place in which people live.

classified as either 'country' or 'terminal' elevators, with terminal elevators further categorized as inland or export types" and that both country and terminal elevators can be subdivided into "two basic types of design: traditional and modern."[8] This perspective is echoed by a third source, but with a twist: "Grain elevators can be divided into two major functional types, 'country' elevator (in Canada, a 'primary' elevator) and terminal elevator, and three more specialized types: receiving elevator, transfer elevator and cleaning elevator."[9] A fourth source lists four major types: "primary elevators" (aka country elevators), "transfer elevators"

Fourth and last, "house" will be a metaphor or figure for the human body, a ruler's kingdom, even human existence itself.

[8] *Air Pollutants 42, Fifth Edition, Volume I*, Chapter 9.9.1-1: Grain Elevators and Processes, issued by the Clearing house for Inventories & Emissions Factors, Environmental Protection Agency, February 1980. "Traditional grain elevators are typically designed so that the majority of the grain handling equipment [...] are located inside a building or structure, normally referred to as a headhouse." Built after 1980, "modern elevators [...] eliminated the enclosed headhouse and gallery (bin decks)" and "employ a more open structural design, which includes locating some equipment [...] outside of an enclosed structure." But "modernity" didn't arrive in 1980, in the form of developments that primarily concerned country elevators. One might more plausibly maintain that "modernity" arrived in the late 1890s and early 1900s, when materials other than wood (tile, steel and reinforced concrete) were first used in the construction of "fireproof" terminal and receiving elevators.

[9] Robert M. Frame III and Jeffrey A. Hess, "Saint Anthony Elevator No. 3," Historic American Engineering Record, HAER No. MN-57, November 1992, p. 9.

(transfer towers and floating elevators), "terminal elevators" (transfer and storage elevators) and "processing elevators" (aka receiving elevators).[10] A fifth source lists five types of elevators: terminal, transfer, country, "private" (aka receiving elevators), and "hospital" (designed to rehabilitate inferior or damaged grain).[11] If we put these sources together, we come up with *ten* distinct types: traditional country elevators (crib or balloon construction); modern country elevators; transfer towers; floating elevators; traditional in-land terminals; modern in-land terminals; traditional export terminals; modern export terminals; receiving elevators; and hospitals.

Further complications arise when one takes into account the building material(s) out of which grain elevators are constructed. Traditional country elevators are built out of wood, and modern country elevators are built out of steel or reinforced concrete.[12] When they were still used (before 1920), both stand-alone transfer towers and floating elevators were made out of wood. Ever since the late 1890s and early 1900s, grain terminals and receiving elevators have been built out of tile, steel and/or reinforced concrete. Though

---

[10] "Grain Elevators in Canada," Table 9, Canadian Grain Commission, 2007.

[11] "Concrete Elevators," Barney I. Weller, *Proceedings of the Ninth Annual Convention, held at Pittsburg, Pennsylvania, December 10-14, 1912*, Vol. IX (National Association of Cement Users, 1917), p. 339.

[12] One of the striking things about Barbara and Bruce Selyem's "The Legacy of Country Elevators: A Photo Essay," *Kansas History*, Spring/Summer 2000, is that it includes so many pictures that show traditional country elevators built out of wood standing next to modern country elevators built of reinforced concrete. The latter are often *twice* the height of the former and distinctly "urban" in character.

there are exceptions, grain elevators built out of wood tend to be small (storage capacities between 40,000 and one million bushels), while those built out of reinforced concrete tend to be immense (storage capacities between one and twenty million bushels).

Let us arrange these elevators according to their position in or along the "grain stream." Furthest "upstream" are the country elevators and hospitals, whose owners receive grain directly from the farmers in the surrounding regions. These primary elevators then ship this grain by railroad to local receiving elevators, where the stream ends, or to "mid-stream" inland terminals, where the grain is either stored for eventual shipment to regional receiving elevators or transferred from rail to barge for transportation to ocean-port terminals, transfer towers and floaters. At these "downstream" ports, the grain is either sent to large-scale receiving elevators, where the stream ends, or to terminals and receiving elevators in other countries, where it continues on.

Except for the floaters – which transship grain from one kind of water-borne vessel to another (for example, from a lake steamer to a canal boat, or from a barge to an ocean-going tanker) – grain elevators all along the stream can receive grain from ground-based forms of transportation. The wagons, trucks and railcars simply drive up to the elevator's receiving shed and dump their respective cargoes into pits, from which bucket-bearing conveyor belts elevate the grain to the top of the building. With the exceptions of the receiving elevators, which stand at "the end of the line," and the floaters, grain elevators all along the stream can load grain into ground-based vehicles (especially railcars) for further transportation "downstream." Some grain elevators – the inland and export terminals and the transfer towers – can load grain into water-borne vessels as well as into ground-based vehicles. But only the grain terminals, transfer towers, floaters and some of the receiving elevators can *unload* grain from ships, barges and boats. Such vessels cannot simply dock and dump their cargoes into receiving pits. Their cargo-bays or "holds" are below sea level, and so require assistance from the grain elevator. They receive it in the form of a "marine leg," which is a bucket-bearing conveyor belt that has been attached to an apparatus that can be lowered down into a ship's hold from the heights of a specially constructed "marine tower" and then retracted back into that tower when the "leg" is not in use.

For a variety of reasons that will be explored at great length in this book, the "marine leg" – far from being an exception or late development, as its position in/on the stream might indicate – was in fact the first type of grain elevator to be invented. To be precise, the very first mechanized (steam-powered) grain transfer and storage warehouse was built in Buffalo, New York, in 1843, by the engineer Robert Dunbar, then employed by the entrepreneur Joseph Dart. By the 1850s, the example of "the Dart Elevator" had been followed in port cities all over the Great Lakes. But it wasn't until after the Civil War, when standardized and uninterrupted railroad service was finally established, that the first country elevators were built. And so here we have a contradiction or "wrinkle" that takes time to examine and smooth out: the first grain elevator *wasn't* built "upstream," on a farm, but "downstream," in a port city. In other words, the history of the grain elevator takes us from the city to the farm, while the grain stream that the grain elevator helped to create moves in the *opposite* direction, that is, from the farm to the city.

As a result, this book has been organized in such a way that the reader is always reminded of the importance of geography, space and spatial practices. Though chronological exposition has been relied upon in most of the chapters that follow, this book isn't so much a *linear* presentation of the history of the American grain elevator from 1843 to 1943, but a *spatial* presentation. It describes the way grain elevators "take up" or consume space and produce new space(s), and it also dramatizes or mimics these very spatial practices. Like grain bins, each chapter of this book can serve as an autonomous unit *and* as a part of the "larger" array. My readers can explore them in any order that they fancy.

What will these readers find, once inside these chapter-bins? Not heaps of fragments, as one finds inside each of the many chapters that compose and subdivide Walter Benjamin's massive *Arcades Project* (from which I have quoted several passages), nor uninterrupted flows of narrative exposition, which is typical of most scholarly works. Instead they will find well-ordered assortments of "kernels" and interruptions. My model here is a pile of wheat: not only does it contain several different varieties of this particular grain, but also "foreign" objects (organic materials) that have been swept up and included in the course of the harvest, such as clumps of soil, dead insects, bits of other plants and so forth.[13]

To help guide the reader, I offer the following slightly enlarged iteration of the Table of Contents: Chapter 1, "Grain Power," identifies the role of grain elevators in the international grain trade; Chapter 2, "The Metaphor of Elevation," widens the discussion to include the symbolic dimensions of grain elevators; Chapter 3, "The Rise and Fall of the Port of Buffalo," tells the story of the invention of the world's first grain elevator, and the effects it had on the city

---

[13] In the analogy thus created, Franco-German Marxism, utopianism and modern poetry correspond to the "foreign" objects that have gotten mixed in somehow.

(and the nation) in which this first grain elevator was located; Chapter 4, "Fireproofing the Tinderbox," describes the work that went into designing and building grain elevators that resisted fires and explosions; Chapter 5, "American Colossus," tries to explain why the grain elevators of the 19th century were thought to be ugly, even evil; Chapter 6, "The European Modernists," details the many mistakes that the European modernists, despite their strong interest in American grain elevators, made when they used pictures of them in their manifestoes; Chapter 7, "Reyner Banham," appreciates and critiques Banham's pioneering book *A Concrete Atlantis*; Chapter 8, "Town and Country," describes and critiques the post-Banham tendency to focus exclusively on country elevators; and Chapter 9, "On Dwelling," touches upon the adaptive reuse of abandoned grain elevators.

I would also like draw the reader's attention to back of this volume, which includes an appendix that lists every grain elevator ever built in Buffalo, a bibliography of sources, a comprehensive index, and a total of seven black and white illustrations.

William J. Brown
12 February 2009
Cincinnati, Ohio

Chapter 1
Grain Power

Thirty years ago, Dan Morgan published *Merchants of Grain*, the first major work on the international grain trade.[1] Originally assigned to write an article for *The Washington Post* on the "well-publicized and controversial sales of American grain to the Soviet Union in 1972," Morgan became motivated to write something more substantial after the OPEC oil embargo of 1973. He writes in his introduction: "This book is intended to contribute to a better understanding of the world that was so suddenly and painfully revealed to us in 1972 and 1973 – a world in which nations all depend on each other for basic needs, and a few giant international companies and banks allocate and distribute the essential raw materials and the capital required to produce them." Elsewhere in *Merchants of Grain*, he refers to "global interdependency (or less charitably, the global dependency on huge multinational companies)."[2] Morgan's book remains relevant today precisely because this world of "global interdependency" still exists: it is *our* world.

At the beginning of his research, Morgan found that "the subject of grain ha[d] not been ignored by academic researchers. I found many useful books, pamphlets, articles, and reports covering pieces of the history – even large pieces." This wasn't at all surprising. After all, "grain is the only resource in the world that is even more central to modern civilization than oil. It goes without saying that grain is essential to human lives and health."[3] Certainly most of the

---

[1] Dan Morgan, *Merchants of Grain*, Viking, New York, 1979.

[2] Dan Morgan, pp. vii-viii and 173.

[3] Dan Morgan, pp. ix and vii.

quotations assembled by Morgan to provide epigraphs for the chapters of his book support this idea: "Grain is the currency of currencies," which is attributed to Lenin; "Dig tunnels deep, store grain everywhere, and never seek hegemony [until the time is right]," attributed to Mao; and "Nobody is qualified to become a statesman who is entirely ignorant of the problem of wheat," attributed to Socrates.[4] Grain lies at the intersection of biology and politics ("bio-politics"): it nourishes or starves the political and economic health of the State, *and* the physical and spiritual health of its individual citizens.

But Morgan found that a great deal was missing. For example, there were no "scholarly works tracing the political and economic history of grain, charting the trade routes, and, perhaps, sketching the profiles of the great traders."

> What I could not find was any work that brought together and gave significance to all these strands of grain's history when European civilization was industrializing and expanding in the nineteenth century (although the French historian Fernand Braudel does so for a period preceding the modern grain trade). As it is, the literature on oil, rubber, timber, or railroads provides more accessible information on the origins of these basic industries than anything I was able to find on grain.[5]

The problem wasn't with the researchers, but with the major grain-trading companies, which had made it a long-standing policy to reveal as little about themselves as possible.

---

[4] *Merchants of Grain*, pp. 1, 255, and 342, respectively. Morgan does not provide citations for these quotations, and I have not been able to find their sources.

[5] *Merchants of Grain*, pp. viii-ix and ix.

"Economy is desirable, but secrecy is essential," one representative of the British merchant house of Baring Brothers wrote to another in 1844.[6] Secrecy, especially secrecy concerning deals being negotiated, profits from past deals and the actual amounts of grain on hand at any one time, gave grain merchants an enormous advantage when it came to profiting from, speculating on, and even cornering the market.[7] It also protected these merchants from both distrust of "middlemen" and anti-Semitism.

> Wanting to blend in, to keep a low profile, is a natural enough instinct in the grain business for the families [that control the big firms] have never felt beloved by the larger society. From the merchant-adventurer days on down to the present, they have been middlemen, suspected by their customers and their supplies alike of shaving pennies on every bushel. Successful merchants quickly learned that it was unwise to go around sporting wealth very ostentatiously – all that did was confirm the worst notions about merchants as greedy profiteers.[8]

Morgan notes that, today, "the code of secrecy that applied in 1844 has not only been perpetuated but fortified as the control of the major companies became centralized in the hands of a few people [...] The grain companies don't presume that the public has a right to know anything about what they are doing – and this despite the fact that they have received billions of dollars in U.S. government subsidies over

---

[6] Quoted in *Merchants of Grain*, p. x.
[7] William Cronon, *Nature's Metropolis: Chicago and the Great West* (WW Norton, 1991), p. 136.
[8] *Merchants of Grain*, pp. 180-181.

the years."[9] In the case of Continental, the company never even published a company brochure. "It was said at Continental," Morgan reports, "that Fribourg would 'rather lose a million dollars than get his name in the papers.' " Over at Bunge, "'public relations' meant keeping Bunge out of the limelight."[10]

Morgan found out that this "code of secrecy" (deliberately created obscurity) was so thoroughgoing and effective that many people didn't even know the *names* of the world's top-five grain companies – Cargill, Continental, Louis Dreyfus, Bunge y Born, and Andre – not to mention the extent of their operations, wealth and power. In the words of Senator Frank Church, chairman of the Senate Subcommittee on Multinational Corporations in 1975, "No one knows how they operate, what their profits are, what they pay in taxes and what effect they have on our foreign policy – or much of anything else about them."[11]

Each of the Big Five achieved and maintained their long-sought "invisibility" by being organized as privately owned companies and operated by the members of the tightly knit families that founded them:[12] the Cargills and MacMillans, in the case of Cargill;[13] the descendants of Simon Fribourg (his sons Jules and Rene Fribourg), in the

---

[9] *Merchants of Grain*, p. x.

[10] *Merchants of Grain*, p. 161.

[11] Quoted in Dan Morgan, *Merchants of Grain*, p. ix.

[12] There is a strong similarity here to the big flour milling companies based in Minneapolis, all of which are dominated by the descendants of Cadwallader Washburn, John Crosby, Charles Alfred Pillsbury and James Bell.

[13] Both founder William Cargill and his son-in-law John MacMillan were Midwesterners. Eventually, Cargill, Inc. was headquartered in Minneapolis, Minnesota.

15

case of Continental Grain;[14] the descendants of Charles
Bunge (his sons Edouard and Ernesto Bunge) and Ernesto's
brother-in-law Jorge Born, in the case of Bunge y Born;[15] the
descendants of Leopold Louis-Dreyfus, in the case of Louis
Dreyfus;[16] and the descendants of Georges Andre, in the case
of Andre.[17] Morgan notes: "Members of these families not
only own most of the stock of the companies, but also serve
as board chairmen, presidents, and chief executives at each of
them [...] In the grain companies, it is possible to observe a
social and economic phenomenon of some historical note: a
functioning oligopoly that has survived right into the
contemporary, post-industrial age." And yet, "mysterious and
obscure as the firms may be, they are near-perfect stereotypes
of the new global corporations that manage the distribution

---

[14] Long based in Paris, thereafter in New York City,
Continental Grain is now called ContiGrain.

[15] Originally based in Belgium, then in Buenos Aires,
and now in Brazil, "the Octopus" is now called Bunge
Limited. It went public in 2001.

[16] Originally based in Paris, Louis Dreyfus is now
headquartered in New York City. Dan Morgan writes: "In the
1930s, the Louis-Dreyfus family had been in the public
limelight. Louis Louis-Dreyfus had been in politics and
owned a newspaper. And what good had it done? It made the
family all too visible at a time when anti-Semitism was on
the rise. Afterward, the family made it a rule to keep in the
shadows" (*Merchants of Grain*, p. 186). But times change.
Note that the actress Julia Louis-Dreyfus, who is world-
famous for her portrayal of Elaine on the very Jewish TV
show *Seinfeld*, did not change her name before going into
show business, even though she is a descendent of this very
rich and powerful family.

[17] Based in Switzerland, the company is now known as
the Andre MaggiGroup.

and processing of basic resources in the late twentieth century."[18]

Comparisons with "Big Oil" are instructive. Thanks in part to *The Seven Sisters: the Great Oil Companies and the World They Shaped*, which the British investigative journalist Anthony Sampson brought out in 1975,[19] the existence and role of the "Big Seven" (Standard Oil of New Jersey, Texaco, Gulf, Standard Oil of California, Mobil, Royal Dutch Shell, and British Petroleum) has been public knowledge for many years. Today, it is common knowledge that Exxon and Chevron – two of the four "super-major" oil conglomerates that resulted from the mergers of the last thirty years[20] – are making the largest corporate profits in American history,[21] and that, thanks to the corporate affiliations of George W. Bush (Texaco, now part of Chevron) and Dick Cheney (Halliburton), Big Oil has been intimately involved in the formulation and implementation of American foreign policy concerning Iraq, Afghanistan, Georgia and Iran, among other nations.

But if one were to ask someone today which *grain companies* are reaping windfall profits from the rising prices of wheat, corn and rice, or helping to formulate American foreign policy concerning agriculture in Cuba, Brazil, the Sudan, Egypt, India, North Korea and China, he or she probably wouldn't know. In the words of Felicity Lawrence, the "trading giants remain shadowy in European perception, despite their colossal footprint." It would appear that

---

[18] Dan Morgan, *Merchants of Grain*, pp. 7 and 5.

[19] Viking, New York, the same house that published *Merchants of Grain* five years later.

[20] The other two are Royal Dutch Shell and BP.

[21] Clifford Krauss, "Exxon's Second-Quarter Earnings Set a Record," *New York Times*, August 1, 2008; Andrea Chang, "Chevron reports record profit of $6 billion," *Los Angeles Times*, 2 August 2008.

Cargill's boast – "99 per cent of our customers have never heard of us"[22] – remains true, even today.

Like the big oil companies, which made themselves indispensable through their control of the refineries and distribution systems, the big grain companies don't own the land on which the grain is grown, nor do they grow the grain itself. Instead, they have invested in grain elevators, transportation (railroads, lake vessels and trans-oceanic tankers) and crushing, processing, milling and oil-extraction plants. The Big Five have also created global communications and information-gathering networks. Dan Morgan's analogy is spot on.

> Soybean price quotations soon flickered over an electronic board in a former living room, and communications and telex machines were crammed into what looks like a butler's pantry. In another room, a map dotted with tiny flags pin-pointed the weather all over the planet. There in the Minnesota woods, Cargill operates its own foreign office, gathering information, keeping in touch with its emissaries in dozens of countries, channeling money into many parts of the world, and assessing the impact of political, financial, and economic developments on Cargill's foreign relations. This is the seat of the 'government of Cargill,' which is like no government in the world.[23]

At the end of the day, "farmers take the risk of falling prices, bad weather, and governmental policies that sometimes depress farm prices," Morgan observes. "The grain

---

[22] Quoted in Dan Morgan, *Merchants of Grain*, p. 161.
[23] Dan Morgan, *Merchants of Grain*, pp. 171-172.

companies, one stage removed from the production process, can make money *whether prices are rising or falling.*[24]

The power – the *grain power* – of the Big Five has only grown since the 1970s. According to Alan J. Thrush, the author of *History, Organization and Strategies for Grain Producers and the Grain Industry,*[25] the Big Five own or control over 50% of the nation's grain-storage capacity and make 70% of the nation's grain sales. There are only small differences between these companies concerning size, location of headquarters, operating costs and transportation costs. The Big Five have strategic advantages over smaller companies concerning control of grain flow through the system, facility locations, processing capabilities and vertical integration. The biggest of the group is Cargill, which is the single largest privately owned corporation in the world. According to Felicity Lawrence, Cargill controls 45% of the global trade in grain, 42% of U.S. corn exports, 33% of U.S. soya bean exports, and 20% of U.S. wheat exports. Its total revenue for 2007 was $88 billion dollars;[26] in 2008, Cargill's annual revenue had grown to $120 billion, more than twice its closest competitor, Archer-Daniels Midland.[27]

Morgan's arguments in favor of governmental scrutiny and oversight of Big Grain are quite reasonable.

---

[24] Dan Morgan, *Merchants of Grain*, p. 6, emphasis added.

[25] Submitted as his Master of Science thesis to the Department of Agricultural Economics at the Michigan State University in 2003.

[26] *Eat Your Heart Out: Why the Food Business Is Bad for the Planet and Your Health* was published by Penguin Books, London, 2008. An extract appeared as "Our Diet of Destruction," in the 16 June 2008 issue of *The Guardian.*

[27] Chris Serres, "Cargill looms as a silent giant," *The Minneapolis Star Tribune*, 4 December 2008.

It is *because* [the grain companies] are "neutral," because they claim not to represent national governments, because they are devoid of a political ideology[,] that they can go everywhere and do everything. [...] In the absence of effective supervision or governmental guidance for the transnational firms – in the absence, in fact, of much hard data on their activities – national interests can get lost in the shuffle. Huge corporations cannot and do not make decisions on the basis of what is in the best interests of the countries where they are represented. This is not to say that the companies always act *against* these best interests. It is just that the companies have a different set of interests from those of individual nations. And because of their immense wealth and their global operations, they can do things that harm a country without any special costs to them.[28]

But this doesn't go far enough. When the multinational grain companies make bad, even disastrous decisions about the intensive use of pesticides, monoculture, hybridization and genetic modification,[29] "national interests" and "individual nations" aren't the only things that are "harmed." Also harmed is the long-term health of the *billions* of individuals who rely upon grain products for their "daily bread"[30] and whose "interests" are all-too-often poorly represented, even or especially on the national level. Precisely because genetically modified soybeans and corn are so widely used in the production of a whole range of secondary food products (cooking oils, starches and sweeteners), it is virtually

---

[28] Dan Morgan, *Merchants of Grain*, p. 247.

[29] Dan Morgan, *Merchants of Grain*, pp. 237-240.

[30] "Give us this day our daily bread" (Matthew 6:11).

impossible to avoid eating "Frankenfoods," even if you consciously attempt to do so.[31] Thus, it should be in the name of protecting human health, not national interests, that the international grain trade – "the mother of all trade"[32] – is brought into the daylight, supervised and regulated.

There is another factor to consider. Unlike the big oil companies, which mostly rely upon *foreign* sources, the Big Five mostly rely upon *domestic* sources. In an era in which it has become cliché to say, "America no longer produces anything," it is easy to forget that America is the only country in the world that produces exportable surpluses of wheat, corn, rice *and* soybeans. And so, intervention into or regulation of the international grain trade isn't simply a matter for the foreign policy experts,[33] but for the experts in

---

[31] "Frankenfood" is a neologism that evokes Frankenstein's monster. In a statement released in 2001, an organization opposed to genetically modified foods called the Organic Consumers Association called on "elected officials, political candidates, state departments of agriculture, and all universities and colleges to oppose the growing of GM wheat" until several things could be proven. One of them related directly to grain elevators: "Shipping and storage systems will be able to keep genetically modified grains separate from other varieties." But such separations are not possible within the current "grain in bulk" system.

[32] See Milja van Tielhof, *The 'Mother of All Trades': The Baltic Grain Trade in Amsterdam from the Late 16th to the Early 19th Century* (Brill, 2002).

[33] Passed by Congress in 1954, Public Law 480 allowed foreign governments to receive loans to buy surplus American grain. Though praised for "helping farmers" and "starving people abroad," P.L. 480 was used to further American foreign policy – providing "food aid" to anti-Communist allies, denying it to others. See Dan Morgan, *Merchants of Grain*, pp. 100-102.

domestic policy, as well. If the Big Five have "grain power," isn't that power really *American* grain power? Shouldn't the American people control the disposition of American grain? And who represents the American people: private companies or the U.S. government?

It certainly bears repeating: grain is essential to human lives and health. It always has been and will no doubt continue to be the primary source of nutrition for most of the world's people. A generic term derived from the Latin *granum*, "grain" refers to the small, hard and coarse seeds or seed-like fruits (*caryopsis*) that come from cereal plants. Classified as grasses (*gramineae*), which do not produce usable quantities of seed-fruits unless they are cultivated, cereal plants include such staples as wheat, wild rice, corn, rye, barley, millet, sorghum, spelt, and oats. "Grain" is also used to refer to the seed-fruits of such pseudo-cereals as buckwheat, amaranth and quinoa. In all of its forms, grain is a living organism and thus *doubly* valuable: it can be consumed as food in the present (if it is properly prepared),[34] and it can be planted to produce food in the future (if conditions are right and the harvest is a good one). The sensible use of grain is easy to divine: eat some now, save some for later.

In the modern grain trade, the three biggest grains are wheat (*Triticum*), corn (*Zea Mays*) and rice (*Oryza*). Because it is a semi-aquatic cereal grass, rice is typically considered separately from the other cereals. In Europe and North America, the most popular grains are wheat and corn. There are currently thirteen different types of wheat classified by the Wheat Genetic and Genomic Resources Center at Kansas State University.[35] For our purposes, there are two main types

---

[34] Depending on what precise cereal plant it is, "grain" can be malted, brewed, distilled, milled or baked.

[35] https://www.ksu.edu/wgrc/Taxonomy/taxintro.html, accessed 17 August 2008.

of wheat: "winter wheat" and "spring wheat," both of which are named according to the time of year in which the seeds are best planted. Brought to Kansas by Russian immigrants in the 18th and 19th centuries,[36] winter wheat is hard, difficult to mill cleanly, and relatively high in protein and gluten content. Once separated from the husks and stalks ("threshed"), the endosperms and embryos of the remaining "wheat berries" are separated out and milled into flours that are used to make cereals, crackers, and many kinds of high-quality breads. Durum is the hardest winter wheat and is primarily used to make macaroni ("pasta") and noodles. (In the United States, durum is often planted in the spring, not in the winter, to maximize total output.) Spring wheat is soft, easy to mill, and relatively low in protein and gluten. It is typically threshed and milled into an all-purpose flour that is used to make cakes, pastries and certain types of bread. Milled corn ("corn meal") can be made into a variety of products, including bread, polenta and breakfast cereals (cornflakes).

Not including human teeth, the first hard things used to crush wheat berries, and thus begin the separation of the husks ("chaff") from the wheat itself, were smooth, hard stones (sarsen or sandstone, mostly). At first powered by the back-and-forth thrusting of human hands, these stones were later revolved within querns, which were pedal-powered devices. When querns proved to be too small or too slow to grind large amounts of wheat, gristmills were required.[37] As early as 60 B.C.E., European gristmills were powered by moving water. In his *Ten Books on Architecture*, Vitruvius reports:

---

[36] The Native Americans did not cultivate wheat, and only cultivated corn for subsistence, not for profit not animal feed.

[37] In Old High German, *grist* means "teeth."

1. Wheels on the principles that have been described above are also constructed in rivers. Round their faces floatboards are fixed, which, on being struck by the current of the river, make the wheel turn as they move, and thus, by raising the water in the boxes and bringing it to the top, they accomplish the necessary work through being turned by the mere impulse of the river, without any treading on the part of workmen.

2. Water mills are turned on the same principle. Everything is the same in them, except that a drum with teeth is fixed into one end of the axle. It is set vertically on its edge, and turns in the same plane with the wheel. Next to this larger drum there is a smaller one, also with teeth, but set horizontally, and this is attached (to the millstone). Thus the teeth of the drum which is fixed to the axle make the teeth of the horizontal drum move, and cause the mill to turn. A hopper, hanging over this contrivance, supplies the mill with corn, and meal is produced by the same revolution.[38]

Approximately a thousand years later, the first gristmills powered by wind were built in Iran, Pakistan and Afghanistan.[39] Later, windmills were built in England,

---

[38] "Water Wheels and Water Mills," Book X, Chapter V, *The Ten Books on Architecture*, translated by Morris Hicky Morgan, Harvard University Press, 1914.
[39] Adam Lucas, *Wind, Water, Work: Ancient and Medieval Milling Technology* (Brill Publishers, 2006), p. 65.

Holland and Spain, where they so vexed Don Quixote, who thought they were "wild giants."[40]

The gradual but clear progressions from manpower to waterpower, and from waterpower to wind-power, not only allowed flourmills to become bigger, faster and more productive, which meant that more people were better fed. This "progress" also made or contained the unspoken promise that manual labor (so closely tied in Judeo-Christian culture to original sin, dispossession, and mortality)[41] would eventually be abolished. "Spare the hand that grinds the corn, O miller girls, and softly sleep," pleads Antiphilos of Byzantium.

> Let Chanticleer announce the morn in vain! Demeter has commanded that the girls' work be done by Nymphs, and now they skip lightly over the wheels, so that the shaken axles revolve with their spokes and pull round the load of revolving stones. Let us live the life of our fathers, and let us

---

[40] Miguel de Cervantes, *Don Quijote*, translated by Buron Raffel (W.W. Norton, 1999): "Look there, Sancho Panza, my friend, and see those thirty or so wild giants, with whom I intend to do battle and to kill each and all of them, so with their stolen booty we can begin to enrich ourselves. This is noble, righteous warfare, for it is wonderfully useful to God to have such an evil race wiped from the face of the earth" (p. 43). One wonders what visions the sight of a truly colossal grain elevator would have inspired in the mind of the Man of La Mancha.

[41] "In the sweat of thy face shalt thou eat bread, till thou return unto the ground; for out of it wast thou taken: for dust thou art out, and unto dust shalt thou return" (Genesis 3:19).

rest from work and enjoy the gifts that Demeter sends us.[42]

This vision of a paradisiacal life on earth, "the life of our fathers," in which men and women "rest from work" thanks to labor-saving devices and finally get to enjoy the fruits of their labor: it persisted and even grew more vivid and alluring as querns became gristmills, and gristmills became powered by water wheels, wind-catching vanes and then wood-burning steam-engines.

Charles Baudelaire's poem "The Ransom" expresses mankind's growing impatience: will paradise never come?

Man has for paying his ransom
Two fields of rich, deep, porous rock
That he must clear and cultivate
With the iron of his reason;

To obtain the sorriest rose
To extort a few ears of grain,
He must water them constantly
With salty sweat from his gray brow.

One is Art and the other Love.
To win the judge's favor
When the terrible day
Of dispassionate justice dawns

He will have to show granaries
Filled with harvests and flowers
Whose forms and colors will
Win the suffrage of the Angels.[43]

---

[42] Quoted by Walter Benjamin, *The Arcades Project*, page 697. Demeter, of course, was the Roman incarnation of the Greek goddess Ceres.

This business-like deal or arrangement in which God rewards those with a "strict work ethic" and destroys those tainted by "corruption, laziness and fraud": isn't it a kind of kidnapping or extortion? Held hostage are both Art and Love, neither of which have anything to do with "work," precisely because both gain by losing (as in, "parting is such sweet sorrow"). The irony here is bitter, like coarse, black bread: the fruits of Art and Love (grain and roses) are not collected and stored for the enjoyment of people. No, they are part of a ransom eternally paid to God.

In the 1960s, the world's farmers produced over 200 million tons of each of the three big grains every year. Today, when there are fewer farmers and larger farms, "agribusiness" annually produces *three times* that amount. And yet hundreds of millions of people are either hungry or starving to death. Bread riots have recently broken out in many countries (including Egypt, Indonesia and Pakistan), as have large protests and demonstrations against rapidly increasing food prices ("tortilla protests" in Mexico and "pasta protests" in Italy). As in the 1970s, there are bread riots in Egypt and soaring gasoline prices at home. The "bad old" days have returned.[44] How is this possible?

Wheat used to be grown in large amounts all over the world: in Canada, the United States, Argentina, Western Europe, Southern Europe (as far east as the Ukraine), Northern Africa, India, China and Australia.[45] Today, wheat

---

[43] First published in *Les Fleurs du mal*, 1863, translated by William Aggeler (Fresno, CA: Academy Library Guild, 1954).

[44] See "Strikes, Unrest, Bread Riots: Return to the Bad Old Days?" *Middle East & Africa Monitor*, April 7, 2008.

[45] Map entitled "World Wheat Acreage in the 1930s," source: U.S. Department of Agriculture, reproduced in Dan Morgan, *Merchants of Grain*, p. 79.

is consumed all over the world, but it is only produced in exportable surpluses in a handful of countries: the United States, Canada, France, Argentina and Australia. The United States and Argentina are the only countries that produce exportable surpluses of corn, and the United States and Brazil are the only countries that produce exportable surpluses of soybeans. Virtually every other country, especially those in Africa, Asia and Latin America, have become net importers of food, no matter how much grain is or used to be grown domestically.[46]

The problem is complex. At the root of it are changes in the world's food-growing practices: virtually everyone has adopted (and become dependent upon) America's over-indulgent tastes for white bread milled from winter wheat and for meat cut from corn-fed cattle, pigs and chickens.[47] That is to say, people in the "Third World" have stopped sustaining themselves on such indigenous crops as rice, maize, beans, and cassava, and have switched over to American or American-style bread and meat.[48] These days, America

---

[46] See Audrey Ensminger, *The Food and Nutrition Encyclopedia, A to H* (CRC Press, 1994), figure C-67.

[47] In America, this mixed system of crop and livestock production was begun very early. In *Nature's Metropolis: Chicago and the Great West* (WW Norton, 1991), William Cronon reports that, "speaking of the fifteen hundred bushels of corn he had raised the preceding year, one farmer in Jacksonville, Illinois, wrote home in 1838 that he would 'not sell a bushel, but feed it all to the stock.' Although he planned to keep raising corn himself, he added, 'Whether we raise too much or too little, we shall give it all to hogs & cattle, as we think it more profitable than to sell the corn' " (p. 223).

[48] In 1994, vegetables, fruits, nuts, legumes, oilseeds, roots and tubers accounted for only 32 percent of the world's food plants. The rest was made up of cereal grains (40.3%)

exports more than 200 million bushels of grain to them every year. This changeover (the "green revolution") was no accident. It was in fact an engineered solution to the problem of grain over-production in the United States after World War II.

> To strategists at the USDA [United States Department of Agriculture], Cargill, and Continental, the solution to the surplus problem was self-evident. It was to get people in other countries to eat the way Americans did. A global economy in which millions of rice-eaters in Asia were converted to wheat bread was one that absorbed some of the perennial U.S. wheat surpluses. And a food system in which affluent countries bought billions of dollars of U.S. corn and soybeans to feed their beef, hogs, and poultry every year was one that helped the American balance of payments and trade.[49]

There were also strong local reasons for the post-colonial world to adopt Western dietary habits. In the words of John Williams, the American agricultural attaché in Zaire in 1973, bread had been "the staple diet of the colonial masters and was adopted by the elite. Because of the effect of imitation, bread consumption identifies [the eater] with progress and modernity for the masses."[50]

To pay for their grain imported from America, the world's other countries have been forced to sell, rather than consume, their indigenous crops and crop-based products (bananas, pineapples, sugar, palm oil, coffee, cocoa, rubber

---

and sugarcane (27.7%). See Audrey Ensminger, *The Food and Nutrition Encyclopedia, A to H*, page 365, figure C-67.

[49] Dan Morgan, *Merchants of Grain*, p. 99.

[50] Quoted in *Merchants of Grain*, p. 229.

and timber) and/or forced to cultivate those crops that were valuable as exports (especially illegal plant-derived substances). As Morgan points out, "food imports have become a means [in these countries] for perpetuating outmoded policies, for continuing feudal social structures, and for maintaining the power and privileges of small ruling business and political groups."[51] Furthermore, "the availability of the imports makes it possible [for the local governments] to postpone radical domestic reform, land distribution, and the redirection of credit to different sectors of society. The sale of imported food on the local economy [...] generates money that can be used to pay the civil servants, police forces, and soldiers who make up the regime's base of political support. And the imported food helps to hold down inflation, which is a primary cause of unrest to the middle class (students, merchants, businessmen)."[52]

Morgan refers to this global phenomenon as "economic recolonization." He writes:

> Flourmills, corn-compounding plants, and soybean-crushing installations often are as much symbols of status and prestige for a country [in the Third World] as an airport and an international hotel. But multinational companies rather than local governments are often in control of these facilities. They supply the capital, procure and install the technology, supervise the operations of the plants, control the procurement of raw materials, and set up the local distribution systems for the dissemination of the processed products.

---

[51] Dan Morgan, *Merchants of Grain*, p. 350.
[52] Dan Morgan, *Merchants of Grain*, p. 355.

In the spread of [such] grain "refineries" (as, indeed, in many other types of processing) it is possible to see the phenomenon of European and American economic recolonization. The same corporate names keep coming up in country after country. They are the major grain companies (the Big Five) plus a few others such as Ralston Purina, Corn Products Corp., Archer-Daniels Midland, Central Soya, Pillsbury, General Mills, and Uniliver. Their products include flour, starch, sweeteners, soybean meal, vegetable oil, and feeds used by poultry, dairy, and cattle and hog farmers the world over.[53]

Morgan's implicit parallel between oil refineries and "grain refineries" is an appropriate and interesting one. In the last forty years, food, just like everything else, has become an industrial product, mass-produced, and available everywhere. Indeed, food for people and fuel for automobiles has come to overlap in the form of ethanol, which is a perfect example of the illogical "rationality" of the profit-driven market: it is "surplus grain" (corn in fact) that is plentiful precisely because petrochemical fertilizers and pesticides were used to grow it, and that gets processed into "food" for cars because petrochemical fuel is reputedly too expensive.

The end result of these developments is that, today, *less than fifty percent* of the two billion tons of grain produced .every year is consumed as food by human beings. Thirty-five percent of it is fed to livestock animals, which are then slaughtered and consumed as meat by those who have a taste for it and can afford to buy it, and slightly more than fifteen percent of the world's grain (corn mostly) is turned into ethanol and burned in combustion engines by those who depend upon them to get around. And so, Morgan concludes,

---

[53] Dan Morgan, *Merchants of Grain*, p. 232.

"People are not starving [...] because the world is running out of food. They are starving because they are poor – poor and beyond the reach of the vast commercial system that produces food and transfers it from one country to another [...] At the present time, it is money, not food[,] that is badly distributed across the planet."[54] The same is true today, thirty years later.

What is the solution? Economic recolonization is indeed a significant development, and Morgan knows that it requires changes in our way thinking about modern society. He writes, "Karl Marx [...] built his thesis around the notion that the control of the 'means of production' was power. He had in mind the factories of England. In the present era of international interdependence, it is necessary to modify Marx's definition somewhat. Today, power is in the hands of those controlling not only the means of production but also the means of distribution, the access to world markets, the necessary technology (the know-how), and the processing capability."[55] But Morgan is not a Marxist, and he lets this thread drop.[56] In its place, he cites the 1977 report by the

---

[54] Dan Morgan, *Merchants of Grain*, p. 345. Contrast this insight with Georg Simmel, *The Philosophy of Money* (third enlarged edition, edited by David Frisby, Routledge: London, 2004), p. 155: "Just as the exchange value of grain can be traced to the fact that there is not enough of it to satisfy all those who are hungry, so the exchange value of the money material is the result of the fact that there is not enough to satisfy all those needs for it additional to the need for money."

[55] Dan Morgan, *Merchants of Grain*, p. 231.

[56] To pick it up, see Guy Debord, *La Societe du Spectacle* (1967), translated as *The Society of the Spectacle* (Black & Red, 1977); "Abat-Faim" (1985), translated as "Hunger Abatement" (NOT BORED! 2004); and

National Research Council: "hunger and malnutrition cannot be addressed solely by food [relief] programs. The processes of social and economic development must be considered, including programs concerned with access to resources, distribution of income, control of parasitic diseases, extension of health services, provision of safe water supplies and literacy and general education."[57] Once again, this is quite reasonable, but, in light of Morgan's reference to Karl Marx, it can be seen as soft "liberal" talk that elides the necessity of truly radical changes in the way world society is organized.

Not surprisingly, references to "wheat" or "corn" appear throughout the Hebrew Bible ("the Old Testament"), the Christian Bible ("the New Testament") and the Koran. Here they are: "thorns [...] instead of wheat" Job 31:40; "the finest of the wheat" (Psalm 81:16); "he makes peace in your borders; he fills you with the finest of the wheat" (Psalm 147:14); "sown wheat and [...] reaped thorns," "ashamed of their harvests because of the fierce anger of the Lord" (Jeremiah 12:13); "what has straw in comparison with wheat?" (Jeremiah 23:28); "he will clear his threshing floor and gather his wheat into the granary, but the chaff he will burn with unquenchable fire" (Matthew 3:12); "but while men were sleeping, his enemy came and sowed weeds among the wheat [...] So when the plants came up and bore grain, then the weeds appeared also" (Matthew 13:25-26); "Simon, Simon: behold, Satan demanded to have you, that he might sift you like wheat" (Luke 22:31); "unless a grain of wheat falls into the earth and dies, it remains alone; but if it dies, it bears much fruit" (John 12:24); "What you sow does not come to life unless it dies. And what you sow is not the body which is to be, but a bare kernel, perhaps of wheat or of some

---

Commentaires sur La Societe du Spectacle (1988), translated as *Comments on the Society of the Spectacle* (Verso, 1990).

[57] Dan Morgan, *Merchants of Grain*, p. 357.

other grain. But God gives it a body as he has chosen, and to each kind of seed its own body. For not all flesh is alike [...]" (I Corinthians 15:36-38); "The parable of those who spend their property in the way of Allah is as the parable of a grain growing seven ears [with] a hundred grains in every ear; and Allah multiples for whom He please; and Allah is Ample-giving" (The Cow, 2.261); "Surely Allah causes the grain and the stone to germinate; He brings forth the living from the dead and He is the bringer forth of the dead from the living; that is Allah! how are you then turned away?" (The Cattle, 6.95); "cornfields and palm-trees having fine spadices?" (The Poets, 26.148); "Cornfields and noble places!" (The Smoke, 44.26).

A set of insistent and conflicting themes emerge from these passages: grain is peace at home, wise investment, plenitude, and great value distinguished from that which has none; grain is wasted effort, danger, evil, sin, judgment, punishment, death and infamy; and grain is rebirth, resurrection and the eternal human soul, which is *the kernel of the human grain berry*.[58] In the words of the Rev. Stephen Jenner, to speak such eternal truths about human life and death is to bring "grain from the granary."[59] For is not the Church itself a kind of Granary of Souls?[60]

---

[58] Note well that America's oldest and most-famous cemetery – it includes the husks of Benjamin Franklin, Paul Revere and Mother Goose, among many others – is called the "Granary Burial Ground." It borders a granary that was used between 1728 and 1784. See *Historical Sketch and Matters Appertaining to the Granary Burial Ground*, published by the Cemetery Department of the City of Boston, 1902.

[59] See *Grain from the Granary: Sermons Preached in the Parish Church of Bekesbourne, Kent* (London, 1882).

[60] In response to reports that there was a "protestant granary in Rome" (that is, a Protestant congregation meeting in an old granary), a writer for *Punch* claimed, "Indeed that

Of course, the intertwined themes of grain, death and rebirth aren't limited to the monotheistic religions. Concerning the Greek and Asian myth of the tree-spirit Attis, James George Frazer writes: "The story of his sufferings, death and resurrection was interpreted as the ripe grain wounded by the reaper, buried in the granary, and coming to life again when it is sown in the ground."[61]

Certainly the best-known references to grain in the Hebrew, Christian and Muslim Bibles are made in the course of the story of Joseph in Egypt. Significantly, these references aren't to grain as such, nor to the planting and harvesting of it, but to *storing* grain for future use. Long-term grain-storage containers must be physically secure (unlikely to be damaged or destroyed by inclement weather); dry and cool, so that the grain doesn't germinate; and impenetrable to evil spirits, other human beings and "vermin" (unwanted consumers such as insects, bugs, small animals and birds).

Three types of ancient storage containers answered these needs: jars made of pottery, which were typically tall and narrow; pits dug in the ground, which were typically circular in shape; and silos (from the Greek word *siros*), which were extensive underground structures in which jars or pits of grain and other foodstuffs were stored). Collared jars (*pithoi*) were called for when "household" amounts of grain were to be stored or moved somewhere else. Deep pits, lined with straw, stone, cement or plaster, were called for if larger amounts were to be stored for the winter. And silos were appropriate if the storehouse was to include an entire

---

granary church may, in its rudeness, in the very nakedness of its poverty, preach the intrinsic purity of Christianity, and may show in beautiful contrast to the Cathedral of St. Peter's." *Punch: Funny, Intelligent, Pleasantly Plump*, 1851, p. 75.

[61] *The Golden Bough: A Study in Magic and Religion*, London: Palgrave, 1914, p. 425.

community's supply and/or remain hidden from thieves, spies or raiders.

The world's oldest granary apparently dates from 9500 B.C.E. and was located in the Jordan River valley. Another one dates from 6,000 B.C.E. and was located in the Indus Valley in Pakistan. Some ancient granaries were very capacious. The silos at Megiddo (725 B.C.E.) reputedly could store 340 metric tons of grain, that is, enough to provide a thousand people with nourishment for a whole year.[62] In China, Korea and Japan, where mostly rice is grown, granaries built upon sturdy wooden posts ("raised-floor buildings") appeared as long ago as 1,000 B.C.E.

By the First Century B.C.E., elevated storage structures had replaced subterranean grain-pits in Europe. In *The Ten Books on Architecture*, the great Roman architect Marcus Vitruvius Pollio (80-15 B.C.E.) writes: "So it is with granaries: grain exposed to the sun's course soon loses its good quality, and provisions and fruit, unless stored in a place unexposed to the sun's course, do not keep long" (Book I, Chapter IV); "Those who do business in country produce must have stalls and shops in their entrance courts, with crypts, granaries, store-rooms, and so forth in their houses, constructed more for the purpose of keeping the produce in good condition than for ornamental beauty" (Book VI , Chapter V); and "Rooms for grain should be set in an elevated position and with a northern or north-eastern exposure. Thus the grain will not be able to heat quickly, but, being cooled by the wind, keeps a long time. Other exposures produce the corn weevil and the other little creatures that are wont to spoil the grain" (Book VI, Chapter VI). In modern times, *all* granaries are elevated structures, not subterranean pits.

---

[62] See Philip King and Lawrence Stager, *Life in Biblical Israel*, the Library of Ancient Israel, 2002, p. 91.

When it is stored in a pottery jar, grain can appear to be or be likened to a liquid: when the jar is tilted, grain literally pours forth from it. When it is stored in a "raised floor building," grain will pour down like a liquid if a door at the bottom of the building is opened up.[63] But when it is poured into and stored within large pits or intricate underground vaults, grain no longer appears to be a liquid; it appears to "go back to" being a solid. Its dominant characteristic is its weight, that is to say, its weight per whatever measuring unit is used. Is the measure taken accurate? Wet grain weighs more than dry grain. Wheat is the heaviest grain, corn the next heaviest, oats the lightest.

When "grain in bulk" (a loose pile of grain) is stored in an elevated structure, and whether the builder or user of that structure knows it or not, the grain *continues* to perform or "act like" a real liquid. In fact, grain in bulk is a "semi-liquid": an incompressible, homogenous, granular mass that has no internal cohesion; the particles within it are held in place by their mutual friction upon each other. Grain piles not only exert pressure downwards, as weight; they also exert pressure laterally (horizontally), as stress against the retaining wall(s). Provided that the amounts of grain held in

---

[63] In some ancient/primitive cultures, such as that of the Dogon of Mali, granary doors bear elaborate carvings that depict, among other wonders, the Nommo, the Dogon's primordial ancestors, who have now descended from heaven to bring fertility to Earth, and stand with their arms raised, praying for rain, rebirth and regeneration. In the words of the catalogue for the auction of Dogon granary doors held at Sotheby's on 12 May 2005 – the bidding started at around $5,000 per item – "the granary itself is often associated with the celestial ark of origins and creation among the Dogon. The door itself can be likened to a heartbeat with its opening and closing[,] signaling the vitality of the granary to Dogon life."

them are not *too large*, granaries that are built on the ground or above it ("barns") can safely be constructed out of piles of cemented-together stones or bricks, lattices of sticks, and/or wood that is nailed together. There is no need to "rationalize" or "theorize" what "too much" grain means for such structures. The mode is simple trial and error: mistakes are never catastrophic (except for individuals); what works is what works.

Agricultural societies have built at least three types of barns: large wooden sheds that are built to accommodate grain that has already been poured into sealed ceramic jars or burlap sacks (an above-ground descendent of the ancient Greek *siros* and a direct descendent of the ancient Roman *horrea*); large wooden sheds in which grain is stored in big piles on the ground (an above-ground descendent of the ancient Mesopotamian pit); and large wooden sheds that have a group of storage compartments within them (an arrangement common at flour mills and breweries, where it is important to keep the different types of grain separate from each other, and to store separate batches of grain, no matter what kind of grain it is, according to who owns it).

So essential are granaries to human societies that they even figure in works of Science Fiction. Take for example *Star Trek*, perhaps the most well-known, popular and influential Sci-Fi story ever told. In the television episode entitled "The Trouble With Tribbles,"[64] the Starship Enterprise is called in to protect a shipment of grain being temporarily stored at K7, a deep-space station located near Klingon (i.e., hostile) space. The following scene occurs early in the action:

Mr. Baris (the Under-Secretary of Agricultural Affairs for the region): "Now, Captain: I want all

---

[64] Episode 44, first aired on 29 December 1967.

available security guards. I want them posted around the storage compartments."

Captain Kirk: "Storage compartments?! Storage compartments?!"

Baris' assistant: "The storage compartments containing the quadro-triticale."

Captain Kirk: "The what? The what? What's . . . quadro-triticale?" (He is shown some.) "Wheat. So what?"

Baris: "Quadro-triticale is not wheat, Captain. Of course I wouldn't expect you or, uh, Mr. Spock to know about such things, but, uh, quadro-triticale is a rather . . ."

Mr. Spock (interrupting): "Quadro-triticale is a high-yield grain. A four-lobed hybrid of wheat and rye; a perennial also, if I am not mistaken. Its root grain, triticale, can trace its ancestry all the way back to 20th century Canada . . . ."

Kirk: "Uh, Mr. Spock: you've made your point."

Lurry (administrator of K7): "Quadro-triticale is the only Earth grain that will grow on Sherman's Planet. I have several tons of it here on the station. Now, it's very important that the grain get to Sherman's Planet safely. Mr Baris thinks that Klingon agents may try to sabotage it."[65]

---

[65] My transcription.

It turns out that the quadro-triticale has in fact been poisoned by the Klingons, but Captain Kirk and the others only learn this after a very large number of small, fuzzy, irresistibly cute (and yet) voracious and rapidly reproducing pets called "tribbles" have gotten into the storage compartments, devoured all of the grain, and died. The horror of discovering the storage compartments to be full of dead animals is successfully dispelled or off-set by the comic spectacle of Captain Kirk (exasperated and suffering from a head-ache the entire episode) standing *underneath* one of the storage compartments and slowly being buried up to his armpits in tribbles as they fall *down upon him*. He has two immediate orders: find the man who brought the creatures aboard, and "Close that door!"

It is possible the grain was stored at K7 in this elevated fashion because the only suitable storage compartments at the space station were the equivalent of our 20th-century "over-head compartments." It is also possible that, in the future, all civilized people store their grain in this way. In any event, if it were not for the elevation of the granary, and Kirk's position beneath it, the scene would be ghastly, not funny.

Granaries are more than places for simple storage: they bring essential supplies together, and keep them safe in the common interest. *The very idea* of possessing a granary is valuable: "But there were ten men among them one who said to Ishmael, 'Do not kill us, for we have stores of wheat, barley, oil, and honey hidden in the fields.' So he refrained and did not kill them with their companions." (Jeremiah 41:8). According to Lewis Mumford, "the granary bin and cellar are village prototypes of the library, archive, museum and vault," and thus the city itself.[66] Writing about modern cities, the New York City politician Henry George declared, "Here are the great libraries, the storehouses and granaries of

---

[66] *The Culture of Cities*, Harcourt, Brace: New York, 1938, p. 274.

knowledge, the learned professors, the famous specialists. Here are museums and art galleries, and all things rare and valuable, the best of their kind."[67]

In their classic dictionary of ancient Greek and Latin words, William Smith and Charles Anthon show that the roots of the modern word "granary" lie in the ancient word *horreum*.[68]

> [A Greek word that] was, according to its etymological signification, a place in which ripe fruits, and especially corn, were kept, and thus answered to our "granary". During the Empire, the name *horreum* was given to any place destined for the safe preservation of things of any kind. Thus we find it applied to a place in which beautiful works of art were kept; to cellars; to depots for merchandise, and all sorts of provisions. Seneca even calls his library a *horreum*. But the more general application of the word *horreum* was to places for keeping fruit and corn; and, as some kinds of fruit required to be kept more than others, the ancients had, besides the *horrea subterranea*, or cellars, two other kinds, one of which was built, like every other house, upon the ground; but others were erected above the ground, and rested upon posts or stone pillars, that the fruits kept in them might remain dry.
>
> From about the year 140 A.D. [*sic*], Rome possessed two kinds of public *horrea*. The one class consisted of buildings in which the Romans

---

[67] *Progress and Poverty*, Book IV, Chapter 2, line 15, first published in 1879.

[68] *A Dictionary of Greek and Roman Antiquities* (Harper & Brothers, 1847), p. 510.

might deposit their goods, and even their money, securities, and other valuables, for which they had no safe place in their own houses. This kind of public *horrea* is mentioned as early as the time of Antoninus Pius, though Lampridius assigns their institution to Alexander Severus. The officers who had the superintendence of these establishments were called *horrearii*. The second and more important class of *horrea*, which may be termed public granaries, were buildings in which a plentiful supply of com was constantly kept at the expense of the state, and from which, in seasons of scarcity, the corn was distributed among the poor, or sold at a moderate price. The first idea of building such a public granary arose with C. Sempronius Gracchus; and the ruins of the great granary (*horrea populi Romani*) which he built were seen down to the sixteenth century between the Aventine and the Monte Testaceo.

The plan of C. Gracchus was followed out and carried farther by Clodius, Pompey, and several of the emperors; and during the Empire we thus find a great number of public *horrea* which were called the names of their founders, e.g. *horrea* Aniceti, Vargunteii, Seiani, Angusti, Domitiani, etc. The manner in which corn from these granaries was given to the people differed at different times.

Thus, save for the fact that they returned no interest, the ancient granaries or *horrea* were forerunners of the modern bank.

What *isn't* the ancient granary forerunner of? In *The City in History* (1961), Lewis Mumford likens the granary to the archetypal mother (the granary is the mother of all public buildings) because *all* buildings are like a mother's womb:

> Women's presence made itself felt in every part
> of the village: not least in its physical structures,
> with their protective enclosures. . . . Security,
> receptivity, enclosure, nurture – these functions
> belong to woman; and they take structural
> expression in every part of the village, in the
> house and the oven, the byre and the bin, the
> cistern, the storage pit, the granary, and from there
> pass on to the city, in the wall and moat, and all
> inner spaces, from the atrium to the cloister.
> House and village, eventually the town itself, are
> women writ large.[69]

And so the granary can be taken as a symbol of humanity itself.

According to the Hebrew Bible (Genesis 41: 1-57), the Pharaoh of Egypt was troubled by nightmares during a period of abundance. In his first nightmare, Pharaoh dreamed that:

> There came up out of the river [Nile] seven cows,
> well-favored and fat-fleshed; and they fed in the
> reed grass. And, behold, seven other cows came
> up after them out of the river, ill-favored and lean-
> fleshed; and stood by the other cows upon the
> brink of the river. And the ill-favored and lean-
> fleshed cows did eat up the seven well-favored
> and fat cows. . . .

In his second nightmare, the King of the Egyptians dreamed that:

---

[69] Lewis Mumford, *The City in History: Its Origins, Its Transformations, and Its Prospects* (Harcourt, Brace: New York, 1961).

> Seven ears of grain came upon one stalk, rank and good. And, behold, seven ears, thin and blasted with the east wind, sprung up after them. And the thin ears swallowed up the seven rank and full ears.

The Pharaoh was so rattled by these bad dreams and their incongruence with reality that he called upon Joseph, an imprisoned Hebrew, because he was rumored to have the ability to interpret dreams. When summoned, Joseph replied, "It is not in me; God will give Pharaoh a favorable answer" (Genesis 41:16). He then declared that the two dreams were actually one (a "double-vision," if you will).[70] Joseph declared that his double-dream meant that Egypt's abundance would only last seven years, and that it would be followed by seven years of severe famine. Convinced by this answer that Joseph was indeed a true soothsayer, the Pharaoh asked him to recommend courses of action, for the import of this double-dream was such that it had to be acted upon immediately.

Joseph's practical recommendations were no less striking than his "theoretical" interpretation of Pharaoh's dreams. Pharaoh's ministers should "take up" and "keep" one-fifth of the produce of the land. Furthermore, the ministers should "gather all the food of these good years that come, and lay up corn [not *maize*, but wheat] under the hand of Pharaoh for food in the cities, and let them keep it." These huge granaries would be "a store to the land against the seven years of famine, which shall be in the land of Egypt; that the land shall not perish through the famine."

If adopted and implemented, these truly radical measures would have immediate and potentially grave consequences. Brand-new granaries would have to be built, perhaps at considerable expense. Once constructed, they

---

[70] cf. Genesis 41:32.

would inevitably attract vermin, and would also be obvious targets for bribery, theft, intrigues and sabotage. And so the Pharaoh would have to organize a brand-new system of grain collection and storage, *and* use some of his soldiers (or recruit more) to fortify and protect that system from its many possible enemies: a doubly expensive operation.

Associations between granaries and military battles remain strong to this day. In the world of fantasy, there is *The Age of Empires*, a very popular computer game made by Microsoft in 1987 and updated many times since then. During the "Stone Age" part of the action, each player must build a Granary, which is an explicitly military – not agricultural – installation that allows players to build fortifications such as walls and towers.

In the world of military history, two examples stand out. First, the Battle of Stalingrad, which was fought between the invading German Nazis and the besieged Russian Soviets between July 1942 and February 1943. A part of this bloody campaign took place in and around a colossal grain elevator built on the banks of the Volga River.[71] The two sides could reportedly hear each other's whispers in and through the structure. A few photographs survive: they show the victorious Russians leading a group of German POWs away, with the ghostly snow-covered grain elevator in the background. The structure still stands, with a statue out in front of it; its main building is painted green. A banner proclaims: "Victory in the name of the Motherland; victory in the name of the living; victory in the name of those who will come after us. Victory!"

Second, the United States' accidental destruction of the grain elevator in Al Basra, Iraq, which took place in early

---

[71] Built in the classic American-style of the 1920s (freestanding cylindrical reinforced concrete grain tanks and a massive workhouse), this elevator appears to have been built in the early 1930s.

June 2003. Built in "the American style" in the early 1950s, this grain elevator was so prized (or its destruction was so embarrassing) that the United States not only offered to rebuild it, and build a brand-new grain elevator in Umm Osar, but also put a picture of the Al Basra Elevator (as it had been) on one of the new *dinars* that were issued in June 2003.[72]

Under Joseph's plan, less land would be cultivated for the production of grain for immediate consumption, and so the possibilities that bad weather or vermin might ruin the Egyptian harvest would be increased. Fears of scarcity or even famine in the near future would inevitably grow, thus leading to hoarding ("if the Pharaoh can store up grain, why can't I?") and monopolization, which would in turn further deplete the available supply of grain. Prices would rise, perhaps too fast and too high (not only for the buyers of grain, but also for the people who employed them and, based upon low grain prices, paid them low wages). There would be insistent, even desperate calls for increased wages; there might even be "bread riots" and open revolt in the cities. The granaries themselves would certainly be the primary sites of conflict. In sum: the Pharaoh might not be strengthening his regime by following Joseph's advice; he might actually be undermining it.

If the "Joseph Idea" failed, all of Egypt might be destroyed. And if it succeeded, Joseph's personal power (both agricultural and military) might become greater than Pharaoh's. The only thing that authorized the Pharaoh to go along with this plan – the only thing that allowed both the Egyptian people and Joseph himself to behave properly – was the certainty that it was God's plan and would play out according to his laws. A believer in God, even if it was

---

[72] See Tom Sawyer, *et al.*, "Plans Laid for Next Phase As Iraq Rebuild Continues," *Engineering News-Record*, 20 October 2003.

Joseph's God and not his own, Pharaoh followed Joseph's radical recommendations; he even put Joseph himself in charge of executing them. "So Pharaoh said to Joseph, 'Since God has shown you all this, there is none so discreet and wise as you are; you shall be over my house, and *all* my people shall order themselves as you command; only as regards the throne will I be greater than you.' And Pharaoh said to Joseph, 'Behold, I have set you over *all* of the land of Egypt'" (Genesis 41:39-41, emphasis added).

In a remarkable passage, Joseph is said to have "stored up food in the cities; he stored up in every city the food from the fields around it. And Joseph stored up grain in great abundance, like the sand of the sea, until he ceased to measure it, for it could not be measured" (Genesis 41:48-49). The Hebrew version is more elegant: "he laid up corn as the sand of the sea, very much, until they left off numbering; for it was without number." A threshold was crossed: there were so many grains (infinitesimally small and individually insignificant particles) in Joseph's granaries that their number reached infinity. The grains of wheat were like the grains of sand on a beach, and the waves of wheat were like the ocean itself.

In a word, the contents of Joseph's granaries were *sublime*. Summarizing Immanuel Kant's *Analytic of the Sublime*, which is Book II of *The Critique of Judgment* (1790), Jacques Derrida writes: "But the sublime, if there is any sublime, exists only by overspilling: it exceeds cise and good measure, it is no longer pronounced according to man and his determinations [...] *Erhaben*, the sublime, is not only high, elevated, nor even very elevated. Very high, absolutely high, higher than any comparable height, more than comparative, a size not measurable in height, the sublime is *superelevation* beyond itself' [...] 'We call *sublime* that which is absolutely large' (sect 25). The absolutely large is not a dimension, in the quantitative sense [...] That is what we call sublime, 'a dimension which is equal only to itself.'"[73]

In *The Socialist Perspective*, the Soviet dissident and committed anti-Socialist Igor Sharfarevich recalls that, in the 1930s, Russian agricultural experts were fascinated by ancient and contemporary Chinese granaries, which they took to be spectacularly successful. He summarizes Russian reports about ancient China (circa 1100 B.C.E.):

> Numerous songs describe agriculture based on the use of large groups of peasants directed by officials who indicate where, when and what to sow. For example, land officials were instructed as follows: "Our ruler summons us all . . . orders you to lead the plowmen to sow grain . . . quickly take your instruments and begin to plow. . . . Let ten thousand pairs go out . . . this will be enough." Elsewhere a similar scene is pictured: "A thousand pairs of people on the plain and on the mountain slope weed and plow the field." Of the harvest it is said: "There are large granaries everywhere. . . . In them, millions of *tan* of grain. . . . A thousand granaries must be prepared. . . . Ten thousand grain baskets must be prepared." Finally, the wang gives his approval – the ultimate goal of labor: "All the fields are completely sown. . . . The grain is truly good. . . The wang was not angry; he said, 'You peasants have labored gloriously.'"[74]

---

[73] Jacques Derrida, *The Truth in Painting* (1978), translated by Geoff Bennington and Ian McLeod, University of Chicago, 1987, pp. 122 and 135.

[74] Originally published in 1975. Translated by William Tjalsma, Harper & Row, 1980.

I know that Sharfarevich is trying to draw the reader's attention to despotic socialism's ruthless exploitation of the peasants, but I keep getting distracted – just as the Soviet leaders of the 1930s and 1940s probably did – by all that grain: ten thousand grain baskets, millions of *tan*, a thousand granaries . . . that makes a billion *tan* (!) The mind swims, gets carried away by the tide.

No matter how large or sublime the quantity of grain that was (or was not) stored in Joseph's granaries, it certainly couldn't top the contents of, say, the DeBruce grain elevator in Hutchinson, Kansas, which is in fact the biggest grain elevator in the world. It can store 20 million bushels of wheat, which is enough to supply the bread-needs of the entire United States for six months. In fact, there have been so many "amber waves of grain"[75] in America for so long that several dreamers have envisioned the country coming close to *drowning* in it. On a tour of the grain elevators at Buffalo, New York, in October 1861, the English novelist Anthony Trollope claimed that he "saw the wheat running in rivers" and "saw the men bathed in corn as they distributed it in its flow." Trollope himself had "breathed the flour, and drank the flour, and left myself to be enveloped in a world of breadstuff." In America, he concludes, "God had prepared the food for the increasing millions of the Eastern world, as also for the coming millions of the Western."[76]

The same metaphor is taken up in Frank Norris' novel, *The Pit*. Drawing upon a true story, Norris's narrator tells the tale of an unsuccessful attempt to corner the market in wheat – the "Niagara of wheat," the thundering "cataract" of wheat

---

[75] A line in "America, the Beautiful," a poem written by Katherine Lee Bates in 1893.

[76] *North America*, edited with notes by Donald Smalley and Bradford Allen Booth, Knopf, New York, 1951, page 158. Excerpts appeared in the *Chicago Tribune* on June 28, 1862.

– that poured "in upon the Pit from Iowa, Minnesota and Dakota, from the dwindling bins of Illinois and the fast-emptying elevators of Kansas and Missouri." The narrator's repeated use of phrase "wheat, wheat, wheat, wheat, wheat" attempts catch the sound of this prodigious river. "It was the Wheat! The Wheat! It was on the move again. From the farms of Illinois and Iowa, from the ranches of Kansas and Nebraska, from all the reaches of the Middle West, the Wheat, like a tidal wave, was rising, rising. Almighty, blood-brother to the earthquake, coeval with the volcano and the whirlwind, that gigantic world force, that colossal billow, Nourisher of the Nations, was welling and advancing."[77]

Though Norris's novel doesn't include such a scene, it gives its reader enough material and inspiration to imagine that "justice" would consist in either throwing the unsuccessful speculator into the mighty river whose course he foolishly attempted to divert for his personal benefit, or forcing him to *eat* the millions of bushels of grain he managed to hoard as part of his attempted corner, and thus driving home the point that grain is *food*, not a plaything for capitalist speculators. But it was only in the late 20th century that the American river of grain was actually portrayed as smothering and lethal. I can only find one such instance, but it is potent: in *The Witness*, a film directed by Peter Weir (1985), one of the "bad guys" gets buried by and suffocates to death in the grain stored an Amish country elevator. And yet there is no "poetic justice" in this death by drowning in grain. It just happens.

---

[77] Frank Norris, *The Pit: A Story of Chicago* (New York, 1903). See as well the very last line of Truman Capote's *In Cold Blood* (New York, 1965): "the whisper of wind voices in the wind-bent wheat."

Perhaps we just can't shake the idea that, though some *granaries* might be haunted,[78] *grain itself* is good and pure, and eternally so. For example, William C. Edgar finds himself obligated to recognize that "it has frequently been asserted that wheat found in ancient Egyptian tombs has been sown and has fructified. There seems to be no foundation for this statement." He goes on to say,

> In his great work, Sir Gardner [Wilkinson] remarks that in the sepulchers of Thebes grains of corn (wheat) and other seeds, have been found entire and preserved as if fresh from the soil [...] Moreover, these grains and seeds were preserved in pits hewn in the rock and sunk to depths ranging from fifteen to seventy feet [...] As a matter of fact, no case of mummy wheat germinating has ever been established [...] Transplanted to America, the germinated mummy-wheat legend has grown to marvelous proportions through the agency of the daily newspapers, those fruitful sources of popular misinformation. The idea of growing wheat from seed found in Egyptian ruins evidently appeals with much force to the imaginations of those whose duty and pleasure it is to prepare the choice

---

[78] See Robert Sadler's "The Haunted Farmer, or The Ghost in the Granary, a Tale," published in 1800. For a more recent example, see "Alberta writer wants Saskatchewan ghost stories," written by Matthew Gauk and published in the 31 October 2008 issue of the *Prince Albert Daily Herald*: "My ideal story is to find a haunted grain elevator," Christensen said, laughing."

literature which appears in the American Sunday newspapers.[79]

Agnes Denes' "earthwork" entitled *Wheatfield – A Confrontation*, which she executed in New York City the summer of 1982, is relevant here, too. In the words of the artist herself:

> After months of preparations, in May 1982, a 2-acre wheat field was planted on a landfill in lower Manhattan, two blocks from Wall Street and the World Trade Center, facing the Statue of Liberty. Two hundred truckloads of dirt were brought in and 285 furrows were dug by hand cleared of rocks and garbage. The seeds were down by hand and the furrows covered with soil. The field was maintained for four months, cleared of wheat smut, weeded, fertilized and sprayed against mildew fungus, and an irrigation system set up. The crop was harvested on August 16 and yielded over 1000 pounds of healthy, golden wheat. Planting and harvesting a field of wheat on land worth $4.5 billion created a powerful paradox. Wheatfield was a symbol, a universal concept, it represented food, energy, commerce, world trade, economics. It referred to mismanagement, waste, world hunger and ecological concerns. It called attention to our misplaced priorities. The harvested grain traveled to twenty-eight cities around the world in an exhibition called "The International Art Show for the End of World Hunger", organized by the Minnesota Museum of Art (1987-90). *The seeds were eventually carried*

---

[79] *The Story of a Grain of Wheat*, McClure, Phillips & Co., 1903, pp. 39-41.

away by people who planted them in many parts of the globe.[80]

Perhaps the sacredness of grain is why so many people have been willing to believe that the "crop circles" (elaborate circle-based patterns) that have appeared in wheat fields in South England since the late 1970s are not the work of hoaxers, but the work of aliens, Unidentified Flying Objects, "earth energy" and/or vortices created by the wind. The miraculous shapes and the nutritious plants in which they appear are each too "beautiful," too "natural," to be the work of mere people.

As foreseen by Joseph, God's spokesperson, the famine did indeed come and Egypt was well prepared – or at least its cities were well prepared – and so survived and even prospered, while many others perished. "All the earth came to Egypt to Joseph to buy grain, because the famine was severe over all the earth" (Genesis 41:57).[81] Where exactly were Joseph's granaries located? They were certainly placed alongside the Nile, the longest river in the world, or in the Delta region, because freight has always been so much easier, quicker and cheaper to transport by water than by land. The wording of the various Bibles is insistent and consistent: Joseph laid up corn "in the cities." This is significant: the first archetypal granaries were *urban* structures, not rural ones; they were located in port cities, not along land-locked

---

[80] http://www.evo1.org/agnesdenes.html accessed 15 August 2008. Emphasis added.

[81] Among these buyers were "ten of Joseph's brothers," who were sent by their father, Jacob, "to buy grain in Egypt" (Genesis 42:3). They do not recognize him. Perhaps he had come dangerously close to renouncing the religion of his father. The Koran has Joseph say: "Surely I have forsaken the religion of a people who do not believe in Allah, and they are deniers of the hereafter" (Yusuf, 12.37).

roads. Lewis Mumford reminds us in *The City in History* (1961) that everything that one imagines to be constitutive of a "modern" city (including a centrally located granary) was already present in the city-states of ancient Mesopotamia.

In her discussion of a 1927 painting of a grain elevator in Lancaster, Pennsylvania, by the American artist Charles Demuth, Karal Ann Marling reminds her readers:

> [there is a] tradition which holds that the [ancient Egyptian] pyramids were grain elevators, not tombs. According to classicist I.E.S. Edwards, the legend predates the fifth century [C.E.], when Julius Honarious quoted an older text to prove that the pyramids were Joseph's granaries, where corn was stored during the seven years of plenty. Although Arab scholars of the ninth century dismissed the story, it turned up again in the chronicles of the Baron d'Anglure in 1395 and is reflected in the mosaic decoration of a dome in the church of San Marco in Venice. The Hertel edition (1758-60) of Ripa's *Iconologica* revived the trope: the *fatto storico sagro*, or scriptural gloss on the classical allegory of Agriculture, in which Joseph interpreted Pharaoh's dream, showed the fat ears of life and the lean ears of death hovering above a pyramid.[82]

Even if it is apocryphal or merely "poetic,"[83] this substitution of granaries (storehouses of living grain) for pyramids (tombs

---

[82] Karal Ann Marling, "*My Egypt*: the Irony of the American Dream," *Winterthur Portfolio* 15:1, Spring 1980, p. 34.

[83] See Pamela A. Bakker's *Pondering Four Controversial Sites in Biblical Archaeology: Eden, Noah's*

of dead pharaohs) is extraordinary. It brings to mind 1) the image of things *contained* within other things, in particular, grain containers contained with a tomb, life contained within death; 2) the idea that, like the great men buried within the Great Pyramids, the kernels of grain in such granaries can look forward to immortality; and 3) the notion that *everyone*, not just the pharaohs, can achieve immortality (or resurrection), because each person contains a unique "kernel" (a soul) within their respective "husks" (earthly bodies).

The problem for Marling's reading of Demuth's painting is that there is a mismatch: despite its dead-giveaway title, *My Egypt* does not resemble or even evoke a huge pyramid.[84] And so, how to interpret the enigma of the title? Marling's best guess is that Demuth was referring to his own death, his own passing into history, his own funereal monument: "The finality of these cool, pristinely modern shapes dictates that the Pennsylvania [grain] elevator would outlast Demuth."[85] But what if she's got it backwards? Instead of memorializing his own death, Demuth might have been saying that the grain elevator in Pennsylvania – even though it was brand-new when he painted it – was already a kind of ruin. There is a possible parallel to America itself: never a young country; always already old and ruined.

Not surprisingly, the story of Joseph in Egypt continues to inspire people. Take for example the following paragraph, which was part of an article entitled "What Muslims Hear at Friday Prayers," published in *Der Spiegel* on 19 April 2006.

Landing, Joseph's Main Granary, the Exodus Crossing Point (Outskirt Press, 2007).

[84] But pyramidal forms do appear in *Box of Tricks* (Demuth's 1919 painting of an industrial warehouse) and Louis Lozowick's *Minneapolis* (a lithograph of grain elevators in Minnesota dated 1925).

[85] Karal Ann Marling, "*My Egypt*: the Irony of the American Dream," p. 33.

"Place me in charge of the granaries of the land, and you will see that I am a clever custodian," Joseph advises the pharaoh in the Koran sura that bears his name. No one has ever been a more efficient manager than Joseph, at least according to the imam from Jakarta [interviewed by *Der Spiegel*]. Today's leaders ought to take a page from Joseph's book, he said, adding that "corruption, laziness and fraud bring about destruction." By contrast, said the Indonesian imam, God rewards professionalism and a "strict work ethic" with happiness and fulfillment.

The reference is to Yusuf, 12.55, which in the translation I consulted does not mention "granaries" at all: "He said: Place me [in authority] over the *treasures* of the land, surely I am a good keeper, knowing well" (emphasis added). Perhaps this is mere quibbling. Are not granaries national treasures?

In the United States, Henry A. Wallace, who was the U.S. Secretary of Agriculture from 1933-1940 and Vice President under Franklin Delano Roosevelt from 1941-1945, was a great champion of what called "the Joseph Idea." Inspired by reading a book about the ancient Chinese, who apparently established an "ever-normal" granary in 54 B.C.E.,[86] Wallace started lobbying for an modern American ever-normal granary in 1918, when he began editing and publishing articles in *Wallace's Farmer* (Des Moines, Iowa). In 1926 and 1927, continuing to refer to ancient China, Wallace laid out the basic principles: when prices are low, the government should buy grain at its "normal" price, so as to benefit the farmers; and when prices are high, the government should sell its grain at its "normal" price, so as to

---

[86] Chen Huan-chang, *History of the Former Han Dynasty*, 1923.

benefit the common people. The key, of course, lies in setting what the "normal" price should be.

Despite Wallace's preference for the exotic (ancient China), there were plenty of modern precedents for such an idea. As Michel Foucault pointed out, the "normalization" of the grain trade has been at the center of government policy in England, Holland and France for more than 200 years. Prior to the 16th century, Europe was like America: there were virtually no public granaries; all of the granaries were privately owned. Steven Laurence Kaplan writes that,

> In place of the victualing systems of prefectoral Rome, Joseph's Egypt, or sixteenth-century Venice, Paris boasted Delmare's *Traite de la police*; foresight was enshrined in the rules and regulations rather than in the storehouses. The government itself undertook provisioning operations only in dire emergencies, at the last minute. For Parisians, the king was the baker of last resort rather than the Pharaoh of lean years and fat years.[87]

In a footnote (number 4) to this passage, Kaplan notes that "contemporaries praised Louis XIV for having done 'more than Pharaoh' in combating the dearth of 1662," and that "Pharaoh imagery remained very much in the minds of local officials who had to deal with everyday problems of provisioning."

The landmarks were the British laws of 1689 and the French laws of 1764, which – instead of insuring social peace (the absence of famines and bread riots) by making sure that

---

[87] "Lean Years, Fat Years: the 'Community' Granary System and the Search for Abundance in Eighteenth-Century Paris," *French Historical Studies*, 1977, Vol. 10, Issue 2, page 198.

prices and wages were always low, that buyers of grain didn't hoard it, and that the cultivation of land was kept limited – tried to ensure social peace by allowing prices to rise to a "normal" level. These laws 1) allowed farmers to export their grain to foreign markets in an indirect attempt to get domestic prices to rise during times of abundance, when prices were traditionally relatively low; 2) placed taxes on grain imported from foreign countries during times of abundance, so that prices would, despite the abundance, remain relatively high; 3) allowed "hoarding," that is to say, the construction and operation of granaries, which would prevent the "over-availability" of grain; and 4) encouraged the extension of areas under cultivation, which served to mitigate any set-backs caused by bad weather or vermin, and thus reduced the risks of generalized or widespread shortages, scarcities and famines. Thus "freed" from constraint, the market would "secure" itself.

Foucault summarizes the turning points: "The event on which one tries to get a hold will be the reality [everything involved in the growing, harvesting, storing and shipping] of grain, much more than the obsessive fear of scarcity [...] In other words, by working within the reality of fluctuations between abundance/scarcity, dearness/cheapness, and not by trying to prevent it [*sic*] in advance, an apparatus is installed, which is, I think, precisely an apparatus of security and no longer a juridical-disciplinary system [...] So, I think we arrive at this idea that is essential for the thought and organization of modern political societies: that the task of politics is not to see to the establishment within men's behavior of the set of laws imposed by God or necessitated by men's evil nature. Politics has to work in the element of a reality that [...] is a physics."[88]

---

[88] Michel Foucault, lecture of 18 January 1978, *Security, Territory, Population: Lectures at the College de*

The system of "free grain" first put into place in England and France in the 17th and 18th centuries, and adopted in America in the 20th century, works as long as three conditions are met when a bad harvest is imminent and prices start to rise: 1) consumers – presumably confident that imported grain will come to relieve them should a shortage occur during the spring (planting season) – agree to put up with some shortages in the interim, and restrain themselves from seizing the granaries, in the name of preventing the situation from getting out of control and threatening the general social peace (scarcity and revolt); 2) granary owners ("hoarders") and foreign grain producers – presumably convinced that the risks of waiting to see what the prices will be as the spring approaches aren't worth taking – agree to sell their reserves at the current price; and 3) society as a whole – presumably seduced by the notions of "civilization" and "progress" – agrees to overlook the facts that there is still "some scarcity, some dearness, some difficulty in buying wheat, and consequently some hunger, and it may well be that some people die of hunger after all," because "the multiplicity of individuals" is less "pertinent" to "the government's economic-political action" than the population as a whole (Foucault, p. 42). In other words, it is a system liable to breakdown at any time.

As Derk Bodde points out in "Henry A. Wallace and the Ever-Normal Granary: Chinese Origin of Wallace's Ever-Normal Granary,"[89] it wasn't until 1934 – a radio address on June 6, 1934, to be exact – that Wallace started mentioning examples of ever-normal, government granaries from "Bible times." It is in "Joseph, Confucius and the Farm Board," a

France, 1977-1978 (Palgrave, London, 2007), pp. 36, 37, and 47.

[89] *The Far Eastern Quarterly*, Vol. 5, No. 4, August 1946, pp. 411-426.

speech Wallace delivered on 19 August 1936,[90] that he first asserts: "Joseph was one of the earliest economic statesmen of history." Thereafter, the ever-normal granary becomes the "Joseph idea." Bodde claims that, compared to the Chinese granary, the "Joseph idea" was of "secondary importance." He's right, at least concerning the political and economic aspects of the ever-normal granary.[91] But he's wrong when it comes to mythology and symbolism. The Judeo-Christian-Muslim figure of "Joseph" allowed Wallace to clothe his ideas in Western dress, and thereby avoid the taint of Eastern despotic socialism. On 16 February 1938, President Roosevelt signed into law the Agricultural Adjustment Act of 1938, which allowed the government to adjust production so that it was more efficient and didn't produce "over-availability" (gluts) of grain, to insure grain that was stored in third-party warehouses, and to balance out existing stocks of grain through commodity storage loans.

Seventy years later, America's ever-normal granary is almost empty and a modern-day Joseph is nowhere in sight.

> WASHINGTON - Larry Matlack, President of the American Agriculture Movement (AAM), has raised concerns over the issue of U.S. grain reserves after it was announced that the sale of 18.37 million bushels of wheat from USDA's Commodity Credit Corporation (CCC) Bill Emerson Humanitarian Trust.
>
> "According to the May 1, 2008 CCC inventory report there are only 24.1 million bushels of wheat in inventory, so after this sale

---

[90] Reprinted in *Henry A. Wallace: Democracy Reborn*, Reynal and Atitchcock, New York, 1944.

[91] Compare with Benjamin Graham, *Storage and Stability: A Modern Ever-normal Granary*. New York: McGraw Hill (1937).

there will be only 2.7 million bushels of wheat left the entire CCC inventory," warned Matlack. "Our concern is not that we are using the remainder of our strategic grain reserves for humanitarian relief. AAM fully supports the action and all humanitarian food relief. Our concern is that the U.S. has nothing else in our emergency food pantry. There is no cheese, no butter, no dry milk powder, no grains or anything else left in reserve. The only thing left in the entire CCC inventory will be 2.7 million bushels of wheat which is about enough wheat to make half of a loaf of bread for each of the 300 million people in America."

The CCC is a federal government-owned and operated entity that was created to stabilize, support, and protect farm income and prices. CCC is also supposed to maintain balanced and adequate supplies of agricultural commodities and aids in their orderly distribution.

"This lack of emergency preparedness is the fault of the 1996 farm bill which eliminated the government's grain reserves as well as the Farmer Owned Reserve (FOR)," explained Matlack. "We had hoped to reinstate the FOR and a Strategic Energy Grain Reserve in the new farm bill, but the politics of food defeated our efforts. As farmers it is our calling and purpose in life to feed our families, our communities, our nation and a good part of the world, but we need better planning and coordination if we are to meet that purpose. AAM pledges to continue our work for better farm policy which includes an FOR and a Strategic Energy Grain Reserve."

AAM's support for the FOR program, which allows the grain to be stored on farms, is a key component to a safe grain reserve in that the supplies will be decentralized in the event of some unforeseen calamity which might befall the large grain storage terminals. A Strategic Energy Grain Reserve is as crucial for the nation's domestic energy needs as the Strategic Petroleum Reserve. AAM also supports full funding for the replenishment and expansion of Bill Emerson Humanitarian Trust.[92]

The CCC Inventory report for August 1, 2008 says there are only 12.2 million bushels of wheat in store, and a whopping 263.8 million bushels of corn![93] The disparity says it all: *Wheat?! Let them eat corn.*

---

[92] "The U.S. Has No Remaining Grain Reserves," published June 10, 2008 in *The TriState Observer*.

[93] http://www.fsa.usda.gov/Internet/FSA_File/wid2a.pdf accessed 21 August 2008.

Chapter 2
The Metaphor of Elevation

The verb "to elevate" and the nouns "elevation" and "elevator" are very rich, and it would be best if we did not rush through them, confident that we know all about their various overlaps and divergences. The verb-form can mean five different things: to lift up or raise above the ground; to raise the pitch or volume of a sound; to raise a person in rank or position, so such a person becomes exalted, dignified or "lofty"; to raise someone to a higher intellectual or moral level; and to raise someone's spirits, to elate or exhilarate. The value judgment is clear, and can be specified by examining the portrait drawn of the "low," which is not just at ground or sea level, but also inaudible, undignified, stupid, immoral and depressed.

Almost all of these meanings are in Charles Baudelaire's poem "Elevation" – the word is the same in both English and French – which was published in *Les Fleurs du Mal* (1862).[1]

Above the ponds, above the valleys,
The mountains, the woods, the lakes, the seas,
Beyond the sun, beyond the ether,
Beyond the confines of the starry spheres,

Mon esprit, you move with agility,
And, like a good swimmer who swoons in the wave,
You gaily furrow the profound immensity
With an inexpressible, male voluptuousness.

---

[1] My translation from the French. Cf. *Les Fleurs du Mal*, bilingual edition (David R. Godine, Boston, 1982), p. 192.

Send yourself quite far from the morbid miasmas;
Purify yourself in the upper air,
And drink, as if it were a pure and divine liquor,
The clear fire that fills the limpid spaces.

Beyond the troubles and the vast sorrows
That task misty existence with their weight,
Happy is the one who can with a vigorous wing
Rush towards the luminous and serene fields!

The ones that the thinkers, like the skylarks,
Towards the heavens take a free flight in the morning,
Who float over life, and effortlessly understand
The language of the flowers and the mute things!

The key word is *esprit*, which can be translated as spirit, mind, intelligence, even wit. True elevation is not possible unless the *esprit*, closely associated here with the "pure" minds of men, leaves and soars above the body, which is implicitly associated with the impure, heavy and wet bodies of women. These "sexist," that is to say, *mythological* associations can be extended to the similarities between "elevation" and "erection": when a man's penis is erect, the head of his penis is elevated; furthermore, during the "heights" of orgasm, his seed *rises* from within his testicles to the top of that head.

The first noun-form of the word ("elevation") can mean eight different things: an instance of elevating or being elevated; a high place or position in a hierarchy; height above ground level; the execution of a leap by a dancer or a basketball player; dignity, eminence or loftiness; a flat, scale drawing of a building; the angular altitude of a airplane, satellite, planet or star above the horizon; and the angle of a gun or cannon with respect to a horizontal vector. The only meaning here that causes a slight disturbance (a kind of stuttering) is the architectural one: one can draw an elevation of an elevator.

The second noun ("elevator") is also rich, and can mean five different things: a person or thing that raises or lifts up; a machine that hoists or lowers passengers or freight in tall buildings or deep mineshafts; a machine that uses buckets on a conveyor-belt to hoist grain; a warehouse for storing, hoisting and discharging grain; and a horizontal rudder on an airplane. We are already familiar with the "stuttering" or repetition here: an elevator is both a component in a grain elevating and storage warehouse, and the warehouse itself. This paradox further complicates architectural drawings of grain elevators. When one shows an elevation of an elevator, what is one actually looking at, the whole or one of its parts? How can the answer be "both"?

Perhaps now we can see some of the linguistic and conceptual complexities of the following questions: What does mean to *elevate the grain*? What is being done when grain is being elevated? What is being symbolized? Why is the phrase, indeed, the very idea of a *grain elevator* so odd and fascinating, and worth dwelling upon?

To anticipate the material discussed at length in the next chapter of this book: one elevates grain to unload it from wheel-barrows, ships or boxcars, and then bring it to the tops of the grain bins; these bins are typically tall and narrow to accommodate the two forces that grain in bulk exerts (dead weight pressing downwards, and lateral pressure against the retaining walls); the entire bin-structure is typically elevated above the ground so that there is sufficient space beneath it for hoppers, horizontal conveyor-belts and the like; a grain elevator built in a harbor like Buffalo actually elevates the grain *twice* (from the depths of the ship's hold to water/ground level, and from water/ground level to the top of the bin-structure).

No matter where they are built, either in the cities or in the prairies, grain elevators are always among the very tallest buildings in the area. Without intending to do so – their great height is required by the way they work and, when they are built in harbors, by limitations on available space on the waterfront – grain elevators rival or even overshadow buildings that were *designed* to be impressive, symbolically rich and unforgettable ("monumental"): cathedrals, palaces and certain public buildings. And so, in addition to their primary functions (unloading, transshipping and storing grain in bulk), grain elevators inevitably find themselves tasked with three others: being visual landmarks; being screens upon which people project their fears, fantasies and memories; and being privileged vantage points from which one can see the entire surrounding region.

"The land is flat," Truman Capote says in the first paragraph of *In Cold Blood: A True Account of a Multiple Murder and Its Consequences*, "and the views are awesomely extensive; horses, herds of cattle, a white cluster of grain elevators rising as gracefully as Greek Temples are visible long before a traveler reaches them."[2] "That's me," says a

---

[2] New York, 1965, p. 3. In the 1967 film version by Richard Brooks, several white clusters of grain elevators can be spotted from time to time, but they are in no way part of the film's action, mood or point of view.

Exactly ten years before Capote's book was published, Kansas (the location in which the murders took place) was the setting for Joshua Logan's film *Picnic*, which stars William Holden and Kim Novak. Before he's invited to the picnic, where the majority of the action takes place, Holden's character (Hal Carter) is given a tour of the immense grain elevators in Hutchinson, Kansas, by Alan Benson, the son of a wealthy grain-elevator owner (played by Cliff Robertson). If he is patient, Hal Carter is told, he could start as a "wheat scooper" and work his way up from there: a doubly daunting prospect, given how dirty, difficult and dangerous wheat-scooping is, and how vain and headstrong Hal Carter is. And so, as in the opening pages of *In Cold Blood*, the appearance of white grain elevators is a harbinger or foreboding of evil (murder or public drunkenness and forbidden love).

character in *Street Wheat*, a play written by Mansel Robinson, "trying to figure out how to get home. But the elevator! It was like a sign from God giving me directions. And I always knew where home was. But they knocked down most of our elevators and I'm driving blind looking for the towns I used to recognize."[3]

There's always an asymmetry in the grain elevator's "unofficial" functions: while everyone can see, and can project themselves upon, the grain elevator, only a few people get to see the view or project themselves *from* the grain elevator. As Walter Benjamin asks, "For in those days who besides the engineer [who built it] and the proletarian [who worked there] had climbed the steps that alone made it possible to recognize what was new and decisive about these structures: the feeling of space?"[4] Only a few get to explore the "galleries" of these elevated spaces.[5] The similarity to a religious, royal or economic elite is striking: only a few can attain the dignity, the eminence and the loftiness – in a word, the *elevation* – necessary to comprehend, appreciate and give proper praises to the *supremely elevated* (God, the sublime, or immortality). Everyone else is doubly low: beneath God's chosen elite and beneath God Himself.

---

[3] *Street Wheat*, Regina, 2003, p. 36.

[4] *Das Passagen-Werk*, published Suhrkamp Verlag, 1982, translated as *The Arcades Project*, Harvard University Press, 1999, p. 156.

[5] "From the palaces of the Italian High Renaissance, the chateaux of the French kings take the 'gallery,' which [...] becomes the emblem of majesty itself. [...] Its [the gallery's] new triumphal advance in the nineteenth century begins under the sign of the purely utilitarian structure, with those halls known as warehouses and markets, workshops and factories." A.G. Meyer, *Eisenbauten: ihre Geschicte und Aesthetik*, Esslingen, 1907, pp. 74-75, quoted in Walter Benjamin, *The Arcades Project*, p. 16.

And yet, at the same time, to elevate the grain is to "raise" the baby from its "crib," so that it can become educated and mature.[6] A remarkable word, *crib* is Old English for a basket, trough or box that holds animal feed, especially for cattle and oxen; it also refers to a small bed with high walls, suitable for a baby. In this context, the use of the phrase *grain crib* suggests that the grain, personified, "sleeps like a baby" while it is inside the barn (the womb), and doesn't "wake up" or "grow up" (germinate) until it is birthed. Given that grain cribs are typically tall and narrow boxes, one might say that the grain sleeps "standing up."

To elevate the grain is to praise the life-nourishing qualities of the grain itself. To elevate the grain, to sit down and "break bread," is to come together to celebrate the fruits of one's labor as both an individual and as a member of a social body. To elevate the grain is to symbolize civilization itself, if not its "upwards" progress, as well. To elevate the grain is to praise, worship and give thanks to God. For example, one elevates the middle piece of unleavened bread ("matzoh") during the annual Jewish Passover ceremony, which celebrates the ancient Hebrews' release from bondage to the Pharaoh; or one raises the Eucharist, saying "The body of Christ," who arose from the dead, and taking communion. To elevate the grain which has fallen (and indeed must fall) is to symbolize the seasons of the year and the eternal return of winter and spring, death and rebirth, decay and regeneration, burial and resurrection, destruction and recreation – not just of one deity or one god, but of *all* souls, *all* men and women, *all* living things.

These apparently contradictory images (the grain elevator as an instrument and symbol of power, and the

---

[6] See the many puns on the French word *élève* that Jacques Derrida makes in *Glas* (Paris, 1974): a seedling, an animal-breeder, a student, and a high, lofty or elevated person.

elevation of grain as a symbol of a free humanity) can be superimposed and re-represented in the "dialectical image" of gravity. When *a grain elevator elevates grain*, it doesn't simply or permanently "defy" or "beat" the laws of gravity. The machines work against these laws, temporarily "master" them, and then derive a great deal of "free" energy from them. That is to say, without any further human intervention or the expenditure of any more energy, the grain that has been elevated to the top of the structure will fall into a garner, which breaks flows of grain into batches, then into a scale that weighs the batches out, and finally into bins for storage. Even in storage bins, grain that has been elevated still possesses "stored energy," which can be released and utilized by simply opening the hopper at the bottom and letting the grain pour down. This reserve of "stored energy" is only emptied when the grain is in piles upon the ground.

Impressive though they are, elevation's victories do not defeat, change or repeal the laws of gravity, which of course remain in effect and have sovereign "jurisdiction" over every building on the planet's surface, even the high and mighty grain elevators! Isn't there endless satisfaction in watching films of buildings being intentionally demolished? Yes, indeed: the bigger they come, the harder they fall. What goes up *must* come down. To "fall" isn't merely to be overcome and lose one's way (one falls in love, in with a bad crowd, under a spell, under the influence, from favor, from grace, etc.). Falling provides unintended humor – a pratfall, "a fall on the buttocks, esp. one for comic effect, as in burlesque" – for one's fellow mortals. To rise, fall on your ass and then laugh about it afterwards shows you are human (obviously) and can admit it.

Chapter 3
The Rise and Fall of the Port of Buffalo

Looking over a map of New York State in, say, January 1815, one would find it virtually impossible that, within a mere 40 years, Buffalo, New York – a small trading and military outpost on the southeastern edge of Lake Erie, known as New Amsterdam before 1811, burned to the ground by the British on 30 December 1813, and lying in ruins ever since – would become the world's most-active port for the shipment of grain, the world's most important commodity. Far likelier candidates would have been one of the two big towns along the Hudson River, which was where most of the state's one million people lived: New York City, situated on the Atlantic Ocean and the beneficiary of one of the greatest natural harbors in the world, or Albany, lying upstate at the meeting of the Mohawk and Hudson Rivers. If one were to try to compete with Montreal, which was located to take advantage of the St. Lawrence River and its access to the Atlantic Ocean, one might have chosen towns in New York State that bordered the St. Lawrence River (Ogdensburg) or Lake Ontario (Oswego or Rochester). Buffalo was at the far-western end of New York State, more than 350 miles from Albany and 400 miles from New York City. An inland port, Buffalo could only communicate with the St. Lawrence River through the Niagara River, which fell from a great height (the world-famous Niagara Falls) before it fed into Lake Ontario. Dunkirk, New York, would have been just as good a choice as Buffalo. At least *its* natural was harbor.

For our hypothetical map-viewer, the improbability of the phoenix-like rise of Buffalo, New York, would not have been lessened by the digging and building of the equally improbable Erie Canal. At a time when America had not yet produced skilled cadres of architects and engineers, this deliriously ambitious canal was designed to be 360 miles long, 40 feet wide at the surface, 28 feet wide at the bottom, and 4 feet deep. It would require the construction of 18 aqueducts and 83 stone-and-wood locks, each 90 feet long, 15 feet wide and capable of accommodating boats weighing up to 100 tons. The longest American canal at the time was only 28 miles long.

Furthermore, as late as 4 July 1817, when construction on the canal began (eight years after the New York Legislature first surveyed its possible routes to Lake Ontario and/or Lake Erie), its terminus point *still* wasn't settled upon. Labor strife, political wrangling, rising costs of building materials and other factors might cause the direction of the canal to turn north at Syracuse and terminate at Oswego, which in fact became a center for flour-milling in the late 1830s; or it could terminate at Rochester, which was a major flour-milling center as early as 1823.

But let us grant that the Erie Canal ended up as it did, terminating at Lake Erie, not Lake Ontario. Buffalo's spectacular rise would *still* not be assured! Unlike the village of Black Rock, which was located a few miles north of Buffalo (at the meeting of the Black Rock and Niagara Rivers), Buffalo did not have a natural harbor. Strictly speaking, it didn't have a harbor at all. In the words of the fur-trader and later county judge Charles Townsend, who arrived in Buffalo in 1811: "There was no harbor here. The mouth of the Buffalo Creek was usually so much obstructed by a sand bar, that small vessels could but rarely enter, and even canoes were sometimes shut out, and footmen walked dry shod across the mouth." Because of this fifteen-foot-deep, sixteen-rod-wide, seasonally reoccurring sand bar, boats coming from Montreal, Toledo and Cleveland had to be "loaded and unloaded at a wharf near Bird Island, at Black Rock."[1]

But let us grant that a "modern" harbor – as well as adequate protection from storms coming off Lake Erie – were in fact built in and around Buffalo: first between 1819 and 1822, at the expense and thanks to the dogged determination of a handful of local businessmen. Furthermore, let us grant that the existence of this harbor (and the "fortuitous" sweeping away of Black Rock's piers during a particularly violent lake-borne storm in 1823) swayed the builders of the Erie Canal to terminate their work at Buffalo, which they eventually did in October 1825.

"Ah, yes," our hypothetical map-viewer from 1815 could then say; "it's all coming into focus now. By 1855, Buffalo will be the most-active grain port in the world, receiving over 60 million bushels of wheat per shipping season. And, by 1900, Buffalo will be the nation's eighth largest city, the first American city to be lit by electric power (ever since 1881), and the location chosen for the upcoming Pan-American Exposition (to be held 6 September 1901). Remarkable!"

Such accomplishments *were* truly remarkable, even heroic. But we have "granted" a lot to attain them. In particular, we have granted that Buffalo became a great city over the course of a mere 40 years, not due to natural resources, geographical location, God's grace or "manifest destiny," but due to what can only be called *violence*: the force of will and the will to use force. The German architect Walter Gropius put it this way:

> Art is made by man and for man; it is a contradiction of nature. It seeks to change the absolute beauty proper to nature, into conscious

---

[1] H. Perry Smith, *History of the City of Buffalo and Erie County* (Syracuse: D. Mason, 1884), p. 47.

relative beauty. This conversion is wrought by the will. What is without will in nature, man strives to affect by means of the will [...] Will thus orders chaos, renders the arbitrary necessary, and the disorderly rhythmic [...] For creator and spectator alike, the work of art reveals a pacification of the confusions of the world.[2]

Standing on the peaceful, unassuming shores of Lake Erie in 1800, Gouverneur Morris – one of America's "founding fathers" and empire builders – declared: "The proudest empire in Europe is but a bauble compared to what America will be, *must be*, in the course of two centuries, perhaps one" (emphasis added). It is precisely because Buffalo was never a natural city, but always an artificial one, that the passage of its time has been so rapid and so devastating. In only 160 years (from 1815 to 1975), Buffalo went from being a tiny outpost in the wilderness, to one of the world's great cities, to part of the American "Rust Belt," an immense tract of half-populated land, previously devoted to manufacturing and heavy industry, that stretches from northern New Jersey to northern Indiana, and from southern Ohio to northern Michigan and Minnesota. Buffalo is not alone in its rapid rise and fall. But it was the first to rise and the first to fall.

Before the arrival of the Europeans (the French, Dutch and British), the place now known as Western New York State was inhabited by the Five Nations: the Mohawks, the Senecas, the Cayugas, the Onondagas and the Oneidas. Founded around 1570 by the Mohawk chief Hiawatha, the Five Nations (the so-called "Iroquois") was considered to be the most powerful and wealthy group of nations in the Eastern Woodlands. They numbered more than 16,000

---

[2] Quoted in Helmut Weber, *Walter Gropius und das Faguswerk*, 1961, pp. 27-28. Translation in Reyner Banham, *A Concrete Atlantis*, MIT Press, 1986, pp. 197-198.

people when the French explorers arrived. According to the English colonist and historian Captain John Smith, writing in the 1620s, the "Iroquois" inhabited "all the land not sold to the English, from the mouth of the Sorrel River, and the south side of Lakes Erie and Ontario, on both sides of the Ohio, till it falls into the Mississippi, and on the north side of these lakes that have territory between the Ottawa River and Lake Huron, and even beyond the straits between that and Lake Erie." To be more precise: the Mohawks inhabited the shores of the great river that now bears their name; the Senecas inhabited the expanse of land between Seneca Lake and Lake Erie; the Oneidas and Cayugas lived on the shores of the lakes that would later bear their respective names; and the Onondagas inhabited the land in between Oneida Lake and Cayuga Lake (the area around what is today called Syracuse, New York).

During the American War for Independence, a military force led by General George Clinton, who later became New York's first Governor and Vice President of the United States under Presidents Thomas Jefferson and James Madison, decimated the Senecas, who, like the rest of the "house" of the Five Nations, had sided with the British. Officially speaking, the Senecas' title to their land in the Buffalo region was extinguished by the 1797 Treaty at Big Tree (now called Geneseo, New York). The participants in the treaty conference were the English-born land speculator Robert Morris (represented by his son, Thomas, and by U.S. Army Captain Charles Wimson), the Senecas (represented by Red Jacket, the half-European Cornplanter, and Farmer's Brother), and the Holland Land Company (represented by the New York City banker William Bayard and by the HLC's land surveyor and future resident agent Joseph Ellicott). Translation was provided by three interpreters who'd been hired by Morris and been instructed by him to make sure that the mile-long strip on the east end of Lake Erie – a kind of Levant that Ellicott had already surveyed and called "one of the keys to the Companies' land" – was relinquished by the Senecas and turned over to the HLC. The United States government also participated in the treaty conference and was represented by Jeremiah Wadsworth, a future railroad baron.

Under the terms of this manifestly unfair treaty, in exchange for almost four million acres of land worth millions of dollars on the international market, the Seneca leaders were compensated as follows: Red Jacket was given $600; Cornplanter $300; Farmer's Brother $100; someone named Billy $100; Little Beard $100; and someone named Pollard $50. These meager funds were not distributed in cash, but were invested in Alexander Hamilton's brainchild, the Bank of the United States, and maintained in the name of the President of the United States; dividends (surely of very small sums) were paid semi-annually. The Seneca women were paid 60 cows. The Nation as a whole was "allotted" a group of plots, located on the Tonawanda and Buffalo Creeks, and totaling 200,000 acres, upon which they were expected to settle and practice the "civilized" pursuit of agriculture. Growing wheat, for example.

In 1799, Joseph Ellicott made sure that the Senecas were not allowed to control the mouth of Buffalo Creek, the short, twisting and shallow tributary that flowed into Lake Erie. Ellicott made a secret deal with one Captain William Johnston. A former member of the British Indian Department who'd married a Seneca woman and become a trader and an interpreter, Johnston had been given two square miles of land at the very mouth of Buffalo Creek by the Senecas. Ellicott not only got Johnston to surrender his own claim to the land, but got him to convince the Senecas that they, too, should abandon their claims. Johnston's gimmick: because the mouth of the Creek silted up every year, the Great Spirit must have cursed it. The trick worked. In exchange for his services, Johnston was given a total of 685 acres of land in the new village that was going to be called New Amsterdam.[3]

Because they were hunters and trappers, not farmers, the Senecas didn't last much longer, limited as they were to twelve meager parcels of land. Though one report has it that, as late as the 1830s, "Red Jacket and his Seneca brethren, dressed in long blue frock coats with bright red sashes about their waists, lounged on the streets of Buffalo," by the early 1840s, the Senecas had either moved, become assimilated or died out. Today, few traces of the once mighty Seneca Nation remains. Note well the pathetic bronze plaque mounted on a boulder in a small park in south Buffalo that reads:

> In this vicinity from 1780-1842 dwelt the larger portion of the Seneca Nation of the Iroquois League. In this enclosure were buried Red Jacket,

---

[3] A different version of these events is relayed in George H. Harris' *The Life of Horatio Jones* (Buffalo Historical Society, 1903). One of the interpreters at the treaty negotiations with the Seneca Nation, Jones claims that the Senecas gave the land at the mouth of Buffalo Creek to his and Jasper Parrish, one of the other interpreters: "We have therefore made up our minds to give them a seat of two square miles of land, lying on the outlet of Lake Erie, about three miles below Black Rock, beginning at the mouth of a creek known by the name of Scoy-gu-quoy-des Creek, running one mile from the River Niagara up said creek, thence northerly as the river runs two miles, thence westerly one mile to the river, thence up the river as the river runs two miles, to the place of beginning, so as to contain two square miles." Quoted in Henry Wayland Hill, *Municipality of Buffalo, New York, A History. 1720-1923* (Lewis Historical Publishing Company: New York, 1923), excerpted by *The Buffalonian*.

Mary Jemison and many of the noted chiefs and leaders of the nation.

In the words of historian George W. Clinton, son of DeWitt Clinton, the twelve parcels of land occupied by the Seneca "soon passed into the hands of the Holland Land Company and, under the liberal policy recommended by their agent, Joseph Ellicott, and adopted by the Company, were rapidly occupied by industrious and intelligent families."

Ever since 1975, another sign has been called for. It would say: "Dear Native Americans. You can have your land back. We're done with it. Signed, the United States of America." But *where* are the descendants of Red Jacket and the other Senecas? If they were alive today, would they even want this land back again? The "Rust Belt" isn't red, the color of financial deficit: it is black and brown, the colors of spilled oil, garbage dumps, "brownfields" and "Super Fund" toxic-waste sites.

When New Amsterdam opened for business in November 1804, the conceptual and practical space of this future metropolis had already been pre-produced in the form of Joseph Ellicott's layout of it. Encouraged by Pierre-Charles L'Enfant's 1800 layout of Washington, D.C. – or at least by its long, wide avenues – Ellicott's layout called for the construction of wide streets that radiated out from the central hub like spokes in a wheel, and that were crisscrossed by equally wide streets, arranged to create a dense gridiron. It is worth recalling that Washington, D.C. was intended to be the nation's capital, and so had to present an air of magnificence. Pierre-Charles drew upon the design of Versailles. He also "worked" the natural environment into his design: the most prominent hills were reserved for the Capitol Building and the President's House (later called the White House), each of which had a spectacular view of the Mall. But New Amsterdam wasn't intended to be a capital city, not even the capital of New York State, and Ellicott didn't "work" the natural environment into his design. He simply imposed his plan upon it,[4] confident that Rene Descartes was right when he declared:

> Thus it is observable that the buildings which a single architect has planned and executed, are generally more elegant and commodious than those which several have attempted to improve, by making old walls serve for purposes for which they were not originally built. Thus also, those ancient cities which, from being at first only villages, have become, in course of time, large towns, are usually but ill laid out compared with the regularity constructed towns which a professional architect has freely planned on an open plain; so that although the several buildings of the former may often equal or surpass in beauty those of the latter, yet when one observes their indiscriminate juxtaposition, there a large one and here a small, and the consequent crookedness and irregularity of the streets, one is disposed to allege

---

[4] See William Cronon, *Nature's Metropolis: Chicago and the Great West*, WW Norton, 1991, p. 102: in "the system which the government had used since 1785 for selling public lands," the nation was subdivided "into a vast grid of square-mile sections whose purpose was to turn land into real estate by the most economically expedient method. By imposing the same abstract and homogenous grid pattern on all land, no matter how ecologically diverse, government surveyors made it marketable. As happened during Chicago's land craze of the 1830s, the grid turned the prairie into a commodity, and became the foundation of all subsequent land use."

that chance rather than any human will guided by reason must have led to such an arrangement.[5]

The trials and tribulations of the construction of a harbor at Buffalo were many, legendary, almost biblical. They are captured in great detail by *The History of the Great Lakes, Volume I.*[6]

> Buffalo harbor was the first constructed on the Great Lakes, and was at first built by private enterprise. The village was made a port of entry by Act of Congress March 3, 1805. In the spring of 1820, when Buffalo had less than 2,000 inhabitants, when there were in reality no harbor facilities, and when there was not yet sufficient business on the lakes to be dignified by the name of commerce, a plan was projected by Hon. Samuel Wilkeson for the improvement of the harbor [...] The harbor was constructed in 221 days, not including Sundays, as the laborers rested on that day, and when completed for that season it was about eighty rods in length. At its extremity the water was twelve feet deep. It was begun, carried forward to completion and completed principally by three private individuals, though they received material assistance from George Coit.
> Even after the completion of this work the mouth of the creek was still obstructed by sand, and vessels could not get in and out without running aground. The schooner Hannah, of 49

---

[5] *Discourse on the Method of Rightly Conducting the Reason, and Searching for Truth in the Sciences*, 1637.

[6] J.B. Mansfield, editor, *History of the Great Lakes*, Volume I (Chicago: J.H. Beers, 1899).

tons, could not get over the bar at the mouth of the harbor, and had to unload her cargo, pass over the bar, anchor outside in the lake, and there be reloaded. This, however, was the only vessel under 50 tons that was compelled to discharge her cargo in order to get out of the harbor; though the schooner Beaver, of 37 tons, stuck fast on the bar, and remained there for some time before being got off; the schooner Red Jacket, of 53 tons, remained thus fast for about half a day, and the schooner Erie, of 78 tons, was on the bar for twenty-four hours [...]

Because of the inadequacies of the Creek and the powerful and sometimes very destructive storms coming off Lake Erie, Buffalo's harbor required constant "improvement" (dredging and widening) all through the 19th century. But the federal government only funded one of the improvements made between 1838 and 1860.[7] The rest of the time, the funds were furnished by local businessmen, trade associations and other interested parties. Pleased by the turn of events seen after 1860,[8] the author of this entry in *The History*

---

[7] General harbor appropriations bill of 30 August 1852, signed by President Millard Fillmore. Thomas D. Odle, *The American Grain Trade of the Great Lakes, 1825-1875*, p. 106. The only other federal appropriations for harbor improvements in Great Lakes that went through 1838 and 1860 (St Mary's River, 7 July 1856 and St Clair Flats, 8 July 1856) were passed over presidential vetoes. See Odle. p. 106.

[8] For example: the harbor appropriations bill for Buffalo dated 6 July 1864 and the general harbor appropriations bill of 23 June 1866. Thomas D. Odle, *The American Grain Trade of the Great Lakes*, p. 107-108.

of the Great Lakes could afford to be generous in his praise.

Since 1826 this harbor has been very greatly improved by the United States Government. At first it was determined to construct piers on the north and south sides of Buffalo creek, and the work has been so carried forward that at the present time the water in the creek for a mile from its mouth is from 12 to 14 feet deep, and its average width is 200 feet. The harbor is protected by a substantial stone pier and sea wall jutting out into the lake, and at the end of the pier is a lighthouse 46 feet high and 20 feet in diameter.

There is also a ship canal 700 yards long and 80 feet wide and 13 feet deep, running nearly parallel with the creek, and nearly midway between the creek and the lake.

The works projected by the United States Government for the improvement of this harbor consist of a masonry sea wall along the lake shore for nearly a mile, running south from the shore end of the south pier, and a channel pier of about 650 feet in length.

The great storm of October 18, 1844, wrought great injury to the south pier, and it became necessary to rebuild the parapet wall. The old wall was but two feet thick. In 1845 it was determined to rebuild in a much more substantial manner. The new wall was of heavy stone averaging four feet in length, and weighing from one to three tons, dressed on the bottoms and joints and having a rough face, and they were laid in hydraulic cement. This wall is eight feet thick at the bottom and gradually becomes thinner until it is only four feet thick at the top, and was crowned by a heavy coping one foot thick.

This work was begun in 1845, suspended in 1846, and resumed in 1853, an appropriation having been made of $14,000 in 1852. During the years 1853 and 1854, there were constructed about 1,000 feet of exterior slope, averaging twelve feet, the top being covered by a broad flagging, over 400 feet of parapet wall raised 5½ feet being completed. Some 300 feet of the old wall were removed, excavations made and a new wall built, completing the parapet within the appropriation made for this purpose [...]

The total amount expended by the United States on the improvement of Buffalo harbor up to June 30, 1898, was $2,896,190, with the result of obtaining and maintaining a very good harbor. The principal features of the harbor work are a north and south pier at the mouth of Buffalo creek, protecting the entrance to the creek, and Blackwell Ship canal, in which the principal part of the business of the port is done; also an outer breakwater, 7,608 feet long, built of timber and stone. The superstructure on 3,879 feet of this length has been replaced with concrete. A seawall 5,400 feet long was also built along the lake shore south of the harbor entrance, and a sand-catch pier of piles and stone built out from the shore 870 feet long. The maximum draft that can be carried June 30, 1898, at mean low water over the shoalest part of the locality under improvement is 20 feet.

Chicago was quite similar to Buffalo in this regard. In the 1830s, "the Chicago River may have been more than a puny brook, but it was rather less than a great waterway: short, shallow, with no current to speak of, and far better suited to canoes than to sailing ships."[9] Indeed, "all of the harbors on the Great Lakes are at the mouths of rivers (except for the natural harbor at Erie, Pennsylvania), and at the entrances to these harbors, which the river current meets the Lake shore current, sandbars are constantly in the process of formation. Consequently, in the period before the Civil War regular dredging was required in order to keep the harbor entrances open to shipping, and if this dredging was not done the commercial interests of the port were apt to suffer."[10]

The history of the Erie Canal is also quite instructive from the standpoint of the imposition of human will upon the natural landscape. In 1807 and 1808 – from the depths of a debtor's prison in Canandaigua, New York – someone named Jesse Hawley signed the ancient and elevated pseudonym "Hercules" to a series of articles for *The Genesee Messenger* that championed a "Genesee Canal." Hawley imagined that this canal would use the route the Mohawks had used for centuries – that is, the Mohawk River – to get from the Hudson River, through the Appalachian Mountains, and to Oneida Lake. From there, the Genesee Canal would chart a new course and, using the Genesee River, cut in a westerly direction through the rest of New York State, all the way to the shores of Lake Erie. The Mohawks were less direct, more patient and less "ambitious" in their route to Lake Erie. They used the Oswego River to go north from Lake Oneida to Lake Ontario, sailed west, and used the Niagara River to get from Lake Ontario to Lake Erie. Hawley was sure that he could see something the Mohawks could not, which was the fact that "the Author of Nature . . . had in prospect a large and valuable canal . . . to be completed at some period in the

---

[9] William Cronon, *Nature's Metropolis: Chicago and the Great West* (WW Norton, 1991) p. 30.

[10] Thomas D. Odle, *The American Grade Grain of the Great Lakes, 1825-1873*, Ph.D. dissertation, University of Michigan, 1951, pp. 101-102.

history of man." That is, when history finds men willing to undertake the Herculean task of building an empire.

In 1811, the New York Canal Commission finally decided that it would recommend the construction of a canal to Lake Erie. Right from the start, this canal was destined to be "grand," to be a "Grand Canal." In the typically grandiose words of Gouverneur Morris, who wrote the Canal Commission's final report:

> And when . . . our constitution shall be dissolved and our laws be lost, . . . after a lapse of two thousand years, and the ravage of repeated revolutions, when the records of history shall have been obliterated, and the tongue of tradition shall have converted (as in China) the shadowy remembrance of ancient events into childish tales of miracle, this national work shall remain. It will bear testimony to the genius, the learning, the industry and intelligence of the present age.

Morris's reference to ancient China isn't as casual as it might appear at first. In 500 B.C.E., a "Grand Canal" was dug in China between Tianjin and the Yangtze River Valley. A thousand miles in length, it was three times longer than the Erie Canal could ever be. But Morris seems to be saying that, in a thousand years, the Erie Canal will make *a better ruin* than the Chinese one. Is this not an odd, even morbid sentiment for an empire-builder whose empire had not yet been built, not to mention lost?

The names of ancient ruined city-states line the route taken by America's "Grand Canal," which went by or through little villages with impossibly grand names such as Troy, Ilion, Utica, Rome, Syracuse, Palmyra and Rochester. Like America itself, the Erie Canal was destined to match and exceed the glorious temples and cities of the ancient, now ruined empires. William Cronon writes:

For American patriots of the nineteenth century, the line from Bishop Berkeley's famous poem was less a cliché than an incantation: 'Westward the course of empire takes it way' [...] The sequence of empires necessarily implied a sequence of cities, and so the boosters, in describing their communities, repeatedly invoked a jumbled handful of classical sites: Babylon, Thebes, Athens, Alexandria, Carthage, Constantinople, and, more frequently than any other, Rome.[11]

Yes, a village called Carthage was founded east of Watertown, New York,[12] despite the fact that the ancient Phoenician city that first bore this name was completely destroyed by the Roman Republic in 146 B.C.E. (Gustave

---

[11] *Nature's Metropolis: Chicago and the Great West*, p. 42.

[12] According to the anonymous author of "Traffic On Lake Ontario," published by *The Rochester Union & Advertiser* on 21 October 1893: "During the [eighteen] 'twenties' there was a rush of boat building both at Charlotte and also at Carthage, that well-night forgotten village which flourished for some time on the east side of the river and near the present north line of the city. [...] The first grain elevator in this vicinity was built at Carthage, and this quickly drew the lake vessels to the Genesee port for loads of wheat and other grain which had rendered the fertile river valley noted. A dozen of the best schooners on the lake also hailed from Carthage, and no better captains could be found than their commanders. Capt. John T.TROWBRIDGE was the owner of the second elevator which was soon afterwards erected, and he also sent out five schooners."

Flaubert once wrote: "Few will suspect how depressed one had to be to undertake the resuscitation of Carthage."[13])

One way or another, as either a failure or a success, the story of the Erie Canal was going to be known the world over. The "Grand Canal" was a kind of wager with history or God himself: it would make famous or infamous the names of those who didn't so much create it as *will it* into being. Like John Winthrop's "Citty upon a Hill," the Erie Canal have "the eies of all people [...] upon us; soe that if we shall deale falsely with our god in this worke wee have undertaken and soe cause him to withdrawe his present help from us, wee shall be made a story and a by-word through the world, wee shall open the mouthes of enemies to speake evill of the wayes of god and all professours for Gods sake; wee shall shame the faces of many of gods worthy servants, and cause theire prayers to be turned into Cursses upon us till wee be consumed out of the good land."[14] Greil Marcus comments: "The depth of the possible betrayal – 'consumed out of the good land,' not driven from it, not abandoning it, but the replacement of God by a demon who, as citizens went about their work or leisure, would suddenly devour them – measures the breadth of the possible achievement."[15]

The Erie Canal was built in the Classical Revival style that was popular at the time in both North America and Europe. Massive and very stately Romanesque arches joined

---

[13] *The Letters of Gustave Flaubert*, 1857-1880, translated by Francis Steegmuller, Harvard University Press, 1982, p. 24. Rome rebuilt Carthage after its forces had destroyed it, and kept the old name.

[14] John Winthrop, "A Modell of Christian Charity," dated 1630 and first published in 1838. Quoted in Greil Marcus, *The Shape of Things to Come: Prophecy and the American Voice*, Picador, 2006, p. 24.

[15] *The Shape of Things to Come: Prophecy and the American Voice*, Picador, 2006, pp. 24-25.

together the piers of each one of the Erie Canal's eighteen aqueducts. The hydraulic weigh-lock building in Rochester had been built to resemble a Greek temple. When completed, these structures and buildings were christened in Freemasonic rituals. On October 6, 1823, the Freemasons of Rochester sang the Masonic ode "The Temple's Completed" upon the completion of the magnificent Romanesque aqueduct that connected the Erie Canal to the west bank of the Genesee River. On June 24, 1825, more than four hundred "brethren of the mystic tie," dressed in full regalia, laid the final capstone at the top of the locks in Lockport, arrayed themselves on the staircase walls so that they were in the shape of a giant pyramid, sang a Masonic ode, listened to the Rev. Francis H. Cuming of Rochester, and watched in reverent silence as the capstone was finally slipped into place.[16]

The official celebrations of the opening of the Erie Canal were among the most spectacular events in the history of the American nation. In Buffalo on 26 October 1825, Governor DeWitt Clinton, the entire Canal Commission, and all of the engineers who'd worked on the canal boarded *The Seneca Chief* and set out for Albany. For this voyage, the boat had been specially decorated by the great American painter George Catlin with a portrait of the Governor wearing a Roman toga. At the head of a "Grand Aquatic Display" that included 46 other ships, *The Seneca Chief* was immediately followed in line by a ship called *Noah's Ark*, which had been specially constructed in the town called Ararat (!) and filled with pairs of live birds, fish, insects, bears and even Senecan

---

[16] Because of this close association of the Erie Canal with freemasonry, the reputation of the former (and many politicians in New York State) suffered between 1825 and 1842, when political anti-masonry swept through Western New York.

youths. All of history, indeed, *all of Creation*, was called upon to witness the Grand Spectacle![17]

As it left Buffalo, the procession was given a "Grand Salute" by a battery of 32-pound cannons. This salute was echoed by batteries of cannons spread out across the entire expanse of both the Erie Canal and the Hudson River; it took a total of 3 hours and 20 minutes for the salute to travel all the way down to New York City and then back again. Cadwallader Colden was so moved by this salute that, in his *Memoirs* of 1825, he demanded, "Who that has the privilege to do it can refrain from exclaiming, 'I too am an American citizen'; and feel as much pride in being able to make the declaration as an inhabitant of the eternal felt, in proclaiming that he was a Roman?" For America and all of its inhabitants were, like ancient Rome, destined to have an eternal place in the history of the world.

The "Grand Aquatic Display" arrived in New York City on November 4, 1825. The next day, the procession set off for Sandy Hook, a New Jersey fishing village on the Atlantic Ocean. To celebrate the world-historical meeting of what DeWitt Clinton called "our Mediterranean seas [the Great Lakes] and the Atlantic Ocean," the assembled celebrants witnessed a spectacular, world-historical "Wedding of the Waters," in which a keg of water taken from Lake Erie, as well as vials of water collected from the Rhine, the Ganges, the Nile and other great rivers of the world, were poured into the Atlantic Ocean. After conducting a "Grand Procession" from the Battery to City Hall, and participating in a "Grand Canal Ball" held therein, the celebrants sent *The Seneca Chief* back on its way to Buffalo, carrying a keg of water drawn from the Atlantic Ocean. The keg, which was marked "Neptune's Return to Pan," was emptied in Lake Erie when the ship finally made it back to Buffalo.

---

[17] Here "spectacle" refers to a visual display that commands attention.

Even before it was completed, the Erie Canal was a great financial and popular success. In its first three years, when it was only open from Albany to Brockport, the Grand Canal took in over $1 million in tolls; it employed the services of 8,000 men, 2,000 canal boats, and 9,000 horses, which were used to pull the boats along through the sluggish water. After its completion, the Erie Canal was even busier because it was open in both directions. Indeed, for those who worked it, the Erie Canal was a kind of circuit. In the words of Thomas Allen's famous song "Low Bridge":

> I've got an old mule and her name is Sal
> Fifteen years on the Erie Canal
> She's a good old worker and a good old pal
> Fifteen years on the Erie Canal
> We've hauled some barges in our day
> Filled with lumber, coal, and hay[18]
> And every inch of the way we know
> From Albany to Buffalo
>
> *Chorus:*
> Low bridge, everybody down
> Low bridge for we're coming to a town
> And you'll always know your neighbor
> And you'll always know your pal
> If you've ever navigated on the Erie Canal
>
> We'd better get along on our way, old gal
> Fifteen miles on the Erie Canal
> 'Cause you bet your life I'd never part with Sal
> Fifteen miles on the Erie Canal
> Git up there mule, here comes a lock
> We'll make Rome 'bout six o'clock

---

[18] A substitution of "hay" for "grain" so that the verse might rhyme with "day."

One more trip and back we'll go
Right back home to Buffalo

Chorus

Oh, where would I be if I lost my pal?
Fifteen miles on the Erie Canal
Oh, I'd like to see a mule as good as Sal
Fifteen miles on the Erie Canal
A friend of mine once got her sore
Now he's got a busted jaw
Cause she let fly with her iron toe
And kicked him in to Buffalo

Chorus

Don't have to call when I want my Sal
Fifteen miles on the Erie Canal
She trots from her stall like a good old gal
Fifteen miles on the Erie Canal
I eat my meals with Sal each day
I eat beef and she eats hay[19]
And she ain't so slow if you want to know
She put the "Buff" in Buffalo

Heading out west on the Grand Canal were streams of
immigrants, who either came to Albany from New England
or the European countries (especially Scotland, Ireland and
Germany) that were experiencing droughts or crop failures at
the time. These immigrants were also accompanied by the

---

[19] Interesting details: both laboring creatures eat very
modestly (no bread for the man, no corn for the mule); and
both eat grain-based foods (beef, presumably corn-fed cattle,
for the man, and hay, presumably wheat or other grain husks
– and not the wheat or grain itself – for "Sal").

large quantities of manufactured goods that they would need after they arrived at their final destinations. In the 1820s and 1830s, these destinations included Ohio (admitted to the Union in 1803), Indiana (admitted 1816), Illinois (1819) and Michigan (1837). In the 1840s and 1850s, they were widened to include Iowa, Minnesota, and Wisconsin, and, in the 1860s and 1870s, to Iowa, Kansas and the Dakotas.

During their stay in Buffalo, no matter how short it was, these immigrants and the workers on the canal boats needed accommodations, food, drink and entertainment. Buffalo thrived by providing these services, and tried to associate itself as closely as possible with the success of the Erie Canal. The seal of the village, adopted in 1828, and later the seal of the City of Buffalo, adopted in 1836, depicted a section of the canal through which a boat was being towed by a team of horses.

Heading back east on the Erie Canal were large shipments of lumber, grain and flour. At first, Western New York State itself was the source of these raw materials. The grain, mostly wheat, was grown on the incredibly fertile farms that had been and were still being established in Genesee County, which lies between Cayuga Lake and Lake Erie. This wheat was of such good quality that "Genesee" served as the gold standard for both wheat and flour (milled in either Rochester or Oswego) until the mid-1860s. Later, in the mid-1830s, the lumber, grain and flour came from the "Great West," which at first meant Ohio, then Illinois, then Minnesota and beyond.

Only 10 years after its completion, the Erie Canal was in fact so congested and painfully slow – the legendary trip from Albany to Buffalo took about a month – that it needed to be enlarged and improved. In 1835 and 1836, the state of New York sold $5.4 million in bonds to finance the enlargement of the entire expanse of the canal. Finally completed in the mid-1840s, these improvements included the creation of a sequence of double-locks just east of

Syracuse and the expansion of the Canal's dimensions (from 40 feet wide to 70 feet wide, and from 4 feet deep to 7 feet deep). Encouraged by these developments, the canal-boat lines steadily lowered their freight rates, from $4.16 per ton in 1830 to $2.96 in 1843. Success! But the similarity with Buffalo's harbor is striking: yet another "unnatural" creation that needed to be constantly re-created. Thomas Allen's "Low Bridge" wasn't written in 1840, as one might expect ("fifteen years on the Erie Canal"), but in 1905, two years after the Erie Canal was scrapped and work on its replacement, the New York State Barge Canal, had begun.

The success of the Erie Canal inaugurated a period of concerted canal-building all around the Great Lakes. In Canada, the Welland Canal was built between 1829 and 1832. A direct all-water connection between Lake Erie and Lake Ontario, this canal placed Port Colborne in direct competition with Buffalo for vessels bound for Rochester, Oswego or Montreal. Between 1842 and 1845, when the Welland Canal was expanded, that competition was intensified. By 1863, there were mechanized grain elevators at both ends of the canal. But large vessels couldn't pass through the canal, and so their cargoes had to be transshipped from lakers to railcars at Port Colborne and then sent north to Port Dalhousie, where they were transshipped from railcars to back to lakers.

In 1833, the State of New York "answered" the Welland Canal with the construction of the Chemung Canal, which connected Seneca Lake with Elmira, a town on the Susquehanna River in south-central New York State. Four years later, New York State constructed the Chenango Canal, which connected the Susquehanna to the Erie Canal. Together, these canals created an all-water route between the main trunk of the Erie Canal and such "faraway" east-coast cities as Philadelphia and Baltimore.

During the 1830s and early 1840s, canals were also constructed in Ohio, Indiana and Illinois. There were four major canals in Ohio alone: 1) the Wabash and Erie Canal (begun in 1827 and completed in 1848), which connected Toledo to Junction (another town in Ohio), and Junction with Terre Haut, Indiana; 2) the Miami and Erie (begun in 1833 and completed in 1845), which connected Cincinnati and Toledo; 3) the Ohio and Erie Canal (begun in 1827 and completed in 1833), which connected Portsmouth to Cleveland; and 4) the Pennsylvania and Ohio (begun in 1840), which connected the Ohio and Erie Canal in Ohio with the Beaver and Erie Canal system in Pennsylvania. (In 1844, the Beaver and Erie Canal system, and thus the Ohio and Erie Canal, was connected to Lake Erie via a 136-mile-long canal called the Beaver and Erie.) Other key canals for grain shipped on the Great Lakes were built in Illinois (the Illinois & Michigan Canal at the Illinois River, completed in 1848) and Michigan (the Saint Mary's Falls Canal between Lake Superior and Lake Huron, built in 1855, and the St Clair Flats Canal in Detroit, built in 1856).

Thanks to this incredible system of canals, traveling out west, becoming a farmer and finding a way to ship your grain to market became much easier propositions than before. In the ever-growing "Great West," the new settlers found some of the best farmland in the world. William Cronon writes,

> The glaciers had left the region west of the Great Lakes unusually well suited to the organisms [plants] and farming techniques that American and European migrants brought with them. [...] Mineral-rich soil had been accumulating for millennia. Atop it, prairie grasses had made their own contribution. They black soil they had produced measured in feet rather than inches and contained well over 150 tons of organic matter per acre in what seemed an inexhaustible fund of fertile earth. [...] Considering the favorable

climate as well, it would be hard to imagine a landscape better suited to agriculture.[20]

But to get at this rich "topsoil," the settlers had to clear the land of *everything* upon it: the trees and stumps; the wild fields of prairie grasses (big bluestem, little bluestem, "Indian" grass, switch grass, cord grass, prairie dropseed, and blue joint grass); and the thick sod of roots beneath those grasses.

> Many farmers hired professional 'prairie breakers' who owned oversized plows to do the initial cutting. The work had to be carefully timed, for if it was done too early the prairie grasses grew back and overwhelmed the [imported] crops; if too late, the turned-over vegetation did not rot soon enough for a successful planting in the fall. Professional prairie breaking was expensive, but well worth the cost for small landowners who could not afford to purchase special breaking equipment themselves [...] Farm families had destroyed the habitats of dozens of native species to make room for the much smaller bundle of plants that filled the Euroamerican breadbasket. As a result, the vast productive powers of the prairie soil came to concentrate upon a handful of exotic grasses [and there was a] deluge of wheat, corn and other grains.[21]

Once exposed, the topsoil wasn't plowed and seeded by hand, as the Native American cornplanters had done, but by teams of animals (oxen and horses). This was a momentous change, because these animals had to be fed, and *the wild*

---

[20] *Nature's Metropolis*, p. 98.
[21] *Nature's Metropolis*, pp. 99 and 145.

grasses upon which they would normally graze had been cleared away to "make room" for the farms. There appeared to be no other choice but to feed the animals one of the cereal grains. Corn was chosen because it was easier to harvest, less profitable as a cash crop and more desirable to the animals themselves than wheat. A kind of hybridized or dual agricultural regime was thus produced: to grow wheat, animals were required; but animals required feed, and so corn was also planted, which in turn required more farm animals to do the work. Conversely, as William Cronon has noted: "The precariousness of grain crops on the arid lands of the High Plains meant that many settlers turned to agricultural regimes better suited to a dry climate. If they could not profitably grow wheat or corn, they could usually raise livestock successfully [...] For Illinois farmers, this meant a steady conversion of [even more] grasslands to cornfields so that animals could eat domesticated rather than wild grain. A mixed crop-livestock system emerged, with the bulk of the region's immense corn production going to feed not people but animals."[22]

Grain grown in the "Great West" could be shipped to market via two all-water routes: the Great Lakes/Erie Canal system, and the Mississippi River, which is 2,340 miles long, fed by tributaries as far north as Minnesota and pours in the Gulf of Mexico. In the early 1830s, most of the grain grown in Ohio and Illinois was sent downriver on one of these tributaries, where via Cincinnati or St. Louis it eventually reached New Orleans. At the time, New Orleans was America's fourth largest city and the world's fourth most-active commercial port (only New York City, London and Liverpool were more active). But the Mississippi River was not an ideal shipping route. Though it was open during the winter months, unlike the frozen shipping routes on the Great Lakes, the "Big Muddy" had such strong currents and eddies,

---

[22] *Nature's Metropolis*, pp. 214 and 222.

and such constantly shifting channels, that grain-laden boats were all too often delayed by detours or the victims of accidents. At two points north of St. Louis (Des Moines and Rock Island), the Mississippi River was full of rapids, which caused two inconveniences. Cargoes had to be unloaded and carried along by land, and the ships themselves had to towed around and beyond these hazardous passages (lighterage and portage, respectively). As a result, the cost of insuring New Orleans-bound grain shipments was sometimes very high. In an effort to keep these costs down, some farmers accompanied their grain on its voyage to market, but this kept them away from their farms when they were needed there (planting season). It also encouraged the use of "flatboats," which were homemade vessels, used as a way of avoiding the cost of hiring one of the established shipping companies, and dismantled and sold off as lumber when the voyage was finished. Such boats tended to clog up traffic at key points and times.

New Orleans was not a developed grain market in the 1830s. The port could only transship grain to places such as Cuba, Central America and western Florida, which had relatively small populations, while Buffalo was only four hundred miles from Boston, New York, Philadelphia and Baltimore. New Orleans was not yet home to banks and insurance companies, which had access to relatively fresh information about crucial factors affecting prices, such as the weather, the fall harvest, supplies and demand in other markets. Buffalo's big brother, New York City, was the banking capital of the whole country and, consequently, was the first place that information about the markets in London and Liverpool was received. As a result, the trip down the Mississippi was doubly perilous: over the course of the voyage from the farm in Ohio to the market in New Orleans, the price might fluctuate so much that a shipment worth thousands of dollars when it was loaded might be worth a fortune or nothing at all when it was unloaded, without the grower or dealer knowing one way or the other until it was *a fait d'accompli*.[23] The market for grain in New Orleans was all-too-often glutted with "surplus" grain that could not find a buyer. As a result, around 1835, the tide of commerce from the northern states began to turn away from New Orleans and towards Buffalo.

Note well that although New Orleans "lost out" to Buffalo in the mid-1850s,[24] the Mississippi River *never* ceased to be a major shipping route. Thanks to the rapid expansion of corn farming in the "southern" states of Missouri, Kansas and Nebraska in the 1890s, Gulf of Mexico ports such as New Orleans, Galveston and Port Arthur became very active. In an article published in June 1897, the grain scholar George G. Tunel correctly deduced that, "as the railroads leading to the gulf have erected or are erecting terminal facilities for the handling of grain on a large scale, particularly at the southern termini, they may be expected to wage a spirited contest for the traffic of the disputed territory, and as a consequence grain rates to the Atlantic seaboard and to the gulf will probably fall in the near future."[25] Tunel was also correct in his forecast that the expansion of grain-growing into the Central West and Southwest of America

---

[23] See the story of John Burrows of Davenport, Iowa, in William Cronon, *Nature's Metropolis: Chicago and the Great West*, p. 105.

[24] William Cronon notes with respect to the southern part of the Great West: "As late as 1850, St. Louis was still handling over twice as much wheat and flour as Chicago [...] Between 1850 and 1854, the net eastward movement of freight shipments via the Great Lakes finally surpassed shipments out of New Orleans." *Nature's Metropolis: Chicago and the Great West*, p. 110.

[25] George G. Tunel, "The Diversion of the Flour and Grain Traffic from the Great Lakes to the Railroads," *The Journal of Political Economy*, Vol. 5, No. 3, p. 371.

would continue to reinforce the demand for the transshipment services of Gulf of Mexico ports. Dan Morgan reports that, today, "in the global chess game of grain, it is essential to be positioned at the mouth of the Mississippi, and all of the dominant merchant houses are. [There are] eight huge steel and cement grain-silo complexes that are spaced out along the lower 160 miles of the river."[26] These elevators are typically built several hundred feet back from the banks of the river, and use long horizontal gantries to reach the ships that must be unloaded or loaded with grain, so that if the water level rises too high the elevator's basements will not become flooded.

Grain shipped to market over the Great Lakes was handled differently than grain shipped down the Mississippi. There were no disposable flatboats; the farmers didn't accompany their shipments, but relied upon the services of professional shipping lines instead. Using wind-powered craft (sail vessels such as sloops, schooners and brigs) and then steam-powered ships (shallow-draught steamboats and screw-propelled steamers) to traverse the lakes, these lines were extensions of or associations with the companies that had been providing canal-boat service on the Erie Canal since the 1820s. As a result, these lines could bring shipments of grain from virtually anywhere on the lower lakes (Milwaukee, Chicago, Toledo or Cleveland), all the way to New York City, even if this all-water voyage required that the grain and the appropriate bills of lading were transfered from larger to smaller vessels at Buffalo or Oswego. Instead of requiring the farmers to buy insurance for their shipments, these companies doubled as "commission and forwarding agents." That is, in addition to forwarding (transporting) shipments of grain from one location to another, these agents also sold grain on behalf of the farmers – who still remained the legal owners of the shipments – in exchange for a

---

[26] *Merchants of Grain*, Viking, 1979, p. 313.

commission (a fixed percentage of the eventual sale price, usually one or two percent). To encourage business, many commission and forwarding agents offered their clients cash advances, which were financed by "bank drafts" from credit institutions in Buffalo, Albany or New York.

In 1831, the brig *John Kenzie* brought several dozen sacks of consigned wheat all the way to the Port of Buffalo from Chicago, which meant that the grain had traversed three of the five Great Lakes: up Lake Michigan, down Lake Huron, and across Lake Erie. In 1836, the *John Kenzie* (which was owned by Dorr & Jones, of Detroit, and commanded by Capt. R. C. Bristol)[27] brought in 3,000 bushels of wheat on consignment from Grand River, Ohio. In 1838, the steamer *The Great Western* brought to Buffalo 39 sacks of Ohio wheat consigned to parties in Oswego. In 1839, the brig *The Osceola* carried 1,678 bushels of wheat from Chicago to Mahlon Kingman's flourmill in Black Rock. In 1840, the schooner *The Gazelle* brought a 3,000-bushel shipment of wheat from Illinois to Buffalo. By 1841, the Port of Buffalo was 1.6 *million* bushels of wheat (in addition to 700,000 barrels of flour and 200,000 bushels of corn), and continued to receive huge amounts in 1842 and 1843.

Due to the physical presence of so much grain – some of it already sold, most of it still for sale – Buffalo became one of the most important grain markets in America. In 1840, every major participant in the grain trade had an agent or an office there: the transportation lines, the commission and forwarding agents, the warehousemen and the flour millers. "By 1850 Buffalo had become the largest grain and flour

---

[27] J. B. Mansfield, *History of the Great Lakes, Volume I* (1899).

market in the United States,"[28] and that it would remain so until 1880, when Chicago finally overtook it.

The physical presence of so much grain also created a *spatial crisis* (i.e., a crisis in spatial practices). There wasn't enough room on Buffalo's crowded streets for all the commission and forwarding agents and all the potential grain-buyers to meet, display and examine samples of grain, calibrate their scales,[29] negotiate prices, and conclude their deals. Nor was there sufficient room on Buffalo's wharves and in its waterfront warehouses, at which hundreds of workers were needed to unload, sort out, and either transship or store the grain shipments themselves. Improvised "granaries" were set up everywhere, and their contents were subject to theft, contamination, and premature germination. Last but not least, there wasn't sufficient room in Buffalo's harbor to accommodate all the vessels (lake vessels and canal boats) waiting to be either unloaded or loaded and sent on their way.

The barrels of flour weren't particularly difficult to transship: they could be rolled down gangplanks and, if need be, rolled along wharves and streets. But the sacks of wheat and corn were quite difficult: the stevedores had to board the boats, negotiate the tortuous passageways that led to the storage bins, lift the sealed burlap sacks (each of which typically contained two bushels of wheat) and then carry them back through those same passageways to the boats' decks. Using a block-and-tackle,[30] the stevedores then had to

---

[28] Thomas D. Odle, *The American Grain Trade of the Great Lakes, 1825-1873*, University of Michigan, 1951, p. 64.

[29] At this time, a "bushel" was a unit of volume (the amount of grain it took to fill up a bushel), not a unit weight (sixty pounds).

[30] The block-and-tackle is an ancient device by which heavy loads can elevated from the ground. Its invention is

elevate the sacks, swung them over, and set them down on the docks to be sorted out.

In the case of the shipment of wheat carried by *The Osceola* in 1839, it took five days to load it, two weeks to take it to Buffalo, and a whole week to unload it. But it could take even longer than a week to unload a shipment if the weather was bad (summer storms often came across Lake Erie) or if their was "trouble" with the stevedores, who could bring the entire unloading process to a standstill if they were displeased with either the local bosses who hired them or the transportation lines that entered into contracts with their bosses. Delays in Buffalo caused delays all the way down the line to Albany and New York, and backed things up in Cleveland, Toledo and Chicago.

The solution lay in the "labor-saving device," that is to say, a *mechanical* device that doesn't so much "save" labor as reduce the need for it, but without actually getting rid of that need entirely. Prior to 1842, steam-powered engines had

---

generally credited to Archimedes, the great Greek mathematician (287-212 B.C.E.). The block-and-tackle had many applications, only some of them mentioned in *Plutarch's Lives* (under "The Life of Marcellus"): launching weapons and attacking walled cities, certainly; but also constructing temples and large public buildings, lowering provisions into ships about to leave, and elevating freight from ships just arrived. Vitruvius speaks of both hand-powered and ox-driven "hoisting machines" at great length in Book X, Chapter II, of the *Ten Books on Architecture*. He writes: "All these kinds of machinery described above are, in their principles, suited not only to the purposes mentioned, but also to the loading and unloading of ships, some kinds being set upright, and others placed horizontally on revolving platforms. On the same principle, ships can be hauled ashore by means of arrangements of ropes and blocks used on the ground, without setting up timbers" (paragraph 10).

been used to power several machines widely used on American farms: Cyrus McCormick's reaper (1831); the Pitt Brothers' thresher (1834); and John Deere's steel-tipped plow (1837). Thanks to a man named Joseph Dart, Jr., the author of "The Grain Elevators Of Buffalo," delivered before the Buffalo and Erie County Historical Society on 13 March 1865, we know that the inspiration for the invention of the steam-powered grain elevator didn't come from rural agriculture, but from urban manufacturing (Oliver Evans' flourmills).

Born in Middle Haddam, Connecticut, on 30 April 1799, Joseph Dart was an apprentice in a hat factory near Danbury, the center of American hat-manufacturing, as a teenager. At the age of 21, he left Connecticut for Utica, New York, with the intention of manufacturing and selling his own fur products. In May 1821, Dart moved to Buffalo and joined up with another fledgling merchant capitalist, Joseph Stockham, who operated a hat manufacturing plant and a fur store on Main Street. Their partnership lasted until 1837, when the financial "panic" that began that year (and lasted until 1844) forced them to dissolve it. It isn't clear what Joseph Stockham did next. Joseph Dart eventually went into the grain trade.[31] It is possible that he did so not out of any

---

[31] On 16 August 2004, someone named Jeremiah Dart confirmed on an on-line genealogy board that, "Joseph Dart, the inventor of the Grain Elevator in 1842, was the brother of Russel Dart the first (1795-1865) who married Matilda Schenck. I've heard from Buffalo they moved to MI and some of my distant relatives started Dart Container Corp. [...] Some extra info: Joseph Dart, the inventor, was son of Joseph Dart (1770 - ?) of Middle Haddam CT, who married Sarah Hurd. His parents where Joseph Dart (1737 - ?) who married Abigail Brainerd. He is son of Ebenezer Dart (1698 - ?) who founded Middle Haddam CT. He came from Bolton, CT and his parents were Daniel Dart (1666- ?) and Elizabeth

great interest in grain, but simply because he had access to bank credit or waterfront property upon which a grain elevator could be built.

Despite its broad title, Dart's essay "The Grain Elevators of Buffalo" is not an honest history of the subject, but an expression of Dart's ultimately unsuccessful attempt – launched approximately three years after the destruction of the pioneering grain elevator that bore his name – to obtain a patent[32] for his invention, which he describes as "a simple apparatus with which all are now familiar, consisting of a series of buckets attached to a leather or canvas and rubber belt revolving upon pulleys." The strategy of Dart's essay is two-fold. On the one hand, it seeks to limit the discussion. Dart does not mention any of the people with whom he worked to build and operate the Dart Elevator, nor does give adequate attention to either water-powered or horse-powered grain elevators.[33] Joseph Dart is only interested in Joseph Dart. He writes:

Douglas. Who was the son of Richard Dart (1635 - ?) and Bethia ?. Son of Richard Dart (1610 or 11 - ?) who was son of Richard Darte (1589 - ?) and Johanne Spicer of Devon England." http://genforum.genealogy.com/dart/messages/ 601.html accessed 30 August 2008.

[32] It is difficult to research patents granted before 1920, but it appears that two grain-elevator-related patents were granted in the early 1880s. U.S. Patent 0,225,531 was granted to John S. Metcalf for a "scoop-shovel for unloading cars" in 1880. Three years later, a "W. Watson" was granted U.S. Patent 0,281,214. One wonders if this is the same Watson (or a descendant) who operated the Watson Elevator in Buffalo, New York, where the first "power-shovels" were used to help speed the unloading of grain boats.

[33] Thomas D. Odle, author of *The American Grain Trade of the Great Lakes, 1825-1873*, p. 47, reports that horse-powered grain elevators were built in Buffalo in 1837

It seemed very clear to me, that such an increasing trade demanded largely increased facilities for its accommodation at this point. [...] I determined, in 1841, to try steam power in the transfer of grain for commercial purposes [...] There were various obstacles to the successful execution of such a plan, and predictions of failure were somewhat freely expressed. I believed, however, that I could built a warehouse, of large capacity for storage, with an adjustable Elevator and Conveyors, to be worked by steam; and so arranged as to transfer grain from vessels to boats or bins, with cheapness and dispatch. Amid many difficulties, discouragements and delays, I began the work of erecting the building on Buffalo creek, at the junction of the Evans' ship canal, in the autumn of 1842, on the spot where now stands the stately Elevator of Hon. D. S. Bennett, which has risen, Phoenix-like, from the ashes of its parent. Indeed, the building I then erected may perhaps be called the parent, not only of the Bennett Elevator, but of all others; for I believe it was the first steam

---

(Mahlon Kingman's flourmill), in Toledo in 1838, and Chicago in 1841. Joseph Dart reports in "The Grain Elevators of Buffalo" that "I am informed, by our worthy townsman, Mr. John T. Noye, that, in 1824, his father rented a flouring mill on Bronx river, near King's Bridge, New York, for the manufacture of flour; attached to which was an Elevator for the unloading of grain from vessels, for the use of the mill. Mr. Noye thinks this mill was erected about ten or twelve years previous to its occupation by his father. But the commercial Elevator grew out of the wants of the grain-shipping interests of this port [Buffalo]." It isn't clear how this elevator in the Bronx was powered.

transfer and storage Elevator in the world. It was
the first successful application of the valuable
invention of Oliver Evans to the commercial
purpose for which it is now extensively employed.

On the other hand, Dart's essay seeks to rank him (now
properly isolated from the rest of his contemporaries) among
America's other great inventors: Robert Fulton, the inventor
of the steamship; Eli Whitney, the inventor of the steam-
powered cotton gin; and Oliver Evans, the inventor of a
steam-powered "elevator calculated by its motion to hoist
wheat or grain from the lower floor to the upper loft of such
mill." Like these men, all of whom were granted patents for
their inventions, Joseph Dart deserves one, too, because, as
he himself says, "an inventor's merit consists not merely in
conceiving an idea of a machine, but also in overcoming the
practical difficulties of its successful operation [...] It is
worthy of remark that some of the most useful inventions
have not been discoveries of new principles or methods of
mechanical action, but new applications of methods and
principles already known."[34]
Dart doesn't say much about how his own elevator
worked during the twenty years in which it was in operation.
In fact, he only speaks of its first few years.

My experiment, from the very first working, was
a decided and acknowledged success. Within a
month after I started, a leading forwarder, who
had confidently predicted that shippers could not
afford to pay the charges of elevating by steam,
came to me and offered double rates for
accommodation, but my bins were all full. The
great saving of time by the use of the Elevator

---

[34] Never granted the patent he so desperately wanted,
Dart died on 28 September 1879 at the age of 81.

was immediately seen. To give an instance that occurs to my mind, the schooner John B. Skinner came into port, with four thousand bushels of wheat, early in the afternoon, and was discharged, received ballast of salt, and left the same evening; made her trip to Milan, Ohio, brought down a second cargo and discharged it; and, on her return to Milan, went out in company with vessels which came in with her on the first trip down, and which had but just succeeded in getting, rid of their freight in the old way. In this case, the freight work of two vessels was done by one, and instances approaching this have not been uncommon. It had been said that eight hundred bushels an hour was the extent to which an Elevator could be driven, and grain correctly weighed. I began with buckets twenty-eight inches apart, holding about two quarts, and raised without difficulty a thousand bushels an hour. I soon put the buckets some twenty-two inches apart, and then sixteen or eighteen inches, till eighteen hundred or two thousand bushels an hour were raised. In some of the Elevators now in use, the buckets hold eight quarts and are only one foot apart, and will raise six or seven thousand bushels an hour, weighing it correctly. The storage of the first Elevator was fifty-five thousand bushels – its capacity was doubled three years after.

In both the passages quoted above and his much more lengthy discussions of how Oliver Evans' flourmills worked, Dart fails to mention two crucial points. First, Evans' "Conveyor" (no doubt also put to use in the Dart Elevator) was in fact a *screw-conveyor*, that is to say, a steam-powered version of the ancient device, invented by Archimedes, that rapidly conducts water from one place to another. (Evans had discovered the screw could also conduct grain as well.) And second, Evans' over-all intention was to automate the entire process of milling of wheat into flour. To this end, and over the course of many years of work, he installed a total of five steam-powered machines that, together, formed a single integrated production line. From start to finish, human hands did not touch the wheat as it was brought forth from a granary to the millstones, ground and separated from the chaff, and then sent along for temporary storage (and shipment) in barrels. But the human hands – the *few* human hands – that worked the machines were able to do the work of five times their number.

Karl Marx was the first to realize that the mechanization of production was also the production of something that might be called "the collective machine."

> Each detail machine supplies raw material to the machine next in order; and since they are all working at the same time, the product is always going through the various stages of its fabrication, and is also constantly in a state of transition from one phase to another [...] The collective machine, now an organized system of various kinds of single machines, and of groups of single machines, becomes more and more perfect, the more the process as a whole becomes a continuous one – that is, the less the raw material is interrupted in its passage from its first phase to its last; in other words, the more its passage from one phase to another is effected not by the hand of man but by the machinery itself.[35]

---

[35] *Das Kapital*, vol. 1, orig. 1864; Hamburg reprint, 1922, p. 344; quoted by Walter Benjamin, *The Arcades Project*, p. 394.

During the writing of *Das Kapital*, Marx was very interested in flour mills. In a letter to Frederick Engels dated 28 January 1863, he writes that the water-powered corn mill was one of "two material bases on which the preparations for machine-operated industry proceeded within manufacture during the period from the 16th to the middle of the 18th century (the period in which manufacture was developing from handicraft into large-scale industry proper)." The other "basis" was the clock.

> Both were inherited from the ancients. As soon as the water mill was invented, the mill possessed the essential elements of the organism of a machine. The mechanical motive power. First, the motor, on which it depends; then the transmission mechanism; and finally the working machine, which deals with the material [...] The theory of friction, and with it the investigations into the mathematical forms of gear-wheels, cogs and so forth, were all developed in connection with the mill; the same applies to the theory of measurement of the degrees of motive power, of the best way of employing it, and so. Almost all the great mathematicians since the middle of the seventeenth century, so far as they dealt with practical mechanics and worked out its theoretical side, started from the simple water-driven corn mill. And indeed this was why the name *Muhle*, 'mill,' which arose during the manufacturing period, came to be applied to all mechanical forms of motive power adapted to practical purposes (pp. 695-696).

But the application of a mechanical technique from the flour milling industry to the commercial transshipment of grain couldn't be undertaken by just anyone (certainly not by

Joseph Dart); it required the work of a professional engineer, someone highly skilled in machine design and construction, as well as carpentry and masonry. Robert Dunbar was the man for the job. Born on December 13, 1812, in Carnbee, Scotland, where he lived until he was 12 years old – at which time his parents moved the family to Pickering, Ontario, in the hope that his father, a mechanical engineer, might find suitable work – Robert Dunbar was also trained to be an engineer.[36] In 1834, he moved to Black Rock, where he eventually teamed up with Charles W. Evans, and designed and built flourmills. In 1839 and 1840, Dunbar built a pair of flourmills that exploited the difference in height between Black Rock River and the Niagara River. One of these water-powered flourmills was built for the Niagara Flour Company, while the other was built for Lewis F. Allen and a Mr. Lord. The latter was especially impressive: designed by Dunbar and constructed by the Jewett & Root ironworks,[37] this flour mill was equipped with two elevating mechanisms, one facing the Black Rock harbor, the other facing the Niagara River.[38]

Work on what came to be called the Dart Elevator began after the close of the 1842 shipping season and went on all winter long. The site was located on the Buffalo River, between Commercial Street and the Evans Ship Canal, which had been dug out and reinforced at private expense between 1831 and 1834. One presumes that the team that designed and built the Dart (Robert Dunbar, G.W. Schwartz, and

---

[36] He was 78 at the time of his death in Buffalo in 1890. See "Famous Inventor: The Death of Mr. Robert Dunbar," *Buffalo Commercial*, September 18, 1890, p. 6.

[37] In 1853, Robert Dunbar, S.S. Jewett and F.H. Root would found the Eagle Iron Works, which later came under the control of Dunbar and his son, George H. Dunbar.

[38] H. Perry Smith, *History of the City of Buffalo and Erie County* (Syracuse: D. Mason, 1884), p. 215.

others)[39] had a well-worked out plan, and constructed the grain elevator from scratch, that is to say, from the ground up.

Great height was inevitable at the Dart Elevator. The heart of the new invention – a looped or "never-ending" conveyor-belt, made out of canvas, upon which large buckets made out of iron had been attached at regular intervals; the whole thing enclosed within a long, straight rectangular box made out of wood and iron – had to be long enough to reach *all the way down* into the hold of a grain-laden vessel and *all the way up* to the top of the warehouse. (Oliver Evans' flourmill began *its* daily workload with wheat that had been elevated to the top of the building, because elevated grain flowed down through the mill's various machines by the simple force of gravity.) As a result, the tower in which Dart's bucket-conveyor was to be housed – dubbed the "marine tower" because it faced the water – had to be *doubly tall*: tall enough for the top-end of the elevating mechanism to "convey" its contents to the highest point of the adjoining warehouse; and tall enough for the bottom-end of the mechanism to come to rest well above the dock when the elevator had been pulled back inside the marine tower.[40]

---

[39] William Wells also "aided in building the first steam elevator." See H. Perry Smith, *History of the City of Buffalo and Erie County*, p. 217. According to "Obituary Notes," *New York Times*, January 23, 1904, "Philo Durfee of Buffalo" was "the builder of the first grain elevator in this country." Perhaps he was a carpenter.

[40] Because of this "stepping" motion – stepping *down* into the hull of the grain boat, stepping back *up* into the tower – the new elevating device quickly came to be called a "leg," which is an anthropomorphism now universally accepted in the elevator business. The bottom of the leg came to be called the "boot," and – in a departure from this otherwise exact

In his discussion of the Dart Elevator, Reyner Banham evokes one of "the end products of a building tradition whose sources were firmly struck [sic] in Europe itself and reached back as far as the later Middle Ages, to the great warehouses of the Hanseatic ports and other multi-story structures for trade."[41] Such buildings were tall, rather than long, because it was much easier and cheaper to raise heavy things with a block-and-tackle than it was to lift or drag them along by brute force. This can be clearly seen at one of the websites that documents Gdansk's *Speicherinsel* (Storage Container Island), which was ruined in World War II.[42] One incredible photograph on this site[43] shows a row of seven-story-tall, wood-timbered granaries, two of which have had modern elevating mechanisms attached to them. The contrast is startling. Great height can also be seen at the official website for the Hanseatic City of Demmin, which says that one of the sights worth seeing in the town is the *Speicherensemble* (the group of storage containers) at the *Peenehafen* (Peene Harbor).[44] A caption explains that the picture on the website shows, moving from our right to left, the *Luebecker Speicher*, built around 1820, the *Berliner Speicher*, built in 1900, and

---

analogy with the human body – the top of the leg came to be called, not the hip or the pelvis, but the "headhouse."

[41] Reyner Banham, *A Concrete Atlantis: U.S. Industrial Building and European Modern Architecture 1900-1925* (MIT Press, 1986), p. 19. It seems that "struck" is a misprint of "stuck."

[42] http://sabaoth.infoserve.pl/danzig-online/dziel/ gde.html accessed 12 August 2008.

[43] http://sabaoth.infoserve.pl/danzig-online/color/ speichr.jpg accessed 12 August 2008.

[44] Hansestadt Demmin, http://www.m-vp.de/1047/ 1047_4.htm accessed 11 August 2008.

an unnamed pair of *Speichern*, built in 1925.[45] Tall though it is (about five stories), the granary from 1820 is dwarfed by the granaries from 1925, which are easily *twice* as tall.

But Reyner Banham insists that, despite the general similarity between the height of Hanseatic granaries and the inevitable height of the Dart Elevator, what marks the latter as different and, indeed, revolutionary, is its mechanical elevating mechanism (the "leg"), not the size of its storage bins. He writes:

> The complete, independently powered assembly, if contained in a building of its own [...] was known as a "stiff" leg if permanently built into the storage structure or a "loose" leg if movable. Early versions of the loose leg were mounted on their own barges or floats and were used for transferring grain between floating vessels [...] This was the only version [of the loose leg] that could be described simply as an "elevator," uncluttered by nonmechanical functions such as storage [...] As far as the pictorial evidence can be read, it seems to show Dart's pioneering leg built on to the front of a fairly conventional wooden shed with a pitched roof, within which the storage bins were located [...] The same is true of other early elevators in the Buffalo area and elsewhere, but as the grain trade grew towards the end of the century, the need for ever larger storage vessels soon created a situation where the bins or cribs became the dominants parts of the installation, and the building envelopes were made – effectively if not conceptually – by simply

---

[45] *Der Speicher gegenüber dem Hanseviertel wurde 1925 errichtet* (the storage container across from the Hanseatic square was erected in 1925), my translation.

roofing and cladding the bins, their headworks, and the "house" containing the bulk of the elevating machinery.[46]

As the reader will see in the chapter of this book that is devoted to the response to Banham's book *A Concrete Atlantis*, too few of its readers have adopted his emphasis.

No doubt a lot of calculation went into the construction of the Dart Elevator. Given the density of wheat (approximately 60 pounds per bushel), and the amount of wheat involved (tens of thousands of bushels), the building *should* have been constructed upon a mortise-and-tenon timber frame. But such frames required a team of experienced carpenters and took years to season or dry – and Dart and Dunbar had neither. And so they went with a much cheaper and easier design scheme. Called "balloon-frame" or studded construction, this form of design had only been invented a few years earlier in Chicago. It called for lightweight, milled lumber to be fastened together with manufactured iron nails, which had also been invented recently. Though Dart and Dunbar couldn't have known it at the time, balloon-frame buildings – especially those with no windows – were vulnerable to grain-dust explosions because there was nothing to stop flames from climbing the vertical timbers, straight to the roof.[47]

---

[46] *A Concrete Atlantis: U.S. Industrial Building and European Modern Architecture*, 1900-1925, MIT Press, 1986, pp. 111-113.

[47] By the 1870s, balloon-framed designs were replaced by "cribs," which were constructed by placing narrow planks of wood (two-by-fours, two-by-sixes or two-by-eights) down on their sides and piling them up in "Lincoln log" stacks, which were then spiked together at the corners with heavy iron nails.

To be stored in a grain bin, grain (wheat or corn) must be removed from its sacks. But when it *is* stored in large quantities in a bin, grain shows itself to more than just a solid, that is, dead weight to picked up and carried. Grain in bulk is also a semi-liquid, that is, a substance that can pool up and flow like water or oil. This might have been an easy fact to determine in 1843, especially if you worked at a farm, shipped grain or designed flourmills for a living,[48] but the scientific literature on the storage of semi-liquids was small and very new at the time.

In fact, it wasn't until the 18th century that Charles Augustin Coulomb (1736-1806), a Frenchman, began to use "soil mechanics" (the laws of physics) to determine the best ways to construct and shore-up retaining walls. Later Coulomb's work was updated and ultimately rejected in favor of a new work by the great Scottish engineer William John Maqoirn Rankine (1820-1872). Rankine's theories were in turn updated and superceded by the work of the Austrian civil engineer Karl von Terzaghi (1883-1963), who is widely

---

[48] "[Grain] can behave almost like a solid at some times, almost like a liquid at others, and the change of state can be extremely sudden. Even in the holds of ships, let alone in more restricted locations, these changes can look *almost* catastrophic. I have watched a twelve-foot cliff of red durum wheat in the hold of a Steinbrenner ship in the Buffalo River, standing at what was clearly steeper than its natural angle of repose, suddenly let go and flow like a wave round the legs of the men working in the hold. Had the flow been deeper, it could have toppled a standing man. Old hands in the trade know when to stand out from under, but I could not understand the piteous tales I used to hear about inexperienced lads being buried and suffocated under falls of grain." Reyner Banham, *A Concrete Atlantis*, pp. 114-115.

reputed to be the "father" of soil mechanics.[49] Furthermore, it wasn't until the 1880s and 1890s that engineers such as Isaac Roberts (1883), F.H. King (1891), H.A. Janssen (1895), Wilfred Airy (1897), Charles F. Haglin (1898), J.A. Jamieson (1900), Henry T. Bovey (1901), Eckhardt Lufft (1902), J. Pleissner (1902-1905) and Alexander See (1905) began to come up with technical solutions to the problem of building truly prodigious grain bins out of relatively new materials such as iron, steel and reinforced concrete.[50] But you didn't need – or at least Robert Dunbar didn't need – to know the precise mathematics of the semi-liquids to build a good grain bin. All he needed was long personal experience, excellent knowledge of the actual conditions in which the structure was to be built and function, and a certain amount of daring and imagination.

At the Dart Elevator, the bins had to be capacious enough to store the entire contents of a fully packed lake schooner (approximately 5,000 bushels), so that the elevator could reassure grain sellers and grain buyers alike that their respective shipments were stored separately. If the shipment or boat-capacity was *less* than 5,000 bushels, it might still be necessary or desirable to store the grain in a 5,000-bushel bin to keep it cool and dry. But was this an economical use of space when it came to shipments of only 1,000 bushels each? No, and so a set of smaller bins would also have to be

---

[49] This is fairly arcane stuff: Terzaghi's first paper on the topic of earth-pressure ends with the following dry-as-dust statement: "The earth pressure against a perfectly rigid wall to be fairly independent of the density of the back-filling. For sand its value is $H = 1/2 \ (0.42) \ w \ h^2$, implying that K_0 is always 0.42."

[50] Milo S. Ketchum's monumental work, *The Design of Walls, Bins and Grain Elevators* (Engineering News Publishing Company, New York, 1911) contains the whole history.

constructed just for them.[51] There might also need to be a group of bins left unfilled in case of unexpected contingencies: grain that was damaged or already germinating, and needed to be segregated; unexpected increases in the number of schooners needing to be unloaded; break-downs along the Erie Canal that might cause shippers to want to store their grain for longer than usual; etc.

This is how the Dart Elevator worked. When a grain-laden vessel had docked alongside it and the bucket-conveyor was needed, the long box (the "leg") that housed it was lowered into position by a system of ropes and pulleys. When the conveyor-belt was turned on, the "Buffalo buckets" (as they came to be called when the invention became famous) bit into, scooped up, and elevated the grain from the vessel's hold to the top of the warehouse.[52] From there, the grain was garnered into batches[53] and weighed. Once it was weighed, the grain was either sent through a chute that conducted it into the main building for storage in a bin, or it was sent down through a chute to whatever vehicle was waiting to carry the grain away: a wheelbarrow, a wagon or a canal boat. (In a truly creative use of its available space, the Dart

---

[51] If each bin in fact contained approximately 5,000 bushels, then there would have been 11 of them in total. More likely there was a mixture of large and small bins, so that the house could store both large shipments and small shipments (under 5,000 bushels), unmixed and stored in their respective bins, but without wasting storage space. And so there might have been nine bins of large capacity (5,000 bushels), and ten of small capacity (1,000 bushels).

[52] At first, the buckets contained two quarts and were placed 28 inches apart; after some experimentation, Dunbar and Schwartz enlarged them to eight quarts and placed them only 12 inches apart.

[53] Note that the word "garner" (to collect or gather) is etymologically linked to "granary."

Elevator was built with a slip underneath it. When the canal boats came there to get loaded with grain, they managed to stay away from and thus "make room" for the larger lake vessels that were being unloaded or wanting to be unloaded by the elevating leg.) When the hold of the vessel was empty, the elevator was turned off and the box that housed it was retracted into the marine tower. The entire operation was powered by a single wood-burning steam engine, capable of producing approximately 100 horsepower, which was no doubt enclosed in a special "fireproofed" room that was made of iron and brick.

As Frank Severance notes, "we have no separate picture of Dart's first elevator," though it "can be made out in some of the early pictures of the harbor."[54] E. Whitefield drew one of these "pictures" (lithographs). It is reproduced in Frank Severance's *Picture Book of Earlier Buffalo*,[55] with the caveat that "the only copy known to the writer […] bears no date."[56] Another undated lithograph that depicts the Dart Elevator is reproduced online with the caption "This lithograph shows the Dart Elevator, located at the foot of Commercial Street ([courtesy of] Buffalo and Erie County Historical Society").[57]

Unfortunately for us, Whitefield's point of view (his "bird's eye view") is so far away from the Dart Elevator that we can just make out a few forms, three of them in total. Moving from left to right, we see an apparently average-sized building with a pitched roof; a large, tall marine tower with .space beneath it; and part of a large building with a pitched roof and many windows. It doesn't appear that any words or

---

[54] Frank Severance, *Picture Book of Earlier Buffalo* (Buffalo Historical Society, 1912), p. 46.

[55] *A Picture Book of Earlier Buffalo*, p. 26.

[56] *A Picture Book of Earlier Buffalo*, p. 25.

[57] http://www.buffalohistoryworks.com/grain/history/dart-elevator-litho.jpg accessed 6 September 2008.

identifying marks were printed upon the Dart. According to the second lithographer, the Dart Elevator bore the words DART'S ELEVATOR upon it in very large letters and encompassed *four* buildings, not three. In this picture, again moving from left to right, we see an apparently average-sized building with a pitched roof; a tall and narrow building – much like a marine tower, but *not* a marine tower, it seems – that is connected to a smaller building that is raised above the ground by pillars; *and* a tall and very narrow building, raised up on pillars, with a vertical slot in it that is clearly for the "leg" to step in and out of.

It seems we are looking at views of the Dart Elevator before and after 1846, when its storage capacity was doubled (from 55,000 to 110,000 bushels) and a second marine tower was added.[58] This impression is strengthened by the re-creation of the Dart Elevator that was made in 1992, on the 150th anniversary of its construction, for display at the Buffalo and Eric County Historical Museum.[59] In this re-creation, we see pretty much what the second lithographer shows us, that is to say, four structures: a small building with a pitched roof; a very tall and narrow marine tower that is elevated above the dock by heavy timbers (the "leg" is sticking out from the tower's midsection); a very large building, also elevated above the dock by heavy timbers, to which the marine tower appears attached or is part of; and a second marine tower, built upon the "shoulder," as it were of the main building. No chutes or spouts for loading canal boats are depicted, so one assumes all of them were placed underneath the elevator, that is, above the slip that had been dug underneath it.

---

[58] H. Perry Smith, *History of the City of Buffalo and Erie County* (Syracuse: D. Mason, 1884), p. 216.

[59] http://www.buffaloah.com/h/dart/image/2.jpg accessed 24 August 2008.

On June 12, 1843, the Dart Elevator serviced its first vessel, the schooner *Philadelphia*, which was carrying 4,515 bushels of bulk wheat loaded into her at Chicago. With William Wells (the son of Joseph Wells, reputedly the very first ex-European settler to father children in Buffalo) in charge of the elevator crew, the Dart Elevator took just one day to unload the *Philadelphia*, which would have taken at least a week to unload at a non-mechanized grain transfer house. Thanks to the speed of the Dart Elevator's leg, the schooner *John B. Skinner* was able to deliver and unload 4,000 bushels of wheat from Ohio to Buffalo, return to Ohio carrying a cargo of salt, and then carry and unload a second 4,000-bushel shipment of wheat at Buffalo – all in the time it took a traditional warehouse to unload and transship just *one* consignment. In other words, the speed of the Dart Elevator enabled the *John B. Skinner* to do the work of two ships. And so, though the Dart Elevator's per-bushel fees for transshipping grain were higher than the shipping companies had been used to paying for warehouse service in Buffalo, the shippers were more than happy to use the new facility, because so much money was saved in reduced turnaround time.

Over the course of the 1843 shipping season (June to October), the Dart serviced more than 70 different vessels (brigs, barks and schooners), and transshipped from lake steamers to canal boats a grand total of 229,260 bushels of grain.[60] No doubt it was a dangerous place to work. The tops of the grain bins were probably left opened, without covering hatches, so that the crew could simply swivel a spout or chute that came down from the garner and scales, and thereby easily direct the grain down into the appropriate bin. A worker could easily have a misstep, fall down into one of the bins, and thus plunge into enough grain to suffocate to death

---

[60] H. Perry Smith, *History of the City of Buffalo and Erie County* (Syracuse: D. Mason, 1884), p. 216.

("drown"). Accidents aside, if the grain didn't flow properly, a worker might have to "walk the grain down," that is, climb into the bin from the top, use his weight to get the flow going, and then climb out before he was swept along with it.

Dangerous or not, another five or six such facilities would have allowed the Port of Buffalo to transship 1 million bushels of grain per year without any difficulty at all.[61] One would think that such facilities were built right away: "Dart's pioneering effort was quickly and widely imitated," says one very reputable source.[62] "After the opening of Dart's elevator in 1843 the grain warehousemen both in Buffalo and Oswego adopted the new mechanical system of handling," says another.[63] But Buffalo didn't have a half-dozen elevators until 1848. As a matter of fact, it took *three years* for a second elevator to be built in Buffalo and *four years* for a grain elevator to be built outside of Buffalo.

Toledo and Brooklyn were the first cities to follow Buffalo's example, building steam-powered grain elevators

---

[61] "It is only by means of such appliances that such enormous shipments of grain take place in short periods as sometimes happens under particular conditions of the market, as for instance, when 13,600,000 bushels of grain were shipped from a single [American] port for Europe in the month of August, 1880." Cf. "Report on the Cereal Production of the United States," *The Tenth Census of the United States, 1880, Volume III*, quoted in Louis Bernard Schmidt, "The Grain Trade of the United States, 1860-1890," *Iowa Journal of History and Politics* (State Historical Society of Iowa, 1922), p. 436.

[62] Henry H. Baxter, *Grain Elevators* (Buffalo and Erie County Historical Society, 1980), p. 2.

[63] Thomas D. Odle, *The American Grain Trade of the Great Lakes, 1825-1873*, University of Michigan, 1951, p. 47.

in 1847.[64] Chicago built one in 1848.[65] By 1851, there were elevators in Fort Wayne,[66] Detroit[67] and Oswego.[68] Two

---

[64] For Toledo, see Thomas D. Odle, *The American Grain Trade of the Great Lakes, 1825-1873*, p. 48, and for Brooklyn, see Henry R. Stiles, *A History of the City of Brooklyn*, Vol III (1870), p. 580: "In 1846, '47 Col. [Daniel] Richards erected upon the North Pier the first steam grain elevator in the port of New York, and at this day nearly all of the grain business of the metropolis is done at Brooklyn, there being no stationary steam elevators on the New York side."

[65] "Small horse-powered elevators were used in Chicago throughout the prerailroad 1840s, but it was not until 1848 that the first steam-powered grain elevator appeared. Built by Robert C. Bristol, it was a four-story brick building measuring 75 feet square and having a total capacity of over 80,000 bushels. Large by the standards of its day, Bristol's elevator was soon dwarfed by larger ones as the flow of grain through the city increased." William Cronon, *Nature's Metropolis*, p. 111. Note that Bristol also worked as the captain of the grain boat called *John Kenzie*. In his *History of Chicago from the Earliest Period to the Present Time in Three Volumes* (A.T. Andreas, 1884), the historian A.T. Andreas states: "No elevators of large size were erected [in Chicago] prior to 1854. That year, the Galena elevator was built as well as the Munger & Armour warehouse, on North Water Street, on the Galena & Chicago Union Railroad track. The Galena & Chicago Union Railroad Company's elevator was built in 1855."

[66] *Fort Wayne Times*, September 1851.

[67] Thomas D. Odle, *The American Grain Trade of the Great Lakes, 1825-1873*, p. 48.

[68] The May 2, 1851 issue of the *Oswego Daily Times* states "Our Harbor presents a most interesting appearance in commercial point of view, crowded as it is with vessels at all

years later, there was at least one elevator in Milwaukee.[69]
But Philadelphia waited until the late 1850s;[70] St. Louis[71] and

---

our docks, warehouses, elevators and mills." The *Daily News*
(Kingston, New York) reported on 26 July 1853 that the Port
of Oswego had "procured floating elevators from N.Y." On 1
February 1854, the paper carried a notice advertising the sale
of "a floating steam elevator, capable of elevating two
thousand bushels of grain per hour, with flower and screen
for cleaning grain." An illustration that was published in
Frank Leslie's Illustrated Newspaper on 22 March 1856, p.
240, shows an eight-story-tall grain elevator. The article itself
"Monster store house capable of containing two hundred and
fifty thousand bushels of wheat besides twenty five hundred
barrels [of flour], the latter on the first floor."

[69] See the *Daily News* (Kingston, New York) for 17
October 1853. Note that Thomas D. Odle, *The American
Grain Trade of the Great Lakes, 1825-1873*, p. 48, says that
"Milwaukee's first elevator was built in 1845." Due to its
placement between Chicago's elevator of 1848 and Detroit's
elevator of 1851, this date is, I believe, a misprint for 1849.

[70] "The Tide Water Grain Elevator," published in the
Philadelphia Independent in April 2004, suggests that
Philadelphia's first elevator might have been built in 1863.
George G. Tunel says that the elevator built by the
Pennsylvania Railroad in 1865 was "probably the first
stationary elevator erected on the Atlantic coast." George G.
Tunel, "The Diversion of the Flour and Grain Traffic from
the Great Lakes to the Railroads," *The Journal of Political
Economy*, Vol. 5, No. 3, p. 346.

[71] Emerson D. Fite, "The Canal and the Railroad from
1861 to 1865," *Yale Review*, Volume 15, May 1906 to
February 1907 (New Haven, 1907), p. 212-213. Note that
Thomas D. Odle, *The American Grain Trade of the Great
Lakes, 1825-1873*, p. 50, says "the first elevators built along
the Mississippi River grain route were built in 1865 in St.

Erie, Pennsylvania, waited until 1861; New York City also waited until 1861 and only used floating elevators;[72]

Louis and in 1868 in New Orleans." Louis Bernard Schmidt, "The Internal Grain Trade of the United States, 1860-1890," *Iowa Journal of History and Politics* (State Historical Society of Iowa, 1922), reports that, as of 1872, "grain elevators have been erected at St. Louis and New Orleans for handling grain in bulk, which has for a longtime period heretofore been altogether in sacks, and is in part handled in sacks at the present time" (pp. 196-197).

[72] Emerson D. Fite, "The Canal and the Railroad from 1861 to 1865," p. 213: "In the first year of the war two of the monster labor-saving machines were set up, five [more] in 1862, the year of the [shovelers'] strike, seven of them throwing two thousand laborers out of work." This is confirmed by "About Grain Elevators," published by the *New York Times* on April 24, 1885, which claims that the first floating elevator in New York City was built by Andrew Luke in 1861; that subsequent floaters were built by "Mr Mills' New York Floating Elevator Company"; and that, by 1864, Edward Annan's company had built twenty-three of them.

According to George G. Tunel, "The Diversion of the Flour and Grain Traffic from the Great Lakes to the Railroads," *The Journal of Political Economy*, Vol. 5, No. 3, p. 346, "New York did not possess a single stationary elevator" in 1870.

Though William Cronon mistakenly believes that New York "did not use grain elevators until the 1870s," his explanation for the city's delay in adopting them is a good one: the city's grain merchants "faced the special problem of matching their own business practices with those of traders in the British Empire, who strongly favored sale by sample rather than by grade" (*Nature's Metropolis*, p. 416).

Portland, Maine, waited until 1866;[73] Minneapolis waited until 1867; New Orleans until 1868,[74] Baltimore until 1872;[75] Green Bay until 1875;[76] Omaha until 1876; Manitoba until 1879; Midland, Ontario, until 1881, Thunder Bay until 1883; Montreal until 1887, etc. etc. It was only in the 1890s that a true Northern American network of mechanized grain elevators was assembled.

What accounted for these unimaginable delays? How could an invention that accelerated the processes of unloading and loading grain boats be adopted so slowly? No doubt most contemporary observers expected that the Dart Elevator would fail: the machines or the engines would break down because they were too complicated; the building itself wouldn't be able to support the combined weight of the machinery and the grain in the bins, and would collapse; and/or the initial investments and operating costs would be so high that Dart would never make his money back and would

---

[73] An image of Portland after the Great Fire of 1866, placed online by the "Maine Memory Network," sponsored by the Maine Historical Society, show that at least one grain elevator was already present (and still standing).

[74] Floating grain elevators were "the only kind used at New Orleans, where, from the methods of shipment, the fluctuations in the river level, and other causes, they are most convenient." Cf. "Report on the Cereal Production of the United States," *The Tenth Census of the United States, 1880, Volume III*, quoted in Louis Bernard Schmidt, "The Grain Trade of the United States, 1860-1890," *Iowa Journal of History and Politics* (State Historical Society of Iowa, 1922), p. 435.

[75] George G. Tunel, "The Diversion of the Flour and Grain Traffic from the Great Lakes to the Railroads," *The Journal of Political Economy*, Vol. 5, No. 3, p. 346.

[76] Dan Morgan, *Merchants of Grain* (Viking, New York), pp. 53-54.

end up a bankrupt. Rather than jump right in, most observers probably preferred to "wait and see" what happened. (In 1846, when the Dart was expanded in both size and elevating capacity, no one could possibly deny that the "experiment" had been a resounding success.) Perhaps some people even *hoped* that the Dart Elevator would fail and were actually disappointed that it didn't. No doubt the Dart was resented and bad-mouthed by Buffalo's mostly Irish stevedores, who saw that this "labor-saving device" would end up putting them out of work (which it in fact did). In his lecture on "The Grain Elevators of Buffalo," Joseph Dart tells the following story about one of the people who expected and perhaps even hoped that "his" new grain elevator to fail.

> To illustrate his opinion, that the plan [of the Dart Elevator] was impracticable, I will mention here, that a short time before my building was completed, Mr. [Mahlon] Kingman, in passing it, said to me in a familiar manner, tapping me on the shoulder: "Dart, I am sorry for you; I have been through that mill; it won't do; remember what I say; Irishmen's backs are the cheapest Elevators ever built." Soon after my Elevator was in operation, he came to me, about two or three o'clock in the afternoon, to get two canal-boats loaded that day. I reminded him of the speech he wished me to remember. His reply was – "Dart, I find I did not know it all."[77]

But Kingman's humiliation before Dart was even greater than this: in 1847, he was forced by circumstances to convert his horse-powered Swiftsure Flour Mill, which was located in

---

[77] Joseph Dart, Jr., "The Grain Elevators Of Buffalo," delivered before the Buffalo and Erie County Historical Society, 13 March 1865.

Buffalo's harbor, into the steam-powered Sterling Grain Elevator. In this light, it is interesting that Dart has Kingman refer to the Dart Elevator as a "mill." Was Dart trying to suggest that, in his apparent ignorance, Kingman confused the new grain elevator with an old-style flourmill? Or did Kingman simply use the word "mill" in its generic sense (any factory or manufacturing house)? Underneath this self-serving retelling ("I, Joseph Dart, knew it all back in 1843")[78] is the suggestion that Kingman confided his doubts to Dart because he, too, was of Irish descent. Would not the overwhelmingly Irish stevedores of Buffalo feel doubly betrayed by being put out of work by a mechanical device built by a fellow Irishman?

Note well the following story that was printed in the *New York Times*.[79] Headlined "The Grain-Shovelers' Strike: A Crusade Against Grain Elevators, Laborers Refuse to Work Where the Machine is Employed," the story reported:

> About two thousand men have been employed in this City, in handling the immense quantity of grain that arrives here from the West. These men are called 'strikers,' 'shovelers' and 'trimmers.' During the last season, there were introduced into the harbor two 'grain elevators,' which readily performed the work of many men, and did it much more rapidly. This season, five more elevators have appeared, so that although the machines in use will perform about two-thirds the work required. The men have therefore formed a Protective Union, and have resolved not to work in connection with the elevators, or for any man who employs them. They contend that the great

---

[78] Mahlon Kingman had been dead for years when Dart made these comments about him.

[79] July 9, 1863, p. 5.

dust which the elevators raise is injurious to life, and furthermore that the manner in which the ships are loaded often causes the cargoes to shift, the ships to roll and ultimately to sink and be lost. [...] The meeting [of the grain shovelers, trimmers and strikers] was addressed by several gentlemen [who] denounced the owners of the elevators as capitalists and speculators, who were robbing the honest laborer of his due [...] They disclaimed any idea of raising a mob, or of interfering with any who choose to work [...] Mr. W.B. Barber, who appeared on behalf of the Committee from the Merchants' meeting, was the most cordially received. He fairly carried the meeting by storm by his praise of labor, particularly of Irish labor, his praise of Irish patriotism, etc.

No such notice appeared in the Buffalo newspapers, but one can be quite sure that similar sentiments, if not similar meetings, were held there, as well.[80]

---

[80] It wasn't until the 1880s that Buffalo's grain scoopers and shovelers became unionized. In May 1899, they went out on strike, but not against the grain elevators (the Western Elevating Association), nor the shipping companies that employed them. They struck against the "boss scoopers," a handful of men who arranged and supervised their work contracts with the shipping companies. Saloon owners as well as prominent citizens, the boss scoopers used their establishments as hiring halls and, based upon their idea of who a good client of the saloon-system was, determined which scoopers would or would not work on any given day. The boss scoopers were also in charge of dispersing the day's pay, which was issued the form of tokens that could only be cashed in (at the boss' own saloon!) for food, drink or

It probably wasn't clear who, exactly, should build Buffalo's second grain elevator, obvious and necessary though such a step might be. Should it be built by a local grain/produce merchant, like Joseph Dart, or by a local flour miller, like Mahlon Kingman? What about the trans-regional forwarding and commission agents, and the two big shipping lines (the Western Transportation Company and the American Transportation Company) that emerged out of a series of mergers and takeovers in the 1840s?[81] One would think that *all* of these participants in the American grain trade would want to own a grain elevator in Buffalo, that is, if they had the money and expertise to build one. No doubt they each hesitated to see who among them would take the very

---

lodging for the night. And so the scoopers, who numbered around 1,500 people, were *totally* dependent upon a handful of boss scoopers for everything necessary for survival: money, food and housing. After the strike, which paralyzed the grain trade all over the Great Lakes, the scoopers joined the International Longshoremen's Association as Local Grain Shovelers Union Local 109. See Brenda Kurtz Shelton, *Reformers in Search of Yesterday: Buffalo in the 1890s* (SUNY, 1976). But grain-shoveling remained what it had been since the 1840s: dangerous and exhausting. Working hours were between 7 am and 6 pm, six days a week (sometimes Sundays, as well), and there was only one assured holiday on Labor Day. See the "Memorandum of agreement, May 24, 1904, between the Buffalo Elevator Employees' Local Union No. 495 and the Western Transit Company," *Annual Report of the Board of Mediation and Arbitration of the State of New York* (1905), II.164.

[81] According to Thomas D. Odle, *The American Grain Trade of the Great Lakes, 1825-1873*, p. 38, "more [lake] vessels were owned at Buffalo and Cleveland than any other ports on the Great Lakes."

same leaps that Joseph Dart took (mechanical, structural and financial).

To the precise extent that it only handled grain in bulk, the Dart Elevator operated *outside* of the established practices of the grain trade. In these practices, grain was shipped from place to place in sealed burlap sacks. William Cronon notes,

> Since grain originated in farms and villages that had only small quantities to sell, it had to start its journey on a modest scale, ideally suited to small groups of sacks. [...] As the sack of grain moved away from the farm – whether pulled in wagons, floated on flatboats, or lofted on stevedores' backs – its contents remained intact, unmixed with grain from other farms. Nothing adulterated the characteristic weight, bulk, cleanliness, purity, and flavor that marked it as the product of a particular tract of land and a particular farmer's labor. [...] Shippers and their customers wanted to know exactly what they were selling and buying, so it made sense not to break up individual shipments or mix them with others.[82]

In other words, the sacks were both the symbol of and the link between grain as a physical object, valued for its capacity to nourish (a "use-value"), and grain as a commodity, valued for its capacity to be converted into money (an "exchange-value"). Because they were sealed at the beginning of the process and only opened at the end of it, sacks of grain were like the coins of the same era: they contained gold (golden wheat or gold the metal) and they could be exchanged for money. Because it broke the sacks open prematurely, even dispensed with the very need for

---

[82] *Nature's Metropolis*, pp. 108, 107, and 109.

them, Dart's elevator must have been perceived in much the same way that paper money was: shadowy, shady, insubstantial, even devilish.[83]

In what follows I single out four key local developments that, taken together, led to the building of more than a dozen steam-powered grain elevators in Buffalo between 1846 and 1855.

#1) By 1846, when the amount of wheat received at the Port of Buffalo crossed the four-million-bushel mark for the first time (it had remained between one and two million bushels since 1839),[84] it must have been clear to everyone that these unbelievable amounts had *not* been the result of a temporary surplus or a situation that only temporarily favored Buffalo. Thanks to its position at the western terminus of the Erie Canal and the importance of that waterway to commerce in New York, Buffalo was continuing and would continue to receive large (and even larger!) amounts of grain that had been shipped over the Great Lakes.

#2) Between 1845 and 1846, Buffalo's flour milling industry was bolstered by the construction of two brand-new steam-powered mills in the area (the Thorton & Chester, and the George Urban, Sr.). These "modern" mills not only increased the demand for grain shipped in bulk along the Erie Canal (and thus the rest of the Great Lakes water system), but

---

[83] Marc Shell, *Money, Language, and Thought: Literary and Philosophical Economies from the Medieval to the Modern Era* (University of California Press, 1982), figures 1, 2 and 3.

[84] Corn receipts crossed the four-million-bushel mark in 1851, after remaining between one and two million bushels since 1846. Oats crossed the seven-million-bushel mark in 1863, after remaining between one and two million bushels since 1851. See Thomas D. Odle, *The American Grain Trade of the Great Lakes, 1825-1873*, p. 144.

they also stimulated the "local" grain market, which, as we have seen, was a central hub in the nation's grain market.

#3) In 1845, a local flour miller named Russell H. Heywood (proprietor of the Venice Flour Mills in Black Rock, New York) led a group of businessmen – Joseph Dart, Charles W. Evans, George W. Tifft, S. W. Howell, John Pease and Oliver Bugbee, among others – who founded the Buffalo Board of Trade (BBOT). The sixth such organization in the country, preceded by boards in New York City (1768), Baltimore (1821), Philadelphia (1833), New Orleans (1834), Boston (1836) and Cincinnati (1839),[85] the BBOT was established, in the words of its first president, Russell H. Heywood, "for the facilitation of the Commerce of Buffalo, and settlement of differences unavoidably arising between its members, particularly at the point where such a multiplicity of transactions take place in the produce market." The BBOT, indeed, *any* Board of Trade, "elevates the character of each member, and of the city – promotes fair dealing and kindly feelings towards each other."[86] In more concrete terms, it passed resolutions and lobbied the state and federal governments to make improvements, and it undertook projects that benefited its the interests of its members.

One such project was the construction of the Merchants' Exchange Building, which was undertaken at the personal expense of BBOT President Heywood. Located on Prime Street (near-by the Dart Elevator), the Merchants' Exchange was a large, four-story warehouse built out of brick and other fireproof materials (a tin roof, iron window shutters

---

[85] Boards of trade would subsequently be founded in Detroit (1847), Cleveland and Chicago (1848), and Oswego, Toledo and Milwaukee (1849).

[86] Russell H. Heywood, quoted in Frank H. Severance, *Historical Sketch of the Board of Trade, the Merchants' Exchange and the Chamber of Commerce of Buffalo*, Buffalo Historical Society, 1909, pp. 247 and 248.

and doors, and copper gutters). The rear wall was made of solid masonry and had no windows. The first floor was taken up with what Frank Severance calls "six good-sized stores," presumably grain stores.[87] The second floor housed a large octagonal room, around which a dozen offices were arranged. There were more offices on the third floor, and the fourth floor contained 20 storage rooms.

Heywood leased the entire second floor to the BBOT for free, thus giving Buffalo's buyers, sellers and merchants a proper place to conduct their business, indeed, *the* place in Buffalo "to exhibit your samples of grain and light articles of merchandise, [and] to place on the bulletin [board] your advertisements of the sailing of your steamboats and vessels and articles of merchandise you have for sale."[88] As a result of this spatial localization ("centralization"), Buffalo's grain booming trade might become more organized, more efficient and more profitable.

On June 5, 1845, Heywood spoke in dedication of the Merchants' Exchange. Because the building itself was clearly a warehouse and not an office building, Heywood felt the need to say a few words on the subject. His remarks were brief, but quite striking, if only because they were so similar to the terms in which, decades later, Walter Gropius, Le Corbusier and other modernist architects praised American industrial structures. "In erecting [the Exchange Building]," Heywood said, "I have endeavored to combine strength, durability, utility and just proportions; the eye has been consulted instead of works on architecture."[89] In other words, the new Merchants' Exchange Building was as much a symbol as it was a place to conduct business. Though not

---

[87] Severance, *Historical Sketch of the Board of Trade*, p. 244.

[88] Heywood, quoted in Severance, *Historical Sketch of the Board of Trade*, p. 247.

[89] *Ibid.*

beautiful by conventional standards, the building was an instance of *good building*, that is to say, a symbol of *good business practices*.

#4) In September 1846, the Morse Telegraph Company installed an electrical telegraph line in the Merchants' Exchange.[90] Operated by the New York, Albany and Buffalo Telegraph Company, which added a second line in early 1847, this line provided general news and market reports from New York, which had been connected by telegraph lines to Boston, Philadelphia and Washington, DC, since 1844. Such information – national grain prices in New York; international grain prices in Liverpool, London and Amsterdam; and surpluses, scarcities, famines or wars anywhere in the world – was crucial to what went on in Buffalo's grain market. According to John Langdale, "most of the subscribers" to the first line into Buffalo "were wheat and flour dealers"; the rest were local newspapers.[91]

Before the installation of the telegraph, the Merchants' Exchange had in Heywood's words "attracted little attention, and discussion had given rise only to worse than unprofitable quarrels, resulting in the defeat of every scheme and project of improvement." Its members had relied upon newspapers (and rumors) for the information that they used to make decisions about how much grain to buy, what kind of grain to buy, and when to buy it. Looking ahead to the installation of a telegraph line in Buffalo, Russell H. Heywood had

---

[90] Invented in 1837 by Samuel F. B. Morse and Alfred Vail as a tool in the control of railroad traffic, the telegraph was soon after put to use as a means of high-speed long-distance communication, both along and independent of railroad rights-of-way.

[91] John Langdale, "Impact of the Telegraph on the Buffalo Agriculture Commodity Market: 1846-1848," *The Professional Geographer*, Volume 31, May 1979, Number 2, p. 165.

reminded his fellow grain merchants that "Many of you take two or three New York papers [which are] in these days of railroads and electricity, very stale, when all your neighbors have it from twenty to thirty minutes before you."[92]

The telegraph greatly accelerated the process by which usable information from the east coast (the first place that news from Europe arrived by ship) was made available in Buffalo. It "reduced the traveling time of New York market reports from more than four days to just under one," William Cronon reports.[93] The telegraph also increased the volume of information that was available in Buffalo, where one could gather reports from several different sources (wherever a terminal was established) instead of a single source (newspapers from New York, relying on the news brought to America by ships from Europe).[94] Some wondered if accelerated communications wouldn't end up burying its subscribers alive.[95]

---

[92] Quoted in Frank Severance, p. 248.

[93] *Nature's Metropolis*, p. 417.

[94] Later, when trans-Atlantic travel became more frequent and highly specialized, ships from England would dock at Boston, while ships from continental Europe would dock at New York. This meant that grain traders in Buffalo needed to receive information from both cities, not just the latter.

[95] "To this end, each of them [our great heads of finance, industry, big business] has nailed up, in a corner of his office, electric wires connecting his executive desk with our colonies in Africa, Asia and the Americas. Comfortably seated before his schedules and account books, he can communicate directly over tremendous distances; at a touch of a finger, he can receive reports from all his far-flung agents on a startling string of matters [...] All this is rapid succession. The poor brains of these men, robust as they were, have simply given way, just as the shoulders of some

John Langdale has shown that the telegraph tended to "reduce the level of uncertainty" in Buffalo's grain trade and "encourage[d] the dispersal of such activity" into other areas.[96] Less "uncertainty" meant that grain buyers in Buffalo, now better informed about prices, could afford to set a certain amount of caution aside and offer or accept "higher" prices (something more closely resembling the real prices) for grain available in Cleveland, Toledo, Chicago, and Milwaukee. This in turn encouraged farmers in the hinterlands of these cities to bring their grain, especially their corn, to market via the Great Lakes, rather than send it down the Mississippi to New Orleans. As a result of its telegraph connections, which were extended through Western Pennsylvania and Ohio, all the way to Detroit, by the Erie and Michigan telegraph Company in 1847, Buffalo soon thereafter became "the leading grain transfer center in the United States."[97]

The invention and widespread use of the telegraph led to important changes in the way business contracts were structured in Buffalo. Prior to the telegraph, when business transactions were negotiated "on the spot" and completed

---

Hercules of the marketplace would give way if he ventured to load them with ten sacks of wheat instead of one." Jacques Fabien, *Paris en songe*, Paris, 1863, pages 96-86, quoted in Walter Benjamin, *The Arcades Project*, page 567. Like Atlas, Buffalo's Herculean shoulders were destined to stay strong.

[96] Langdale, "Impact of the Telegraph," p. 165.

[97] Langdale, "Impact of the Telegraph," p. 166. In January 1849, a telegraph line was installed in Chicago, which allowed the Chicago Board of Trade to communicate directly with New York, without having to "go through" Buffalo to get their information or arrange their contracts. As a result, "by the 1850s Buffalo declined in importance as a [futures] market for grain and flour and its function reverted to that of a storage and transshipment center," p. 169.

face to face (either on the street or in an office in the Merchants' Exchange Building), such contracts stipulated that a certain amount of grain would be exchanged for a certain amount of cash, right then and there. The basis of the transaction was the current price of a bushel of grain,[98] which of course could be sampled and evaluated by the potential buyer. Tried and true though it was, this arrangement was subject to cycles of glut and scarcity, in which prices plummeted then soared. After the harvest,[99] when farmers had grain to sell, commission and forwarding agents weren't buying, because they had no idea what prices would be like when winter came. And so prices fell, the market was glutted with cheap grain and the farmers lost money. Then, during the winter and spring months, when agents and other grain-buyers *were* interested in making big purchases, the farmers didn't have any grain because they didn't have the facilities or financial resources to store it for such long periods of time. And so prices rose, grain was hard to find and the ultimate consumers of grain in bulk (flourmills in the case of wheat, and distilleries and feed mills in the case of corn) lost money.

Once they could be negotiated "telegraphically" over long distances by parties who did not need to be in face-to-face contact, contracts were structured so that the farmer or commission and forwarding agent agreed to deliver a certain quantity of grain on a certain date *in the future*, and the buyer agreed to pay a price that was acceptable to the seller at that very moment for grain. Called "to arrive" contracts, these agreements worked to the advantage of all the parties involved.[100] Farmers and their agents could sell their grain

---

[98] Measured by volume, not weight.

[99] In the United States, the harvesting of grain starts in the south in May and works its way up north by November.

[100] In *Merchants of Grain* (Viking, New York, 1979), Dan Morgan takes the phrase "to arrive" to mean as-of-yet-unsold. "Odessa merchants usually shipped wheat to England

when prices were "high" and buyers could receive their grain shipments when they needed them.[101] Nobody needed to lose money again, provided, of course, everyone had ready access to sufficient amounts of credit. For example, if the harvest turned out to be a poor one and grain was unexpectedly scarce, the farmer or agent who had signed a "to arrive" contract still had to deliver the specified amount of grain, all of it, when the contract came due. Conversely, if there were a shortage of funds when the contract came due, the grain-buyer who entered into it would still have to pay the agreed-upon amount in full and forthwith. In either case, some kind of loan or credit line would be necessary, and that required banks that were willing to grant or arrange it in time.

There was another problem, one that required more than a decade to solve. In the absence of face-to-face transactions, grain samples could not be inspected at the time the contract was signed. Even if they were arranged telegraphically, contracts still relied upon grain samples being sent by lake vessel from to Buffalo and then by canal boat from Buffalo to Rochester, Albany or New York. To speed the process up, or to at least reassure grain-buyers while they waited for their samples to arrive, some farmers and agents issued certificates of general quality. Even if these certificates were genuine, which they were not on occasion,

---

without any idea of the price it would fetch when samples of it finally were laid out on tables in London's Mark Lane several months later. The grain was dispatched unpriced – 'to arrive' – which meant that it often was floating on the high seas, en route to Western Europe, without a customer" (pp. 28-29).

[101] According to William Cronon, " 'to arrive' contracts were common enough at Buffalo during the late 1840s that they already constituted almost a full futures market," that is, *twenty years* before the advent of a full futures market in Chicago." *Nature's Metropolis*, p. 418.

they still had to be delivered, and so they did not solve the underlying problem.

A peculiarity of the new grain-in-bulk system – which would have been impossible without the introduction and gradual acceptance of paper money, which started in the United States in the late 1830s[102] – was the creation of "elevator receipts." As if the grain elevator were a kind of bank, these receipts were issued when the grain was "deposited" at the elevator and could be "cashed in" (exchanged for the same *quantity* of grain, but not for the original deposit itself) at any time by anyone in possession of them. This arrangement made building a brand-new grain elevator a much more attractive proposition. Because elevator receipts entitled their bearer to "withdraw" a specific amount of grain, but not necessarily the very same batch of grain that had been originally deposited, grain shipments could be freely mixed together when in storage. Grain elevators no longer needed to be built with large numbers of small bins; and once built, they no longer needed to keep some of their bins partially filled. Instead, the elevator operators could construct a few very large "common" bins in which several batches were mixed together and filled right to the top. Thus a new form of property was created: private property was brought together into a common pool and yet remained privately owned. In the words of an anonymous newspaper reporter, "It dawns on the observer's mind that one man's property is by no means kept separate from another man's."[103]

---

[102] Marc Shell, *Money, Language and Thought: Literary and Philosophical Economies from the Medieval to the Modern Era*, University of California Press, 1982, pp. 5-23.

[103] "The Metropolis of the Prairies," *Harper's New Monthly Magazine*, volume 61 (1880), p. 726; quoted in Cronon, *Nature's Metropolis*, p. 116.

Like paper banknotes, elevator receipts became commodities in their own right, and could be bought or sold at will, even used as collateral for a loan. "The money was good as long as there was grain corresponding to each receipt," William Cronon notes. "But if elevator operators illegally issued counterfeit receipts for grain that did not exist, they could mint themselves a fortune without anyone's ever knowing."[104] In the absence of regulation by the federal government, which regulated all the other banks, a greedy or unscrupulous operator could sell – for as much money as he or she dared – as many elevator receipts as he or she dared to print, confident that no one would question an operator's knowledge of how much grain was actually in his or her elevator. The sale of these fraudulent receipts could raise enough money for the operator to "corner" all the grain actually in storage and keep it off the market, thereby creating an artificial shortage, which prevented others from meeting their contractual obligations. With the demands for both elevator receipts and actual grain at their highest points, the crooked elevator operator could buy back his fraudulent receipts from the people to whom he'd sold them, but at much lower prices, thereby creating a "windfall" profit. Then and only then would the crooked operator meet his or her contractual obligations and deliver the grain. Detecting or proving the existence of such fraudulent activity would be nearly impossible because, at the end of the scam, it was the crooked elevator operator who had final possession of the receipts, which were the only evidence of his or her crime.

Elevator operators weren't the only ones to run corners on the market, of course; so did grain traders and "bullish" speculators. But the participation of a grain elevator operator was essential in running a successful corner, because only he or she knew how much grain was actually on hand and how

---

[104] *Nature's Metropolis*, p. 136.

many paper contracts were impossible to fulfill.[105]
Furthermore, elevator operators were unlikely to charge
themselves for storing the grain while the corner was being
run.

When paired with "to arrive" contracts, elevator
receipts created the basis for what today is called the futures
market: the buying and selling of *promises* to deliver grain,
not grain itself. In this "abstract" or virtual market, which
existed alongside or "above" the market in real grain
(elevator receipts), a speculator could enter into a contract
without actually possessing any grain at that moment; he or
she could sell "short," that is, enter into "to arrive" contracts
on the speculative possibility that, by the time the contracts
came due, he or she could buy the specified amount of grain,
but at prices that were lower than those at the time that the
contracts were negotiated. Indeed, a speculator could meet
the obligations of the "to arrive" contract without *ever*
coming into possession of any grain. On the specified
delivery date, the speculator could simply deliver elevator
receipts that totaled the amount of grain specified in the
contract. Same thing with the buyers: they might enter into a
contract without the slightest intention of ever receiving any
grain, which would be shipped to or picked up by someone
else. In the words of Morton Rothstein, the futures market
was a series of transaction in which "men who don't own
something are selling that something to men who don't really
want it."[106]

---

[105] For example, on April 17, 1875, the *Chicago Tribune*
estimated that the trade in futures (some $2 billion per year)
was *ten* times larger than the trade in physical grain. A
decade later, the volume on the futures market was *twenty*
times that of the cash grain business. Cf. Cronon, *Nature's
Metropolis*, p. 126.

[106] Morton Rothstein, "Frank Norris and Popular
Perceptions of the Market," *Agricultural History*, volume 56

As a result of the developments of 1845 and 1846, the "rush" to build and operate steam-powered grain elevators in Buffalo began. In 1846, BBOT member and flour miller Oliver Bugbee built the City Elevator, and the commission and forwarding agent Henry M. Kinne[107] built the Buffalo. In 1847, seven more grain elevators were built: Wadsworth,[108] the Evans,[109] the Reed, the Hatch, the Hollister (owned by George Tifft), the Sternberg and the aforementioned Sterling (formerly Mahlon Kingman's horse-powered Swiftsure elevator). Three of the new elevators (the Sterling, the Reed

---

(1982), p. 58; quoted in Cronon, *Nature's Metropolis*, p. 125. In the words of Georg Simmel, *The Philosophy of Money* (third enlarged edition, edited by David Frisby, Routledge: London, 2004), p. 194: "[At our modern commodity exchanges] both [buyer and seller] know exactly, when they agree to a contract for a certain standardized quality of wheat or petrol, that they are obliged to deliver an objectively fixed standard of the commodity – a standard that has no regard for personal uncertainties and deficiencies. There has thus been established a mode of bargaining at the peak of the money economy which lightens the burden of responsibility for both parties but transposes the subjective basis of the transaction into an objective one and alleviates the disadvantage of one party at the expense of the other."

[107] Kinne was also the owner of the schooner *Wyndham*, which was constructed in 1839 and capable of holding 10,000 bushels of grain.

[108] It is possible that the Wadsworth, later known as the Seymour & Wells, was built in 1846.

[109] H. Perry Smith, *History of the City of Buffalo and Erie County* (Syracuse: D. Mason, 1884), p. 219, says the Evans was "built from old warehouses in 1847." A drawing of the Evans Elevator appears in Frank Severance, *Picture Book of Earlier Buffalo* (Buffalo Historical Society, 1912), p. 33: it was sandwiched between a flourmill and a grain-retail store.

and the Hollister) were built in the vicinity of the Dart, while the other six were built further up Buffalo Creek. The Sternberg, the City and the Wadsworth were built along its northern shore; and the Evans, the Hatch and the Buffalo were built on its southern shore.

Robert Dunbar designed the machinery and general plan of five of these nine elevators.[110] Abram Schwartz designed one elevator (the Hollister); it isn't clear who designed the Buffalo, the Wadsworth, and the Hatch. The marine legs in the new elevators were capable of moving at least 2,000 bushels of grain an hour, and sometimes as many as 2,500 bushels. At the Marine Elevator, which was designed by Robert Dunbar and built in 1848[111] to replace the Hatch Elevator, which exploded in 1847, there were *two* marine towers, each one equipped with a "fast" leg (high-speed elevating mechanism). All of the new elevators had bigger over-all storage capacities than the Dart Elevator, even after it was expanded. The smallest of the new elevators, the Wadsworth and the Hatch, could store as many as 150,000 bushels each, while the largest, the City, could store up to 375,000 bushels.

---

[110] In addition to designing the Dart, the Evans, the Reed, the City, and the Sternberg, Robert Dunbar would go on to design the following elevators in Buffalo: the Watson, the Merchant Transfer Tower, the Wilkeson, the Bennett, the Coburn, the Richmond, the Excelsior, the Sturges, the Fulton Transfer Tower, the Marine, the Sternberg A, the Niagara B, the Ohio Basin, the Connecting Terminal and the Coatsworth Transfer Tower. Thomas D. Odle, *The American Grain Trade of the Great Lakes, 1825-1873*, p. 50, claims that "the first elevators built in Europe were built by Robert Dunbar," as were "many other elevators on the Great Lakes."

[111] Note: other sources say that the Marine was built in 1853.

As their respective names indicate, the elevators of 1847 were owned and operated by prominent local businessmen. But new players had arrived on the scene since 1843. In addition to flour millers (Oliver Bugbee and Mahlon Kingman) and commission and forwarding agents (Charles W. Evans, C.M. Reed, and James Hollister),[112] railroad stockholders and directors (Israel T. Hatch, James Wadsworth, and P.L. Sternberg) were now in "the elevator business."

First used for commercial purposes in England in 1829, the steam-powered locomotive was introduced to New York State in 1831, when the former Erie Canal engineer John B. Jervis designed and built *The DeWitt Clinton*, and set it in motion along the newly laid tracks of the Mohawk and Hudson River Railroad. Over the course of the 1830s, the State of New York built the infrastructure of an emerging railroad system through a series of public works projects, worth over $12 million in bonds. By 1842, Albany was linked to Buffalo by way of an awkward combination of seven short passenger lines: the Mohawk and Hudson; the Syracuse and Utica; the Saratoga and Schenectady; the Utica and Schenectady; the Auburn and Syracuse; the Auburn and Rochester; and the Buffalo and Rochester. One might say that there was a nearly religious zeal with which these railroads were constructed.[113] But it wasn't until the 1850s

---

[112] Hollister later sold his elevator to William Wells, who renamed it after himself.

[113] "One can compare the zeal and the ardor displayed by the civilized nations of today in their establishment of railroads with that which, several centuries ago, went into the building of cathedrals [...] If it is true, as we hear, that the word 'religion' comes from *religare*, 'to bind' [...] then the railroads have more to do with the religious spirit than one might suppose." Michel Chevalier, "*Chemins de fer*," *Dictionnaire de l'economie politique*, Paris, 1852, p. 20,

that these various lines (each with their own gauges) were unified into a truly regional rail system. And so, until then, the grain trade in and through Buffalo was exclusively conducted over water routes.

The creation of a grain elevator district in Buffalo sent the historian George W. Clinton into paroxysms of enthusiasm. "That Buffalo is destined to be one of the greatest cities of the Union is universally admitted," he proclaimed in 1848, a year of collapsing empires and revolutions in France, Germany and elsewhere in Europe.

> All things are full of promise for her [Clinton went on]. The convulsions of the old continents are unfelt in this [continent]. European capital will seek investment where alone it seems secure; and affrighted multitudes will flee for shelter to the only country in the world where peace can be secure, and where war can wreak comparatively little injury. The prosperity of the United States

---

quoted in Walter Benjamin, *The Arcades Project*, p. 598. To a Marxist, this "religious spirit" was not the desire to worship God in a new, more "modern" way, but the faith or belief that it was both possible *and* desirable to abolish private property and instaurate collective ownership. In the words of one Marxist, "Railroads [...] demanded, besides other impossibilities, a transformation in the mode of property [...] Railroads had need of such massive amounts of capital that it could no longer be concentrated in the hands of only a few individuals. And so a great many bourgeois were forced to entrust their precious funds, which had never before been allowed out of their sight, to people whose names they hardly knew." Paul Lafargue, *"Marx' historischer Materialismus,"* *Die neue Zeit*, 22 no. 1, Stuttgart, 1904, p. 831; quoted in Benjamin, *The Arcades Project*, pp. 576-577.

must be greatly augmented, and, whether the East is invigorated, or the West developed, Buffalo will surely reap a rich share of the harvest. Manufacturers, purged of all debasement and oppression, are rising in her bosom; honest labor is happy in innumerable employments; prudent enterprize [*sic*] is expanding her resources; capital is flowing in; and, above all, a commerce, boundless as the West, limitless as the necessities of man, fertilizing as the Nile, and humanizing in all its tendencies, and which can never be diverted, warrants and confirms our most exalted hopes.

Washed, indeed cleansed of "all debasement and oppression" by the great amber-colored river of commerce,[114] Buffalo approached the 1850s – the troubled decade that began with the Missouri Compromise and ended with the beginning of the Civil War – securely at peace with itself and the world around it.

Between 1848 and 1855, four more new steam-powered grain elevators were built in Buffalo: the 100,000-bushel Erie Basin Elevator, located at the meeting of the Erie Basin and the Peacock Slip, and built by a railroad company (the

---

[114] William Cronon notes: "The boosters embraced the common American notion that free commerce and an enlightened democratic government would together create an expanding empire in which there were no subjects, only citizens. At least in theory, people joined the Republic by choice, and they would trade with its metropolis in much the same way. America's cities had grown by *commercial* power, not the tyrannical power of the state [...] The booster vision of imperial destiny presupposed no exploitation." *Nature's Metropolis: Chicago and the Great West* (WW Norton, 1991), p. 44.

Delaware, Lackawanna and Western Railroad, an affiliate of the New York Central & Hudson River Railroad); the 500,000-bushel Brown Elevator, built by James W. Brown and located on the south shore of the Creek, opposite Lloyd Street; the 200,000-bushel Main Street Elevator (later called the Hazard), located on the south shore of Buffalo Creek, along Peck Slip; and the 100,000-bushel Holley & Johnson, located on the north shore of the creek, at the base of Chicago Street. In 1855, Buffalo had a dozen grain elevators, the combined storage capacity of which was over 2 million bushels.

The 1848 to 1855 period also saw the construction of the first "floaters" and "transfer towers," both of which were pure transshipping elevators that didn't store any grain at all.[115] Installed upon small boats, the floaters were pulled into place between lake steamers and canal boats. In a single operation, they unloaded grain from the former and loaded it directly into the latter. Tall marine towers set upon small boats,[116] the floaters didn't much resemble their land-based counterparts, and perhaps were even stranger looking.[117]

---

[115] The first floating elevator was "invented and patented by Mr. A.S. Bemia of Buffalo for discharging and weighing grain from vessels into canal boats and warehouses. It is constructed after the style and model of dredging machines and floats in the harbor. One is to be built and launched ready for Spring service." *Scientific American*, Vol. 2, No. 25, March 13, 1847.

[116] At one floater in Buffalo, built by Nimbs and Clifford, the marine tower was set upon a revolving 16-foot-wide "turntable" that was raised 15 feet above the deck. See "New Floating Elevator in Buffalo," *New York Times*, December 29, 1863.

[117] See the photograph by N.M. Hinshelwood entitled *Floating grain elevators, Port of Montreal, QC, about 1915*, at the McCord Museum: http://www.mccordmuseum.qc.ca/

Useful though they were, the floaters added to the congestion of Buffalo's harbor, and so only a handful of them were in use at any one time. They were eventually phased out.[118] But transfer towers – marine towers without warehouses attached to them – were built upon dry land and took up very little space. By the 1870s,[119] there were nearly a dozen of them in Buffalo, and many remained in use at the dawn of the 20th century.

---

en/collection/artifacts/MP-1985.31.83 accessed 18 August 2008.

[118] It appears that the first "American-style" grain elevators built in England were floaters. An engraving published in a 1880 issue of *The Graphic: an Illustrated Weekly Newspaper* shows "The American grain elevator on Thames Off North Woolwich." An engraving from an 1883 issue of the same newspaper shows what appears to be the same elevator over the caption, "The new grain elevator, 'International,' being towed across the North Sea to Antwerp."

[119] Thomas D. Odle, *The American Grain Trade of the Great Lakes, 1825-1873*, p. 134, notes that "the year 1873 serves as a convenient point of demarcation in terms of both the emergence of a new pattern of commerce in the grain trade and of the beginning of changes which were to end the predominance of grain-growing in the East North Central area [of the United States]. The changes in the grain trade brought about by the telegraph and railroad were gradual in their development, but the new pattern of commerce had clearly emerged by 1873. In addition this same year serves as a convenient point to mark the beginning of another gradual development: the westward movement of the center of grain production into the trans-Mississippi River area." 1873 was also the year in which the Suez Canal was opened, and thereby provided a new and more direct route by which Indian wheat could reach England.

All through this period, Buffalo's artificial harbor remained a liability. To accommodate both the new grain elevators and the ships that crowded in front of them, the Buffalo Board of Trade endorsed and successfully lobbied the State of New York for the excavation of a ship canal that would begin at the center of the harbor and cut a strip, pointing to the southeast, into the land between the southern bank the Buffalo Creek and the eastern shore of Lake Erie. First called the Blackwell and then the City Ship Canal, this two-mile-long slip – started in 1848, "finished" in 1852 and widened and deepened in 1873 – opened up maneuvering-room for ships and boats, and permitted the digging of lateral slips between it and Buffalo Creek. New waterfront structures, including several grain elevators, would soon be built along such lateral slips as the Main & Hamburg, the Peck, and the Peacock.

Thanks to other BBOT initiatives, two large basins were excavated in Buffalo's harbor between 1848 and 1852. The Erie Basin was excavated above the mouth of the harbor, along the Niagara River between Buffalo and Black Rock. Protected by a sea-wall made of wood, stones and gravel, the Erie Basin was designed to provide shelter for waiting or docked ships. It also provided another access route to the Erie Canal, to which the Erie Basin was connected by a slip. The Ohio Basin, by contrast, was excavated far to the east, way up the Buffalo Creek. A huge rectangle, the Ohio Basin was connected by slips to Buffalo Creek and the Main & Hamburg Slip, and, through the latter, to the terminus of the Erie Canal. As a result of these improvements, Buffalo's cramped harbor district grew by a total of 100 acres.

It was in the pages of the 1855 edition of *The Commercial Advertiser Directory for the City of Buffalo* that the wonderful news was first reported: based upon the previous year's tallies, the Port of Buffalo was "the largest grain depot in the world"! In 1854, Buffalo's grain elevators – the Brown, the Dart, the Evan and Dunbar, the Fish, the

Hatch, the Holley & Johnson, the Hollister, the Richmond, the Seymour & Wells, and the Sterling – transshipped a grand total of 20,044,463 bushels of wheat and flour, almost seven million bushels more than Chicago, which was reputed to be the world's second "largest" (that is, most active) grain depot. In order of their ranking, the other top grain depots were New York City (9 million bushels), the Romanian twin-cities of Galatz and Ibrelia (8 million), the Russian ports St. Petersburg and Odessa (7 million each), and St. Louis, Missouri (5 million). Not surprisingly, it was the advent of the Crimean War (March 1854-February 1856) that alerted Buffalo's boosters to the existence of Europe's major grain ports: during this conflict, American wheat exports to Europe first doubled, then tripled in size.

Of course, other sources report other figures. Some sources have self-contradictory information, as is the case with J.B. Mansfield's *History of the Great Lakes*, vol. I (Chicago: 1899). Under the heading of "Chicago," Mansfield reports that, in 1854, the grain capital of the world was Chicago, which shipped exactly 30 million bushels. The rest of the world falls out in this way: Archangel, 9.5 million bushels; Galatz & Brailow, 8.32 million; St Petersburg, 7.2 million; Odessa, 7.04 million; Danzig, 4.4 million; and Riga, 4 million. But under the heading of "Buffalo," he reports that, in 1854, Buffalo shipped out 19.5 million bushels (5 million of wheat, 10 million of corn, 4 million of oats, half-a-million of rye).

Apparently Buffalo's top position wasn't a fluke. *The 1856 Commercial Advertiser Directory for the City of Buffalo* reported that, for the second year in a row, the Port of Buffalo was the world's "largest" grain depot. In 1855, Buffalo's grain elevators had transshipped a total of 19,788,473 bushels of wheat and flour, 3 million bushels more than Chicago, which again came in second place. The other top grain depots were the port on the White Sea, Archangel (9 million), Galatz and Ibrelia (8 million), St.

Petersburg, on the Sea of Finland (7 million) and Odessa (7 million).

Perhaps more so than other collections of statistics, these reports must be taken with a proverbial grain of salt. In particular, one should question the reporters' access to accurate information from around the world. Why is it that both London and Liverpool are consistently missing? Where is New Orleans? Rotterdam? Danzig?[120] Why is it that New York City and St. Louis feature in the first tally, but not in the second? Is it likely that the statistics from the ports on the Black Sea (Odessa and Galatz & Ibrelia) were really from the years 1854 and 1855, which was when the Crimean War was being fought? Is it likely that the tallies for two different ports (St. Petersburg and Odessa) are exactly the same for both 1854 and 1855? Doesn't combining the figures for barrels of flour (converted in bushels) and grain shipped in bulk tend to exaggerate the activity in Buffalo, whose grain elevators could not transship barrels?

Perhaps this is quibbling. The essential fact remained: though it was only a cramped inland port in Western New York, Buffalo was a city of international importance. Half of all the grain grown in the American heartland (the emerging breadbasket of the world) went through its elevators. J.B. Mansfield shows that between 1858 and 1862, the total amount of grain transshipped through Buffalo (wheat, corn, oats and rye) went from 28.5 million to 58 million bushels per year. By 1897, those totals had reached 181 million bushels. The rewards for this prominence were rich and varied, and included the creation of the University of Buffalo (1846), the Buffalo Fine Arts Society (1862), the Buffalo and Erie County Historical Society (1865), the State University of

---

[120] Also known in Polish as Gdansk, Danzig (its German name) had been one of Europe's most active grain ports for five hundred years.

New York at Buffalo (1867), and Delaware Park, designed by Frederick Law Olmstead (1867).

In 1884, A.T. Andreas' book *History of Chicago*[121] included a recently-drawn print that claimed to represent the "First Shipment of Grain from Chicago's first dock," which allegedly took place sometime in 1830 (figure 1). In particular, this print claimed to depict "Loading grain into the OSCEOLA of Buffalo from Newberry & Doles Chicago warehouse." I am not so much interested in the accuracy of the date (which seems dubious), as in the depiction of the action. It appears that only five workers were needed to load this brig with its shipment of grain in bulk (no sacks are depicted): one in the warehouse to pour grain into the spout that carries it down to portable trunks on the dock, and two pairs of workers to empty these trunks into the hold of the brig. Except for a half-dozen onlookers, the dock is virtually deserted. Surely at work in this odd depiction is something like the exclamation "If only they knew what they were starting!" (See Siegfried Giedion's notion that "wherever the nineteenth feels itself to be unobserved, it grows bold."[122]) But there is also something "spectacular" about this unassuming scene, in the precise sense given to this word by the art historian T.J. Clark: the absence of crowds and the "unexpected desolation" of individuals in modern cities.[123]

The grain elevators constructed in Buffalo and elsewhere after 1843 were "spectacular" in the exact same sense. For example, in "The City of Buffalo: A Glance At Its

---

[121] A.T. Andreas, *History of Chicago from the Earliest Period to the Present Time in three volumes* (Chicago, 1884).

[122] *Bauen in Frankreich*, 1928, p. 33, quoted by Walter Benjamin, *The Arcades Project*, p.154.

[123] *The Painting of Modern Life* (Knopf, 1986), p. 15. See also Guy Debord, *La Societe du Spectacle*, 1967, translated as *The Society of the Spectacle* (Detroit, Black & Red, 1977).

Progress Down to the Present Time," published in 1862, Sanford B. Hunt lamented the fact that, as a result of the grain elevator, "gradually the bustle ceased."

> Laborsaving devices drove away a host of longshore men. The elevators usurped the function of the Irishman. . . . [A] larger commerce diffused over a larger surface made a smaller exhibit than before. The region of the waterside grew dull when the buckets of the elevator, propelled by steam, lifted three thousand bushels of grain per hour from the hold of a vessel. The trade was there, but the hurrah was gone, and it fed fewer mouths.

Hunt wasn't alone in lamenting the passing of the noisy bustle of the stevedores and expressing discomfort with the eerie calm of the newly mechanized waterfront. In 1857, a writer for *The Chicago Daily Press* reported that, "All this [moving of grain] is done without any noise or bustle; and with but little labor, except that of machinery." Calm, but not quiet, the air was now filled with the inhuman sounds of grain elevators, which shook, creaked and groaned when their mechanical legs were working, when the rivers of grain were flowing within them, and when the bins were being emptied or filled.

The "victory" of the mechanized grain elevator (grain transshipped in bulk) over the traditional practices of grain handling (grain transshipped in sacks) can be dated fairly precisely.[124] Between 1856 and 1859, the Chicago Board of

---

[124] Note that Cronon states "the railroads changed all this," that is to say, changed and/or ended the traditional system of "sack-based shipments." *Nature's Metropolis*, p. 109. While it is true that "shippers and railroad managers soon came to think of grain shipments not as individuals

Trade (CBOT) – in an attempt to prevent the State of Illinois from regulating the city's grain trade – took it upon itself to do the job. First, the CBOT decided to officially subdivide "wheat" into spring wheat and two kinds of winter wheat (red and white). Then it subdivided spring wheat into grades that were ranked from high to low quality: "Club Spring" (the best), "No. 1 Spring" (wheat that weighed more than 59 pounds per bushel) and "No. 2 Spring" (wheat that weighed between 56 and 59 pounds per bushel). Shortly thereafter, a fourth category was created: "Rejected," which was wheat that weighed under 56 pounds per bushel. In the words of one CBOT member, "much of the grain that was heretofore passed as standard in this market" would be rejected "to improve the [overall] character of our grain."[125] In time, the main four grades were applied to winter wheat and each the other major grains (corn, oats, rye and barley).[126] Because of the strong demand for it among flour millers, spring wheat would eventually be separated into ten different grades.[127]

'sacks' but as 'carloads' consisting of about 325 bushels each" (p. 110), such shipments of grain-in-bulk couldn't be unloaded without mechanized elevators.

[125] Quoted in Cronon, *Nature's Metropolis*, p. 118. During the nationwide depression that began in 1857, the "good name" of grain transshipped through Chicago was tainted by farmers who, seeking to get a better price for their grain, either watered it down, didn't clean it thoroughly or mixed it with other grains to make it weigh more.

[126] Note that oats, rye and barley hadn't been cultivated as cash crops in the United States before 1860. In comparison to wheat and corn, these grains – which were used primarily at distilleries, breweries and livestock farms – simply weren't dense enough to ship in bulk. But with their inclusion in the grading system, these grains soon became profitable as exported products.

[127] Today, there are eight "classes" of wheat: Durum

Though they weren't accepted everywhere right away,[128] these changes were nothing short of momentous. They meant that telegraphic "to arrive" contracts could be signed and executed without the buyer receiving a small sample of the grain in advance. Instead, the buyer and seller simply agreed that, on a certain date, in exchange for a certain sum of money, a certain amount of grain of a specific grade was to be delivered. And so the speed of the telegraph, which moved faster than physical samples could be sent, could at last be fully utilized.

These changes also meant that grain elevator operators could not only mix different shipments of grain together in common bins, and thus maximize the size and number of

---

wheat, Hard Red Spring wheat, Hard Red Winter wheat, Soft Red Winter wheat, Hard White wheat, Soft White wheat, Unclassed wheat, and Mixed wheat. Durum, Hard Red Spring, and Soft White are further divided into sub-classes. See "U.S. Standards for Grain," established on May 1, 2006, by the Grain Inspection, Packers & Stockyards Administration, United States Department of Agriculture.

[128] The Milwaukee Board of Trade adopted them in 1858, the Buffalo Board of Trade adopted them in 1860, and the Toledo Board of Trade adopted them in 1863. But it wasn't until 1876 that the New York Produce Exchange adopted its own system of grading. Winter wheat was subdivided into white winter wheat, amber white winter wheat, and red winter wheat; and spring wheat was subdivided into Northwest spring wheat and spring wheat. Each of these subdivisions was in turn divided into five grades (Extra, No. 1, No. 2, No. 3 and Rejected). Corn, oats, rye and barley were also divided into kinds and each kind was graded. See "Grades of Grain, Established by the Committee on Grain of the New York Produce Exchange," *Report of the New York Produce Exchange for the Year 1879* (New York: Jones, 1880), pp. 181-182.

their grain bins, but could also mix *dissimilar* grades together, and thus maximize their profits. For example, an elevator operator could take a large amount of "Rejected" grain and mix it with just enough "No. 1 Spring" grain to artificially elevate its grade to "No. 2 Spring." Or he could take a small amount of "Club Spring" and mix it with a large amount of "No. 2 Spring," thereby creating a batch of "No. 1 Spring." Either way, the elevator operator would strive to cross the lower boundary of the grade, but go no "higher" than that.

As William Cronon points out, "distinction among grades inevitably depended to a considerable degree on subjective judgment [...] There was plenty of room for disagreement in these standards."[129] Disagreements and even suspicions of corruption broke out when country elevators gave higher grades than the elevators in Chicago for grain that came from the same farm and was shipped in exactly the same condition. And so, between 1857 and 1860, the CBOT began to appoint "official" inspectors to make sure that its rules were being followed and that fraud was not being perpetrated. Within the next decade or so, official grain inspectors were also appointed by the Boards of Trade in Buffalo, Detroit, St. Louis, Cleveland and Toledo. But these inspectors were drawn from the ranks of the grain business itself, and so they had agendas of their own. Furthermore, because they reported to the CBOT, which was still a private membership organization, the inspectors were more likely to .be deceived, incompetent, biased or corrupt than someone working for the state government.

It would certainly take an honest man and a skilled inspector to spot and report some of the frauds that the owners of grain elevators could perpetrate. For example, a grain bin that contained 10,000 bushels of "Rejected" could appear to better quality than that if someone at the elevator

---

[129] *Nature's Metropolis*, p. 118.

covered it over with a few bushels of "No. 1 Spring." Or an elevator's scales might be adjusted so that a shipment came up a few bushels short, just enough to change the shipment's grade from a higher to a lower one.

Other "tricks of the trade" were not obviously unethical. With the invention of grain-drying and grain-cleaning machines in the 1850s and 1860s, elevator operators could remove excess water and foreign particles from shipments of grain.[130] Elevators in Buffalo used Marsh caloric grain-dryers as early as 1863.[131] Though grain that had been dried and cleaned weighed less than the original

---

[130] The following information appears on the website of the Mount Washington Cog Railroad: " 'A perfect safeguard against the heating of corn has been discovered by our fellow citizen, Sylvester Marsh,' reported the *Chicago Tribune*, describing his new 60-foot tall grain kiln. 'Having secured a handsome fortune, he ceased packing beef and pork in 1853. For the last several years he has devoted a large share of his time, and not a little of his income, to experiments upon drying corn [...] The effect of his discovery upon the demand of our great staple in Europe can scarcely be over-estimated.' Of eleven U. S. Patents Marsh received, six were for grain dryers. 'Marsh's Caloric [meaning using heat] Grain Dryers' and his grain shipping company provided him a substantial income." http://www.cog-railway.com/smarsh.htm accessed 18 August 2008.

[131] In the lithograph entitled "Bird's Eye View of the City of Buffalo," dated 1863, a building bears the words "Marsh Coloric [*sic*] Grain Dryer" upon it stands next to the Reed Elevator. In "Our State Institutions. – XVIII: The Buffalo Grain Trade," *New York Times*, January 22, 1872, a writer named "J.B." confirms that the Reed Elevator used a Marsh surface dryer, and informs his readers that George Clark-made driers were in use at the Richmond and Hazard Elevators and that a Beach was in use at the Union.

shipment, and would therefore rate a lower grade, it was more valuable to flour millers, many of whom couldn't afford or didn't have room to install such expensive in *their* facilities. As a result, when the deal was finally closed, the dried and cleaned grain fetched a higher price than its original grade indicated it was worth. The effects of this kind of technological disparity were clear. While a grain elevator's capital investments in the newest grain-handling machines quickly paid for themselves, farmers couldn't afford to purchase such machines and so were effectively locked out of the cycle of productive technological renewal.[132]

Motivated by a rising tide of anger amongst farmers, who had not been satisfied with the CBOT's attempts to regulate the grain trade on its own, the Illinois legislature passed the Warehouse Act of 1867.[133] According to William Cronon, the Act "proved ineffective from the beginning," because most of its key provisions and the methods of

---

[132] But grain dryers are not without their drawbacks. For example, they create even more grain dust, which increases the possibility of fires and/or explosions. "Grain dryers present a difficult problem for air pollution control because of the large volumes of air exhausted from the dryer, the large cross-sectional area of the exhaust, the low specific gravity of the emitted dust, and the high moisture content of the exhaust stream. The rate of emission of PM [particulate matter] from grain dryers is primarily dependent upon the type pf grain, the dustiness of the grain, and the dryer configuration (rack or column type). The particles emitted from the dryers, although relatively large, may be very light and difficult to collect." *Air Pollutants 42, Fifth Edition, Volume I*, Chapter 9.9.1-14: Grain Elevators and Processes, issued by the Clearing house for Inventories & Emissions Factors, Environmental Protection Agency, February 1980.

[133] That same year, the *New York Times* published an expose on what it called "The Tricks in the Grain Trade." See issue dated January 20, 1867.

enforcing them had been removed by legislators who were "bribed" or otherwise coerced by the elevator operators.[134] It was repealed in 1869. The next year, the Illinois Constitutional Convention voted to an "elevator bill" in the state's constitution. Under Article 13, all grain elevators in Illinois were defined as "public warehouses," even when privately owned, which meant that the State had the power to regulate their transactions. The owners of the elevator were compelled to post weekly notices concerning how much grain of each grade was in store and to keep a public registry of all outstanding elevator receipts that had been issued. Grain from different grades could only be mixed together after government approval had been given. To give these regulations teeth, the state legislature also created a Railroad and Warehouse Commission, thereby cutting the CBOT out of the inspection business.

Challenges were soon forthcoming. Ira Y. Munn, who owned and operated grain elevators in both Chicago and Buffalo, claimed that the State had overreached its proper authority and thus refused to take out a license for his grain elevators. He was prosecuted and convicted of operating without a license in June 1872. Munn appealed his conviction, and claimed that the Warehouse Act was unconstitutional to the extent that it separated him from his property without "due process," as guaranteed by the Fourteenth Amendment. "The public outcry about the case was so strong that voters changed the composition of the Illinois Supreme Court to make sure that the Warehouse Act and other new 'Granger laws' would be declared constitutional."[135] Munn lost, appealed to the United Supreme Court in 1876, and lost again.[136] The next year, the

---

[134] William Cronon, *Nature's Metropolis*, p. 138.

[135] William Cronon, *Nature's Metropolis*, p. 142.

[136] From the majority opinion in *Munn v. Illinois* (94 U.S. 113): "Property does become clothed with a public

United States Congress passed the Interstate Commerce Act, which established the Interstate Commerce Commission and its mandate to oversee and regulate the nation's domestic trade.

Something similar took place in New York, but years later. In 1881, after holding hearings on the allegedly excessive rates charged by the Western Elevating Association,[137] the New York State Legislature introduced a bill that was intended "to regulate and control the elevating business by law; the act was introduced but failed of passage in the Senate."[138] Similar bills and introduced and defeated in 1882,[139] 1884/1885[140] and 1885/1886.[141] Finally, in June

---

interest when used in a manner to make it of public consequence and affect the community at large. When, therefore, one devotes his property to a use in which the public has an interest, he, in effect, grants to the public an interest in that use, and must submit to be controlled by the public for the common good, to the extent of the interest he has thus created. He may withdraw his grant by discontinuing the use; but so long as he maintains the use, he must submit to the control."

[137] Those who were called or volunteered to testify were Alonzo Richmond, Chandler J. Wells, William H. Abel (the president of the "Western Elevating Association") and P.G. Cook, its Secretary. "Buffalo Grain Charges," *New York Times*, April 2, 1881.

[138] H. Perry Smith, *History of the City of Buffalo and Erie County* (Syracuse: D. Mason, 1884), p. 218.

[139] "The Senate's Disposal of Bills," *New York Times*, June 2, 1882.

[140] "Grain Elevator Charges," *New York Times*, February 27, 1885.

[141] "The Measure to Reduce Elevator Charges Defeated," *New York Times*, April 28, 1886.

1888, the "McEvoy Reduction Bill" became Chapter 581 of the Laws of the State of New York.

The new law set a limit to the price that grain-elevator operators could charge for the elevation of grain (five-eighths of a cent per bushel) and required that the operators only charge their clients for the actual costs of shoveling. Though some thought that the "elevator men" were "clever enough to entirely dodge the provisions of the bill,"[142] they were in fact angry enough to directly confront it. In Buffalo, J. Talman Budd of the Wells Elevator refused to follow it, as did Brooklyn's Edward Annan, the owner of a floating elevator, and Francis Pinto, the owner of a land-based grain warehouse. All three men were indicted, tried and convicted. In response, Budd challenged the new law's constitutionality. In October 1889, his challenge was rejected by the Court of Appeals,[143] and in March 1892, it was rejected by the United States Supreme Court.[144]

Back in 1856 and 1857, while the Chicago Board of Trade was establishing its revolutionary grain-grading system, important events were also taking place in Buffalo. But these were secret events, not public ones. In response to the general recession of 1856, which thereafter became "the Panic of 1857," the Buffalo Board of Trade decided to reorganize itself as a New York State corporation (previously it had been a private membership organization). After the incorporation of the BBOT on March 3, 1857, commission and forwarding agents who had strong ties to water-based shippers dominated it. For example, its new president, George S. Hazard (owner of the Hazard Elevator) wrote a series of articles that argued that the federal government should take charge of repairing and rebuilding the canal.

---

[142] "Elevator Men Angry," *New York Times*, June 14, 1888.

[143] *People v. Budd*, 117 N.Y.1, 22 N.E., Rep 670.

[144] *Budd v. New York*, 143 U.S. 517 (1892).

Evidently convinced that the BBOT could no longer be counted on to fairly represent their corporate interests, which had grown considerably over the course of the 1850s,[145] Buffalo's railroad men founded their own association, called the Western Elevating Company (WEC).[146]

Like any other private membership organization, the WEC didn't need to disclose its gross revenues, dividends, expenses, or taxes to the public.[147] As a result, it is difficult to learn much about how it came together and how it operated. In fact, it is impossible to establish with any certainty the year in which the WEC was founded. Some sources say 1857, while others say 1859.[148] In his testimony in front of

---

[145] Between 1851 and 1853, both the New York & Erie Railroad and the New York Central Railroad provided "through connections" between Buffalo and the Hudson River.

[146] The name of the company is noteworthy. Wouldn't "Buffalo Elevating Company" have been truer to the company's location? Buffalo wasn't a "western" city, but one that looked *to* the west for the grain that it received. In point of fact, the Western Elevating Company was affiliated with the Western Transit Company, an affiliation of Erie Canal/Great Lakes shipping companies with strong ties to the New York Central Railroad.

[147] When asked by the United States Industrial Commission on Agriculture, "Would you be willing to give the Commission a copy of the [Western Elevating Association] agreement?" its Secretary, P.G. Cook, responded, "I [would] hardly like to, because that is a sort of a private paper." *Report of the Industrial Commission on Agriculture and Agricultural Labor, including Testimony, with Review and Topical Digest thereof*, Volume X of the Commission's Reports (Washington, DC, 1901), p. 1019.

[148] In J.B. Mansfield, *History of the Great Lakes*, Volume I (Chicago: J.H. Beers, 1899), the date is 1857, and

the New York Commerce Commission, Philos G. Cook, then secretary of the Western Elevating Association (the name the WEC took after reconstitution in 1897), says "Well, I don't know [how long the WEC/WEA has existed]; there was an association back in the early sixties and there has been an association most of the time since."[149] Two years later, in 1901, in his testimony to the United States Industrial Commission on Agriculture, he said the WEA was formed "way back in the sixties somewhere."[150] Cook's feigned ignorance of the origins of his own company (he'd been with the WEC since 1880) was part of a longstanding and universally adopted policy among monopolists: divulge as little information about yourself as possible,[151] even when called to testify before the government.[152] As a result, much

---

in H. Perry Smith, *History of the City of Buffalo and Erie County* (Syracuse: D. Mason, 1884), it is 1859 (p. 217).

[149] *Report of the New York Commerce Commission, Volume II, transmitted to the legislature January 25, 1900* (Albany, 1900), p. 1225.

[150] "Statement of Mr. P.G. Cook, Secretary of the Western Elevating Association," May 27, 1901, *Report of the Industrial Commission on Agriculture and Agricultural Labor, including Testimony, with Review and Topical Digest Thereof*, Volume X of the Commission's Reports (Washington, DC, 1901), p. 1017.

[151] Note the discussion of the "code of secrecy" in Chapter 1, "Grain Power."

[152] See the testimony of Gibson L. Douglass, the Vice President and General manager of the Western Transit Company (closely affiliated with the New York Central Railroad) in front of the New York Commerce Commission. Commissioner Smith: "I don't suppose that you think the arrangement between the elevators here [in Buffalo] is any injury to the commerce?" Mr. Douglass: "I know it is not; I know it is a benefit." Commissioner Smith: Inasmuch as this

of what "we" know about this particular monopoly and how it operated in the 1850s and 1860s comes from the 1890s, when the WEC/WEA was investigated by both state and federal commissions for its role in artificially inflating the rates for elevating and storing grain in Buffalo.

William Wells, a well-known citizen of the city and a key player in Buffalo's grain business, is said to have been the WEC's founder. Wells' father, Joseph Wells, settled in Buffalo in 1802 and had remained there ever since. Born in Buffalo in 1806, William Wells – the oldest male native-born resident of Buffalo for his whole life – seems to have helped build the Dart Elevator, and he was that elevator's first foreman. He also appears to have owned a steam-powered lake vessel.[153] His younger brother, Chandler J. Wells, designed several grain elevators in Buffalo, including the Wells (built in 1858, later called the Wheeler), the Coburn (built in 1860), and the C.J. Wells (built in 1861), and was the Mayor of Buffalo from 1865 to 1867. In 1872, the two brothers purchased and rebuilt the Williams Elevator, which thereafter was known as the William Wells Elevator.[154]

Commission does not know what you know and is in doubt on that point, how are we going to satisfy our doubts until we do know?" [...] Commissioner Fairchild: "Is Mr. Smith's question not very pointed? How can this Commission arrive at any proper conclusion regarding that business unless each and every one of those elements to which you refer are made known on the record here to the Commission?" Mr. Douglass: "I don't see where it interests you." *Report of the New York Commerce Commission, Volume II, transmitted to the legislature January 25, 1900* (Albany, 1900), p. 1207.

[153] "Obituaries," *The New York Times*, September 7, 1885.

[154] See Michael Rizzo, *Through the Mayor's Eyes: The Only Complete History of the Mayors of Buffalo, New York*, 2003, on-line: http://www.buffalonian.com/history/industry/

The WEC was intended to accomplish four related tasks: 1) allow all five of the big trunk lines (the New York Central, the Erie, the West Shore, the Delaware, Lackawanna & Western, and the Lehigh Valley) to participate in and profit from the grain transshipment business, even if they didn't own any grain elevators in Buffalo;[155] 2) systematically drive out of business those grain elevators that were canal-only and had no rail connections, and so were especially unlikely to join "the association"; 3) allow these trunk lines, working in concert, to obtain and exert monopoly control over all of the grain elevators in Buffalo, which was (no one had forgotten) the single biggest grain-transfer point in the country; and 4) charge as much as possible for the elevation and short-term storage of grain.[156] For example, if the WEC charged one cent per bushel on the 50 million bushels that came through Buffalo every year, it stood to make a half-million dollars annually, and this very large sum of money did not include the profits from its grain-scooping and grain-loading operations.[157] In the sunny words of one of

---

mayors/Wells.htm accessed 5 September 2008.

[155] All but the New York Central and the Erie did not own any elevators in Buffalo.

[156] There was "no established rate [for elevating and temporary storage]," Cook explained to the State of New York in 1899, "just what we could get." *Report of the New York Commerce Commission, Volume II* (Albany, 1900), p. 1232.

[157] "These little charges of an eight and a quarter [of a cent], while they do affect, and you can figure them up in so many hundreds of thousands of dollars, they are spread over so much territory that people don't feel it." Statement of Mr. Spencer Kellogg, proprietor of the Kellogg elevator, Buffalo, N.Y., May 27, 1901, *Report of the Industrial Commission on Agriculture and Agricultural Labor, including Testimony,*

its secretaries, Philos G. Cook, the Western Elevating Company prevents price "cutting" and "puts everyone on an even footing in handling grain or in putting grain through here [Buffalo]."[158]

For the WEC to perform well, each and every grain-elevator owner in Buffalo would have to join the WEC. No one could be allowed to operate independently. And that meant: *once and for all*. To make sure no one broke ranks or a new elevator didn't "come along" to threaten its monopoly, the WEC changed its rates frequently[159] and reconstituted itself at the beginning of each and every shipping season.[160]

To become a member of the WEC, one had to relinquish control of one's grain elevator(s) and "all the machinery, docks and appurtenances thereunto pertaining, useful and necessary for working of the same." This transfer

---

with Review and Topical Digest thereof, Volume X of the Commission's Reports (Washington, DC, 1901), p. 1016.

[158] Statement of Mr. P.G. Cook, Secretary of the Western Elevating Association, May 27, 1901, *Report of the Industrial Commission on Agriculture and Agricultural Labor, including Testimony, with Review and Topical Digest thereof,* Volume X of the Commission's Reports (Washington, DC, 1901), p. 1018.

[159] "Last season, Mr Bennett of Buffalo offered to transfer grain at ¼ cent per bushel, the regular price being ¾ cent, and the pool at once did it for nothing, forcing him back into the pool." "Excessive Elevator Charges," *New York Times,* March 21, 1885.

[160] "[News Sent] By Mail & Telegraph," *New York Times,* May 21, 1872: "The Buffalo Grain Elevator Association was broken up today." In 1881, the Western Elevator Company broke up and was replaced for a single shipping season by the Western Elevating Association. In 1883, the Western Elevator Company was reconstituted. "Buffalo Wants to Store Grain," *New York Times,* June 6, 1885.

of control gave one the opportunity to buy shares in the WEC. It was according to the number of shares owned that members would receive their respective dividends, that is, after the organization's treasurer had deducted the costs of purchasing fire insurance,[161] paying taxes, making repairs, and hiring scoopers and power-shovels to assist in and speed up the unloading of lake vessels. In 1899, when there were twenty shareholders in the WEC, the average dividend would have been between twenty and thirty-five thousand dollars per year.[162]

Though monopoly control over Buffalo's grain transshipment facilities could have been obtained if each grain-elevator owner purchased a single share (or, rather, one share per elevator he owned), a handful of owners purchased very large numbers of shares. In 1881, four of the WEC's thirty-five shareholders – Israel Hatch, George W. Tifft, Dean Richmond and James Wadsworth – owned a combined total of 262 shares, with the remaining 278 shares almost equally divided among the other 31 shareholders. This meant that, unless every single one of the other shareholders sided against them, the Big Four could do as they pleased. This same situation existed in 1899, when a handful of elevators owned by the railroad companies (five out of a total of twenty-one elevators) controlled 48% of the WEA's shares.[163]

---

[161] "Should his elevator be destroyed by fire within the said term," the WEC's articles of agreement stated, "then he shall be entitled to receive of and from the said company the rents [to which he is entitled]."

[162] Cf. testimony of Carleton T. Ladd, the manager of the Watson Elevator, in *Report of the New York Commerce Commission, Volume II* (Albany, 1900), p. 1170.

[163] In his testimony in front of the New York Commerce Commission, Philos G. Cook, secretary of the WEA, revealed that there were *five* factions within the

In 1881, when the Connecting Terminal (a brand-new, railroad-owned grain elevator) was brought into the WEC, its secretary, Philos G. Cook proclaimed, "The entire elevating interest of this port is now substantially in the control of the Western Elevating Company, and such has been the case during its existence; when new elevators have been erected, such arrangements have been made with their owners as to induce them to place their elevating property in the hands of the company."[164] No doubt the "inducements" to join the WEC could take negative as well as positive forms.[165] Failure to join the WEC meant that one would have to pay one's own

---

organization, each with their own respective agreements: 1) elevators affiliated with the New York Central and New York & Erie (23 percent of total shares issued); 2) elevators affiliated with the other railroad companies (25 percent); 3) elevators affiliated with local flour millers (37 percent); 4) elevators that could only load canal boats (9 percent); and 5) elevators owned by the Wells family (5 percent). *Report of the New York Commerce Commission, Volume II* (Albany, 1900), p. 1236. Note well that one of the Wells' elevators (the C.J. Wells) transshipped three million bushels in 1899, while his other elevator (the Bennett) was kept inactive. *Report of the New York Commerce Commission*, p. 1218.

[164] Quoted in H. Perry Smith, *History of the City of Buffalo and Erie County* (Syracuse: D. Mason, 1884), p. 217.

[165] "The contract [that punished the Kellogg Elevator] was made after they [the WEA] had attempted several times to get the Kellogg elevator into the association and the Kellogg elevator refused to go in; refused to be dictated to; so after that they started to put on the screws." Statement of Mr. Spencer Kellogg, proprietor of the Kellogg elevator, Buffalo, N.Y., May 27, 1901, *Report of the Industrial Commission on Agriculture and Agricultural Labor, including Testimony, with Review and Topical Digest thereof*, Volume X of the Commission's Reports (Washington, DC, 1901), p. 1015.

taxes, as well as pay for one's own repairs, grain-scoopers, and fire insurance (without the benefits of group discounts), as well as. Furthermore, if one's elevator *did* happen to be destroyed by fire, one would only be compensated for loss of property, not for loss of business, as well.

As if the point needed proving, a great many of Buffalo's grain elevators caught fire or exploded during the WEC's first few years of existence. In fact, a total of sixteen grain elevators (most of them newly constructed) were destroyed by fire between 1858 and 1867: the Hollister, the Reed, the City (twice), the Grain Dock, the Sternberg,[166] the Wilkinson, the Sterling (again), the Evans (twice), the Coburn, the Main Street, the Corn Dock, the Sturges, the Ohio Basin, the Erie, and, last but not least, the Dart.[167] It is *certain* that some of these elevators caught fire and exploded because someone unintentionally ignited a cloud of grain dust.[168] Because Buffalo's elevators were built so closely to each other, a fire or explosion at one quickly spread to

---

[166] Built in 1861 by Charles F. Sternberg, the Sternberg "A" elevator burned in September 1863. According to "Destruction in Buffalo," New York Times, September 27, 1863, the insurance on the building was $40,000 and was covered by 36 separate policies.

[167] The site of the old Dart Elevator was occupied by the Bennett Elevator, named after its new owner, the railroad baron David S. Bennett, who moved to Buffalo from Syracuse in 1853. In time, Bennett would pay designers and builders to erect three more grain elevators in Buffalo: the Tifft, operated in partnership with George W. Tifft; an elevator built in partnership with A. Sherwood; and the Union Elevator, built in 1867 at the very edge of Buffalo's harbor.

[168] I return to this subject in Chapter 4, "Fireproofing the Tinderbox."

another.[169] It is *possible* that avant-garde Confederate commandos burned several of them down.[170] But it is *likely* that some of these fires were caused by arsonists.[171] An arson attack on a grain elevator full of someone else's grain could be used to punish certain elevator owners who wouldn't join the group, to intimidate members who had joined but wanted

---

[169] Indeed, a fire at a grain elevator could spread to one of the ships that it was unloading, as happened when the Sturges burned on 31 July 1866.

[170] In the words of a letter sent to Governor Seymour by several prominent Buffalo businessmen, and reprinted under the Title "The Defence of Buffalo" in the *New York Times* on August 22, 1864, one need "only to look at the twenty-seven elevators filled with grain, and which are indispensable to transfer for the thirty or forty millions of bushels that must arrive here before the close of navigation, to see that, if these be destroyed, it will be a national calamity, the effects of which will be felt to the remotest part of the United States; and they are necessarily of that combustible material [that is] easily ignited, and once on fire they are so high that there can be little hope of extinguishing the flames." According to the writers of this letter, "rebels from Canada" want "to burn our city and plunder its inhabitants." Other dangerous parties include "a marauding force composed of rebels from the Southern States and deserters from our own army, many of whom, we are informed, are utterly depraved, in most destitute circumstances, and ready for an expedition that promises devastation and plunder with a hope of escape."

[171] In reference to the fire of May 22, 1858, which "broke out in the Hollister Elevator, on Ohio street," and which destroyed the Hollister itself along "with two dwelling houses, the Elevator office, and a saloon adjoining," the *New York Times* stated "these fires were all unquestionably the work of incendiaries." See "Incendiary Fires in Buffalo," *New York Times*, May 22, 1858.

to leave, and/or to cash in on the WEC's generous insurance provisions.[172]

With the WEC in full control of Buffalo's grain elevators, and the WEC under the control of pro-railroad factions, the railroad companies were able to take giant steps towards monopolizing something that had previously eluded their grasp: the transshipment of grain in bulk through Buffalo. Between 1854 and 1860, only 20 percent of the grain in bulk that was received at the Port of Buffalo was sent to cities on the east coast by railroad; the other 80 percent was transported along the all-water, Erie Canal/Hudson River route.[173] But the railroads had exerted monopoly control over the transshipment of barrels of flour since the early 1850s. In 1856, for example, the New York Central or the New York & Erie Railroad combined to transship to New York City virtually all of the 1.2 million barrels of flour that had been received by the Port of Buffalo.

A number of factors had allowed the railroads to take over and monopolize the transshipment of barreled flour, which in the 1850s was still done in the "traditional," block-and-tackle fashion by large gangs of stevedores. Unlike the curved surfaces of a ship's hold, the flat bottoms of railcars were ideally suited for transporting barrels of flour. Because they, too, were flat-bottomed, these barrels (unlike sacks of

---

[172] "Deterrence is as relevant to relations between friends as between potential enemies [...] The deterrence concept requires that there be both conflict and common interest between the parties involved [...] We can equally well call it the theory of precarious partnership or the theory of incomplete antagonism." Thomas C. Schelling, *The Strategy of Conflict* (Harvard University Press, 1980 edition, pp. 11 and 15.

[173] Thomas D. Odle, *The American Grain Trade of the Great Lakes, 1825-1873* (University of Michigan, 1951), p. 86.

grain) could be stored by stacking them up, one upon another, to form a sturdy column. Rows and rows of such columns could be placed inside a railcar. Unlike the lake vessels and canal boats, the railroads could operate during the winter months. They even had an advantage during the summer, because produce of all kinds (grain and flour included) was better off in airy railcars than in the dank holds of ships. Farmers and forwarding and commission agents preferred the railroads to lake vessels and canal boats because, unlike the later, the former assured safe delivery and thus obviated the need for transportation insurance. The railroad companies also such low prices that the shipping companies could not match them, and so they were forced out of business or into selling their companies to the railroads.

The WEC used some of the same tactics to divert the flow of grain in bulk away from the Erie Canal and towards the railroad companies that were in competition with it. Though it kept elevating and storage fees as high possible, the WEC transshipped grain to canal boats for free. When the water-based shipping companies couldn't compete any longer and closed down or sold off their grain elevators, the WEC or its allies in the railroad companies purchased them. Once they were owned by the WEC, these elevators would be used to transship grain from lake-to-rail. If they couldn't be used in this fashion, they weren't used at all and their share of the WEC's profits was diminished (they received none of the profits from the WEC's grain-loading or grain-scooping operations). Elevators that were unused quickly fell into disrepair or even ruin.[174] And so the pro-canal men within the

---

[174] According to Carleton T. Ladd, the manager of the Watson Elevator, one year out of commission was enough to ruin a grain elevator for good. In 1899, the Richmond and the Brown had been out of commission for five years; the Lyon had only been used for "two seasons" even though it had

WEC were made an offer they couldn't refuse: they could stay inside the WEC, draw their modest dividends for doing little or no work, and help undermine the Erie Canal in favor of the railroads, or they could leave the WEC, try to use a ruined grain elevator, and draw no dividends at all.

The strategy worked.[175] In 1872, the railroads carried to New York City as much wheat and corn in bulk as the Erie Canal did (30 million bushels). In 1895, when a record-breaking 162 million bushels of grain arrived in the Port of Buffalo, 142 million of them were transported to market by the railroads, and only 20 million by the Erie Canal. In 1900,

---

been built twenty years previously; and the Swiftsure hadn't been used for "twenty years." See the *Report of the New York Commerce Commission, Volume II* (Albany, 1900), pp. 1170-1174.

[175] At least it did until 1897, when "the Export elevator and the [Great] Northern could not agree on sharing, and the Electric elevator, too, and the result was it all went to pieces." See testimony of Carleton T. Ladd, *Report of the New York Commerce Commission*, Volume II (Albany, 1900), p. 1179. See also "To Build a Steel Elevator: The Great Northern Railway to Make an Experiment," *New York Times*, March 1, 1897: "The Great Northern elevator, besides being the largest and almost the only modern elevator in Buffalo, will be free from the pool and will make, it is understood here, such charges as will do more to break the combine than any legal enactment made in New York State." In "No Graft on His Road, declares J.J. Hill," *New York Times*, November 22, 1906, Hill reported that, in 1897, the WEC was charging 1.5 cents per bushels to elevate and store, while the Great Northern wanted to charge only 0.5 cents per bushel. After the WEC disbanded in 1897, it re-formed as the Western Elevating Association in 1898. Unlike the WEC, the WEA was exclusively composed of rail-friendly elevators and included no canal-friendly elevators at all.

all of the grain that came into Buffalo by lake vessel left by railroad car.

The State of New York wasn't at all happy with these developments, nor was the federal government.[176] In 1884, New York State had stopped collecting tolls on the Erie Canal to help it compete with the railroads. In 1895, it had spent $9 million to repair, improve and expand the canal. In 1898, then-Governor Black asked the New York Commerce Commission to find out why commerce was suffering. Two years later, the Commission recommended the construction of a barge canal system, which was in fact undertaken between 1905 and 1918 at the cost of almost $100 million. But by 1960s, the entire "New York State Barge Canal System," unable to compete with the railroads and truck companies, was no longer used for commercial shipping. Today, New York's many canals are only open for recreational uses.

In 1860, after reviewing the "gratifying" volume of grain and other shipments over the Erie Canal during the previous year, an anonymous writer for Buffalo's *Commercial Advertiser Directory* contended that it must be remembered that the Erie Canal's "common enemy, the railroads, have, by every means which ingenuity could invent, sought to render it unpopular and deprive it of that legitimate business of which, in justice to the people of the State, should be the sole possessor." References to the railroad companies as the "enemies" of the Erie Canal

---

[176] "Bitter complaints are made of combinations among the grain warehouse, not only at such important transfer points as Chicago and Buffalo, but also throughout the wheat growing region of the Northwest." "Review of the evidence: Elevators," *Report of the Industrial Commission on Agriculture and Agricultural Labor, including Testimony, with Review and Topical Digest thereof*, Volume X of the Commission's Reports (Washington, DC, 1901), p. XLVIII.

continued to appear for the rest of the 19th century. "Once let that superb work [the Erie Canal] fall into the hands of its enemies, the railroads, or into desuetude," one writer predicted, "and the knell of Buffalo's commercial supremacy will soon be heard; her glory will have departed, and from her proud position of Queen of the Lakes she will descend into a mere way-station on the trunk railroad lines; her elevators will rot as they stand, her wharves go to ruin, and scarcely a sail will dot or a steam-tug ripple the bosom of her beautiful bay." It took a century, but this dire prediction eventually came true, and paints an unnervingly accurate picture of what Buffalo has been like for the last 40 years.

The first major series of "blows" to Buffalo's importance in the international grain trade came between 1905 and 1908. In 1905, the Dominion of Canada – anticipating the Imperial Conference of 1907, which officially granted the former British colony the right to self-government – built the first of five large-scale grain elevators in Montreal. Work on these elevators, and the concurrent modernization of Montreal's harbor, would last through the mid-1920s. Because these new grain elevators were publicly owned and financed, they could work just as fast as, and yet charge lower prices than, those privately owned (railroad-owned) grain elevators in Buffalo. In the words of the anonymous author of "*Les Mysteres d'un Elevateur a Grains*":

> According to the statistics, millions of bushels of grain are produced in the West, the majority of it sent by water-routes to the East and from there to Europe [...] The exporters have realized that the transport of grain by water, by the Great Lakes to Montreal, allows them to save 1.5 cents of freight per bushel; while the shipment by rail to the United States, with at least two transshipments [along the way], not only does not permit sensible

economics, but also causes many troubles and sometimes congestion. This is no doubt why the Port of Montreal receives more and more shipments, all principally by water [...] The grain-exporters who use [the government's elevator] only pay for the work necessitated by the unloading of the grain, while the elevator [operator] is not remunerated for loading the ships and trains that carry Canadian cereals. This generosity is intended, one assures us, to facilitate trade and the sale of Canadian grain. In brief, it is a gratuity that our government gives to the [Canadian] trade in cereals.[177]

In 1908, the Goderich Elevator Company built a brand-new grain elevator in Goderich, Ontario, to replace an older one (built in 1898) that had exploded the prior year. Over the course of the 1910s and 1920s, this elevator would be expanded and equipped with faster equipment several times. Located on the south shore of Lake Huron, Goderich was in an excellent position to divert all Montreal-bound traffic from the lower Great Lakes (Lakes Erie and Ontario) in favor of a more direct route by railroad.

A small but nevertheless important event took place in 1911, when the huge Canadian flour company Maple Leaf opened a flourmill in Port Colborne. Located on the Lake Erie side of the canal (the Welland) that connects Lake Erie with Lake Ontario, Port Colborne had long competed with Buffalo for grain that was headed to Rochester and Oswego, both of which were entrances to the New York State Barge Canal and flour-milling centers in their own right. The opening of a flourmill at this rival transshipment point both

---

[177] *Album Universel* on 21 October 1905, pp. 784-785, my translation from the French.

increased the pressure on Buffalo and extended it to Rochester and Oswego.

In the aftermath of World War I, during which Buffalo transshipped over 40 million bushels of grain,[178] there were clear signs that the nation's grain trade was moving elsewhere. In 1922, the Federal Trade Commission took stock of the twenty-three most important grain ports in the United States and grouped them by geography. There were five regions: the Atlantic Ocean (Portland, Boston, New York City, Philadelphia, Baltimore, Newport News and Norfolk); the Gulf of Mexico (New Orleans, Galveston, Port Arthur, and Texas City); the Great Lakes (Buffalo, Chicago, Milwaukee and Duluth); the Pacific Ocean (Seattle, Tacoma, Portland, Astoria [Oregon] and San Francisco);[179] and the Interior (Kansas City, Fort Worth and San Antonio).[180] While the Great Lakes region could store a total of 111 million bushels of grain, which was four to ten times more than could be stored in any other region of the country,[181] the bulk of America's grain was being shipped through the Interior. From 1919 to 1922, the amount of grain received at Kansas City grew from 116 million to 126 million bushels. During

---

[178] Henry Baxter, *Buffalo's Grain Elevators* (Buffalo and Erie Country Historical Society, 1980), p. 21.

[179] San Francisco was the port from which "the grain king," Isaac Friedlander, exported wheat.

[180] At this time, sacks of grain were still in use in the Pacific Ocean area and in Fort Worth and San Antonio. They were stored in elevators with "flat capacity." *Report of the Federal Trade Commission on the Methods and Operations of Grain Exporters* (Washington, DC, 1922), p. 260.

[181] Chicago, 44 million bushels of capacity; Duluth, 36 million; Buffalo, 24 million; and Milwaukee, 5 million. *Report of the Federal Trade Commission on the Methods and Operations of Grain Exporters* (Washington, DC, 1922), p. 255.

that same period, the amount of grain received at Duluth, Chicago, New York City, New Orleans, Galveston, and Portland, Oregon also increased (though none of them topped 60 million bushels per year). In Buffalo, grain receipts declined from 11 million to only two million bushels.[182]

The second series of major blows to Buffalo's position came between 1929 and 1932. First, "the Interstate Commerce Commission gave Oswego [New York] the right to charge a preferential [railroad] rate to New York and Boston, lower than the Buffalo rate for both domestic and export, and John, Jr. [MacMillan] wrote his father, 'this […] will establish a precedent for demanding similar rates out of Ogdensburg [New York] and it seems to all of us here [at Cargill] that it will definitively mark the end of Buffalo as an important transfer point.'"[183]

Three years later, in 1932, Canada renovated and greatly expanded the Welland Canal on the occasion of its centenary.[184] Because it connected Lake Erie to Lake Ontario, the Welland permitted shippers a variety of transfer points other than Buffalo: Rochester or Oswego, both of which were connected to the New State York State Barge Canal, which opened in 1925 on the centenary of the Erie

---

[182] See *Report of the Federal Trade Commission on the Methods and Operations of Grain Exporters* (Washington, DC, 1922), pp. 255 and 263.

[183] Wayne G. Broehl, *Cargill: Trading the World's Grain* (University Press of New England, 1992), p. 324.

[184] Note well that the Welland Canal had been steadily improved since the late 1890s, when the Canadian government spent $80 million to deepen the canal from 10 to 14 feet, and to deepen the St. Lawrence River to 14 feet, thereby opening it to large ocean-going vessels. "Canadian Trade Conditions," *New York Times*, January 1, 1900.

Canal; and Ogdensburg, New York,[185] or Montreal, both of which were on the St. Lawrence River and thus accessible by ocean-going vessels.

Buffalo was also threatened by the "trade preferences" that Great Britain established for Canadian wheat in 1932. To qualify for this six-cent-per bushel subsidy, Canadian wheat had to be shipped to Great Britain from Canadian ports (Montreal and the other ports along the St. Lawrence River). In the words of Dan Morgan, "This made it difficult for New York merchants to bring Canadian grain through Buffalo and other American Great Lakes ports because it was difficult to prove [to the British] that the cargo was Canadian."[186]

The further encourage all-Canadian routes for Canadian grain, the Dominion government built a colossal lake-to-ocean transshipping terminal near Port Prescott, just across the St. Lawrence River from Ogdensburg. Built in the long, tall and narrow style of Buffalo's Concrete Central Elevator,[187] this massive terminal bested its predecessor by having a larger storage capacity (five million bushels) and a total of *four* loose legs. This elevator still stands, and has been photographed by amateur photographers who have posted their shots on-line.[188]

---

[185] Ogdensburg's grain elevators had been built in the 1890s by railroad companies (the Rutland & Lake Michigan and the Ogdensburg & Lake Champlain). A photograph of the latter's elevator appears on-line http://www.ogdensburg.info/webphotos/dgrainel.jpg accessed 20 August 2008.

[186] *Merchants of Grain*, Viking, 1979, p. 81.

[187] See the following photograph on the website hosted by the Halton Hills Public Library in Ontario, Canada: http://www.hhpl.on.ca/GreatLakes/GLImages/FullImage.asp?ifid=4902&number=4 accessed 20 August 2008.

[188] http://www.ogdensburg.info/webphotos/dma15.jpg accessed 20 August 2008.

Paradoxically, perhaps, the Port of Buffalo was extremely busy all through the late 1920s and 1930s. During this period, Buffalo displaced Minneapolis[189] as the nation's single most productive flour-milling city, a distinction that Buffalo maintained through the rest of the 20th century. At least eight major flour companies leased or owned grain elevators and flourmills in Buffalo: Washburn-Crosby, which later became part of General Mills; Pillsbury, which purchased the Great Northern Elevator; Russell-Miller, which purchased the American Elevator and extended it in 1931; Hecker-Jones-Jewell, later known as the H&O Oats Company, which erected a steel-binned grain elevator in Buffalo in 1931; Husted, which owned the Superior Elevator, which was extended twice in the 1920s; Spencer-Kellogg, which built an extension to its main elevator in 1936; and

---

[189] Centered upon St. Anthony's Falls, the only waterfall on the Mississippi River, where a large difference in levels allowed water-powered mills to operate, the flour-milling district of Minneapolis took shape in the 1860s. Future giants of the flour industry, such as Washburn-Crosby and Pillsbury, were founded there, as was the grain trader, Cargill. It seems the city's first large-scale flour mill was built in 1863 by Cadwallader Washburn and that its first grain elevator was attached to the Washburn "A" Mill in 1874. This elevator exploded in 1878 and was rebuilt in 1879, the same year that the Great Northern Railroad built a large, wood-binned elevator in St. Anthony's Falls. Other early elevators in the "Midway" – that is, mid-way between Minneapolis and St. Paul – were built in 1888 (the huge, wood-binned, ironclad Saint Anthony #1) and 1892 (the small, wood-binned, ironclad Saint Anthony #2). By 1896, thanks to the tremendous amounts of wheat being grown in western Minnesota and the Dakotas, Minneapolis' mills were producing more flour than any other city in the country (almost 13 million barrels a year).

three locally based milling companies (Thorton & Chester, and George Urban, and J.A. Walter). Buffalo was also home to at least seven large-scale feed mills: Park & Pollard; Mapl-Flake; Maritime; Eastern States, which built a large grain elevator in Tonawanda in 1934; Ralston-Purina, which built a steel-binned elevator in Buffalo in 1907; and the Grange League Federation (GLF), which took over the marine elevator previously owned by Wheeler and built a new one in 1936.

As a matter of fact, Buffalo remained a dominant grain port all through the 1940s, a hundred years after the construction of the Dart Elevator. The war forced American shippers to avoid Montreal and route all their grain through Buffalo. More than 200 million bushels of grain passed through Buffalo's elevators every year during World War II: some of it bound for the city's own flour mills, feed mills and breweries, some of it bound for New York City and other port cities on the Atlantic coast; most of it bound for Europe. Demand for temporary storage in Buffalo was in fact so great that extensions or annexes were added to the Eastern States Grain Elevator in 1941, the Standard Elevator in 1941, the GLF elevator complex in 1942, and the Electric Elevator in 1942.[190]

The third major blow to Buffalo as an international transshipment hub came in 1959, when Canada officially opened the St. Lawrence Seaway, which widened and deepened the St. Lawrence River so that it could accommodate the huge tankers then becoming active upon the Atlantic Ocean. Because it helped Montreal compete with New York City for shipping to and from Europe, the St. Lawrence Seaway undermined the desirability of the entire Erie Barge Canal/Hudson River shipping route. In a way, the

---

[190] The last extension in Buffalo was made in 1954. It was made to the Connecting Terminal Elevator, the first section of which was built in 1914.

rise of Montreal as an international grain port also undermined the strategic position of the Great Lakes, which could now be avoided if the grain traders used an all-rail, all-Canadian route to reach the Atlantic Ocean. A sign of the times was the sudden international prominence of Port Cartier, at which a modern elevator was built that could elevate grain at the rate of 88,000 bushels an hour and could store over 10 million bushels.

The fourth and knock-out blow came in 1965, when, after three years of wrangling, the Interstate Commerce Commission decided to end the freight-rate system in which Buffalo had received preferential treatment to compensate it for the collapse of trade on the New York State Barge Canal in the 1950s. Without artificially low freight rates, Buffalo no longer presented any advantages to grain merchants in the Midwest, who now could afford to avoid the Great Lakes entirely and ship all their grain to the east coast ports by railroad cars or trucks.

Almost immediately after the ICC's decision, Buffalo's grain elevators began to close. The Marine A was the first to go, only 40 years after it was built. The Eastern States Elevator and Feed Mill was abandoned in 1966, a mere twenty-five years after *its* construction. When the Connecting Terminal exploded, it was simply closed down and abandoned. Continental closed and abandoned of the Concrete-Central in 1967, and Cargill did the same with its elevators (the Electric, the Superior and the Pool) shortly thereafter. In the 1970s, both the H&O Oats cereal plant and the GLF/Agway feed mill were closed and abandoned. Pillsbury kept the Great Northern open until 1981, when it was finally closed down. Today, in 2008, the only grain elevators active in Buffalo are affiliated with either General Mills or Archer-Daniels-Midland.

The maps that Dan Morgan published as the front and back endpapers to *Merchants of Grain* neatly illustrate the Port of Buffalo's demise from the heights of the 1850s. In the first map, entitled "Major World Grain Routes, 1880," the grain in question is American wheat, and it is shipped from Duluth and Chicago via the Great Lakes. A curved arrow indicates that this grain is transshipped through an unnamed inland port (that would be Buffalo) before it arrives by rail or boat at Portland, Baltimore, Philadelphia or New York City.[191] The grain's final destination is Liverpool, which also receives corn from Buenos Aires, Argentina and wheat from Adelaide, Australia.

In the second map, entitled "Major World Grain Routes, 1978," the grain in question is both Canadian and American, and it is transported from three of locations: 1) Vancouver, Canada and Portland, Oregon,[192] from which all

---

[191] According to Exhibit 11 in the *Report of the New York Commerce Commission*, volume II, transmitted to the legislature January 25, 1900 (Albany 1900), the big grain ports on the American east coast in 1898 were Portland (Maine), Boston, New York, Philadelphia, Baltimore, Newport News (Virginia), and Norfolk. Other ports mentioned were Montreal, New Orleans, and Galveston (Texas).

[192] Thanks to its location – at the meeting of three rivers (the Columbia, the Willamette, and the Snake) and relatively close to the wheat-growing areas of Montana, Idaho and North Dakota – the Port of Portland, Oregon, has long been a major grain port. According to one on-line source, there were a total of nine "grain docks" and four flour mills in Portland in 1900. Large-scale grain elevators built of out reinforced concrete were erected in 1912 by the Globe Grain & Milling Company and in 1919 by the municipal government. http://www.portlandwaterfront.org/1900_1939.html accessed 23 August 2008. The city's elevators transshipped over 200 million metric tons of grain in 2002, and are projected to transship 600 metric tons by 2011. See

kinds of North American grains (wheat, corn, barley, sorghum, rice, and soybeans) are shipped to Japan, China, the Philippines and India; 2) New Orleans, Louisiana and Houston, Texas, from which various grains are shipped to Europe and Asia, respectively; and 3) Montreal and Quebec, which from grain is sent to Western Europe, Eastern Europe and Northern Africa. Present but unnamed in the first map, Buffalo isn't even "on" the second one.

In 1976, there was a tragedy at the Concrete Central. A local kid who was climbing around in it fell to his death. No doubt he didn't fall *off* the elevator, but into one of its grain bins, which were uncovered (this has been the case in so many other instances). Despite the semi-hopeful headlines,[193] the Concrete-Central wasn't torn down. Given the size of the building and the materials used to construct it, the 60-year-old structure couldn't be demolished by hitting it with a wrecking ball. It would have to be exploded, which was a very expensive proposition, especially for a "Rust Belt" city like Buffalo, which was the midst of a recession. The City chose instead to seal the Concrete Central's basements and remove all of its ladders and staircases, which effectively prevented all but the most intrepid explorers from climbing it. Over the years, this same treatment was given to the Superior, the Marine A, and the Eastern States, among others. Unfortunately for the elevators themselves, no measures were taken to protect them from "the elements" (Buffalo's acidic rain and snow) or shore up their foundations (the reinforced concrete dock at the Concrete Central has been seriously compromised for over 20 years).

Like Buffalo, Minneapolis has also seen many of its abandoned grain elevators become "attractive nuisances" in

---

http://www.portofportland.com/MTMP_Facts_Figrs.aspx accessed 23 August 2008.

[193] "Buffalo may seek to aid to tear down tragedy elevators," *Courier Express*, 13 April 1976, page 1.

which people fall to their deaths. In his essay from 2004, *Vanishing Giants: The Grain Elevators of Minneapolis and Their Legacy*, William E. Stark reports: "An abandoned South Minneapolis elevator on Garfield Avenue was demolished following incidents where several youth fell to their deaths in the late 1970s and early 1980s. Similarly, following a series of killings and violent crimes at the General Mills elevators at Second Street and 10th Avenue South in Minneapolis, the City Council voted to raze the structure in 1997. At the Bunge y Born Elevator, the proliferation of graffiti on and in the structure just since its closure in 2002 is testament to the lure these buildings provide. In 2006, a University of Minnesota student tragically fell to her death one night while exploring its inner workings. Similar incidents at other elevators occur with regularity."

But unlike Minneapolis, which has had the money to demolish nearly all of its abandoned grain elevators (at the cost of about $1 million each), Buffalo has been unable to do so or, rather, has only managed to destroy a few. Unfortunately, each one was a historically significant grain elevator: the Dakota, which was demolished in 1966 to "make room" for an elevated portion of the motorway that encircles the City; the Dellwood Elevator, which was demolished in 1973, when the Archer-Daniels-Midland company left Buffalo, in the hope of making this "waterfront" property more desirable; and the Electric Elevator, which was demolished in 1984 for the same stupid reason (and because its steel grain tanks could be carved up and sold off!). And so, by virtue of two *accidents of history* – the fact that the first mechanized grain elevator was built in Buffalo, not somewhere else, and the fact that the Buffalo has long been unable to either reclaim or demolish its abandoned elevators – this city has long possessed the biggest collection of *ruined grain elevators* in the world.

184

Gouverneur Morris got what he wanted for New York, the "empire" state: monumental ruins, ruins worthy of a great civilization. But these ruins arrived *prematurely*, not "after a lapse of two thousand years," which is what he hoped for, but "in the course of [only] two centuries," which was the time he thought it would take for the American nation to become a great empire. I can't help but think here of Walter Benjamin's comments on the title that Charles Baudelaire gave to his 1863 collection of poems (*Les Fleurs du mal*), because they suggested the title of this book ("American Colossus"):

> With this title, in which the supremely new is presented to the reader as something 'supremely old,' Baudelaire has given the liveliest form to his concept of the modern. The linchpin of his entire theory of art is 'modern beauty,' and for him the proof of modernity seems to be this: it is marked with the fatality of being antiquity one day, and it reveals this to whoever witnesses its birth. Here we meet the quintessence of the unforeseen, which for Baudelaire is an inalienable quality of the beautiful. The face of modernity itself blasts us with its immemorial gaze. Such was the gaze of Medusa for the Greeks.[194]

---

[194] Walter Benjamin, *The Arcades Project*, pp. 22-23.

Chapter 4
Fireproofing the Tinderbox

Grain kernels are dry and multi-layered; when large quantities of them are assembled and moved around in bulk, they rub against each other and produce a lot of dust, approximately 25 pounds of it for every ton of grain. Because these dust particles are very small and light, they hang in the air as well as accumulate on surfaces. As little as a one-eighth of an inch (.32 cm) of grain dust is an unacceptably dangerous accumulation by today's standards. A mixture of grain particles and "foreign" substances such as mold, fungi, soil, live microorganisms and pieces of dead insects, this dust is very unhealthy if inhaled, especially for people who smoke tobacco. Grain dust can cause asthma, bronchitis, and even a form of fever. In the mid-1860s, the Charity Organization Society was founded to help Buffalo's grain scoopers, who worked in the midst of grain dust day after day, and suffered mightily from it.

But the worst danger posed by clouds of grain dust is that they can burst in flames and cause the explosion of the building in which they are trapped.[1] It isn't known what precise precautions Robert Dunbar took to prevent clouds of

---

[1] See "Grain-dust explosions," in *Engineering News*, Volume 72, 1914, p. 821: "Grain-dusts are more explosive and produce higher explosion pressure, and at lower temperatures, than standard coal-dust (from the Pittsburg experimental mine); some dried dusts yielded 16 times the pressure of the undried dusts. Explosions are caused by open lights, conflagrations, foreign materials in grinding machines (particularly dangerous), and electric sparks from motors, switches, circuits, and belts."

grain dust from forming in such likely places as the marine tower and the area above the grain bins, but he certainly must have been aware of the problem. On the one hand, Dunbar had to place the wood-burning engine that powered the machines in the Dart Elevator in a spot that was sufficiently far enough away from the flows of grain that the inevitable sparks and cinders coming from the controlled burn wouldn't set off an explosion. On the other hand, that spot couldn't be so far away that the engine had difficulty powering the machines, which were connected to it via shafts. Furthermore, since the entire structure of the grain elevator rocked, shifted and re-settled when it was being used, it was inevitable that one or several of the steam shafts or machines would get jarred out of line, and thus create a potential source of metal-to-metal contact and sparks.

Inexperience or lack of adequate training on the part of any member of the crew might also create potential sources of sparks. An operator working under a very tight deadline might try to clear a clogged or "choked" leg by "jogging" the belt, that is, stopping and starting the conveyor in an effort to clear the passage. He might try to engage in "hot work" (the welding, brazing or cutting of metal) in an area filled with grain dust. Or he might fire up an oil lamp to see things better, light up a cigarette or a pipe to relax, or simply flick an ash.

So little has changed since 1863! The damn things *continue* to explode.[2] Writing in the aftermath of the five deadly explosions that took place at American reinforced-concrete grain elevators in the month of December 1977, Dan

---

[2] See, for example, "The Erie Elevator Fire," *The New York Times*, August 26, 1882: "Timothy Driscoll [one of five workers who were killed], was not burned. He blown out of the building and so seriously injured that he cannot recover." This explosion took place only three years after the Erie was constructed.

Morgan reported: "From the outside, a modern grain elevator looks like a simple enough concrete structure, but inside it is a labyrinth of pipes, ducts, ventilators, belts, and shovel lifts, all controlled from a command room complete with console and flashing, colored buttons [...] A fine, choking dust fills the air, clogs the lungs, and covers clothing, reminding a visitor that a century after Cadwallader Washburn's A Mill exploded in Minneapolis with a thunderclap, the problem of grain dust has yet to be solved. Grain elevators are still volatile, explosive places – mines above ground."[3]

According to the Occupational Health and Safety Administration, there were at least 14 more grain elevator explosions between 1979 and 1981. Dozens of such explosions took place in the 1980s and 1990s. The most spectacular one was on 8 June 1998, when the DeBruce Grain Elevator in Hutchinson, Kansas, then listed in *The Guinness Book of World Records* as the single biggest grain elevator in the world (it could store a total of 20 million bushels), exploded, killing several workers, most of them trapped in the elevator's basement.

And so I must insist: the invention of the mechanized grain elevator was also the invention of the grain elevator explosion. "The concept of progress must be grounded in the idea of catastrophe," Walter Benjamin claims. "That things are 'status quo' is the catastrophe. It is not an ever-present possibility but what is in each case given."[4] Here we might also cite the French theorist Paul Virilio, who has been advocating the creation of a "Museum of the Accident" since the 1980s.[5]

Between the 1860s and the 1910s, the *increasingly less futile* search for a "fireproof" grain elevator largely

---

[3] *Merchants of Grain*, p. 314.

[4] *The Arcades Project*, p. 473.

[5] See his most recent book, *The Original Accident* (Cambridge: Polity, 2007).

concerned the materials out of which the bins and buildings themselves were made. Ironically, many of the elevators that exploded in the late 1850s and early 1860s *had already been fireproofed.* Or, rather, they were "more fireproof" than the elevators built in the 1840s and early '50s. In the mid-1860s, it became common for grain elevators in Buffalo to have heavy wooden lids for the tops of the grain bins, which not only reduced the amount of grain dust in the air and the likelihood of fatal slip-and-fall accidents, but also served to contain explosions that might otherwise spread, from one bin to the other, through the air. Another improvement involved the extensive use of stone and brick in the construction of the foundations, and iron cladding in the construction of the walls that housed the cribs, which were still made out of wood.

In the 1859 version of the New York Central & Hudson River Railroad's "City Elevator," for example,[6] the mainhouse was built on a foundation of 128 stone piers, mostly constructed out of stone and brick, and completely clad in fire-proof sheet-iron. In the eyes of *The 1860 Commercial Advertiser Directory for the City of Buffalo*, the City Elevator was a truly "modern" elevator: "The intermediate space between the its [supporting] piers is to [be] occupied by mason work, surmounted by inverted arches running at right angles from the piers, and connected with them in such a manner as to prevent the building from settling." In Charles Magnus' lithograph "Bird's Eye View of

---

[6] At the time of its explosion in November 1859, the old (first) version of the New York Central elevator contained 137,000 bushels of wheat, 56,000 bushels of oats, 24,000 bushels of corn, 17,000 bushels of barley and 1,500 bushels of rye. The elevator was insured by eleven different polices, which totaled $172,000. See "Conflagration at Buffalo," *New York Times*, November 10, 1859.

the City of Buffalo, NY," dated 1863,[7] the City has a very unusual marine tower. Raised up on pillars, it looks to be three separate structures that led back to the mainhouse. One has a slot that suggests it houses the marine leg itself; the other two gabled towers might contain shipping bins or machinery. In 1865, only six years after it was constructed, the City Elevator was destroyed by an explosion.

Undeterred, the railroad company built a new City Elevator in 1866. Called the "City A" after an even bigger and more modern elevator was built next to it in 1890, this grain elevator possessed a massive four-story brick and stone main house, the tin-clad ridged-roof of which rose to the height of 105 feet. Inside this huge windowless building were 152 wooden cribs, each 42 feet deep, altogether capable of storing 600,000 bushels of grain. The elevator's 400-horsepower coal-fired engine and boiler were housed in a separate, four-story-tall, ironclad wooden building that was located at the far side of the main house. Facing the water (that is, at the near side of the main house) was the elevator's marine tower. Rising 140 feet above the ground level, this tower was one of the tallest erected in Buffalo in the 19th century. A photograph of the City A and City B elevators taken sometime after 1890 and published in Frank Severance's *A Picture Book of Earlier Buffalo* shows that the City A wasn't simply tall.[8] It was also a very wide structure. The side of the building that faces the river was apparently full of machinery: there are windows on all of its four floors.

---

[7] Available on-line http://www.buffaloah.com/h/maps/map1863 accessed 21 August 2008.

[8] Frank H. Severance, *The Picture of Earlier Buffalo* (Buffalo Historical Society, 1912), page 41. But the City A wasn't nearly as tall or narrow as the City B, which was equipped with two very tall marine towers: one stiff, the other loose.

The tower as a whole is raised up on timbers and protrudes out over the dock, thus creating space underneath it.

At its prime, which came in 1889, the City A transshipped a total of 10,890,500 bushels of grain in a single shipping season. The elevator enjoyed a long and productive life, more than twelve to fifteen years, which was commonly accounted as the average life for such a building. Indeed, the only reason that the City A was decommissioned and destroyed was because, in 1908, the New York Central Railroad wanted to construct a freight depot in its place.

The Watson was another elevator built to be fireproof and remained standing until it was no longer needed. Erected in 1863 upon on the very tip of the peninsular land mass that had been created by the digging of the City Ship Canal, the Watson Elevator lasted until 1906, when it and the very ground upon which it stood were removed so that Buffalo's ever-cramped harbor could be expanded once again. Centrally located as far as water-borne shipping was concerned, and yet hard to reach by railroad, the Watson focused exclusively on transshipping grain from lake vessels to canal boats, and was the only major grain elevator in Buffalo to do so. It could store a total of 600,000 bushels of grain.

Two innovations allowed the Watson to succeed in a harbor increasingly dominated by lake-to-rail transshipments: its unique main house, which was raised up over the ground in such a way that canal boats could "slip" underneath it and receive loads of grain from its spouts; and the power-scooper, which the owners of the Watson patented in 1865. Still in use at some grain elevators today, though it is now powered by electricity and not by steam engines, the power-scooper is a device that, from within a ship's hold and drawing its power from the elevator leg itself, drags piles of loose grain towards the boot of the leg. A "labor-saving device" like the elevating leg itself, the power-scooper dramatically reduced (but did not eliminate) the need for manual laborers, who still had to operate the machine and clear blockages.

The unusual location of the Watson Elevator also made it a kind of unofficial city landmark. It was in fact the very first thing seen by the crew and passengers of each and every boat that came into Buffalo's harbor. The effect of the Watson's visibility was compounded by the elevator's unusual appearance. Atop the Watson's flat roof, there was a small shed, upon which in turn there was a cupola. An architectural element most commonly found atop churches and residential buildings, but never before seen on a grain elevator in Buffalo, this cupola housed a belvedere. It is likely that only a few (the elevator's owners and their guests) were allowed to enjoy the view from it.

Massive, boxy, darkly colored and almost completely windowless, the Watson Elevator's huge main house had the words WATSON ELEVATOR printed upon it in letters so large they might have been visible from Toledo. But here the Watson wasn't unique. Every grain elevator built in Buffalo in the 19th century had the same method of self-identification: "I am the [blank] elevator, [blank] because I was built by [blank, always a businessman's last name], and 'elevator' because I am a grain elevator." One is reminded of the naming of Roman *horrea* after their wealthy sponsors.[9]

An additional fireproof grain elevator built in Buffalo in 1863 deserves mention: the Bennett. Originally built "on the ashes" (in the *approximate* location) of the burned Dart Elevator, the Bennett was a large elevator, capable of storing 600,000 bushels in its 52-foot-tall wooden cribs. It occupied 150 feet of dock space and was 98 feet wide. The Bennett survived until 1912, when it was finally taken down to make room for a NYC railroad freight depot.

---

[9] Note that by 1900, almost all of Buffalo's grain elevators were named after the corporations that owned them, not private individuals.

An excellent photograph of the Bennett was published in Frank Severance's *A Picture Book of Earlier Buffalo* (page 38). In it we see a classic grain elevator of the 19th century: a form that would later be adopted by other grain elevators, both in Buffalo (the Brown and the Reed, for example) and elsewhere. Laid out alongside the Buffalo River and facing the Evans Slip, the Bennett Elevator was a narrow and very tall structure, with sheer windowless ironclad walls, a steeply pitched gable roof, and a long, window-lined clerestory (the slip-side of which proclaimed BENNETT in very large letters). The entire structure rested upon a stone masonry foundation that came up a full story above the ground. On the "first floor," facing the river, there was an arched opening protected by two swinging fire doors.

There were two marine towers attached to the main house. One tower faced the Buffalo River, was raised upon pillars, and protruded out towards the water from the very mid-point of the structure. It is clear from the "super tower" atop it that this marine tower contained the retractable leg, which could elevate grain at the rate of 5,000 bushels an hour (five times faster than the Dart Elevator). The super tower was just a few feet away from a very tall and narrow smokestack, which suggests the approximate placement of elevator's steam-powered engine (probably generating more than 400 horsepower): *within* the main house, and not set off to the side of it, and as close as possible to the machines in the marine tower. The second tower stood between the main house and the Evans Slip, and faced the water. Raised upon a series of pillars and fairly tall in its own right, this tower no doubt contained all the garners, scales and spouts necessary to send the right amount of grain down to the right canal boat. This tower was the farthest away from the center of the structure (the boiler room) because its operations required no power from it at all.

In the 1850s and 1860s, a largely unknown engineer named George H. Johnson designed at least *three* pioneering "fireproof" grain elevators: the Grand Point Storage Company's "Washington Avenue Elevator" in Philadelphia, Pennsylvania (begun in 1859 and completed in 1866); the U.S. Warehousing Company Grain Elevator in Brooklyn, New York (aka "the Brooklyn Iron Elevator," begun in 1860 and taken down in 1902);[10] and the Plympton Elevator in Buffalo, New York (built in 1868 and taken down sometime between 1890 and 1902).[11] Reyner Banham reports that Buffalo's Plympton "seems to have been forgotten in that city,"[12] but this might be because the name of its owner was

---

[10] This elevator was either built alongside the Gowanus Canal, which was constructed between 1867 and 1869, or on the Atlantic Dock (located on the waterfront, below the future location of the Brooklyn Bridge). In 1870, Henry R. Stiles reported in his *History of the City of Brooklyn*, Vol III, that there were a total of "nine first class steam elevators, some of which exceed anything of the kind in this way or any other country: the principal [elevator] being capable of accommodating two millions of bushels of grain" (p. 575). The following year, on 11 April 1871, *Harper's Weekly* published two illustrations of a single grain elevator/dryer on the Atlantic Dock: one captured the elevator from the eastern side, and depicted its marine tower to be a very tall and narrow building, while the other captured the elevator head-on, as it would have been seen from Manhattan, and depicted it as shorter and wider than before. In both cases, the storehouse that stood behind the marine tower was depicted as a much larger and more impressive structure.

[11] According to H. Perry Smith, *History of the City of Buffalo and Erie County* (Syracuse: D. Mason, 1884), p. 220, "Mr. Johnston" also designed the Niagara A elevator (1867).

[12] Reyner Banham, *A Concrete Atlantis: U.S. Industrial Building and European Modern Architecture, 1900-1925* (MIT Press, 1986), p. 134.

actually Plimpton.[13] Later the name of the elevator was changed to the Tifft (after its new owner, George W. Tifft).

All of these elevators were revolutionary. In the case of the elevators built in Philadelphia and Brooklyn, the revolutionary feature was the use of wrought iron and the brand-new iron alloy called "Bessemer" steel to construct the grain bins. In 1858, an American named Henry Bessemer invented a process by which molten pig iron could be converted into a hard, strong but "plastic" metal alloy on an industrial scale. One of his early adherents was Alexander L. Holley[14] who was born and operated Bessemer steel plants in nearby Troy, New York, during the 1860s.

Unlike the bins in, say, the Dart Elevator – tall and narrow boxes made of wood – those in Johnson's Philadelphia and Brooklyn elevators were cylindrically shaped, vertically oriented metal tanks that had, in fact, been modeled on the boilerplate tanks in use in steam engines. Being a semi-liquid, grain was well suited for storage in such tanks, which improved upon rectangular grain bins to the extent they didn't have "corners" and thus air pockets in which grain-damaging heat, insects, bacteria or fungi might collect. It is unfortunate that we do not know how Johnson solved the problem of maximizing the use of space when one is storing *cylinders* in a *rectangular* building. What did he do with the spaces inevitably left open between the tanks themselves (the "interstitials"), and between the tanks and the building that enclosed them?

A photograph of the Brooklyn Iron Elevator has survived, and was published in a book by its builder, Daniel

---

[13] "Our State Institutions. – XVII: The Buffalo Grain Trade," *New York Times*, January 22, 1872.

[14] Not the Holley in "Holley & Johnson," which was a grain elevator in Buffalo owned by Samuel J. Holley.

Badger.[15] Of course it is too much to ask that it shows the
arrangement of the bins inside (each reputedly 50 feet tall
and a foot in diameter) or is accompanied by a detailed floor
plan! Predictably and quite understandably, it limits itself to
an exterior elevation and shows a massive six-story building.
The brick face of the building is divided into a regular grid
by cast-iron columns and arches. There's a tall cupola at one
end: it is no exaggeration to say that the Brooklyn Iron
Elevator resembles a Gothic cathedral.

Walter Benjamin would have loved it. "For the first
time since the Romans," he writes, "a new artificial building
material appears: iron. It will undergo an evolution whose
pace will accelerate in the course of the century. This
development enters a decisive new phase when it becomes
clear that the locomotive – object of the most diverse
experiments since the years 1828-1829 – usefully functions
only on iron rails. The rail becomes the first prefabricated
iron component, the precursor of the girder. Iron is avoided
in home construction but used in arcades, exhibition halls,
train stations – buildings that serve transitory purposes"; "For
the first third of the previous century, no one as yet
understood how to build with glass and iron. That problem,
however, has long since been solved by hangars and silos."[16]

The Plympton was an even more radical breakthrough
than the elevators Johnson built in Philadelphia and
Brooklyn. Its bins were made of brick,[17] cylindrically shaped,

---

[15] Daniel Badger, *Illustrations of Iron Architecture*
(New York: Baker & Godwin, 1865-1867).

[16] *The Arcades Project*, pp. 16 and 155.

[17] The elevator design was patented "and employed a
double wall of bricks specially designed to interlock
vertically using projecting knobs or dowels on the bottom
that fit into recesses in the top of the brick below, or that is
what published drawings illustrate." Robert M. Frame and
Jeffrey A. Hess, "Northwestern Consolidated Elevator A:

and stood completely unenclosed. Perhaps the novelty of the *combination* of these revolutionary features in a single elevator blinded Johnson's contemporaries to their respective desirability, because "there is no indication that [the Plympton] inspired other builders [...] Of all the structural materials used in grain construction, brick has turned out to have been the least used."[18] Freestanding, cylindrically shaped brick bins wouldn't be built again until the early twentieth century. The Cleveland Elevator Building Company of Minneapolis constructed an experimental one between 1902 and 1903, the same years that S.H. Tromanhauser built small but complete brick-binned

---

Written Historical and Descriptive Data," Historic American Engineering Record, HAER No. MN-16, January 1990, p. 7.

[18] Robert M. Frame and Jeffrey A. Hess, "Northwestern Consolidated Elevator A: Written Historical and Descriptive Data," pp. 8 and 7. The authors go on to point out that, "for reasons that are not readily apparent, brick seems to have been used more extensively in other countries than in the United States. In his 1903 survey of fireproof elevator construction for the *Northwestern Miller*, E.P. Overmire stated that 'brick grain elevators have been built successfully in Europe for many years, on both the bin and warehouse systems . . . Several large elevators with brick bins have been built at Odessa and Novorosissk, on the Black Sea in Russia.' He also described a recent 1,500,000-bushel square-bin brick elevator erected in Liverpool, England. Of the handful of brick examples in the 1913 edition of *Plans of Grain Elevators*, published by *Grain Dealers Journal*, the most impressive is the 4,500,000-bushel round-bin brick elevator built in 1904 in Buenos Aires, Argentina" (p. 8). A one million-bushel brick-binned elevator called the Northwestern Consolidated Elevator A was built in Minneapolis in 1908.

elevators in Rushford, Minnesota, and Watertown, South Dakota.[19]

"One may guess," Reyner Banham offers, "the slow adoption of the steel-tank bin had four main causes [...] The comparatively high cost of the material and the specialized skills required to fabricate it [...] Rust and corrosion; steel's poor performance as a thermal insulator; and lastly the geometrical problems of packing circular bins into a rectangular building without leaving a lot of wasteful and awkwardly shaped spaces between them."[20]

Nevertheless, George H. Johnson left an impressive legacy. In 1869, he obtained a U.S. patent for hollow prismatic tiles that, when laid down in a staggered fashion, in the style of masonry and held in position by internal terra-cotta clamps, could be used to construct fireproof grain bins. George's son Ernest V. Johnson went on to found Johnson & Record, which obtained key patents for the designs of tile-binned grain elevators in 1895. Four years later, after performing a few tests, the Barnett & Record Company of Minneapolis, Minnesota, started building them. Were it not for the fact that neither father nor son designed any grain elevators made out of reinforced concrete, the Johnsons would have pioneered every innovation in grain bin design undertaken before and after 1900: brick, tile and steel.

While some engineers were working on the problem of fireproofing the grain storage bins, other engineers were concerned with getting the grain elevating machines to go faster and faster, to move more and more grain per hour. Between the 1860s and 1880s, at least two major innovations were made in the field of "materials handling": 1) the installation of steam-powered screw-conveyors and,

---

[19] Robert M. Frame and Jeffrey A. Hess, "Northwestern Consolidated Elevator A: Written Historical and Descriptive Data," p. 10.

[20] *A Concrete Atlantis*, p. 117.

eventually, steam-powered horizontal conveyor-belts into the area above the grain bins, and 2) the invention of the "loose" leg.

Prior to 1868, when the pioneering Niagara Elevator was built, some grain elevators in Buffalo had horizontal conveyor-belts installed in their "basements," that is, below their grain bins. Such conveyors brought grain dumped down on them to a boot, from which a lofting leg elevated the grain to the top of structure. It wasn't strictly necessary to have such a conveyor – the spouts and chutes could simply send their grain directly from the bottoms of the bins to the boot – but this might involve a great tangle of spouts and chutes, if not the need for a second (or third!) lofting leg to accommodate them all.

At the Niagara Elevator, which was designed by George H. Johnston, horizontal conveyor-belts were installed both above and below the grain bins. The walls and foundations of the building were able to accommodate all that weight – the combined weight of the grain bins themselves, their contents, and two floors' worth of machines – because they were laid down upon newly driven piles, more than a thousand of them, which secured a solid place for the Niagara on the otherwise weak, marshy banks of the Buffalo River. Like the Bennett Elevator before it, the Niagara had a solid masonry foundation and ironclad wooden walls and grain cribs. But unlike the Bennett, it could store 800,000 bushels, not 600,000.

The key feature of the steam-powered conveyor belt that ran alongside the tops of the grain bins was the "trimmer" or "tripper," a device that deflected the flow of grain off the belt, and down and into a particular grain bin. (See figure 5.) The ingenuity, that is, the *usefulness*, of the trimmer lay in the fact that it could be unlocked, moved up or down the line, and then locked into position above a different grain bin. This meant that the number of big turn-heads and spouts previously needed to conduct the grain down from the garner and scales in the marine tower to the tops of the bins could now be drastically reduced; the whole procedure could be simplified. Same thing for the basement of the elevator, even though the trimmer didn't play a part down there: thanks to the steam-powered conveyor belt, the number of spouts and chutes leading down from the bins to the boot of the lofting leg could be reduced. The cramped space of such basements could now be "freed up." But "freed up" spaces came with a cost: conveyor belts exposed more grain to the air, and thus created more fugitive grain dust than did the spouts, unwieldy though they were.

As a result of the lateral "reach" of the new conveyor-belts, elevator operators and designers began to re-conceptualize the way that grain bins *might be* organized. Instead of locating the bins close to or even around the spouts that came down from the marine tower – which was a spatial practice that tended to make and keep the elevators' main houses tall and boxy (sometimes even round) – the designers began to array the bins in long straight rows that led away from the marine tower. This meant that large-scale elevators no longer needed to be centralized like the Watson or oriented along conflicting lines, as in the case of the Bennett Elevator (one line ran from the marine tower at the Evans Slip side of the elevator to the other end of the building, i.e., *along* the Buffalo River, while another line ran from the boiler room and the primary marine tower *to* the Buffalo River). New elevators could now be built in a long, narrow and tall row, perpendicularly to the river, which not only "freed up" space along the wharf, but also created space for the railroads to lay down little feeders that led to their trunk lines. These new elevators could not only transship grain from lake to canal, but from lake to rail, as well.

The second major innovation in the field of grain-handling techniques between the 1860s and 1880s was the invention of the loose leg. Reyner Banham is right when he says, "Early versions of the loose leg were mounted on their own barges or floats and were used for transferring grain between floating vessels," but he is dead wrong when he says that the Electric Elevator, constructed in Buffalo in 1897, "has the very considerable distinction of being the first elevator to be electrically powered and therefore the first, also, to be equipped with a [true] mobile loose leg" and that the Electric, "in introducing electric power, the loose leg, and the freestanding cylindrical bin, [...] effectively introduced the modern elevator."[21]

The invention of the loose leg did *not* need to wait for the introduction of electricity into the Buffalo area, which took place in 1895. According to J.B. Mansfield, writing a few months before the construction of the Electric Elevator, the Marine Elevator "*has* two legs, a portable tower, a vertical engine, thoroughly modern cleaning machinery usually not found in transfer elevators, and in short all the necessary modern improvements. It is owned at present by the Marine Elevator Company."[22] But it isn't clear *when* the "portable tower" was built.[23] An undated picture of the Marine reprinted in Thomas E. Leary and Elizabeth C. Sholes' *Images of America: Buffalo's Waterfront* does indeed show a marine tower that looks like it could be moved along a track about 20 feet long.[24]

There's another consideration. Floaters (floating grain elevators) can also be considered portable towers. Conical or

---

[21] Reyner Banham, *A Concrete Atlantis*, pp. 111, 124 and 130, respectively.

[22] *History of the Great Lakes*, vol. I, Chicago: 1899, emphasis added.

[23] Charles Magnus' lithograph "Bird's Eye View of the City of Buffalo, NY" (dated 1863) does not depict a portable tower, so it must have been installed between 1864 and 1897. Available on-line http://www.buffaloah.com/h/maps/ map1863 accessed 21 August 2008.

[24] Buffalo: Arcadia Publishing, 1997, p. 18.

pyramidal little ships, floaters were elevating legs that could be pushed or pulled into place to transship grain directly from one boat to another. And they'd been in use in Buffalo since the 1850s.

Strictly speaking, then, the loose leg was invented in 1882 by none other than Robert Dunbar, who'd been tasked by the Connecting Terminal railroad company with designing, building and installing two marine towers for the company's brand-new lake-to-rail "Connecting Terminal Elevator."[25] Dunbar's many problems included the fact that, despite the existence of more than *two dozen* high-speed, steam-powered grain elevators, there *still* wasn't enough time to unload and store all of the grain that had been brought to the Port of Buffalo before the winter came and everything was frozen over. And so a large number of vessels simply sat in the harbor, unloaded, and waited the winter out. Once the spring thaw came, this "winter fleet," as it came to be known, would be the first to be unloaded.[26] The size of the winter fleet grew

---

[25] On December 7, 1881, the *New York Times* reported "the work on driving piles on the new elevator for the connecting terminal [sic] railroad of this city has commenced." On 26 September 1882, Dunbar patented the "loose leg" (original Patent No. 264, 938). In the words of District Judge Coxe, who adjudicated *Dunbar et al v. Eastern Elevating Company, et al* (Circuit Court, N.D., New York, July 20, 1896), a suit filed by Dunbar's son, George H. Dunbar: "The idea of moving the elevator leg to the hatch of the vessel instead of moving the hatch of the vessel to the elevator leg was, certainly, a brilliant and ingenious one. It was entirely new with [Robert] Dunbar. No one had thought of it or anything like it in connection with grain elevators."

[26] Some of these vessels had already been loaded with grain and either didn't have time to get out of Buffalo before the winter ice arrived or were simply biding their time. "The export companies based in New York kept 'winter books' on

steadily in the last decades of the 19th Century, which made Buffalo's infamously congested harbor congested all year around, not just during but also after the shipping season.

Dunbar's solution wasn't simply to accelerate the speed at which the elevator's legs scooped up and unloaded grain in bulk, which is something he tried to do with every new elevator leg he designed, but to try to accelerate the speed at which the *really* big grain lake steamers that were starting to come into the Port of Buffalo (some storing as much as 50,000 bushels each) could be unloaded and sent on their way. He would use *two* marine towers to unload them, not just one. Rather than build these towers right next to each other, which would limit the range of their deployment, Dunbar set one of them on a set of rail tracks. Powered by a steam engine, this loose leg could be moved up to thirty feet, which meant it could either work alone or in tandem with the other leg, the "stiff" one. (See figure 2.) This arrangement must have been a success, because it wasn't until 1914 that the Connecting Terminal Elevator exploded and had to be replaced. By 1893, there were three elevators in Buffalo with loose legs.[27]

A building on wheels! Why not a whole city on wheels? Do such marvels exist today? As late as 1953, when a half-mad French painter named Ivan Chtcheglov wrote his "Formulary for a New Urbanism" (excerpted in

the Great Lakes – grain stowed aboard vessels or in port elevators ready to move to Europe as soon as the waterways unfroze." Dan Morgan, *Merchants of Grain* (New York: Viking, 1979), p. 71.

[27] "Three [of Buffalo's 32 elevators] have movable towers which allow the legs to be adjusted at such a distance apart as will correspond to a vessel's hatches." Frederick J. Shepard, "The City of Buffalo," *New England Magazine*, April 1, 1893. On page 239, there is a photograph captioned "Elevator with Movable Tower," but this elevator isn't identified.

Internationale Situationniste #1, June 1958), buildings on wheels were still a utopian's dream.

> The state of technique allows permanent contact between the individual and cosmic reality by suppressing its unpleasant features. A glass ceiling allows one to see the stars and the rain. A mobile house turns with the sun. Its sliding walls allow vegetation to invade life. Mounted on rails, it could go down to the sea in the morning, and return in the evening to the forest.[28]

After the introduction of electricity generated by hydroelectric plants, which took place in the Niagara River/Buffalo area in 1895, the search for a fireproof grain elevator became urgent. The days of the steam engine (burning either wood or coal as fuel) were over! "It is a new century, and electricity is its god," proclaimed Henry Adams.[29] The entire flour milling industry would want to become electrified. In 1896, the George Urban Flour Mill in Buffalo became the first flourmill in the world to become electrically powered. Grain elevators would inevitably be electrically powered, too, at least in Buffalo, where even 27 steam-powered elevators were having difficulty unloading the colossal amounts of grain that were arriving by lake (240 million bushels in 1897 alone). A new, more modern source of power seemed to call for a new, more modern building material. But what should that material be? Something fireproof, which would allow the burgeoning insurance companies to lower their premiums, and which would encourage the banks to make loans towards the building of grain elevators without requiring fire insurance during their construction.

---

[28] My translation from the French.

[29] *Letters, 1892-1918*, Vol. 2, Boston: 1938.

By the late 1890s, Bessemer steel had already been used to create the frames of several well-known multi-story "skyscrapers" built in Chicago, New York City, Buffalo and Cincinnati. (Because of the presence of electric elevators, which made building beyond the height of five stories possible, these structures were sometimes called "elevator buildings.") But using steel in the construction of fireproof grain tanks posed several unique problems, most of which already came up in the 1860s with George H. Johnson's experiments: cylindrical, boiler-plated tanks took a great deal of time and expertise to design and construct. (As did cylindrical wooden bins, which were first constructed in the 1890s by F.H. King, a professor of the University of Wisconsin, and subsequently known as "King" or "Wisconsin" silos.) The costs of constructing grain bins made of steel not only included the steel itself, which had to be made-to-order and transported to the building site, but also the "priceless" services of dependable engineers and builders. These experts had to deal with technical questions concerning grain pressures, interstitial spaces, keeping grain cool in the summer (when there was a risk of it germinating or being damaged by heat), and economic questions concerning the speed and overall costs of construction.

Almost inevitably, it was a railroad company that first attempted to build grain bins made out of steel. The first real consumers of large amounts of iron and steel products were the railroad companies, which not only needed them to build their locomotives, but also to form the rails on which they ran. Only a railroad company would have the capital and/or access to credit necessary to build a structure made out of steel, which would certainly cost hundreds of millions of dollars.

Based in St Paul, Minnesota, which was where James J. Hill (its Canadian-born founder and chief executive officer) had taken up residence in 1856, the Great Northern Railroad Company had previously concentrated on the western parts of the United States and Canada. Around 1895, the company decided it was going to get involved in the grain trade in the east. Towards this end, it started building grain elevators in West Superior, Wisconsin, which along with its twin city Duluth, Minnesota, was (and still is) the single biggest collection-point for American grain[30] to be shipped over the "upper" Great Lakes. By 1898, there were two such elevators in West Superior: the Great Northern "A," capable of storing 1.8 million bushels, and the Great Northern "X," capable of storing 1.5 million bushels.[31] That same year, the company undertook to build a grain elevator in Buffalo, New York. Such an elevator would allow the company to operate on both sides of the Great Lakes: transporting grain from country elevators all over Canada and the United States to West Superior, and transporting grain from Buffalo to markets on the east coast.

Once referred to as "undoubtedly the greatest structure of its kind in the world,"[32] the Great Northern Elevator in Buffalo (250 Ganson Street) cost $1,000,000 to build[33] and required the work of a small team of experts. D.A. Robinson, a builder from Chicago whose firm specialized in grain-elevating equipment, created the general plans and the

---

[30] The Canadian counterpart would be the twin port cities of Fort William and Fort Arthur, now called collectively referred to as Thunder Bay, Ontario. Both sets of twin cities are on the same lake: Lake Superior.

[31] J. B. Mansfield, "Grain Traffic," *History of the Great Lakes*, Volume I (Chicago, J.H. Beers &Co., 1899). The "A" Elevator burned down in 1907. The "X" Elevator still stands.

[32] J. B. Mansfield, "Grain Traffic," *ibid.*

[33] In "No Graft on His Road, Declares J.T. Hill," *New York Times*, November 22, 1906, Hill is quoted as saying that the Great Northern elevator cost $1 million to build, that it earned $2 million its first year, and that Hill sold it shortly thereafter for $300,000 more than it cost.

machinery (for which he was careful to get patents). Max Toltz, an engineer with the Great Northern Railroad Company who specialized in steel bridges, created the specific plans and acted as construction supervisor. The contractor for the steelwork in the main house was the Riter-Conley Company of Pittsburgh, Pennsylvania, while the Penn Bridge Company of Beaver Falls, Pennsylvania, furnished the material for the marine towers. And Newcomb Carleton, an electrical engineer from Buffalo, designed the electrical plant, which was installed under the direction of Albert Vickers.

Save for the fact that its walls were made out brick, not ironclad wood, the outward appearance of the Great Northern Elevator wouldn't necessarily startle someone familiar with grain elevators. As at every grain elevator since the Dart, the main house was essentially a huge shed in which a system of grain bins had been installed. As at the Bennett Elevator, the building was constructed parallel with the waterline and there was a very tall and narrow clerestory that provided a roof for the gallery floor that housed the horizontal conveyors. And, as at the Connecting Terminal Elevator, there was a "loose" leg, actually *three* of them in this case, all 125 feet tall and electrically powered, all very fast, each one capable of elevating 20,000 bushels of grain per hour. Anyone who happened to walk by and see the Great Northern Elevator would certainly be struck by its colossal size (300 feet long, 90 feet wide and 150 feet tall), the haughty grandeur of its legs, and the pleasing simplicity of its overall appearance.

Like George H. Johnson's pioneering elevators of the 1860s, the Great Northern Elevator could only be fully appreciated by someone who ventured *inside* it. Max Toltz had come up with a serviceable solution to the problem of packing cylindrical tanks into a rectangular building without wasting space: he inserted 18 "interstitial bins" (each 15 feet in diameter and capable of storing 18,000 bushels) between the 30 "main bins" (each 40 feet in diameter and capable of storing 85,000 bushels). Raised up on steel pillars and capable of standing on its own, this massive structure actually supported the 2 ½-foot-thick brick wall that surrounded it, and not the reverse. The conveyor floor and the clerestory above it were independently supported by a frame of huge steel I-beams.

Servicing the Great Northern's grain bins were 10 internal lofting legs, each one 168 feet tall, powered by its own 50 HP engine, and capable of matching the unloading speed of the external, loose legs. Such a large number of lofting legs was necessary because neither Toltz nor Robinson thought it necessary to install a horizontal conveyor-belt system in the elevator's basement. Pneumatic collectors and sweepers kept the areas around the lofting legs' boots and heads (relatively) clean of grain dust. In total, there were 17 motors generating 940 horsepower.

Buffalo's Great Northern Elevator was put into service on 29 September 1897, just a few months after the plans were drawn up and construction began. Thanks to the power and reach of its corporate owner, the elevator was an immediate success and transshipped as many as 20 million bushels of grain every year of the first decade of the twentieth century. But it wasn't until a natural disaster struck – a severe storm that came off Lake Erie in 1922 – that the appreciable weaknesses of the Great Northern were revealed and fixed. First and foremost, the storm knocked down one of the three loose legs, all of which were eventually removed and replaced by new, more secure loose legs, designed and installed by the Monarch Engineering Company of Buffalo, New York. Furthermore, the boots of the elevator's lofting legs were located below ground level, which meant that they sometimes became flooded and had to be pumped out, as happened in 1922. Finally, it was decided that more grain tanks needed to be added in the spaces between the existing tanks and the curtain-brick wall. Twenty-six of these "outer" bins were added, bringing the total storage capacity of the elevator up to 2.5 million bushels.

Contrary to what Reyner Banham claims, the Great Northern Railroad Company did not build *three* steel-binned grain elevators between 1898 and 1900.[34] It only built two: the Great Northern in Buffalo and the Great Northern "S," which was built in West Superior, Wisconsin, in 1900 and put into service in 1901.[35] There were great differences between these two elevators: while the former enclosed cylindrical grain bins inside a brick shell, the latter enclosed *rectangular* grain bins inside a shell made of *corrugated iron*. Rather than putting the elevator "boots" down in subterranean pits, as was done in Buffalo, the lofting legs at West Superior (all nine of them) were elevated so far above

---

[34] *A Concrete Atlantis* (MIT Press, 1986), pp. 117-118: "All were designed by Max Toltz, the bridge builder and presiding engineering genius of the golden age of the Great Northern Railway, which served Minnesota and the western Great lakes area. One of them was in Duluth, Minnesota; one in West Superior, Wisconsin; and the third was at the other end of the lake-shipping trade, at Buffalo, New York. All were enormous, with capacities of better than two million bushels, and were housed in brick shells of handsome architectural aspect." Banham's mistake no doubt derives from thinking that Duluth, Minnesota and West Superior are two different places, not one.

[35] *Engineering News*, XLVI (August 1, 1901): 210. "Perhaps one of the best, and certainly one of the latest examples of elevator construction which deserve [sic] mention, is the 3,000,000 bushel terminal elevator put in operation at West Superior, Wis., in February of this year. This elevator was built by the Great Northern Railway and is designed to eclipse in every way the mammoth steel elevator built by the same company at Buffalo, New York, in 1897-98." Quoted in Reyner Banham, *A Concrete Atlantis*, p. 118.

the ground that each required its own mini-tower.[36] Whereas the Buffalo elevator was designed to transship from lake to rail and so had no "canal spouts" (spouts to conduct grain to canal boats), the elevator in West Superior was designed to transship in the reverse direction (rail to lake) and so had fifteen of them.[37] It should no go with mention that, unlike the Great Northern in Buffalo, which closed down in 1981 and has not been used since, the Great Northern in West Superior – thanks to a series of three reinforced-concrete annexes built in the 1920s – remains part of a thriving grain terminal.[38]

The second steel-binned elevator to be built in Buffalo was also constructed in 1897. Erected at 40 Childs Street for a grain trader from Buffalo named Edward W. Eames, the Electric Elevator was designed by W.S. Winn, who was the chief engineer at the Steel Storage and Elevator Construction Company of Cornersfield, Indiana, which specialized in oil tanks. Because grain behaves likes a semi-liquid, Winn was able to use his knowledge of and experience with cylindrical steel tanks (found to be the best shape and material to store oil) to construct grain bins and elevators.

Though he didn't *invent* the loose leg, as has been claimed, Winn did in fact install two truly remarkable legs at the Electric: one stiff, the other loose. In a touch that was either hesitation in the face of momentous changes or an intentional "pun" on visual resemblances, the stiff leg – the one on the right, closest to the bins – was flush with the front

---

[36] See the postcard published by the Detroit Publishing Company in 1902 and stored in the New York Public Library's Digital Gallery: call number MFY 95-29, Digital Image ID 62786.

[37] See the photograph in the Library of Congress: call number LC-USF34-063845-D.

[38] See this photograph: http://duluthsuperior.railfan.net/ images/GN_Grain_Dock.jpg accessed 25 August 2008.

façade of the tall, square workhouse. Since both legs *and* the top of the workhouse had small, double-pitched roofs, this gave the Electric Elevator a curious, unprecedented and never repeated double-gabled profile.

Furthermore, Winn didn't follow the pattern originally broken by the Niagara Elevator and yet maintained by the Great Northern Elevator, that is, constructing the elevator alongside the Buffalo River. His hand forced by the especially cramped space occupied by the Electric Elevator, Winn erected the grain bins *behind* the workhouse and its legs, not next to them. To cap his achievements off, Winn didn't enclose these bins in a building of any kind, as every grain-elevator designer before him had done. All 19 of the Electric's bins – 7 cylindrical steel tanks that were 60 feet tall and 50 feet in diameter, each capable of storing 100,000 bushels, and aligned in a row, and 12 cylindrical steel tanks that were 60 feet tall and 25 feet in diameter, each capable of storing 25,000 bushels, and aligned in a row of their own – stood directly upon foundation pads that were made of reinforced concrete. They were freestanding and exposed, not only to the elements, but to the sight of passersby, the curious, and dreamers.

No matter what grain bins looked like (square or round) or what they were made of (wood, steel or reinforced concrete), the moment of their appearance into the realm of visibility would have been spectacular. Remember that, in Buffalo, grain bins had been hidden from sight ever since the time of the Dart Elevator, and that, in Western civilization, granaries had been hidden from sight, either buried below the ground or raised up into sanctuaries above it, for thousands of years. Inevitably, given the emphasis that our "society of the spectacle" places on visibility, a certain amount of mystery had come to surround what exactly went on *inside* these mysterious and colossal structures, but not inside huge tanks of water or oil, precisely because their contents were so prosaic, at least in comparison to grain (the edible seed). At the Electric Elevator, and for the first time anywhere, grain bins were out in the open, not just revealed but *exposed* to sight, standing on their own, as if with pride. The "ancient secret" (if there was one) could now be known by anybody who desired to know it. It was easy, all one had to do was *look*.

It is either ironic or fitting that these some of these bins in fact contained storage compartments that could not be seen from the outside. These mini-storage bins, which were blocked off from each other by small, horizontal steel floors, allowed the operators of the Electric Elevator to keep grain shipments separate from each other, no matter what size they were. It also allowed them to subdivide large grain shipments, should that be desirable.

The "naked" grain tanks at the Electric Elevator were connected to the workhouse by conveyor-belt systems that were installed both under the ground in specially dug tunnels and high above grade-level in slightly inclined overhead gantries. This unusual separation between workhouse and bin-structure was deliberate and, in fact, precisely intended to prevent any fire or explosion in the workhouse from damaging or igniting the grain in the bins. Fires in the workhouse were deemed completely unlikely. Everything in them, the beams, the floors, the walls, the stairs and the machines themselves, of course, were made of iron or steel. (The Export, a one-million-bushel elevator that was built out of wood and iron in Buffalo in 1895, also kept the workhouse separate from the bin-structure as a fireproofing measure.)

Because its reinforced-concrete foundation was built upon solid rock, which was only seven feet below the surface where it stood, the Electric Elevator was the first elevator built in Buffalo with a real subterranean basement. All of the previous ones had been built upon foundations that were in turn built upon hundreds, even thousands of piles, which had been driven into the ground. As a result, the bin-structures of these elevators had to be elevated above ground level. But at the Electric Elevator, there were subterranean tunnels that contained conveyor-belts that traveled underneath the freestanding bins. Between 1900 and 1912, another five freestanding tanks, each 60 feet tall and 66 feet in diameter, and serviced by both overhead and subterranean conveyor-belts, were installed at the Electric. This brought the elevator's total storage capacity up to 1.8 million bushels.

During its busiest shipping seasons (1913 and 1914), the Electric transshipped a total of 5 million bushels, a large amount when compared to the loads transshipped by the old-time elevators, such as the Connecting Terminal, but small when compared with the amount transshipped by the Great Northern. In 1942, an entire annex of grain storage tanks – this time made out of reinforced concrete – was attached to the Electric Elevator by its then-owner, Cargill, Inc. I will return to this annex, which could store an incredible *six million bushels of grain*, after the subject of reinforced concrete has been properly introduced.

For the moment, I must note that many photographs of the original Electric Elevator were taken and almost all of them have survived. They show a building that isn't aesthetically pleasing. "If not handsome, the Electric […] acquired a certain grimy conviction about its forms; their functionality was as strikingly manifest as the technical innovations that underlie the design," says Reyner Banham.[39] But the Electric Elevator was *worse* than "not handsome": it was grim-looking (the marine towers and headhouse, the first things one saw, were square and dark); it was impersonal (the words ELECTRIC and ELEVATOR appeared in large letters at the top of the loose and stiff legs, respectively); and the layout of the steel tanks looked decidedly awkward. Take for example for the photograph originally published in *The Industrial Empire of Niagara* (1919) and reprinted in Reyner

---

[39] *A Concrete Atlantis*, p. 124.

Banham.[40] The meanness of the elevator is emphasized by the sight of the whole structure reflected back in the dark polluted waters of the Buffalo River.

In the first decade of the 20th century, about a dozen steel-binned grain elevators were constructed in America – eight of them in Buffalo.[41] Both (1) the Raymond Elevator and (2) the Jan Kan Malting Elevator are commonly overlooked because there were built in Black Rock, not Buffalo. This is unfortunate, because both seem to have been an extraordinary buildings. Built in 1897 by Robert J. Reidpath for George H. Raymond, the Raymond Elevator could store 600,000 bushels in its steel 32 rectangular bins, which were 12 feet by 24 feet, and 73 feet tall. Raymond was also involved in another very innovative arrangement: in 1897, he and A.M. Kalbfleisch of Brooklyn, New York, brought a floater on shore, attached it to a previously existing transfer tower, and thereby created a "new" grain elevator. The Jan Kan Malting Elevator was designed by J.F. Dornfeld (Milwaukee) and built in the manner of the Great Eastern Elevator.[42]

(3) The Great Eastern was built in Buffalo in 1901. It stood on the City Ship Canal, next to the Dakota, until 1948, when it was intentionally demolished. (See figure 3.) The Great Eastern was built by the Eastern Grain Corporation to replace its huge wood-binned elevator, which was built in

---

[40] *A Concrete Atlantis*, p. 125.

[41] In 1902, the Lackawanna Steel Company began operating just south of Buffalo's harbor, and was certainly a source of much of the steel that was used in the construction of these elevators. Twenty years after its founding, Lackawanna Steel became one of Bethlehem Steel's plants outside of Pennsylvania. Today the site is abandoned, derelict and extremely dangerous due to the presence of toxic chemicals.

[42] Cf. HAER No. NY-239, p. 96.

1895 with three marine towers (one of which was automotive)[43] and destroyed by a grain-dust explosion just four years later. The new elevator was designed by Harry R. Wait, then employed by the Steel Storage and Elevator Construction Company, which had built the Electric Elevator in 1897. (Wait would later go on to found his own company, Monarch Engineering.) The steel for the Great Eastern was produced and erected by the Indiana Bridge Company of Muncie, Indiana. The new elevator had two loose legs and could store 2.5 million bushels in its sixty-eight freestanding, 70-feet-tall, cylindrical grain tanks, which were set down on reinforced concrete slabs and arrayed in a rhomboidal shape due to space limitations. A picture of the Great Eastern appears in Wayne Broehl's book about Cargill.[44] In it, we see a few of the elevator's large grain tanks, surmounted by two horizontal gantries. Only one of the marine towers is visible: it is very tall. One is reminded of the awkward layout of the Electric Elevator.

(Note that a Great Eastern Elevator was also built in Minneapolis sometime before 1910. A photograph at the Minnesota Historical Society[45] shows that the workhouse of this unusual elevator was erected right in the middle of a long straight row of nine large steel bins, five on one side, four on the other. There was a great deal of space left between the workhouse and these tanks, no doubt to minimize the possibilities of fires or explosions traveling between them. The horizontal conveyor-belt that serviced these tanks was installed through the tops of these tanks, not above them.)

---

[43] See photograph taken between 1890 and 1910 by the Detroit Publishing Company and in the collection of the Library of Congress (LC-D4-32072).

[44] Wayne G. Broehl, *Cargill: Trading the World's Grain* (University Press of New England, 1992), p. 555.

[45] MH5.9 MP3.1G p30, negative number 39237.

(4) The Dakota was also built in 1901, and it also stood on the City Ship Canal. (See figures 3 and 4.) The Dakota was destroyed in 1965 to "make way" for an elevated "skyway" portion of a highway for automobile traffic. It was built by the Lehigh Railroad to replace their old "Dakota Elevator," which had been a huge one-million-bushel affair, made out of wood, built in 1887, and the victim of a grain-dust explosion in 1901. The new elevator was designed by Ballou & Shirley (a local team of engineers), and built by the Buffalo-based Eagle Iron Works.[46] The Dakota had two loose legs and could store 1.25 million bushels in its many grain tanks, which were rectangular, not cylindrical; raised above the ground, not set down upon it; and completely enclosed in a tall and narrow corrugated-iron house. The gallery above the tanks was itself two stories tall and surmounted by a clerestory, which gave the entire structure a distinctive but odd, hammer-headed silhouette.

(5) The Iron Elevator was built in Buffalo in 1902 and demolished in 1940. It was both designed and built by the James MacDonald Engineering Company of Chicago, Illinois. The Iron Elevator could only store 500,000 bushels in its 82 bins, but the elevator was a "fast house," that is, it had very fast grain-elevating and transferring machines.[47] The Iron Elevator was also noteworthy because its interstitial and outer bins were *triangular*.

---

[46] In *Buffalo Architecture: A Guide* (MIT Press, 1981), p. 313, Reyner Banham and Francis R. Kowsky incorrectly claim that the Dakota was designed by R.J. Reidpath & Sons.

[47] "The Power Equipment of the New Iron Elevator of the Iron Elevator and Transfer Company, Buffalo, N.Y.," *Electricity Review*, August 9, 1902. In the words of "Invention and Its Progress," *The Washington Post*, August 24, 1902, the Iron elevator was "the most notable institution of the kind in the country, because of the exceedingly up-to-date methods pursued in the handling and storage of grain."

(6) The Monarch was built in 1905 and demolished in 1950. It was designed by H.R. Wait and built by the Steel Storage and Elevator Construction Company. The name "Monarch" is striking, because Wait would later be the chief engineer for the Monarch Engineering Company of Buffalo, New York, which specialized in the construction of grain elevators made of reinforced concrete. Like the Great Eastern and the Iron Elevator, the Monarch was built upon a reinforced-concrete basement, in which bracketed, reinforced-concrete pillars were used to support the concrete slabs on which the iron hoppers and steel bins rested. After additional grain tanks were added sometime after 1917, the Monarch could store over 800,000 bushels (twice its original capacity).

(7) The Ralston Purina was built in 1907 and demolished in the early 1980s. It was designed and built by the James MacDonald Engineering Company for the Ralston Purina Company of St. Louis, Missouri, which operated a feed mill in Buffalo. A small elevator that could only store 400,000 bushels, it contained 18 main bins, 10 interstitial bins and 14 outer bins. In 1917, the A.E. Baxter Engineering Company of Buffalo, New York, added an annex that contained 36 rectangular bins made of reinforced concrete.

(8) The Riverside Malting Elevator (aka as Fleischmann's Elevator) was built in Buffalo in 1907 and demolished in 1965. It was designed and built by the Steel Storage and Elevator Construction Company. Small because of its limited function, the Riverside Elevator could store 200,000 bushels of grain in 32 tanks (20 main bins and 12 interstitials).

At least two major steel-binned grain elevators were built in Minneapolis.[48] The Pioneer Steel was a two-million-

---

[48] Other pioneering steel-binned elevators were built by the West Shore Railroad in Weehawken, New Jersey (1901), by the Grand Trunk Railroad in Portland, Maine (1902), by

bushel elevator erected at 2547 Fifth Street NE for the local grain merchant George Frank Piper. It was designed by the Gillette-Herzog Company and built by Barnett-Record in 1901. A photograph at the Minnesota Historical Society[49] shows that the Pioneer Steel Elevator possessed a total of 22 steel bins: 12 large ones in a row; 10 smaller ones in a row in front of the others. A conveyor-belt installed in a narrow horizontal gantry was laid on top of the row of main bins.

The Electric Steel was a four-million-bushel elevator erected at 600 Twenty-Fifth Avenue SE for the Frank Peavey Company. It was designed by Lewis S. Gillette and built in two stages by the American Bridge Company (1901) and the Minneapolis Steel & Machine Construction Company (1903).[50] Photographs at the Minnesota Historical Society[51] show that the Electric Steel Elevator was a part of the Russell Miller Flour Mill and was connected to various other buildings in this complex by horizontal gantries. There were 12 main bins at the Electric Steel and they were lined up in a row leading straight back from the workhouse. Unlike the Pioneer Steel, which was razed in 1996, despite being listed in the National Registry of Historic Places in 1990, the Electric Steel still stands.

Finally, at least two major steel-binned grain elevators were built in Montreal by the Dominion government. The first was the Harbour Commission's Elevator #1, which was

---

the Southern Pacific Railroad in Galveston, Texas (1903), and by the Board of Commissioners ("the Stuyvesant Elevator") in New Orleans (1904).

[49] MH5.9 MP3.1P p80.

[50] It appears to be the first stage of the Electric Steel Elevator that is depicted in William C. Edgar, *The Story of a Grain of Wheat* (New York: McClure, Phillips & Co., 1903), p. 119, over the caption "A Steel Tank Elevator, America."

[51] MH5.9 MP3.1E r5 and MH5.9 MP3.1R p24 negative # 91951.

built by the Steel Storage & Elevator Construction Company between 1904 and 1905. According to the anonymous author of an article entitled "*Les Mysteres d'un Elevateur a Grains*," which was published in the *Album Universel* on 21 October 1905, Elevator #1 was "a veritable miracle of applied mechanics" that cost approximately 700,000 dollars to build. Part of the complex was "an immense building," "made of iron (for reasons easy to understand, no wood was used in its construction) and 200 feet tall from its base to its summit." Composed of a total of 78 cylindrical steel bins (36 main bins, arranged in three rows of 12, plus 22 outer bins and 20 interstitials), this main house could store 1 million bushels of grain. There was enough room underneath it for railroad cars. Adjoining this tall structure, "in which one could suppose the entire population of a large village could live,"[52] there was a "building of the same height and on rails, so it can be moved along the south side, on the side of the [St. Lawrence] river." In addition to documenting the presence of this loose leg – this *marine leg*, "as the English call it" – this article also reports the use of portable iron towers ("of the 'Eiffel' type") to support and direct the flow of grain coming from spouts, and the existence of a total of 17 floating elevators (each an "Eiffel-style framework" on a boat) in Montreal's harbor (pp. 784-786).[53]

Between 1903 and 1906, the Canadian engineer John S. Metcalf's company designed and constructed the Harbour Commission's Elevator #2 at the Grand Trunk Railroad Company's terminus in Montreal. Like the Great Northern Elevator in Minneapolis, Elevator #2 was a massive and tall rectangular structure made out of reinforced concrete, filled with rectangular steel bins, and built straddling two railroad tracks. But unlike the Great Northern, Metcalf's elevator had

---

[52] For more on this striking image, see Chapter 9: On Dwelling.

[53] My translation from the French.

windows all along its first floor, which demonstrated to the viewer, casual or attentive, that the entire structure was raised a story or two above the ground. This elevated effect – a physical effect for the grain and a visual one for someone standing on the ground – was all the more intense when either grain or eye reached the top of the elevator's towering workhouse. Tall and very narrow, this workhouse was flat at the top, except where it was bested in the search for the highest point by the elevator's six rectangular lofting legs, each of which was enclosed in its own steel tower.

In the first decade of the twentieth century, elevator designers and builders also experimented with hollowed-out tile, which is the only truly fireproof building-material: it doesn't even conduct heat. Between 1901 and 1902, the Barnett-Record Company built a huge tile-binned elevator, the Saint Anthony Elevator #3, for the Washburn-Crosby Company in Minneapolis.[54] Powered by steam until 1950, when it was finally electrified, the Saint Anthony #3 made use of two lofting legs in its six-story tall workhouse and could store a total of 4 million bushels in its 16 tile bins. Divided into two groups – twelve large ones and four smaller ones – these grain tanks were serviced by a gallery that ran through the bins' tops and by two subterranean conveyor-belt systems.[55]

---

[54] It appears that the four immense tile bins pictured in William C. Edgar, *The Story of a Grain of Wheat* (New York: McClure, Phillips & Co., 1903), p. 109, over the caption "Fire-proof Tile Grain Tanks, America," is the St. Anthony #3.

[55] A photograph at the Minnesota Institute of the Arts (accession number 82.126.11) confirms that the Saint Anthony Elevator #3 was built next to the Saint Anthony Elevator #2, which was a small, wood-frame elevator built in 1892. The Saint Anthony #1 was a large wood-cribbed

Between 1903 and 1904, tile-binned grain elevators were built in Buffalo, where nine tanks were made out of tile by the Barnett-Record Engineering Company for the Washburn-Crosby Flour Mills, and in Buenos Aires, Argentina, where an unknown European firm (possibly Belgian) built a huge grain elevator with tile bins for the Bunge y Born Grain Company. Back in Minnesota, two large-scale grain elevators with tile bins were built by the Barnett & Record Company between 1907 and 1909: a 700,000-bushel transfer elevator in Duluth for the Peavey Grain Company,[56] and a 400,000-bushel receiving elevator in Minneapolis for the Pillsbury "A" Mill.

But it was the use of reinforced concrete that first brought international attention to grain elevators in Minneapolis. In 1899, the Minneapolis-based businessman Frank H. Peavey, known throughout the Dakotas, Iowa and Minnesota as the "grain elevator king,"[57] hired a local engineer, Charles F. Haglin, to design and build an

---

elevator built in 1888. Unfortunately, all three Saint Anthony Elevators were razed in 1992.

[56] A photograph taken by the Historic American Engineering Record before the elevator was demolished in 1998 shows a structure with a great number of darkly colored, narrow and tall bins. See HAER MN-97-A1.

[57] A former flour miller in Iowa, Peavey acquired this nickname in the mid-1870s and early 1880s, when he built grain elevators along the rail lines that linked Sioux City, Iowa to Yankton, South Dakota (to the north) and St. Paul, Minnesota (to the northeast). Ten years later, Peavey would start building terminal elevators in Minneapolis, to which he moved in 1885. When he died in 1901 at the age of 55, he owned steamships, railroad lines, banks, real estate and, of course, dozens of grain elevators. Stephen George, Enterprising Minnesotans: 150 Years of Business Pioneers (University of Minnesota Press, 2005), p. 31.

experimental grain silo made of reinforced concrete. "Ferroconcrete" had been invented in France in 1867 by Joseph Monier, and later developed in Europe by Auguste Perret, Francois Hennebique, Eugene Freyssinet and others. "Reinforced concrete has been employed in Europe for constructing grain-elevator bins for about twenty years, and some of the European grain-elevators of this material are of considerable size and importance, even when judged by American standards."[58] As a matter of fact, as far as Europe was concerned, "the year 1898 may be considered as the end of what has been referred to as the early and heroic times of reinforced concrete designing, and particularly of reinforced concrete silo designing."[59]

But in 1898, no European builder had used reinforced concrete to construct a *cylindrical* silo.[60] According to Thomas E. Leary and Elizabeth C. Sholes, "the cylindrical bin [no matter what the construction material] made little impact upon the European scene until the 1920s," when "the

---

[58] Charles S. Hill, *Reinforced Concrete: Part Two: Representative Structures*, second edition (Engineering New Publishing Company, New York, 1906), p. 317.

[59] T.J. Gueritte, "Reinforced Concrete Grain Silos: A General and Historical Survey," *The Structural Engineer*, March 1933, p. 107.

[60] And yet, in *Architecture: Nineteenth and Twentieth Centuries* (1958; Yale University Press, 1987), Henry-Russell Hitchcock claims that "the prototypes for the great monuments of Buffalo, Minneapolis and Duluth [the grain elevators] were certainly French. These monolithic cylinders are, of course, very different from the motor-car factories with their post-and-lintel construction, but that of the elevator seems to have been nearly parallel to that of the factory" (p. 617n).

American model" became widely accepted.[61] Not only did Haglin construct a cylindrical tank out of reinforced concrete, he also abandoned the "fixed form" method favored by the Europeans, and invented (and patented) his own method of using "slip forms." Thanks to the relative speed of the slip-forming technique, Haglin's silo – 20 feet in diameter at the base and 68 feet tall – went up in record time. It was later extended to a height of 125 feet. Today, the silo is a National Historic Landmark and a National Historic Engineering Landmark.

In the fall of 1899, the silo, already dubbed "Peavey's Folly" by local wags, was ready to be filled with grain and sealed for the winter. The next spring, Peavey and Haglin supervised the discharging of the silo's grain, accompanied by a small crowd of on-lookers. Since the grain was in good condition and the silo didn't collapse while or after being emptied, success was declared. Almost immediately, if not actually beforehand, the Peavey Grain Company began the construction in Duluth, Minnesota, of a large-scale grain elevator. First came a group of 15 grain bins, all 104 feet tall and 33 feet in diameter. But before a second group of identical bins could be added, a well-publicized partial collapse took place. A second collapse took place shortly afterwards.[62] It seems that the accidents derived from faulty

---

[61] "Buffalo Grain Elevators," Historic American Engineering Record No. NY-239, p. 28.

[62] One source claims that the concrete in the silos wasn't sufficiently reinforced by the rings of strap-iron that wrapped them. See "The Failure of a Concrete-Steel Grain Elevator at Duluth, Minn.," *Engineering News*, 27 December 1900. (Note the transition signified by the phrase "concrete-steel," which was also used in "An Accident to a Concrete-Steel Grain Bin," *Engineering Record*, June 1, 1901.) Another source claims that, "It was, in fact, the use of these [interstitial] spaces, without full knowledge of how the grain

design, hasty construction or poorly mixed aggregate, and not the suitability of reinforced concrete for such a building, which is how the accidents were occasionally presented in the newspapers and trade publications.

Not everyone was put off from reinforced concrete. Haglin certainly wasn't. He went on to build pioneering elevators in Duluth in 1902;[63] Fort William, Ontario, in 1901 and 1902; Minneapolis in 1902 (the Woodworth) and 1906 (the Washburn-Crosby #1); and Jamestown, North Dakota (a receiving elevator for the Russell-Miller Company) and New Ulm, Minnesota (a receiver for Eagle Rollers Mills) in 1907.[64]

Another firm believer in reinforced concrete was the Canadian-born engineer John S. Metcalf. In 1901, he designed and built four cylindrical grain tanks of modest height (only 47 feet) for the George T. Evans Milling Company of Indianapolis. In 1903, he built an elevator with nine cylindrical tanks of greater height (90 feet) at Port Arthur, Canada.[65] The next year, he designed and built an

---

in them would act, which primarily caused the various collapses." R.P. Durham, "Development of Concrete Grain Elevator Construction," in *Proceedings of the Ninth Annual Convention, held at Pittsburg, Pennsylvania, December 10-14, 1912*, Vol. IX (National Association of Cement Users, 1917), p. 327.

[63] In this case, wire mesh as well as steel tie rods were used to reinforce the concrete. See "A Concrete Grain Elevator," *Iron Age*, April 3, 1902.

[64] C.F. Haglin Company Papers, Northwest Architectural Archives, Manuscript Division, University of Minnesota Libraries.

[65] "The Canadian Pacific Grain Elevator at Port Arthur, Ontario," *Engineering Record*, April 9, 1904, credits this elevator (or perhaps an adjoining one or extension of the first?) to the Barnett-Record Company.

elevator with ten 80-foot-tall cylindrical tanks, arrayed in a single row, for the Missouri Pacific Railroad in Kansas City, Missouri. Metcalf also built elevators for the Santa Fe Railroad in Chicago, Illinois, in 1906,[66] the J.H. Tromanhauser Company in Goderich, Ontario, in 1907, and the Grand Trunk Railroad in Tiffin, Ontario, in 1909.[67]

The historian and industrial archaeologist Robert M. Frame III has offered the following useful guidelines for these years in his essay "Grain Elevators in Minnesota to 1945."[68] Between 1906 and 1912, there was a period of experimentation and novelty; and between 1912 and 1928, a period of acceptance and mastery. Quite obviously, grain elevators continued to be made out of reinforced concrete after 1928; indeed, there were significant developments in elevator design around 1942. But the majority of the elevators built between 1928 and 1942 adopted the "classic" forms that had been worked out in places like Buffalo and Minneapolis in the early 1900s.

Since a great many silo-complexes were built out of reinforced concrete in the first half of the twentieth century, I'll limit myself here to three, all built in Buffalo: an

---

[66] A photograph taken by the Detroit Publishing Company (no. 072296) before this grain elevator exploded and was rebuilt in 1932 shows a very long and tall structure serviced by a single, stationary marine tower. See Library of Congress (no. LC-D4 72296).

[67] Both of the elevators built in Ontario use rectangular grain bins, not cylinders. R.P. Durham, "Development of Concrete Grain Elevator Construction," in *Proceedings of the Ninth Annual Convention, held at Pittsburg, Pennsylvania, December 10-14, 1912*, Vol. IX (National Association of Cement Users, 1917), p. 328.

[68] National Registry of Historical Places – Multiple Property Documentation Form 1990, Section F, Page 7, dated 1989.

experimental grain elevator built between 1906 and 1912; a masterful one built between 1913 and 1928; and one built in 1942, at the end of the line of elevator-design begun almost a century previously by Joseph Dart and Robert Dunbar.

The American Elevator was the first reinforced-concrete grain elevator built in Buffalo. Erected in 1906, it still stands at 87 Childs Street, just east of the site of the Electric Elevator. Designed and built by the James Stewart Engineering Company of Chicago, the American was also the first grain elevator in America to be constructed using continuously poured concrete "slip forms." (The first such elevator in *the world* was the "King Elevator," built in Port Arthur, Canada, in 1903.)

Charles F. Haglin had been the first engineer to use slip forms, which he patented during work on Peavey's Folly in 1899. Haglin had allowed each "form" *a full day* to dry before moving the "slips" up and pouring a new section of concrete. Though this was fast by European standards, which called for pouring the concrete all at once and waiting several weeks for it to dry, it was slow by American standards, especially those of 1906, when there were new and better materials (concrete aggregates, cements and reinforcing bars) with which to work.

In the method of slip forming practiced and patented by James Stewart, the four-foot-tall forms were moved up as soon as the concrete had been poured. At the American Elevator, Stewart's company built 48 cylindrical main bins, each 25 feet in diameter and 90 feet tall, in record time. Laid out in four parallel but not interlocking rows, these concrete tanks both stood alone and tangentially made contact with each other. To maximize the elevator's use of space, three rows of bins (33 in total) were built within the interstices thus created. Capable of storing a total of 2.25 million bushels of grain, the entire bin-structure was raised 14 feet above ground level by reinforced concrete pillars. This allowed the horizontal conveyor-belts running underneath the bin-bottoms (equipped with conical steel hoppers) to be placed directly on the building's reinforced-concrete foundation. (See figure 6.) The gallery that contained the conveyors running *above* the bins was made of a variety of materials: a structural-steel frame; a reinforced-concrete floor; corrugated-iron walls; and a book-tiled roof.

Because of its cramped location on the banks of the Buffalo River, the American Elevator was constructed in a line that ran perpendicular to the water. First came the elevator's one marine tower, a "stiff" leg 125 feet tall and connected to the bin-structure behind it through spouts at its feet. (Today, it is the oldest surviving leg in Buffalo.) Then came the bin-structure. Finally, there was the workhouse, an immense steel-framed structure that was 98 feet long, 42 feet wide, and 196 feet high. Alongside the workhouse, there was a train shed capable of unloading railcars at the rate of 3,500 bushels of grain per hour.

The corporate history of the American Elevator is quite instructive. The elevator was originally built to unload barley from lake vessels and store it until needed by the adjoining brick-and-steel malt house, which had also been built by James Stewart. Both were owned and operated by the American Malting Company, a huge, illegal combine of malt houses organized and protected by J.P. Morgan, among others. The construction of the American Elevator and the adjoining malt house allowed this monopoly to close its plants in Ohio (Cleveland and Hamilton) and Pennsylvania (Erie), and run its entire east-coast operations from Buffalo.

After the passage of the Volstead Act in 1919, and the resulting prohibition of the production, distribution and sale of beer and other alcoholic beverages all through the United States, the American Elevator was sold to the Electric Elevator Company, a subsidiary of the Minneapolis-based Russell Miller Company (the makers of "Occident Flour"). In 1923, the malt house was demolished and a flourmill was built in its place. To handle the in-coming wheat, Russell

Miller built an additional leg, a loose one, along side the old stiff one.

In 1931, the burgeoning flourmill hired H.R. Wait and Monarch Engineering to build a huge annex of reinforced-concrete grain tanks. Capable of storing a total of 1.4 million bushels, they were generally similar to the tanks in the old structure: four rows of six 125-foot-tall cylinders that touched tangentially and were linked together by walls to form space for an additional 15 interstitial bins. But Wait went a step further (a step that had grown common since 1906) and used convex, quarter-walls to create 16 "outer" bins. Because of these outer bins, it was nearly impossible to someone standing outside the new structure to divine the actual layout by simply counting the numbers of "cylindrical" forms that presented themselves. In 1933, Russell Miller brought in the R.S. McManus Steel Construction Company (Buffalo) to built a second workhouse, and brought back Monarch Engineering to build a huge horizontal gantry that would connect the Russell Miller complex with its neighbor, Perot Malting. Once again because of cramped space (and the American Elevator's perpendicular line to the water), this gantry had to be built 150 feet above the ground.

In 1954, Russell Miller was purchased by the Peavey Company, which continued to run the elevator from its headquarters in Minneapolis. Thus, the American Elevator is sometimes called "the Peavey." The Peavey Company was eventually purchased by ConAgra, an up-and-coming corporate giant that operated the American Elevator from the 1970s until 2001. Like three other elevators in its immediate vicinity – the Lake & Rail (built in 1927), the Perot (1909) and the Marine A (1925) – the American was purchased in 2007 by a company that intends to use it for the storage of corn and the production of ethanol. And so the corporate history of the American Elevator is decidedly controversial (that is to say, typical of American capitalism). One mustn't forget this, even as one appreciates the historical and architectural importance of the elevator "itself."

The Concrete Central Elevator was built at 175 Buffalo River in five stages between 1915 and 1917. All five stages were designed by Harry R. Wait and built by Monarch. At the Concrete Central, Wait not only *extended* what he had accomplished and learned at the Dellwood "A," the Connecting Terminal, and the Superior "A" elevators – all built out of reinforced concrete in Buffalo in 1914 – he also perfected his craft as a producer of standardized designs. When it was completed, the Concrete Central was the single biggest grain elevator in the world: it could store a total of 4.5 million bushels in its 268 cylindrical grain tanks, and it was truly colossal, occupying 960 feet of dock space on the Buffalo River, standing 72 feet wide and 150 feet tall at the top of the gallery (187 feet tall at the top of the workhouse).

According to Thomas Leary and Elizabeth Sholes, the authors of a comprehensive report on the Concrete-Central and Buffalo's other grain elevators, submitted to the Historic America Engineering Record in 1991, the Concrete-Central was built and first operated in secrecy and under the protection of the federal government.[69] Not only were there concerns about America's enemies in World War I (fought between 1914 and 1918) and their ability to sabotage the nation's grain elevators; but there were also concerns about cash-poor farmers and their "IWW allies," who, according to the President of the New York Stock Exchange, one Herbert .C. Hoover, were suspected of being behind the rash of grain-elevator explosions in the Midwest in 1916 and 1917.

In Zane Grey's novel *The Desert of Wheat*, published in 1919, the Industrial Workers of the World (IWW) are behind the destruction of grain elevators in the Columbia Basin in "early July [1917], exactly three months after the United States had declared war upon Germany."

---

[69] HAER, NY-243, p. 13.

"Hello, Dorn! Ain't this hell? They got your wheat!" he said hoarsely.

"Olsen! How'd it happen? Wasn't anybody set to guard the elevators?"

"Yes. But the I.W.W.'s drove all the guards off but Grimm, an' they beat him up bad. Nobody had nerve enough to shoot."

"Olsen, if I run into the Glidden I'll kill him," declared Kurt.

"So will I. . . . But, Dorn, they're a hard crowd. They're over there on the side, watchin' the fire. A gang of them! Soon as I can get the men together we'll drive them out of town. There'll be a fight, if I don't miss my guess." […]

"Well, my neighbor, Olsen, managed the harvest. He sure rushed it. I'd have given a good deal for you and Miss Anderson to have seen all those big combines at work on one field. It was great. We harvested over thirty-eight thousand bushels and got all the wheat safely to the elevators at the station. . . . And that night the I.W.W. burned the elevators!"

As a result of these attacks, the great wheat fields in the Pacific Northwest became deserts of wheat: "Here was grown the most bounteous, the richest and finest wheat in all the world. Strange and unfathomable that so much of the bread of man, the staff of life, the hope of civilization in this tragic year 1917, should come from a vast, treeless, waterless, dreary desert!" [70]

I don't mean to scare anyone or encourage round-ups of domestic "subversives" and "terrorists" by mentioning that

---

[70] http://infomotions.com/etexts/gutenberg/dirs/ 1/0/2/0/10201/10201.htm accessed 28 August 2008.

allies of the downtrodden are *still* adamant in their desire to blow up the granaries, at least symbolically. In "Agents of Change: Primal War and the Collapse of Global Civilization," which was published in *Species Traitor No. 4* (2005), Kevin Tucker writes:

> Like the old saying goes: The boss needs us, we don't need the boss. But we can apply that more widely: Replace boss with machine, fields, work, god/s, economy, politics, or civilization. We've lived without all of these things and we don't need them. They are killing us. The city and the countryside stand between us and a society that can support the next generations. Work stands between us and life. Progress stands between a healthy livable world and a suffocating one. Those who built the temples of god-kings, those who filled the granaries, those who worked in the fields, those who built roads, cut forests, those who crushed opposition, all of them hit a point when it was painfully obvious that they were putting far more into the system than they were getting in return.
>
> Most of them always knew this. Just like most of us still know this. But what is different is that they realized they could do something about it. Tired of waiting for god, they stopped civilization. Whether it was through killing elites, sabotaging tools, burning granaries, homes and temples, symbolic destruction, ignoring or torching the fields, or simply stopping production through walking away: They took back their agency.

"What? Sacrifice everything?" Victor Hugo asks in *Paris incendie*, which was written in the aftermath of the crushing of the Commune of Paris (June 1871); "Even the granary?"

Compared to the bin-structure in the original American Elevator, the internal structure of the "Concrete Elevator" (1915) was quite complex: not only were there interstitial bins (16 in total) constructed between the main bins (27 in all), but there were also 20 "outer bins" that were formed by building convex, one-sixth-cylinder linking walls. Each outer bin could hold 4,200 bushels; each interstitial could hold 16,000 bushels; and each main bin could hold 26,000 bushels, for a grand total of 1.05 million. Precisely because they followed a single plan, and weren't constructed in piecemeal fashion, the additions of the "Central Elevator" in 1916 and the three additions made to the Central Elevator in 1917 repeated the same basic design – even though the banks of the Buffalo River required that the "Concrete-Central" elevator to become narrower as it spread out.

Like the Great Northern, the Concrete-Central was equipped with three electrically powered movable marine towers, which at 156 feet were the tallest legs (loose or stiff) ever built in Buffalo. None of them ever blew down, and the legs now rusted-out but still standing at the Concrete-Central are the originals. Because of the elevator's exceptionally long wharf, these legs could get as close together as 4 feet and as far away as 192 feet. Each one could elevate grain from the hold of a grain-laden vessel (even the same grain-laden vessel, if it was big enough, as many lakers were in 1917) at the rate of 25,000 bushels an hour. Unlike the Great Northern, the Concrete-Central had a fourth marine leg, a "stiff" one. Made of reinforced concrete and iron, and set off a little from the fifth and last section of the main building, this short rectangular tower was designed to receive grain via a subterranean tunnel, elevate it and load it into canal boats or barges.

The eastern side of the Concrete Central was dominated by a huge railroad shed, made of structural steel and corrugated iron, and capable of unloading five different boxcars at the same time through a total of four below-grade conveyor belts. Once inside, the grain could be elevated by one of eight high-speed lofting legs. Because of its quite varied capabilities (transshipments from lake to rail, lake to canal, rail to canal and even rail to rail, if necessary), because of the incredible speed with which it handled grain, and because it could accomplish all of these tasks at the same time, the Concrete-Central was the single most active grain elevator ever built in Buffalo. In 1918, its first shipping season, the Concrete-Central transshipped a staggering 22 million bushels of grain. During the 1920s, when the amount of grain arriving at the Port of Buffalo was at its all-time highest (some 400 million bushels per shipping season), the Concrete-Central would transship a tenth of the total on its own.

The Concrete-Central was built and operated by the Eastern Grain Mill & Elevator Corporation, which was founded and controlled by the local businessmen Nisbet Grammer and John J. Rammacher. Over the course of the next 30 years, the EGM&EC would own and/or operate a total of seven grain elevators in Buffalo, including the Standard (built in 1928), the Connecting Terminal (1914), the Iron Elevator (1902), the Export (1899), and the Electric (1897). In 1945, the Concrete-Central was sold to Continental Grain, which had just recently moved its headquarters from Paris to New York City.

In 1967, scared by various recent trends – the increase of railroad demurrage fees in 1963, the absence of Commodity Credit Corporation surpluses in 1964, and the ending of Buffalo-favorable preferential rail rates in 1965 and 1966 – Continental Grain closed the Concrete-Central, announced it was looking for buyers, apparently found one, but then reopened it in 1968, only to abandon it completely in 1973. It was auctioned off for back taxes in October 1973, purchased by someone not in the grain business, and eventually looted of a quarter-million dollars' of machines, valuable metals and office furniture.

As part of its "unglamorous but smart" strategy to "put [its] money into the basics of grain transportation and storage,"[71] the Cargill Grain Company leased several grain elevators in Buffalo in the late 1920s: the Electric Elevator, the Superior, and the Saskatchewan Pool.[72] In 1942,[73] Cargill added a colossal, six-million-bushel "annex" to the Electric. Designed by an in-house engineer, H.G. Onstad, the Electric Annex was unlike every other grain elevator built in Buffalo. Its only predecessors were the elevators that Cargill itself had constructed in Omaha, Chicago and Albany between 1931 and 1933.[74] Each one of these facilities had dispensed with "grain bins" and had returned to the days of the "flathouse," in which a grain warehouse was a big, empty building in

---

[71] Dan Morgan, *Merchants of Grain*, p. 84. By 1975, "Cargill and Continental [another huge grain trading company] owned or leased about half of all the grain storage space in the sixty-seven elevators at American ports, and Cargill had an estimated 7 million tons of space worldwide" (p. 235).

[72] Wayne G. Broehl, *Cargill: Trading the World's Grain* (University Press of New England, 1992), p. 326. Cargill would relinquish their options on all of these elevators by 1929 (p. 381).

[73] This is the date listed in the chart created by Henry Baxter for *Reconsidering Concrete Atlantis: Buffalo's Grain Elevators* (edited by Lynda Schneekloth), The School of Architecture and Planning at SUNY at Buffalo, 2006, p. 14). Elsewhere in this collection, the date provided is "1940 and 1941" (p. 54). For his part, Reyner Banham says the date of construction was 1940 (*A Concrete Atlantis*, MIT Press, 1986, p. 174).

[74] Wayne G. Broehl, *Cargill: Trading the World's Grain*, pp. 384-389.

which sacks of grain and barrels of flour were stored. Only this time, there were no sacks, just towering piles of grain in bulk, and the barn was built of reinforced concrete, not wood. At both the Omaha and Albany elevators, there were only 4 of these grain storage areas, but each one could store approximately one million bushels of grain. At the Chicago version, there was a single, 1,300,000-bushel room. But while Cargill had to pay for its Chicago and Omaha elevators, the Albany elevator was "paid for by the Port Authority [of New York] and built according to Cargill's specifications."[75]

From the outside, the Electric Annex in Buffalo appeared to be an immense collection of 80-foot-tall cylinders, laid out in seven parallel rows. But these cylinders were in fact both the self-buttressing walls that contained the Annex's six colossal storage compartments, each of which could store 1 million bushels, and a system of "outer" bins that could contain equipment and machinery. Even the internal partitions were made of ranks of cylinders and partial cylinders. But *despite* all these cylindrical forms, and speaking quite strictly, the Electric Annex wasn't a grain elevator at all. It was simply a granary made out of reinforced concrete that received grain through a horizontal transfer coming from the Electric Elevator. Once instead the Annex, the grain was scooped up by "power shovels" or transported

---

[75] Morgan, *Merchants of Grain*, p. 84. Built by the James Stewart Company, the elevator in Albany had a storage capacity of 13.5 million bushels, which made it the biggest elevator in the world at the time. It is still in operation: "More than 500,000 tons were shipped overseas last year from the massive grain elevator operated at the port by Cargill Co." Eric Anderson, "Energy fuels Port of Albany growth: Steam turbines, generators, ethanol all part of cargo mix," *The Times Union*, September 21, 2008.

around, from hall to hall, by small gasoline-powered front-loaders. But it was never elevated again.

And so the construction of the Electric Annex was part of a development that marked the beginning of the end of the "classic" grain elevator. In today's grain transshipment and storage warehouses, the grain isn't shipped in bulk, but in sealed containers made of steel; it isn't elevated by bucket conveyors, but "sucked" through pneumatic tubes; and these unloading machines are not part of the grain warehouse, but the grain-laden vessel itself.

Chapter 5
American Colossus

One of the very first visual depictions of a grain elevator in Buffalo was in an advertisement. Published in the same edition of the *Commercial Advertiser Directory* that reported that the Port of Buffalo was the biggest grain port in the world, this ad was for the Reed Elevator, one of the first to be built. Because of the drawing's composition (the schooner is docked right in front of the elevator), the viewer can't see what is truly distinctive about it: the marine tower and the elevating leg inside it. Such an image would have been better suited for the shipping company that owned the schooner, rather than the Reed Elevator.

In 1859, a detailed drawing entitled "Buffalo Harbor, From the Light House" was published in *The State Gazetteer*. A half-dozen grain elevators were depicted, but none of them were shown loading or unloading grain, and none of them had the names of their respective owners printed upon them in huge letters, as was the universal custom. And so, from the lighthouse, the grain elevators – supposedly so modern – seem to be ordinary albeit strangely shaped warehouses.

This inability to adequately visualize the new invention sometimes became comically literal. In two large and very detailed engravings of the Buffalo harbor (executed and published in 1853 by J. W. Hill and in 1859 by J. H. Cohen, respectively), not a single grain elevator was depicted, though there were at least ten of them in the harbor at the time! In fact, it would take until 1863, when Charles Magnus published a "Bird's Eye View of the City of Buffalo, NY," for the city's grain elevators to finally come into focus.[1] In this hand-colored, three-sectioned lithograph of the village's harbor, there were at total of eighteen grain elevators, and each one clearly has the name of its owner printed upon it in Brobdingnagian-sized words. Without any trouble, one can see, spread out all over the harbor, the BENNETT, the CITY, the CUTTER & AUSTIN, the C.W. EVANS, the ERIC BASIN, the EXCHANGE, the MARINE, the REED, the STERNBERG, and the WATSON. In Harley's 1870 drawing "Ship Canal, Buffalo," the Buffalo harbor is a small area crammed full of grain elevators, seven in total, all of them clearly visible and named.

Quite obviously, the grain elevators weren't invisible and the creators of the images of the Buffalo harbor in the 1850s weren't blind. There was something about these buildings (these machine/building hybrids) that *repelled* visual attention. People looked away from them. What was it? Why did they look away? William Cronon provides an explanation in his discussion of similar phenomena in Chicago and St. Louis:

> So hemmed in [crowded] was the [Chicago] river that it did not figure very prominently in people's mental image of the city. Visitors to Chicago [...] scarcely seemed to notice the river's wharves and piers. Perhaps because Lake Michigan was so much more powerful as a visual icon, the Chicago River dominated people's sense of Chicago much less than the Mississippi shaped perceptions of St. Louis. In St. Louis, the wharves were the heart of the town, so much so that few visitors – most of whom arrived by boat – failed to comment on them. The city's buildings sat well back from the

[1] Available on-line http://www.buffaloah.com/h/maps/map1863 accessed 21 August 2008.

riverfront to escape the Mississippi's annual rise during spring floods.[2]

In the case of Buffalo, the Buffalo River, along which all the grain elevators were located, was far less powerful as an icon than either the Erie Canal or Lake Erie. As in St. Louis, Buffalo's important buildings (City Hall, for example) were set back from both the River and the Lake, the latter of which could carry terrible storms at any time of year.

We must also remember that Buffalo's grain elevators were buildings without doors. You couldn't just look or walk into a grain elevator the way you could with a barn. While it was true that these grain elevators had doors (somewhere or another), they were rarely open and thus didn't give passersby and the curious a glance into what was going on inside. Furthermore, the walls that enclosed the grain bins had no windows in them, once again depriving outsiders of a look inside the *sanctum sanctorum*, which remained hidden and inaccessible. The fact that the grain elevators or, rather, the machines inside them, made loud humming sounds when they were in operation surely only emphasized the mystery of the goings-on within.

Walter Benjamin has an interesting take on windowless buildings. "What stands within the windowless house is the true," he writes. "What is true has no windows; nowhere does the true look out to the universe."[3] In this view, windowless grain elevators aren't hiding from outsiders or protecting a secret (shameful or glorious) that only they know. Instead, they are "saying" that there is nothing out there for them (the elevators themselves) to see, that is, nothing that is true.

---

[2] William Cronon, *Nature's Metropolis: Chicago and the Great West* (WW Norton, 1991), pp. 106-107).

[3] Walter Benjamin, *The Arcades Project*, translated by Howard Eiland and Kevin McLaughlin (Harvard University Press, 1999), page 532.

Looking out at the world would only show them what is false.

Windowless buildings also have a very complex relationship with what Benjamin calls "the interior."

> For the private individual, the place of dwelling is for the first time opposed to the place of work. The former constitutes itself as the interior. Its complement is the office. The private individual, who in the office has to deal with reality, needs the domestic interior to sustain him in his illusions. This necessity is all the more pressing since he has no intention of allowing his commercial considerations to impinge on social ones. In the formation of his private environment, both are kept out. From this arise the phantasmagorias of the interior – which, for the private man, represents the universe. In the interior, he brings together the far away and the long ago. His living room is a box in the theater of the world [...] The interior is not just the universe but also the *etui* of the private individual. To dwell means to leave traces. In the interior, these are accentuated. Coverlets and antimacassars, cases and containers are devised in abundance; in these, the traces of the most ordinary objects of use are imprinted. In just the same way, the traces of the inhabitant are imprinted in the interior.[4]

Benjamin goes on to say that "The shattering of the interior occurs via Jugendstil [a modern architectural movement] around the turn of the century."[5] This may have been true in Europe, but not in America, where the "interior" of "the

---

[4] Walter Benjamin, *The Arcades Project*, pp. 8-9.
[5] Walter Benjamin, *The Arcades Project*, p. 9.

private individual" was first rattled, if not "shattered," by the grain elevators of the 1840s and 1850s. The grain elevator confronted this individual with a premature vision of mass society, a hundred years before such a society was finally organized or recognized as such. (Referring to what Siegfried Giedion calls "despised, everyday constructions," Walter Benjamin says, "In these constructions, the appearance of great masses on the stage of history was already foreseen.")[6] The unbroken "mass" of the grain elevator presented a real interior, not an illusory one, and so the private individual felt naked when he tried to look at it. It was easier for him to simply turn away.

In *Technics and Human Development*, Lewis Mumford tries to explain other historians' neglect of "technics" (today we would called them "technologies") that perform their functions in enclosed spaces, and their concomitant over-emphasis of technical functions that take place in open ones.[7] Mumford implicates Puritanism and its aversion to the human body, especially the female body and its reproductive organs, which of course are internal rather than external. Though men have "storage compartments" of their own (stomachs and scrota) and women have functioning "extensions" from which liquids flow (breasts), this analogy can be helpful. It certainly explains why floating or flying storage compartments ("ships") are almost always referred to as "she" and thought to be temperamental. More narrowly, this analogy explains the early attempts to *look away* from the grain elevators (as if they were Medusa heads) as well as the later attempts to look at them directly and denounce them as ugly and monstrous (as if they were the Devil). Unlike skyscrapers, grain elevators weren't comfortingly erect

---

[6] Walter Benjamin, *The Arcades Project*, p. 455.

[7] Lewis Mumford, *Technics and Human Development: Myth of the Machine, Vol. 1*, New York: Harcourt Brace Jovanovich, 1967, p. 140.

phalluses or phallic "symbols," but terrifying enlarged wombs pregnant with unknown offspring. One of the least frightening visions of what could be born from such creatures was relayed by Walter B. Herbert: "An English visitor once said that he watched expectantly for a 40-foot soldier to emerge from each elevator, so much did these buildings [country elevators] appear to him as giant sentry boxes before an imaginary Buckingham palace."[8]

When the British novelist Anthony Trollope came to America in October 1860, he wasn't primarily interested in American agriculture, but in slavery and the impending Civil War between the North and the South. To write his mammoth book on the subject, entitled *North America*, he spent more than a year traveling the country and staying in cities and towns both large and small. He came to Buffalo, of course: his mother, Frances Trollope, had visited and written about the town in 1825, just after the Erie Canal opened.[9]

Like his mother, Anthony Trollope had, in the words of Henry James, a "complete appreciation of the usual," a keen sense of irony, and a strong interest in politics and urban culture. And so, unlike the other famous 19th century authors who either visited or lived in Buffalo (Rudyard Kipling and Mark Twain come to mind), Anthony Trollope took serious interest in the city's grain elevators and placed several long, detailed and very insightful passages about them in *North America*.[10]

---

[8] "Castles of the New World," *Canadian Geographical Journal*, vol. 6, no. 5 May 1933, p. 243.

[9] Frances Trollope, *Domestic Manners of the Americans* (1832), edited by Donald Smalley, New York: Knopf, 1949.

[10] Anthony Trollope, *North America*, edited with notes by Donald Smally and Bradford Allen Booth, Knopf, New York, 1951, pages 168-169. Excerpts appeared in the *Chicago Tribune* on June 28, 1862.

Kipling visited Buffalo in 1889. His comments on the city's grain elevators, which included a fanciful comparison between the elevating leg and an elephant's trunk, were certainly colorful, but they were also very brief and superficial.[11] Shortly after they were reprinted in Buffalo, a local newspaperman complained, "Kipling was evidently in a little bit of a hurry when he made his grain elevator observations [...] Had he taken a little more time, he would have been able to explain . . . more in detail the *modus operandi*." Unfortunately, much of the accolades that Buffalo's grain elevators were to receive, especially from Europeans who saw photographs of them, were also hasty and unconcerned with how the elevators actually worked. As for Mark Twain, he lived in Buffalo for many years, but appears to have written nothing on the subject of the elevators or the grain trade.

Unfortunately, 20th century editors of Trollope's *North America* – in the name of sparing the reader from "long dull areas and technical discourses of little interest now" – have done worse than bore the reader. They have denied him or her the opportunity to read what Trollope actually wrote. In particular, they have removed Trollope's extended and detailed descriptions of the workings of Buffalo's grain elevators. Precisely because (as Trollope himself notes) "over and beyond the grain elevators there is nothing specially worthy of remark at Buffalo," modern versions of *North America* make it seem that he wrote almost nothing at all about the city. After redaction, all Trollope says about Buffalo is that, "It is a fine city, like all other American cities of its class. The streets are broad, the 'blocks' are high, and cars on tramways run all day, and nearly all night as well."

---

[11] See *The Writings in Prose and Verse of Rudyard Kipling: Letters of Travel*, volume 24, New York, 1920, p. 173.

The removal of the passages on Buffalo's elevators also causes problems with Trollope's discussion of Chicago. Despite the fact that *Buffalo* was America's most active grain port, Trollope refers to Chicago as "the Metropolis of American corn – the favourite city haunt of the American Ceres." In a passage not deleted by the editors, Trollope writes that it is in Chicago that

> [t]he goddess seats herself . . . amidst the dust of her full barns, and proclaims herself a goddess ruling over things political and philosophical as well as agricultural. Chicago was intended as a town of export of corn, and, therefore, the corn stores have received first attention. While I was there, they were in perfect working order.

Precisely because the book proceeds in chronological order and because its author visited Chicago *after* he'd been to Buffalo, Trollope obviously expected that anyone who read his comments on Chicago would have already read his comments on Buffalo, the American Ceres' other "city haunt," known to Trollope as "the great gate of the Western Ceres." Had this not been Trollope's expectation, he surely would have described Chicago's "corn stores" and how they work in great detail. But he didn't, and so the passage on Chicago seems hasty and superficial. The book as a whole suffers: it no longer shows an acute appreciation for the grain elevator, which was a key factor in America's miraculous transformation from an ex-colony into an agricultural and political giant over the course of the 19th century.

Trollope's use of the word "haunt" was really quite skillful, not only because the worship of Ceres, the ancient Roman goddess of grains and "cereals," centered upon rites for the dead. Several of this word's meanings were echoed in this passage: a place that is often or continually visited; a home or hamlet; a ghost or spirit that dwells somewhere in particular; and a lair or feeding-place for animals. These meanings give Trollope's image of the re-birth of Ceres in a modern, dusty grain bin something of a mystical or spectral light. Not only was Ceres reborn in Buffalo and Chicago – a statue of her was in fact erected upon the roof of the Chicago Board of Trade in 1930 – she was also reborn a leader of domains outside of her own (politics and philosophy). Does this not represent an historic triumph for women, agricultural workers and other "plebes"?

Significantly, the passages that were excised by the modern editors of *North America* include Trollope's candid admission that he himself had difficulties with "technical discourses of little interest," and so, rather than delete them, he tried to translate and understand those discourses into human terms. The first abstraction to be understood in this way was the staggering quantities of grain arriving in Buffalo at the time. No doubt repeating what he was told by his tour-guide (and Trollope certainly had one), the British author begins his discussion of the city's grain trade by repeating the spectacular statistics of the day: 51,69,142 bushels of wheat, corn and flour transshipped in 1859. "I confess that to my own mind statistical amounts do not bring home any enduring idea," Trollope writes.

> Fifty million bushels of corn and flour [he goes on] simply seems to mean a great deal. It is a powerful form of superlative, and soon vanishes away, as do other superlatives in this age of strong words.

That is to say, without already knowing or being told that 50 million bushels of grain means a year's worth of food for 10 million people, that is, the entire population of a European country, Trollope (or anyone else, for that matter) can only focus his or her attention on the "fifty million" in the phrase "fifty million bushels of corn and flour," and not on the words "corn and flour." And once it has focused on "fifty million," the mind quickly asks itself and dwells upon how much *money* all that grain is worth on the market, and not upon how much *hunger and suffering* such a vast quantity of grain might alleviate.

For Trollope, another abstraction to be understood in human terms was the grain elevator itself. In Trollope's definition, the grain elevator was as "ugly a monster as has yet been produced."

> In uncouthness of form it outdoes those obsolete old brutes who used to roam about the semiaqueous world, and live a most uncomfortable life with their great hungering stomachs and huge unsatisfied maws. The elevator itself consists of a big movable trunk, – moveable as is that of an elephant, but not pliable, and less graceful even than an elephant's. This is attached to a huge granary or barn; but in order to give altitude within the barn for the necessary moving up and down of this trunk . . . there is an awkward box erected on the roof of the barn. . . . When [the elevator's] head is ensconced within its box, and the beast of prey is thus nearly hidden within the building, the unsuspicious [lake] vessel is brought up within reach of the creature's trunk, and down it comes, like a mosquito's proboscis, right through the deck, in at the open aperture of the hold, and so into the very vitals and bowels of the ship. When there, it goes to work upon its food with a greed and avidity that is disgusting to a beholder of any taste or imagination.

Here, in the course of six sentences, the grain elevator undergoes a series of rapid and fantastic transformations. First, it's a dinosaur, then an elephant, and finally a mosquito. These transformations drastically reduce the grain elevator's size from the mammoth to the minute, and yet Trollope has no fear that the monster will cease to disgust and terrify his readers. That's because he has brought it both closer to today and closer to home. First, it's in pre-historic times, then in Africa or Asia, and finally wherever there is standing water in which mosquitoes can breed. In sum, the monster starts off big enough to crush and devour someone whole, and ends up small enough to penetrate the skin and destroy from the inside (the bloodstream).

It is telling that Trollope insists on the grain elevator's "greed," on the way it "goes to work upon its food" and "devours and continues to devour, till the corn within its reach has been swallowed, masticated and digested." Neither dinosaurs, elephants, nor mosquitoes are known for their greed; none of them continue to eat even after they are no longer hungry. Only human beings are selfish enough to do that; and so it is easy to imagine that, behind Trollope's kaleidoscope of metaphors, there is plain disgust with monopoly capitalism. Just a few years later, during the debates concerning the Illinois State Constitution, part of which regulated the grain-elevator business, the editor of the *Chicago Tribune* would proclaim:

> The fifty million bushels of grain that pass into and out of the city of Chicago per annum, are controlled absolutely by a few warehouse men and the officers of railways. They form the grand ring that wrings the sweat and blood out of the producers of Illinois. There is no provision in the fundamental law [as it is today] standing between the unrestricted avarice of monopoly and the common rights of the people; but the great, laborious, patient ox, the farmer, is bitten and

bled, harassed and tortured, by these rapacious, blood sucking insects.[12]

Disgust with capitalism isn't hidden or disguised in Ken Kesey's novel *One Flew Over the Cuckoo's Nest*, which was first published in 1962. Set in a mental institution in the Pacific Northwest, the novel is narrated by Chief Bromden, a Native American who suffers from both mental illness and the policies of the United States government, which built a huge hydroelectric dam across the Columbia River. Apparently delusional, but also quite lucid about the machinations of power, Chief Bromden refers to his oppressors as "the Combine." He doesn't simply mean an association for unethical commercial or political purposes, but also the mechanical device that harvests and threshes grain. Chief Bromden would have been well acquainted with combines, because the areas around the Columbia River were big producers of grain, especially when he would have been a boy (the 1920s or 1930s).

The highlight of the novel (it does not appear in the 1975 cinematic version directed by Milos Forman) is the Chief's nightmare. "[The night attendant at the institution] twists a knob, and the whole floor goes to slipping down away from him standing in the door, lowering into the building like in a grain elevator!" Once inside the bowels of this building – "the light of the dorm door five hundred yards back up this hole is nothing but a speck, dusting the square sides of the shaft with a dim powder" – the Chief gets to see the machines that power it. "A whole wall slides up, reveals a huge room of endless machines stretching clear out of sight, swarming with sweating, shirtless men running up and down

---

[12]   Joseph Medill of Cook County in Illinois Constitutional Debates, quoted in William Cronon, *Nature's Metropolis: Chicago and the Great West* (WW Norton & Company, 1991), p. 140).

catwalks, faces blank and dreamy in firelight thrown from a hundred blast furnaces." The workers are themselves machines: they "all move at the same smooth sprint, an easy, fluid stride." They both work the machines and are food for them. "A workman's eyes snap shut while he's going at full run, and he drops in his tracks; two of his buddies running by grab him up and lateral him into a furnace as they pass. The furnace whoops a ball of fire and I hear the popping of a million tubes like walking through a field of seed pods. This sound mixes with the whirr and clang of the rest of the machines." The Chief sees one of his fellow inmates grabbed up, carried off and cut open by a pair of workers, "but there's no blood or innards falling out like I was looking to see – just a shower of rust and ashes, and now and again a piece of wire or glass."[13]

When the Chief wakes up, he doesn't remember the grain elevator. "If I was fool enough to try and tell anybody about it they'd say, Idiot, you just had a nightmare; things as crazy as a big machine room down in the bowels of a dam where people get cut up by robot workers don't exist."[14] Perhaps this grain elevator – like the equally monstrous one in Anthony Trollope's book – has simply undergone one of its metamorphoses.

Like Chief Bromden, Anthony Trollope paid careful attention to the Combine's "robot-workers." In the hold of a lake vessel anchored next to the greedy monster, Trollope writes,

> [only] three or four labourers are at work, helping
> to feed the elevator. They shovel the corn up
> towards its maw, so that at every swallow he

[13] Ken Kesey, *One Flew Over the Cuckoo's Nest* (New York, 1962), pp. 79-81.

[14] Ken Kesey, *One Flew Over the Cuckoo's Nest*, pp. 79-82.

should take in all he can hold. Thus the troughs, as they ascend, are kept full, and when they reach the upper building they empty themselves into a shoot, over which a porter stands guard, moderating the shoot by a door, which the weight of *his finger* can open and close. Through this doorway the corn runs into a measure, and is weighed. By measures of forty bushels each, the tale is kept. There stands the apparatus, with the figures plainly marked, over against *the porter's eye*; and as the sum mounts nearly to forty bushels he closes the door till the grains run thinly through, hardly a handful at a time, so that the balance is exactly struck. Then the teller standing by marks down his figures, and the record is made. The exact porter *touches* the string of another door, and the forty bushels of corn run out at the bottom of the measure, disappear down another shoot, slanting also towards the water, and deposit themselves in the canal-boat. (Emphasis added.)

Here we are close to the objections raised by Sanford B. Hunt the year after Trollope was in North America: "Laborsaving devices drove away a host of longshore men [...] fed fewer mouths." Apparently, the only people employed at this particular grain elevator were the "exact porter," the teller, and the three or four scoopers working in the laker. Everybody else had been put out of work.

But Anthony Trollope saw or hinted at things that escaped Sanford B. Hunt. It was *boring* to work in such a place. "*Ever, ever, ever* is the unvarying word thundering in your ears from the automatic equipment which shakes even the floor," the historian Jules Michelet writes about those "true hells of boredom" – the spinning and weaving mills – in

Le Peuple.[15] "One can never get used to it." Furthermore, it was *alienating* to work in a grain elevator. The tool-handling worker "could still recognize in every contour of the finished product the power and precision of his own formative touch," Hermann Lotze wrote. "The participation of the individual in the work of the machine, by contrast, is limited to [...] manual operations which bring forth nothing directly but merely supply to an inscrutable mechanism the obscure occasion for invisible accomplishments."[16] Finally, it was *dehumanizing* to be an elevator operator. That "exact porter," for example: though he is weighing out batches of grain that weigh hundreds of pounds each – more than any one man could lift – he does his highly specialized job with but one eye and one finger. His finger touches *this*, and his eye watches *here*; then his finger touches *that* and the process starts again. The porter doesn't need the rest of his body; he doesn't use it. And look at that teller, whose function is also hyper-specialized and detached from the whole: his eye looks *there*, and he writes down what he sees *here*. That's it; that's his job.

If it means anything, transshipping 50 million bushels of grain through Buffalo in a single year means that workers such as the porter and the teller – or, rather, their eyes and fingers – must learn to repeat the same actions over and over again, all day, "weekday and Sunday, day and night incessantly," as Trollope notes. These workers must resist the urges to day-dream and to smoke, and so they must be supervised by an American boss, who, as Trollope notes elsewhere in *North America*,

---

[15] First published in 1846 and quoted in Walter Benjamin, *The Arcades Project*, p. 109.

[16] *Mikrokosmos, vol. 3*, published in 1864 and quoted in Benjamin, *The Arcades Project*, pp. 272-272.

knows nothing of hours, and seems to have that idea of a man which a lady always has of a horse. He thinks that he will go for ever. I wish those masons in London who strike for nine hours' work with ten hours' pay could be driven to the labour market of western America for a spell. And moreover, which astonished me, I have seen men driven and hurried, as it were, forced at their work, in a manner that to an English workman would be intolerable.

To use just one of these metaphors: the grain elevator is a mechanical horse that can never be worked to death. *It can explode,* but this is something Trollope doesn't seem to know (wasn't told?).

"I should have stated," Trollope writes, perhaps calming himself down, knowing that both he and his readers need to be adequately prepared for what follows, "that all this wheat which passes through Buffalo comes loose, in bulk."

Nothing is known of sacks or bags. To any spectator at Buffalo this becomes immediately a matter of course; but this should be explained, as we in England are not accustomed to see wheat traveling in this open, unguarded, and plebeian manner. Wheat with us is aristocratic, and travels always in its private carriage.

Here Trollope hit the nail on the head, just as he did when he located the unique aspect of the grain elevator in its "leg" ("the elevator itself consists of a big movable trunk"), not in its storage bins or the shapes that the buildings take. What made the grain elevator a revolutionary invention, one with international consequences in both agriculture and commerce, was the fact that it moved grain in bulk, not sacks or barrels. By playing upon the analogy between "American-

English" and "plebeian-aristocratic," Trollope suggests that the grain elevator "represents" a revolution in politics as well as in the grain trade. Like grain, we will all travel together one day.

In this vision of utopia, the *sumptuousness* of American grain shines out. It glows with the light of the Divine Plan. "Here in the corn lands of Michigan," Trollope writes, "and amidst the bluffs of Wisconsin, and on the high plains of Minnesota, and the prairies of Illinois, has God prepared the food for the increasing millions of the Eastern world, as also for the coming millions of the Western." At the Port of Buffalo, he saw

> the wheat running in rivers from one vessel to another, and from railroad vans up into the huge bins on the top stories of the warehouses; – for these rivers of food run up the hill as easily as they go down. I saw the corn measured by the forty bushels measure with as much ease as we measure an ounce of cheese, and with greater rapidity. I ascertained that the work went on, weekday and Sunday, day and night incessantly; rivers of wheat and rivers of maize ever running. I saw the men bathed in corn as they distributed it in its flow. I saw bins by the score laden with wheat, in each of which there was space for a comfortable residence.[17] I breathed the flour, and drank the flour, and felt myself to be enveloped in a world of breadstuff.

Has Trollope breathed in too much grain dust? Is he coming down with a case of grain dust fever? He is seeing giants, beings so large that forty bushels of grain is the size of an

---

[17] Note: this striking theme will be taken up in Chapter 9: On Dwelling.

ounce of cheese to us. Right before his own eyes and in the course of a few sentences of his writing, the magical *river of grain* changes from wheat to corn, from corn to maize, from maize to flour, and from flour to breadstuff. It moves and channels itself, both uphill and downhill, without any help from gravity (or any other force of nature), human beings, or elevating machines. It cannot be watched passively. One cannot be a spectator in front of this river. Like the teeming City of London, the river of grain must be *experienced*, bathed in, drunk down, even inhaled. "But endlessly pacing and flowing at my back I was aware of another river, a river of the blind eternally in pursuit of [its] immediate material object," Paul Valéry wrote. "This seemed to me no crowd of individual beings, each with his own history [...] rather I made of it – unconsciously, in the depths of my body, in the shaded places of my eyes – *a flux of identical particles*, equally sucked in by the same nameless void, their deaf headlong current pattering monotonously over the [London] Bridge."[18] But unlike dirty old congested London, the American river of grain – *liquid* in two senses of the word[19] – was both nourishing and cleansing. It sustained and even elevated the human body and soul.

And yet, despite his ecstatic embrace of the notion that the American heartland is divinely favored, Anthony Trollope had no illusions about the ability of Americans to

---

[18] *Choses tues*, published in Paris in 1930 and quoted in Walter Benjamin, *The Arcades Project*, p. 453.

[19] Both a physical substance and a financial asset. See William Cronon, *Nature's Metropolis: Chicago and the Great West, WW Norton*, 1991, p. 145: "By severing physical grain from its ownership rights, one could make it abstract, homogenous, *liquid*. If the chief symbol of the earlier marketing system was the sack whose enclosure drew boundaries around crop and property alike, then the symbol of Chicago's abandonment of those boundaries was the gold torrent of the elevator chute."

handle their awesome responsibility as "owners" of that land.
Or at least he no longer had illusions on that score. Once he
had personally experienced the river of grain flowing through
Buffalo, he "knew then what it is like for a country to
overflow with milk and honey, to burst with its own fruits,
and be smothered in its own riches." And so the secret he
discovered in Ceres' dusty bins was that America is both
divinely favored *and* cursed. In this double vision, America
will be or already is the New Canaan, a re-birth of the
Biblical Canaan (the "land flowing with milk and honey," the
"land of corn and wine"). And yet it will also drown or
already is drowning in its riches, not prospering because of
them.

Anthony Trollope certainly wasn't alone in thinking
that Buffalo's grain elevators, though firm and commodious,
were far from "delightful."[20] In the words of a journalist for
the *New York Times*, writing in 1872,

> Of all the ugly designs that business architectural
> minds [have] ever perpetrated an elevator is the
> most abominable. An elevator always looks to me
> like a great overgrown windmill, whose sails have
> been carried away in a gale of wind. Poor Buffalo
> is disfigured with no less than thirty-one of these
> eye-sores.[21]

In the words of a local journalist, writing in 1891, the
elevators in Buffalo were:

---

[20] According to Vitrivius's classic treatise, *The Ten
Books of Architecture*, all buildings need to be *firmitatis*,
utilitatis and *venustatis*.

[21] "Our State Institutions. – XVIII. The Buffalo Grain
Trade," *New York Times*, January 22, 1872.

indescribably ugly structures, which loom up along the harbor slips and shock the artistic eye with their hideously grotesque angularity and their utter lack of symmetry in their conformation. They rear their ungainly heads, high above the warehouse roofs and ship masts that break the sky line, like huge chunks of darkness set up, in a spirit of travestie [sic], by some mocking builder-daemon bent on setting at naught all regard for architectural ethics and producing the most horrible extreme to "a thing of beauty and a joy forever", in the way of an edifice to be seen in the whole wide world [...] These [are] nightmare buildings.[22]

Though several of these characterizations are clearly over-stated and designed to entertain a local audience,[23] we must

---

[22] "Ugly But Profitable: The Grain Elevators of Buffalo: Examples of Hideousness in Architecture – A Wonderful Branch of the City's Commerce – Its Inception and Development," *The Buffalo Commercial*, 2 April 1891, page 10. An echo of the phrase "ugly but profitable" appears in Frank Severance, *Picture Book of Earlier Buffalo* (Buffalo Historical Society, 1912), p. 46: Buffalo's elevators are "uncouth but potential piles."

[23] There were, of course, people who found the grain elevators to be inspiring, but their praises speak loudly in favor of the arguments of the elevators' detractors. For example, the author of "Our Buffalo Letter," published in *The American Architect*, No. 1, April 1870, p. 22, says: "We are deafened by the roar of their machinery, blinded and choked by their dust and chaff, with feelings of the most ecstatic bliss and inward satisfaction [...] To look upon their blank, unrelieved walls and box-like proportions, is 'a joy forever' to every Buffalonian's heart." Note that phrase "joy

not fail to see the "big picture" being painted here: if their builders are "mocking [...] daemon[s]," then the grain elevators must be more than merely monstrous and "indescribably ugly": they must also be evil.

If we compare the photograph that George Barker took of the entrance to Buffalo's harbor in 1883 and the anonymous illustration that was based upon it in 1885,[24] we see a clear slide towards darkness. In Barker's photograph, it is daytime, and the sky is partly sunny. There is plenty of light to see the words WATSON ELEVATOR written upon the immense, cupola-topped combination grain elevator and small island of that name, and to see that a smaller elevator (the unmarked Union Transfer Tower) stands upon dry land in the foreground. There is a lot of thick, dark smoke in the air, but it is clearly coming from the various steam-ships that are in the water. But in the illustration, it is a very cloudy day: neither "blue" (clear) sky nor sun can be seen. In this darkness, all one can see of the Watson Elevator is huge blurry slab of oddly shaped darkness (the Union has become part of it) from which black smoke is billowing and mixing with or causing the equally dark clouds in the sky. One is immediately put in mind of William Blake's "dark, satanic mills,"[25] if not the visions of Stephen Leacock, in which the "huge [grain elevator] system, complicated in its outline and ramifying in its relations, spread out from the Head of the

---

forever" is an allusion to the first line of John Keats' poem, *Endymion:* "A thing of beauty is a joy forever."

[24] Published under the title "Among the Elevators. From a photograph by George Barker, *Niagara Falls*," [sic] this illustration accompanied Jane Meade Welch's article, "The City Of Buffalo," published in *Harper's New Monthly Magazine* (July 1885), p. 197. See frontispiece.

[25] William Blake, "And did those feet in ancient time," 1804. See also D.H. Lawrence's bitter quip, made more than 100 years later: "The dark, satanic mills of Blake / How much more darker and more satanic they are now!"

Lakes to the confines of the grain country" can be viewed as "either a thing of beauty or of horror, a work of God or of the Devil, according to the type of mind you have."[26] In Joseph Pennell's untitled engraving of a grain elevator in Hamburg, Germany, dated 1914, one of these devilish things is brought to life. Here the grain elevator – a towering bottle-shaped block of darkness, equipped with four or five very long arm-like appendages (canal spouts?) and several other, thinner stalks that extend high above its head – is completely surrounded in smoke, clouds and darkness. At its feet, a tiny craft is being battered by dark waves.

Why are grain elevators satanic? Perhaps Charles Baudelaire gives us a clue.

> Commerce is *satanic* by its essence.
> Commerce is the already-made, available with the implication: *Give me more than I give you.*
> The spirits of all merchants are completely polluted.
> Commerce is *natural*, thus it is *squalid.*
> The least squalid of the merchants is the one who says: "Let's be virtuous so as to gain more money than the idiots who are vice-ridden."
> For the merchant, honesty itself is a financial speculation. Commerce is satanic because it is a form of egoism, the most base and the most vile.[27]

Grain elevators are satanic because they store colossal quantities of grain, which everyone needs to survive, and so they are the very embodiment of commerce's selfish needs to possess and to possess things in *surplus.*

---

[26] Stephen Leacock, *My Discovery of the West*, Boston and New York, 1937, pp. 80-81.

[27] *Mon cœur mis à nu* ("My Heart Laid Bare"), published 1887, my translation.

The anonymous author of "Ugly But Profitable: The Grain Elevators of Buffalo" added an element that was missing from Anthony Trollope's portrait of the monster: a comparison between grain elevators and the human body ("They rear their ungainly *heads*"). Rudyard Kipling drew this same parallel two years earlier when he spoke of the "high-shouldered, tea caddy grain elevators."[28] In 1918, the same image would come to the American poet Carl Sandburg, whose poem "Prairie" envisioned the "hunched shoulders" of the grain elevators in the American Midwest.[29]

Though they imply or are based on the erroneous idea that the human body is purely functional, that it "contains" no parts or organs that serve no essential function – what about earlobes, body hair, vestigial organs and appendages, nipples on men, *et. al*? – comparisons between grain elevators and human bodies are inevitable. On the one hand, artists and dreamers have long associated *houses* (assumed to be unornamented or at least reduced to their basic features) with the human body. For example, in *The Interpretation of Dreams,* Sigmund Freud writes:

> Indeed, Scherner believes – though Volkelt and others do not follow him here – that the dream-imagination has a certain favourite way of representing the whole organism, and that this is as a *house*. Fortunately, though, it does not seem to confine itself to this subject-matter for its representations; contrariwise, it can use large numbers of houses to designate one particular organ, for instance, a very long street of houses for the stimulus from the intestines. At other times

---

[28] *The Writings in Prose and Verse of Rudyard Kipling: Letters of Travel*, vol. 24 New York, 1920, p. 173.

[29] Carl Sandburg, *Cornhuskers* (Henry Holt & Co., New York), 1918.

particular parts of the house represent in reality particular parts of the body; for example, in a head-ache dream the ceiling of the room (which the dreamer sees covered with disgusting, toad-like spiders) represents the head. [...] I am acquainted with patients who have, it is true, preserved the architectonic symbolism of the body and the genitals [...] To them, pillars and columns signify legs (as in the *Song of Songs*);[30] every gateway reminds them of one of the body's orifices ('hole'); every water-supply pipe of the urinary apparatus; and so on.[31]

On the other hand, the jargon of the grain elevator business has long been sprinkled with such quaint, even childish, anthropomorphisms as "marine legs," "elevator boots" and "elevator heads." [32] If we put these two visions together, we

---

[30] "His legs are as pillars of marble, set upon sockets of fine gold" (Song of Songs, 5:15).

[31] Sigmund Freud, *Die Traumdeutung* (1899), translated by Joyce Crick (Oxford: London, 1999), pp. 72 and 259-260, respectively.

[32] Following Georg Simmel, we might say that designers and operators who anthropomorphize (parts of) grain elevators are not as they appear, that is, they are not simply men of science, who do their calculations according to certain "natural" laws (the laws of physics and economic rationality). No, they are also believers in myths. "The illusions in this sphere are reflected quite clearly in the terminology that is used in it," Simmel writes. "Although [...] this seems to be just a matter of terminology, it does lead astray those who think superficially in the direction of anthropomorphic misinterpretations, and it does show that the mythological mode of thought is also at home within the natural-scientific worldview." *Philosophie des Geldes*

get the dream-like, possibly nightmarish, image of the grain elevator as a Giant: a mythological being in human form, but possessing super-human size and strength. Since the grain elevator is a gigantic human form that *stands*, but does not *walk upon* its legs, let's call it a Colossus.

"Originally the word [colossus] has no implication of size," Jean-Pierre Vernant writes. "It does not designate, as it will later for accidental reasons, effigies of gigantic, 'colossal' dimensions. In Greek statue vocabulary [...] the term *kolossos*, of animate genre and of pre-Hellenic origin, is attached to a root *kol-*, which can be connected to certain place names in Asia Minor (Kolossai, Kolophon, Koloura) and which retains the idea of something [standing] erect, upright."[33] And so, to speak properly, *the modern grain elevator is a gigantic, evil Colossus.* "The demons are growing colossal," a German poet once said of modern times. "The horns on their heads draw blood from the sky."[34]

Following Thomas Hobbes, we might be tempted to say that the grain elevator, like the society that produced it, is an "Artificial Animal."

> Nature (the art whereby God hath made and governs the world) is by the art of man, as in many other things, so in this also imitated, that it can make an Artificial Animal. For seeing life is but a motion of Limbs, the begining whereof is in some principall part within; why may we not say, that all Automata (Engines that move themselves

---

(Leipzig, 1900), quoted in Walter Benjamin, *The Arcades Project* (Harvard, 1999), pp. 661-662.

[33] *Myth and Thought Among the Greeks* (1965; translated into English, London: 1983), p. 305.

[34] Georg Heym, "Demons of the Cities," in *Dictungen* (Munich, 1922), p. 19, quoted in Walter Benjamin, *The Arcades Project*, pp. 356-357.

by springs and wheeles as doth a watch) have an artificiall life? For what is the Heart, but a Spring; and the Nerves, but so many Strings; and the Joynts, but so many Wheeles, giving motion to the whole Body, such as was intended by the Artificer? Art goes yet further, imitating that Rationall and most excellent worke of Nature, Man. For by Art is created that great LEVIATHAN called a COMMON-WEALTH, or STATE, (in Latin CIVITAS) which is but an Artificiall Man; though of greater stature and strength than the Naturall, for whose protection and defence it was intended; and in which, the Soveraignty is an Artificiall Soul, as giving life and motion to the whole body; The Magistrates, and other Officers of Judicature and Execution, artificiall Joynts; Reward and Punishment (by which fastned to the seat of the Soveraignty, every joynt and member is moved to performe his duty) are the Nerves, that do the same in the Body Naturall; The Wealth and Riches of all the particular members, are the Strength; Salus Populi (the Peoples Safety) its Businesse; Counsellors, by whom all things needfull for it to know, are suggested unto it, are the Memory; Equity and Lawes, an artificiall Reason and Will; Concord, Health; Sedition, Sicknesse; and Civill War, Death. Lastly, the Pacts and Covenants, by which the parts of this Body Politique were at first made, set together, and united, resemble that Fiat, or the Let Us Make Man, pronounced by God in the Creation.[35]

---

[35] Thomas Hobbes, *Leviathan or the Matter, Forme, & Power of a Common-Wealth Ecclesiastic and Civill* (Andrew Crooke, 1651).

But unlike the "Leviathan," or the bearded giants in Francisco de Goya's paintings,[36] *the body of the grain elevator* isn't complete. It is an "artificiall man," but it is missing several organs or parts normally found in real human bodies and the imaginary bodies of Giants. The grain elevator has extremities (legs, boots, shoulders and a head), but no hands, no arms, no neck, no chest and no back. It apparently has a mouth and a stomach – Anthony Trollope said it "devours and continues to devour, till the corn within its reach has been swallowed, masticated and digested" – but it isn't clear if the elevator has a lower gastrointestinal tract, urinary tract or anus. It certainly doesn't "waste" anything.

And so what we have before us is not really a Giant (an extreme *exaggeration* of the human form), but a Monster (an extreme *deformation* of the human form). We might well say that the grain elevator is an architectural version of Frankenstein's monster: an immense, deformed creature, made out of a clever, even fiendish, mixture of human body parts and inanimate objects; a man-machine. Significantly, both monsters contain no extraneous parts whatsoever: their respective bodies, deformed and monstrously ugly though they might be, are completely devoted to their primary purposes: *to function*, in the case of the former; and *to live*, in the case of the latter.

The problem of what to do if an "Artificiall Man" turns into a Monster is in fact at the heart of the ancient legend of Coriolanus. Told in different forms by several different authors – Plutarch, in Volume I of *Plutarch's Lives* (75 C.E.); Litus Livius (aka Livy), in Book II of *The History of Rome* (28 B.C.E.); Niccolo Machiavelli, in his *Discourses on*

---

[36] See *The Colossus* (1808-1812), commonly but incorrectly attributed to Francisco de Goya, and *Saturn Eating His Children* (1819-1823), which was in fact painted by him.

Livy;[37] and William Shakespeare in *Coriolanus* (1600), among others[38] – this legend concerns the rise and fall of a great but tragic Roman soldier, who was celebrated for his great abilities, heroism and accomplishments in war, but hated for his arrogant contempt for the common people and their attempts to win political power. The bone of their contention: grain.

Plutarch reports that, after the Roman defeat of the Volscians, circa 490 B.C.E., "a great part of the country was left unsown and untilled, while the war gave no opportunities for importation from other countries. The demagogues, therefore, seeing that there was no corn in the market, and that even if there had been any, the people were not able to buy it, spread malicious accusations against the rich, saying that they had purposely produced this famine in order to pay off an old grudge against the people." There were riots, bread riots, in the city. "While this was the state of affairs at Rome, a large amount of corn arrived there, some of which had been bought in Italy, but most of it sent as a present from Sicily by Gelon the despot; which gave most men hopes that the famine would come to an end, and that the quarrel between the patricians and plebeians would, under these improved circumstances, be made up."

There was a spirited debate in the Senate. Should the gift be divided among the plebeians, each receiving their portion of grain *gratis*, for free? At what rate should the other grain be sold? A lowered ("normal") price would certainly silence the common people, who were suffering from widespread scarcities and famines, but it would also discourage them from returning to farming and raising crops of their own. Coriolanus advocated that the gift should be

---

[37] See *Discourses on Livy* (1551), Chapter 7, Book I.

[38] See also Heinrich Joseph von Collin in *Coriolan* (1804), which inspired Ludwig van Beethoven to compose *Overture C-minor, "Coriolan"* (1807).

kept by the government and that the other grain should not be sold at all, but kept in an official and secure storehouse, as a kind of ransom, until the commoners returned the rights and privileges they had won three years previously. It was precisely the extremism of this position and Coriolanus' refusal to modify it that galvanized the political opposition to him and eventually forced him into exile, where, embittered, he organized an army amongst his former enemies to fight against Rome. (Confronted by his mother, wife and children, he finally relented, only to be assassinated shortly thereafter. The Romans did not mourn his death.)

The key to understanding this story, I think, is the fable that one of Coriolanus' supporters, Menenius Agrippa, used to quiet an angry mob, in the midst of a bread riot, before the war against the Volscians had started. This is how the fable is presented in Plutarch, as translated by Aubrey Stewart and George Long:

> Once upon a time, said he [Menenius Agrippa], all the members revolted against the belly, reproaching it with lying idle in the body, and making all the other members work in order to provide it with food; but the belly laughed them to scorn, saying that it was quite true that it took all the food which the body obtained, but that it afterwards distributed it among all the members. "This," he said, "is the part played by the Senate in the body politic. It digests and arranges all the affairs of the State, and provides all of you with wholesome and useful measures."

This analogy between the human body and the body politic (a good example of what Michel Foucault has called "biopolitics") doesn't quite stand up (so to speak). Wouldn't it be more suitable, more flattering, if the Senate were represented by or compared with the head? Is not the head

the leader of the whole body, and the stomach a mere
follower? After all, the belly only "digests and arranges"
what is fed to it by the hands, under the direction of the head.
But in *this* fable, it is the (not lazy!) stomach that leads,
perhaps like an army, which supposedly travels on its
stomach.

Here is the same passage from Plutarch, as translated by
John Dryden:

> "It once happened," he said, "that all the other
> members of a man mutinied against the stomach,
> which they accused as the only idle,
> uncontributing part the whole body, while the rest
> were put to hardships and the expense of much
> labour to supply and minister to its appetites. The
> stomach, however, merely ridiculed the silliness
> of the members, who appeared not to be aware
> that the stomach certainly does receive the general
> nourishment, but only to return it again, and
> redistribute it amongst the rest. Such is the case,"
> he said, "ye citizens, between you and the senate.
> The counsels and plans that are there duly
> digested, convey and secure to all of you your
> proper benefit and support."

Here a nice pun on "digested" has been introduced: digested
by the stomach (physical processing), and digested by the
mind (intellectual understanding). And so, despite the fact
that it is still not the head of the body, the stomach has
"plans," and so the other members of the body (politic) need
not be alarmed.

In Livy (as translated by D. Spillan), the fable of the
belly is presented in a more elaborate form:

> "At a time when all the parts in the human body
> did not, as now, agree together, but the several

members had each its own scheme, its own language, the other parts, indignant that every thing was procured for the belly by their care, labour, and service; that the belly, remaining quiet in the centre, did nothing but enjoy the pleasures afforded it. They conspired accordingly, that the hands should not convey food to the mouth, nor the mouth receive it when presented, nor the teeth chew it: whilst they wished under the influence of this feeling to subdue the belly by famine, the members themselves and the entire body were reduced to the last degree of emaciation. Thence it became apparent that the service of the belly was by no means a slothful one; that it did not so much receive nourishment as supply it, sending to all parts of the body this blood by which we live and possess vigour, distributed equally to the veins when perfected by the digestion of the food." By comparing in this way how similar the intestine sedition of the body was to the resentment of the people against the senators, he [Menenius] made an impression on the minds of the multitude.

Once upon a time, the body was not ruled by the "agreement" provided by the head, but was in a state of anarchy and civil war. – Such a rapid evolution from Plutarch to Livy! Or, rather, such a growing desire to .distance the present from the past! The motivation seems clear: in the past, the (social) body was *suicidal*, that is to say, the other members were willing to starve the belly to the point that the whole body was threatened with death. And it wasn't the belly's retorts that convinced the other members to be patient, as in Plutarch, but the workings of a self-conscious mind: "Thence it became apparent." No retorts were made, and none were necessary. But to which part of the body did it become apparent? It could only have been the mind. Again, the fable fails to convince: I thought you said the head wasn't yet in control of the (social) body! Then how else could what was self-evident become apparent?

Significantly, perhaps, this fable doesn't appear at all in Machiavelli's version of the tragedy. It just wasn't relevant to his primary and sole concern, which was the importance of Coriolanus being put on trial instead of being killed by an angry mob, and so he simply dropped it from his extended summary of Livy.

In Shakespeare's *Coriolanus*, the fable of the belly plays an enlarged role. It is told in the play's very first scene. And, by virtue of the fact that a nameless "citizen" (identified only as "first citizen" in the stage directions) interrupts and prompts Menenius, the fable is told by two people, not one. Before and as Menenius comes onstage, this citizen says, among other things with which a modern audience might have strong sympathies:

> Let us kill him [Coriolanus] and we'll have corn at our own price. Is't a verdict? [...] We are accounted poor citizens, the patricians good. What authority surfeits on would relieve us; if they would yield us but the superfluity, while it was wholesome, we might guess they relieved us humanely; but they think we are too dear: the leanness that afflicts us, the object of our misery, is as an inventory to particularize their abundance; our sufferance is a gain to them. Let us revenge this with our pikes, ere we become rakes: for the gods know I speak this in hunger for bread, not in thirst for revenge [...] [The helms of state] ne'er cared for us yet: suffer us to famish, and their store-houses crammed with grain; make edicts for usury, to support usurers; repeal daily any wholesome act established against the rich, and provide more piercing statutes daily, to chain up

and restrain the poor. If the wars eat us not up,
they will; and there's all the love they bear us.
(Act I, Scene 1, lines 11-90.)

The contrast here isn't between a human body and the body
politic (between one abstraction and another), but between
classes of real people (supposedly) living within the same
social body. The poorer classes or, rather, the bodies of poor
people, are "lean" due to hunger, which is the cause of their
misery. Their only store-house is metaphorical: it is the sum
total of (the varieties of) their misery, which are "an
inventory to particularize their [the others'] abundance."
Significantly, the "first citizen" does not contrast the leanness
of the poor with the fatness of the bodies of the rich. He
doesn't not mention rich people's basic possessions or their
daily requirements (no matter how exaggerated), but only
their extra-corporeal superfluities, surpluses and "storehouses crammed with grain" that they selfishly and cruelly
will not share. If and/or when war comes, *it* will certainly
consume ("eat") the rich's surpluses. But, having no *real*
surpluses of their own, the poor will have to pay the price of
war with their very (real) bodies.

Menenius is foolish enough to try to retort such a
brilliant exposition with the fable of the belly, which even he
knows is "stale" (I.i.95).

There was a time when all the body's members
Rebell'd against the belly, thus accused it:
That only a gulf it did remain
I' the midst o' the body, idle and inactive,
Still cupboarding the viand, never bearing
Like labour with the rest, while the other
instruments
Did see and hear, devise, instruct, walk, feel,
And, mutually participate, did minister
Unto the appetite and affection common

Of the whole body. The belly answer'd – (I.i.99-
109)

Here Menenius is interrupted by the impatient first citizen
("What answer made the belly?") and quickly resumes his
story (note the continued exposition in verse, not prose).

> Sir, I say tell you. With a kind of smile,
> Which ne'ev came from the lungs, but even thus –
> For, look you, I may make the belly smile
> As well as speak – it tauntingly replied
> To the discontented members, the mutinous parts
> That envied his receipt; even so most fitly
> As you malign our senators for that
> They are not such as you. (I.i.110-118)

Menenius is again interrupted by the first citizen, but this
time in a very meaningful way. He heckles:

> Your belly's answer? [Is] what?
> The kingly-crowned head, the vigilant eye,
> The counselor heart, the arm our soldier,
> Our steed the leg, the tongue our trumpeter,
> With other muniments and petty helps
> In this our fabric, if that they – (I.i.118-123).

This interruption (a kind of expositional burp) calls attention
to what's been absent all along from this ancient fable: a
proper head atop the social body, not a stomach that has been
placed in charge, but a thinking head that rules over all the
members, even/especially the stomach. Clearly the citizen
who has interrupted thinks that the analogy between the
human body and the body politic is *corny* (he seems to have
heard it so often he can now rattle it off or imitate it without
difficulty), and that Menenius' fable is *monstrous* (it presents

us with an anthropomorphic representation, the "body politic," in which one member – the belly – can "smile as well as speak," as if it had a mouth of its own and was part of a body in its own right, that is to say, a body within the stomach of another body).

Before Menenius can resume, the citizen lets fly an insult against the belly: he sarcastically calls out that the other members "should by the cormorant belly be restrain'd, who is the sink o' the body" (I.i125). After order is restored, Menenius completes the fable.

> Your most grave belly was deliberate,
> Not rash like his accusers, and thus answer'd:
> 'True is it, my incorporate friends,' quoth he,
> 'That I receive the general food at first,
> Which you do live upon; and fit it is,
> Because I am the store-house and the shop
> Of the whole body: but, if you do remember,
> I send it through the rivers of your blood,
> Even in the court, the heart, to the seat of the brain;
> And, through the cranks and offices of man,
> The strongest nerves and small inferior veins
> From me receive that natural competency
> Whereby they live: and though that all at once,
> You, my good friends' – this says the belly, mark me –

"Ay, sir; well, well," the citizen calls out.

> 'Though all at once cannot
> See what I do deliver out to each,
> Yet I can make my audit up, that all
> From me do back receive the flour of all,
> And leave me but the bran.' What say you to 't?
> (I.i.131-150)

And so this double-voiced, hiccupping version of the fable has a punch line! And it's not a contemptuous retort to the other members: it's a bit of comic self-deprecation. Something like: "I give you flour, not just coarse wheat berries, and all I get to keep is the bran, that is to say, *shit*." (Note well the echo of this in Menenius' friendly caricature of Coriolanus's way of speaking: "Since he could draw a sword, and is ill school'd in bolted language; meal and bran together he throws without distinction" [III.i.320-322].) The joke disarms the citizen, who then says: "It was an answer: how apply you this?" [I.i.150]). This question allows Menenius to easily change both the subject at hand and the object of his deprecations ("What do you think [now], you, the big toe of this assembly?" [I.i.159]). And so, the monstrous image of a body within the stomach of another body (the "kingly crowned belly") is quietly and conveniently forgotten, and the hungry, riotous crowd is dispersed.

Chapter 6
The European Modernists

Given the unanimous conclusion that the grain elevators of the 19th century were monstrously ugly, one might reasonably expect that the same conclusion was reached in the next century, when grain elevators became larger, faster and dustier. But it wasn't: in fact, the "artistic eye" of the 20th century consistently found grain elevators to be beautiful, even sublime. Mind you: not just the allegedly "male" grain elevators of the 20th century (the rows of freestanding cylindrical tanks made out of steel or reinforced concrete), but also the putatively "female" grain elevators of the 19th (the dark and massive windowless enclosures).

We will have cause to wonder about this. What happened to the ugliness and monstrosity? What happened to the emotions that went along with those heated denunciations? Where did the feelings of panic, fear and dread go? Were they dispersed or displaced? It seems that they might have been suppressed by sheer willpower: "Everything that functions well, looks well," the German architect Bruno Taut asserts in one of five definitions of "the new movement" made in *Die Neue Baukunst in Europa und Amerika*. "We simply do not believe that anything can look unsightly and yet function well."[1]

The first person to praise *the grain elevator* (and not *a particular grain elevator*) was the architect and designer Walter Gropius. Born in Berlin in 1882, Gropius joined the *Deutscher Werkbund* (German Work Federation) in 1908, a year after the founding of this influential association of

---

[1]   1929, translated that same year as *Modern Architecture*, London: the Studio, p. 9.

product manufacturers, artists and architects who wished to "modernize" German capitalism and keep it competitive with the American variant. Other notable architects in this association were Peter Behrens (born in 1868), Charles-Edouard Jeanneret (born 1887) and Ludwig Mies van der Rohe (born 1886). Gropius stayed with the *Werkbund* until 1910, when he formed a partnership with Adolph Meyer. Between 1911 and 1913, they co-designed and built the Fagus shoe factory (Alfeld, Germany), which is commonly considered to be one of the very first "modernist" buildings in the world.

What made the *Faguswerk* modernist? It was built out of the newest building materials (glass, steel and reinforced concrete); the forms of the new buildings were simple (cubes and cylinders, no pitched roofs); and none of the buildings were elaborately adorned. Of course, one could say the exact same things about most of the "experimental" fireproof grain elevators built in Buffalo, Minneapolis and Montreal between 1897 and 1912. Indeed, just like them, the *Faguswerk* was a deliberate change from and a challenge to the dominant spatial practices of the day. In the case of the former, the custom was constructing grain bins out of wood and enclosing them in an ironclad warehouse; and, in the case of the latter, the custom was reviving the "classical" architectural styles of the past and combining them in an attempt to come up with something new. There was a key difference between them, of course: while the builders of modern grain elevators wanted to avoid buildings that caught fire and/or exploded, and didn't really care what the final results looked like, the designers of the modernist *Faguswerk* wanted to avoid buildings that took a lot of time and money to make, and then looked ugly or out of place when completed.

Like so many other dreamers in the years before World War I broke out, Gropius and Meyer believed that modern times were fundamentally different from previous eras: the availability of commercial electricity, the invention of structural steel, and the widespread use of machines had inaugurated an era of utopian dreams and confidence in the future. In *The Modern Urban Landscape*, Edward Relph argues that "Machine Age" utopianism began with the publication of Edward Bellamy's *Looking Backward* in 1888. Since Bellamy apparently saw himself as a socialist and a partisan of the "recently formulated philosophies of Karl Marx," as did William Morris, the author of *News From Nowhere*, published in 1890,[2] I see no reason why the era of machine-based utopianism wasn't inaugurated much earlier, in 1848, with the publication of Marx & Engel's "Manifesto of the Communist Party."

Gropius and Meyer were certainly among the first to explicitly state that the new, modern society would need, indeed, presupposed the existence of a truly modern architecture. (Perhaps the very first to do so were the Dutch group of "anti-revivalists" who designed the austere and largely unornamented Amsterdam Stock Exchange Building, built in 1890, and the members of the Vienna Secession Group, which included Adolph Loos and Otto Wagner, and built the Secession Building in 1895.) In practical terms, the advent of "modern architecture" meant that those who had been building in the style(s) of classical revivalism (the university-trained architects) needed to *step aside* and let others have their turn.

Which others? It depended on the social space to be worked. In the cities, the new buildings would be designed and constructed by "radical" industrial engineers (people like Gropius & Meyer, Peter Behrens, Adolf Loos, Louis Sullivan, and F.T. Marinetti, among others). But in the rural areas, the buildings, indeed, entire villages, would be designed and built by artists working in the vernacular and

---

[2] Edward Relph, *The Modern Urban Landscape*, Johns Hopkins University Press in 1987, pp. 11-15.

with other "conservative" craftsmen (Frank Lloyd Wright, Ebenezer Howard, the members of the German group *Die Brücke*, the Dutch *Jugendstil* movement, and the English Arts & Crafts movement). Note that modernism couldn't maintain this internal split after the rise of fascism in Italy in the 1920s and Germany in the 1930s. Fascism was rooted in the myths of the agrarian world, waged war against urban society (and thus modernism of Gropius' type), but rejected the vernacular and its craftsmen in favor of the cult of the great architect and neo-classical or "revivalist" forms of architecture.

As Walter Benjamin points out in *The Arcades Project*, the city-based conflict between engineers (builders) and architects (decorators) broke out a hundred years before the *Faguswerk* was built. Benjamin quotes two relevant passages from Siegfried Giedion's *Bauen in Frankreich* (*Building in France*): "The complicated construction (out of iron and copper) of the Corn Exchange in 1811 was the work of the architect Bellange and the engineer Brunet. It is the first time, to our knowledge, that architect and engineer are no longer united in one person"; and "The new 'architecture' has its origin in the moment of industry's formation, around 1830 – the moment of mutation from the craftsmanly to the industrial production process."[3] Thereafter, Benjamin himself says, "the rivalry begins between builder and decorator."[4] Of course, it was more than a mere "rivalry," which sounds personal and petty. This was a *class struggle* between two socio-economic groups (those who design and own the

---

[3] Walter Benjamin, *The Arcades Project*, translated by Howard Eiland and Kevin McLaughlin, Harvard University Press, pp. 154-155. Note that Benjamin doesn't mark the presence of the grain trade (in the form of the *Corn Exchange*) in the birth of this engineering-based "new 'architecture.'"

[4] Walter Benjamin, *The Arcades Project*, p. 4.

"master plans," and those who simply execute them), and also a *political struggle* between two forms of capitalism (one based on patronage and the aesthetic preferences of the elite; the other based on sales to clients who deal directly with the masses).

While the *Faguswerk* was being built, Gropius wrote a kind of manifesto. Entitled "Die Entwicklung Moderner Industriebaukunst" ("The Development of Modern Industrial Building"), it was eventually published in the 1913 edition of the *Jahrbuch des Deutschen Werkbundes* (*The Yearbook of the German Work Federation*).[5] Addressed to his fellow architects (his "generation"), Gropius' text does not in fact trace the development of modern industrial building, but celebrates the appearance in Germany of industrial buildings that "convey the impression of a coherent architecture which has at last discovered the right dress for the life style of the times and firmly rejects the romantic residue of past styles as cowardly and unreal." In a well-calculated gesture of self-interested praise, Gropius mentions buildings and corporate sponsors associated with his mentor, Peter Behrens.

There should be more of these buildings and more commissions given to young architects such as myself, Gropius is saying. According to Reyner Banham, Gropius tried to convince his audience by making "a close reading of recent writings on aesthetics and an appeal to the industrial prestige of the United States."[6] Those writings certainly included Wilhelm Worringer's highly influential book, *Abstraktion und Einfuhlung* [*Abstraction and Empathy*]

---

[5] A questionable English translation appears in *Form and Function: A Source Book for the History of Architecture and Design, 1890-1939*, edited by Tim and Charlotte Benton (London: 1975), pp. 53-55.

[6] Reyner Banham, *A Concrete Atlantis: U.S. Industrial Building and European Modern Architecture, 1900-1925* (MIT Press, 1986), p. 196.

(Berlin, 1908), which was in turn strongly influenced by the work of Alois Riegl. The "new art historical perceptions of Riegl and Worringer," which contributed to his own ideas about "monumental art," are praised at the very beginning of Gropius' lecture on *Monumentale Kunst und Industriebau* [*Monumental Art and Industrial Building*], delivered in April 1911 at the Folkwang Museum in Hagen.

According to Banham, "the illustrations noted for that lecture are reported to contain examples of *Silogebaude* [silo buildings] (though it is possible that this might have been a European example [not an American grain elevator] by, say, the well-known German concrete firm of Wayss und Freytag)."[7] In a footnote to this passage, Banham refers his readers to an example of a European grain elevator, but not necessarily the one depicted by Gropius: the elevator built in Wurms, Germany, in 1908 by the Wayss & Freytag Company, which held the rights to the original Monier patents for reinforced concrete. (Other sources say that the Wurms elevator was constructed in 1910, the same year Wayss & Freytag built an elevator in the *Osthafen* of Berlin; and that the only elevator-related work the company did in 1908 was to extend a grain elevator in Genoa, Italy, originally built by Francois Hennebique's firm in 1901.) Banham reproduces a photograph of the Wurms elevator in *A Concrete Atlantis.*[8]

---

[7] Reyner Banham, *A Concrete Atlantis*, p. 195.

[8] *A Concrete Atlantis*, p. 212. Here I must point out the existence of a glaring and persistent typographical mistake in Banham's book: the photo of the Wurms elevator wasn't originally published in 1929 in *Bauten der Arbeit und des Werkehrs*, but in *Bauten der Arbeit und des Verkehrs* (Buildings of Work and Transport). The "word" *Werkehrs* doesn't exist in German! Elsewhere in Banham's book, *Bauten der Arbeit und des Verkehrs* is identified as "the first volume of Walter Muller-Wulckow's *Blauen Bucher* series"

The Wurms elevator is an odd sight, at least to my American eyes. Though the building is a square and moderately tall structure, clearly built out of reinforced concrete (concrete bins set down upon a concrete basement), it is covered by a high-pitched, double-pediment roof that *might* have been built atop an American "country elevator" (a rural grain elevator built out of wood), but would *never* have been built atop any American elevator made out of concrete. On the first floor of the side of the elevator that faces us, there are other "revivalist" anomalies, including stone cladding, three neatly arched windows, and small panes of hand-made glass.

On the next page,[9] there is a photograph of a "grain silo, Barby an der Elbe, Germany, by Wayss und Freytag, 1922." As Banham notes, this reinforced-concrete grain elevator "has its ranked cylindrical bins arranged in two parallel rows in a format and under headworks that would have passed unnoticed in Minneapolis or Buffalo by that time. The notes below the caption remark specifically that its (allegedly) unconventional design is *nach amerikanischen Vorbild* – on the American model.[10]" Banham claims that this American-style grain elevator was a manifestation of "the parallel effect that the new American designs, particularly for elevators, were having on European engineers, presumably for 'objective' functional reasons that did not involve rhetoric or aesthetics."[11] I think it shows something else: it took German designers more than *fifteen years* to catch up with .what was going in Minneapolis and Buffalo in 1906. By 1929, when *Bauten der Arbeit und des Verkehrs* was

---

(p. 214). The full title was *Deutsche Baukunst der Gegenwart*, volume I, published in Leipzig by Langewiesche, 1929, and the photo appeared on page 60.

[9] Page 61 in the original and p. 213 in Banham.

[10] Reyner Banham, *A Concrete Atlantis*, p. 214.

[11] *Ibid.*

published, American designers had already created grain elevators that were *ten times bigger* than the one at Barby an der Elbe.

Was Gropius' interest in grain elevators (German or American) originally sparked by the work of Wayss & Freytag in 1908/1910? Quite possibly. Another possibility or "contributing factor," if you like, was the work of Hans Poelzig. Born in Berlin in 1869, Poelzig moved to Poland in 1903 to teach at and direct the Wroclaw Art Academy (*der Kunst- und Gewerbeschule Breslau*). While in Wroclaw, Poelzig designed several industrial structures, including a *Getreidesilo* that was built in the Markthalle of Lublin, Poland, in 1911.[12]

Because of Lublin's longstanding cultivation of hops, it is quite likely that Poelzig's "grain silo" was designed for the storage of this key ingredient in the making of beer. From what I can see in the "virtual" tour of Lokietek Square offered by the City of Lublin on its official website, this buildings still stands, and resembles other German granaries constructed before (and sometimes after) 1930: a tall building that resembles a church or a house, complete with highly pitched roof, but no windows.

As for Gropius' inspirations among contemporary theorists of art: Wilhelm Worringer's *Abstraction and Empathy* was an attempt to show that "modern aesthetics, which proceeds from the concept of empathy, is inapplicable to wide tracts of art history" – that is to say, to the art made by "savage," non-European peoples, both in the ancient past and in the present – because this aesthetics fails to account for art that proceeds from mankind's "urge to abstraction." Modern aesthetics can only become a truly "comprehensive aesthetic system" when the two forms of *Kunstwollen*

---

[12] Note that no such building is mentioned in Julius Posener's *Hans Poelzig: Reflections on His Life and Work* (MIT Press, 1992).

(artistic will) are brought together into their proper "antithetical relation." Worringer declares: "Just as the urge to empathy as a pre-assumption of aesthetic experience finds its gratification in the beauty of the organic, so the urge to abstraction finds its beauty in the life-denying inorganic, in the crystalline or, in general terms, in all abstract law and necessity." While empathetic art finds itself "in relation to the cosmos, in relation to the phenomena of the external world" and "inclines towards the truths of organic life, that is, toward naturalism in the higher sense," abstract art embodies "the suppression of life," the "exclusion of life," and "the self-alienative impulse." In sum, abstract art "seeks to suppress precisely that in which the need for empathy finds its satisfaction."[13]

The stunning ignorance, arrogance and racism of these apparently enlightened positions on non-European primitive art seem to have escaped notice because they are disguised by a "psychology" that is tautologically based upon "scientific" examinations of inanimate works of art, and not on personal contact with the actual human beings and societies who made them. "The extent to which the urge to abstraction has determined artistic volition we can gather from actual works of art," Worringer writes, echoing Alois Riegl, who was able to reach definitive "conclusions" (over-reaching generalizations) about the art and psychology of the ancient Egyptians based upon his examinations of textiles discovered in an Austrian museum collection.[14] "We shall then find that the artistic volition of savage peoples, in so far as they possess any at all, then the artistic volition of all primitive epochs of art and, finally, the artistic volition of certain culturally developed [modern-day] Oriental peoples,

---

[13] Translation in *Art in Theory*, p. 66-68.

[14] cf. *Die ägyptischen Textilfunde im Österreicher Museum* [*The Egyptian Textile Discovery at the Austrian Museum*], 1889.

exhibit this abstract tendency," Worringer claims. "Thus the urge to abstraction stands at the beginning of every art and in the case of certain peoples at a higher level of culture remains the dominant tendency."[15]

In Worringer's mind, "savages peoples" – *all* savage peoples – are mentally deranged. "We might describe this state [of mind] as an immense spiritual dread of space [...] Comparison with the physical dread of open places, a pathological condition to which certain people are prone, will perhaps better explain what we mean by this spiritual dread of space [...] Tormented by the entangled inter-relationship and flux of the phenomena of the outer world, such peoples were dominated by an immense need for tranquility [...] Their most powerful urge was, so to speak, to wrest the object of the external world out of its natural context, out of the unending flux of being, to purify it of all its dependence upon life, i.e., of everything about it that was arbitrary, to render it necessary and irrefragable, to approximate it to its absolute value."[16]

This "theory of modern art" exerted a powerful influence, not only on Walter Gropius' early texts, but also directly or indirectly on Filippo Tommaso Marinetti's "The Foundation and Manifesto of Futurism" (1909), Umberto Boccioni's "Futurist Painting: Technical Manifesto" (1910), Franz Marc's "The 'Savages' of Germany" (1912) and August Macke's "Masks" (1912) – all of which praise and celebrate both "abstraction" and the "neo-savages" of the emerging modernist movement. Let us also include here the Russian artist Aleksandr Shevchenko, who in 1913 –

---

[15] *Form and Function: A Source Book for the History of Architecture and Design, 1890-1939*, edited by Tim and Charlotte Benton (London: 1975), pp. 67-68.

[16] *Art in Theory, 1900-2000: An Anthology of Changing Ideas*, edited Charles Harrison & Paul Wood, Blackwell Publishing, 2003, p. 68.

influenced by Marinetti, not Gropius – declared himself to be favor of "the simple, unsophisticated beauty of the *lubok*, the severity of the primitive, the mechanical precision of construction, nobility of style, and good color brought together by the creative hand of the artist-ruler – that is our password and our slogan."[17] *Lubki* were posters that were "primitive in content, and aimed at a wide and tasteless audience."[18]

Two aspects of Worringer's theory are unappealing to me. First and foremost, it quite simply has everything backwards. The "savages" *aren't* the ones who fear and dread nature, who are alienated from it and from themselves, who obey "law" and "necessity," and who "deny" life and try to "exclude" and "suppress" it in their art. It is the allegedly "civilized" peoples of Europe who suffer from such severe psycho-social problems! After all, "civilized" invaders from Europe exterminated hundreds of millions of "savages" all over the world between the "discovery" of America in 1492 and the publication of *Abstraction and Empathy* in 1908, *not* the other way around. Second, the rapid and widespread acceptance of Worringer's theory boded ill, even evil, for Europe's future. What would things be like when the allegedly "civilized" people of Europe decided to start acting like savages? "We will sing of great crowds excited by work, by pleasure, and by riot," Marinetti wrote in 1909. "We will sing of the multicoloured, polyphonic tides of revolution in the modern capitals."[19] But what if tides of *counter-*revolution came to Moscow, Rome and Munich? What if

---

[17] "Neo-Primitivism: Its Theory, Its Potentials, Its Achievements," in *Russian Art of the Avant Garde*, edited by John E. Bowlt, Thames and Hudson, 1976, p. 45.

[18] Edward J. Brown, *Mayakovsky: A Poet in the Revolution*, Princeton, 1973, p. 110.

[19] *Art in Theory, 1900-2000*, edited Charles Harrison & Paul Wood, p. 148.

Edward Bellamy's machine-based utopianism was hijacked or recuperated by Russian bureaucratic socialism, Italian fascism or German National Socialism? Keep singing the same song? Kill the "savages" *inside* European society, as one had done previously with the "savages" who were outside of it?

In addition to referring to and summarizing "recent writings on aesthetics," Walter Gropius tried to sell the idea of modern architecture by making an "appeal to the industrial prestige of the United States."[20] Gropius' reference to America comes at the start of the last paragraph of "The Development of Modern Industrial Building": "Compared to the rest of Europe, Germany seems to have taken a considerable stride ahead in the field of artistic factory design, but in America, the Motherland of Industry, possesses some majestic original constructions which outstrip anything of a similar kind in Germany."[21] Note well that the translation that appears in the English-language version of Siegfried Giedion's *Space, Time and Architecture* is both different and obviously much better: "In comparison with the other countries of Europe, Germany seems to have gone far ahead in the field of factory design. But in America, the motherland of industry, there are great industrial structures which, in their unconscious majesty, are superior to even our best German buildings of that type."[22]

One can easily imagine why America could be defined as the "motherland of industry." Not only were the inventions and products of American industries well-made, durable and relatively inexpensive, but "the Americans" themselves were

---

[20] Reyner Banham, *A Concrete Atlantis*, p. 196.

[21] As translated in *Form and Function*, p. 54, and repeated by Reyner Banham, *A Concrete Atlantis*, p. 202.

[22] Siegfried Giedion, *Space, Time and Architecture*, German original, 1941, published by Harvard University Press, 1976, p. 343.

widely praised for their industriousness. With the exception of the Civil War, the Americans had *apparently* managed to avoid the "labor problems" – the sabotage, strikes, riots, insurrections and revolutions – that had beset European capitalism since the 1810s. How did they manage to do this? It wasn't simply a matter of their famous "protestant work ethic." It also had to do with the way American employers treated their workers. In particular, the way in which they designed and built their factories. In his 1911 lecture at Folkwang Museum, Gropius summarized, not so much the reality of what had been accomplished in America, but the latest propaganda from management concerning the Americanized workplace:

Work must be established in palaces that give the workman, now a slave to industrial labor, not only light, air, and hygiene, but also an indication of the great common idea that drives everything. Only then can the individual submit to the impersonal without losing the joy of working together for the common good previously unattainable by a single individual. This awareness in every worker could even ward off the kind of social catastrophe that seems to be brewing daily in our present economic system. Farsighted managers have long known that with the satisfaction of individual workers, the common work spirit also grows, and with it the efficiency of the whole plant. The sophisticated calculations of the industrialist will take all profitable steps to relieve the deadening monotony of factory work and alleviate its constraints. That is, he will attend not only to light, air, and cleanliness in the design of his buildings and work spaces, but will also take

cognizance of those basic sentiments of beauty
that even uneducated workers possess.[23]

Banham says that these lines "embrac[e] all the liberal and
progressive viewpoints on trade, industry, and design then in
good currency."[24] But the motivations for espousing such
viewpoints weren't "economic" or humanitarian in nature,
but political: from the perspective of the State, it is cheaper to
have companies pay their workers *five dollars a day* (as
Henry Ford starting to do just a few months after Gropius'
article was published) than it is for both the State and the
corporate sector to suffer the wrath of hungry, angry mobs.

When Gropius mentioned "America, the Motherland of
Industry," he had specific examples of its *Majestat* in mind:
"The compelling monumentality of the Canadian and South
American grain elevators [*Getreidesilos*], the coaling bunkers
[*Kolensilos*] built for the leading railway companies and the
newest work halls of the great North American industrial
trusts can almost bear comparison with the work of the
ancient Egyptians in their overwhelming monumental power.
Their unique individuality is so unmistakable that the
meaning of the structure becomes abundantly clear to the
passer-by."[25] In the Harvard translation: "The grain elevators
of Canada and South America, the coal conveyors of great
railway lines, and the more modern industrial plants of North
America are almost as impressive in their monumental power
as the buildings of ancient Egypt. They present an
architectural composition [*ein architektonisches Gesicht*] of

---

[23] Quoted in Banham, *A Concrete Atlantis*, pp. 198-199.
[24] Banham, *A Concrete Atlantis*, pp. 201-202.
[25] *Form and Function*, p. 54, and Reyner Banham, p. 202.

such exactness that to the observer their meaning [*der Sinn des Gehauses*] is forcefully and unequivocally clear."[26]

But these examples of "monumental" American industrial buildings were rather vague ("Which *particular* grain elevators in Canada and South America?"). The half-hearted comparison with "the buildings of ancient Egypt" (presumably the Great Pyramids of Gizeh, built around 2600 B.C.E.) only confused things ("How can these grain elevators be thoroughly modern *and* comparable to now-ruined ancient structures?"). There were no illustrations in sight – due to limited funds, they had been printed en bloc on the pages that *preceded* Gropius' essay – and so the reader had to continue on, with only his or her imagination as a guide.

To conclude the paragraph and the text as a whole, Gropius stated: "But the impact of these buildings does not depend on their sheer material size alone. That is certainly not where to look for an explanation of their monumental originality. It seems to lie rather in the fact that American builders have retained a natural feeling [*naturliche Sinn*] for large compact forms fresh and intact. Our own architects might take this as a valuable hint and refuse to pay any more attention to those fits of historicist nostalgia and other intellectual fancies under which European creativity still labors [*truben*, literally "clouds up"] and which frustrate [*im Wege*, "lead astray"] our true artistic naiveté [*kunstlerischer Naivitat*]."[27] Here the Harvard version isn't very good: "The natural integrity of these buildings resides not in the vastness of their physical proportions – herein the quality of a monumental work is certainly not to be sought – but in their designers' independent and clear vision of these grand, impressive forms. They are not obscured by sentimental

---

[26] *Form and Function*, p. 343. Note that *der Sinn des Gehauses* literally means "the meaning of the housing."

[27] *Form and Function*, p. 55, and Reyner Banham, p. 202.

reverence for tradition nor by other intellectual scruples which prostrate our contemporary European design and bar true artistic originality."[28]

This is Worringer's influence again: instead of locating and simply *asking* the designers of these buildings about their "vision" of their forms and their attitudes towards "tradition" and "other intellectual scruples," Gropius chose to engage in the following irrefutable and quite false tautology: *monumental and abstract structures such as grain elevators, coal conveyors and modern industrial plants could only be built by savages, who, despite their lack of consciousness, obviously retain the very things we moderns have lost, which is why we haven't managed to make such structures on our own.*

By far the strongest part of Gropius' sales pitch was the group of reprinted photographs that "accompanied" it (these reprints were in fact printed separately, and not intermixed, as I have mentioned, and were published with inadequate captions).[29] There were five images of large American factories, and nine images of *Kanadischer und Sud-amerikanischer Getreidesilos* (Canadian and South American grain silos). All fourteen images were drawn from Gropius'

---

[28] *Form and Function*, p. 343.

[29] This split between image and caption has remained a permanent feature of the discourse on grain elevators. For a very recent example, see "Saving Buffalo's Untold Beauty: the Home to Some of the Greatest American Architecture Tries to Balance the Past with the Future," written by Nicolai Ouroussoff and published by the *New York Times* (as the cover story for the Sunday "Arts & Leisure" section) on 16 November 2008: the Marine "A" grain elevator is depicted by a very large color photograph, but the caption simply refers to "grain silos," which – the article itself goes on to say – became "architectural pilgrimage sites for European modernists like Erich Mendelsohn and Bruno taut, who saw them as the great cathedrals of Modernity."

personal collection. Winfried Nerdinger claims that Gropius' began collecting such images in 1911 at the request of Karl-Ernst Osthaus, who was going to curate an exhibit called *"Der west-deutsche Impuls 1900-1914"* at the Museum zwischen Jugendstil und Werkbund.[30] According to Reyner Banham, "Gropius corresponded for a year with sources in the United States and Canada for illustrations for the 1913 article [...] The pictures seem to have come largely from the American concrete industry, a term which for convenience may be taken to include the offices of the various [Louis] Kahn operations in Detroit and of the Atlas Portland Cement Company."[31] But it is clear that there must have been other sources.

In a footnote,[32] Banham himself reports that the photograph of the Bunge y Born Elevator in Buenos Aires (see below) was originally published in *The Northwestern Miller*.[33] Mark Jarzombek says that this photo was reprinted in the *Illustrite Zeitung* in 1909, which is perhaps where Gropius saw it.[34] As I first pointed out in 1993, the "photograph" that depicted the Dakota and Great Eastern Elevators was actually a brightly colored picture postcard that was printed in 1903 by *The Buffalo Evening News*.[35] This particular postcard – as well as postcard pictures of the Great Northern Elevator in Buffalo, the Concrete Elevator in

---

[30] *The Architect Walter Gropius*, Bauhaus-Archiv, expanded 1996 edition, p. 9.

[31] Reyner Banham, *A Concrete Atlantis*, p. 195.

[32] Reyner Banham, *A Concrete Atlantis*, p. 257.

[33] *The Northwestern Miller* 56: 21 (November 25, 1903): 1156.

[34] "The Discourses of a Bourgeois Utopia 1904-1908, and the Founding of the Werkbund," *Rethinking German Modernism*, National Gallery of Art exhibition catalogue, 1996, p. 131.

[35] "Walter Gropius and Grain Elevators: Misreading Photographs," *History of Photography*, Autumn 1993, p. 306.

Minneapolis, and two huge 19th-century-style grain elevators in Chicago operated by the Armour Grain Company – are reproduced in *American Architecture: A Vintage Postcard Collection.*[36]

A total of eleven grain elevators can be seen in Gropius' *Jahrbuch* illustrations. Half of them were in fact built in the United States. There's the Dakota and Great Eastern Elevators, built out of steel in Buffalo, New York, in 1901; the Washburn-Crosby Complex, built out of tile and reinforced concrete in Buffalo between 1903 and 1909; a Washburn-Crosby elevator made out of reinforced concrete in Minneapolis, Minnesota; a reinforced-concrete elevator operated by the Baltimore and Ohio Railroad in Baltimore, Maryland; the Grand Trunk Pacific Elevator, built out of steel in Montreal, Canada, in 1903; the Grand Trunk Pacific Elevator, built out of reinforced concrete in Thunder Bay, Canada, between 1908-1910; an elevator in Buenos Aires, Argentina (an immense tile elevator, supposedly designed by a European engineer, built for the Bunge y Born company in 1904, and demolished by the local government in 1998); two colossal elevators made out of steel at Bahia, Argentina (possibly designed by John S. Metcalf, who designed Montreal's Grand Trunk Pacific Elevator); and an unknown reinforced-concrete elevator made somewhere, Gropius believes, in "South America."

It seems that one of the images in Gropius' collection didn't make the cut. Supposedly depicting a very large *Amerikanischer Getreidesilo*, this image is actually a painting that must have been based upon a photograph. The tip-off is the "handling" of the clouds in the sky above the elevator.[37]

---

[36] Edited by Luc Van Malderen, Australia, 2000, pp. 31 and 66-67.

[37] See *The Architect Walter Gropius*, an exhibition catalogue, edited by Winfried Nerdinger, Bauhaus-Archiv, 1985, expanded 1996 edition, p. 10.

It would also appear that Gropius had a favorite grain elevator picture: the one of Montreal's Grand Trunk Pacific Elevator, which was used in at least one public exhibition.[38]

Though all eleven of Gropius' grain elevators were built after 1900, they hardly presented a coherent view of "modern" grain elevator design as it was practiced in North and South America in the early 1910s. The period between 1906 and 1912 was an experimental one, in which grain bins were made out of several different building materials (tile, brick, steel or reinforced concrete). As late as 1912, when the Pennsylvania Railroad erected the Girard Point Elevator along the Schuylkill River in Philadelphia, 19th-century style grain elevators (big windowless houses clad in corrugated iron) were still being built in the Motherland of Industry.[39] Freestanding tanks made out of reinforced concrete only came to be "universally" accepted *after* 1912. It is precisely this experimentation, this sense of *transition*, which is captured by Gropius' pictures: we see both freestanding cylindrical tanks (some made of tile, some made of steel, some made of concrete) and colossal structures that enclose their (hidden) bins within walls of steel or ironclad wood. And that's a serious problem or, rather, it is the central

---

[38] See image captioned "Northern American grain silos," in *The Walter Gropius Archive*, Vol. 1, an illustrated catalogue, edited by Winfried Nerdinger, Harvard University Press, 1990, p. 10, plate 2.8.

[39] See postcard captioned "Turret-Deck Steamer Loading Grain for Export, Girard Point Elevator, Schuylkill River," reproduced in John Mayer, *Workshop of the World* (Oliver Evans Press, 1990). There was also a large elevator in Port Richmond operated by the Philadelphia & Reading Railroad, but "at no time" during War War I "was the operation of the elevator railroad facilities to meet the prompt disposal of grain to vesslers," says E.J. Cleave in *Philadelphia in the World War, 1914 to 1919* (New York, 1922), p. 506.

problem with what Gropius is trying to do. As a matter of fact, these grain elevators *do not* "have an architectonic face of such exactness that the clear meaning of their housings strike the inspector with convincing force" (my translation). The clear meaning of "their housings" [*des Gehauses*] can only be ascertained by someone 1) who has actually visited these buildings "in person," and 2) who has had access to an "expert," that is, someone who knows how the damn things work.

The plain fact is *some* of Gropius' grain elevators are not or do not have "housings" of any kind: they are freestanding tanks and independent workhouses. Furthermore, some of these freestanding tanks are actually "outer" grain bins, not fully formed cylindrical tanks, which is what they appear to be from the outside. At grain elevators where the grain bins *are* in fact enclosed in a "house," the "observer" or "inspector" doesn't actually see *Getreidesilos*, but the walls that protect the silos and the various types of machines that are required for the enterprise to work.

At some of Gropius' grain elevators, for example, the Grand Trunk Pacific Elevator in Thunder Bay, Canada, and the unknown elevator somewhere in South America, these machines are installed in tall structures of their own ("workhouses"). At other grain elevators, for example, the Dakota in Buffalo and the Washburn-Crosby in Minneapolis, the workhouses are built on top of the bin-structure and so have been called "headhouses." The machines that actually elevate the grain – the "grain elevators" themselves – are typically located in the workhouse, but thy can also be located in the headhouse, which must contain special roof-top towers to accommodate each one (as at the incredible steel elevators built in Montreal and Bahia, Argentina), or in marine towers, which – in the case of the Dakota – are actually *buildings on wheels.*

According to the Oxford English Dictionary, a grain elevator is a "machine used for raising corn or flour to an upper storey." The O.E.D. goes on to explain that, in American English, a "grain elevator" is a large building (containing one or more elevating machines) used for the storage of grain. At least in 19th-century America, "grain elevator" was shorthand for "grain elevating, transfer and storage warehouse." And so, in Anglo-American English, a "grain elevator" is an unusual hybrid, both architecturally and linguistically: both a grain-elevating machine and the architectural complex that houses it; both the part and the whole.

Not surprisingly, this hybridization is difficult to capture in languages other than English. In German, for example, "grain elevator" is *Getreidesilo* (grain silo); *Getreidespeicher* or *Kornspeicher* (grain container); one never says *Getreideaufzug* (*aufzug* means "elevator," and is exclusively reserved for *passenger* elevators). I have seen references to *Getreide-Elevatoren*, but not often. And so, when Reyner Banham explains in *A Concrete Atlantis: U.S. Industrial Building and European Architectural Modernism, 1900-1925* (Cambridge: MIT Press, 1986) that "what makes a grain elevator a grain elevator is not that it occupies a particular building form, but it has machinery for raising the grain to the top of the storage vessels," the German translation by Kyra Stromberg renders "grain elevator" as *Getreidespeicher*![40]

But this same inability to distinguish clearly between the machine and the building that houses it also affects those poets, painters, photographers and other dreamers who remain on the *outsides* of these uncanny machine-buildings, and do not venture inside, which is precisely where most of the machines (and the grain itself) are housed. As the French sociologist Henri Lefebvre points out in *La production de*

---

[40] *Das gebaute Atlantis: Amerikanische Industrie bauten und die Fruhe Moderne in Europa*, Basel: Birkhauser Verlag, 1990, p. 109.

l'espace,[41] the difficulty here isn't limited to grain elevators and isn't so much cultural, linguistic or perceptual as it is spatial. The movement from *silo* to *elevator* requires a change in or deepening of one's understanding of space "itself." A grain silo need only be 'conceived of' for it to be known and understood. It may be *helpful* to see photographs of a silo, perceive its form, and locate it in physical space; and it might be *nice* to actually visit and experience a silo; but none of this is really necessary. But the same cannot be said for a grain elevator, which must be experienced first-hand, in person, to be "known." If one relies on photographs, one inevitable makes silly mistakes that could have been easily avoided.

Unlike grain silos, which embody and encourage a simple opposition between the container (silo) and what is contained (grain), the walls of grain elevators both contain and are pierced by the machines housed "inside." Unlike grain silos, which can be full, empty or half-full/half-empty, grain elevators are *never* empty, even when there is no grain inside them. The elevator complex or "assemblage" is always already full of silos and machines. Finally, unlike grain silos, whose inner space is homogenous and can easily be sub-divided into smaller compartments of homogenous space, grain elevators contain a heterogeneous space of silos and machines that can't be easily or consistently be sub-divided.

In addition to being a simple container, a silo is self-contained. It can be placed virtually anywhere, and can literally "stand alone." To function, a silo doesn't need, involve or connect to anything else: it just needs to be filled with or emptied of grain. But like the commodity itself, a grain elevator cannot "stand alone." Lefebvre writes,

---

[41] Henri Lefebvre, French original 1974, translated by Donald Nicholson-Smith, *The Production of Space*, Blackwell, 1991.

As for the commodity in general, it is obvious that kilograms of sugar, sacks of coffee beans and meters of fabric cannot do duty as the material underpinning of its existence. The stores and warehouses where these things are kept, where they wait, the ships, trains and trucks that transport them – and hence the routes used – have also to be taken into account [...] It has [also] to be remembered that these objects constitute relatively determinate networks or chains of exchange within a space. The world of commodities would have no 'reality' without such moorings or points of insertion [in space], or without their existing as an ensemble. Without the 'space' of the commodity (containers, warehouses, routes and means of transport), there is no commodity.[42]

The grain elevator is embedded in, works with and depends upon a wide variety of pre-existing networks – sources of grain, grain markets, transportation routes and the vehicles that travel them, communication hubs, financial institutions, labor pools and energy sources – which in turn means that a grain elevator is only built and operated at certain carefully chosen places and at certain fortuitous times.

The single worst instance in which Walter Gropius misread one of the photographs he was reprinting was the Washburn-Crosby elevator in Buffalo, New York. Reyner Banham devotes more than ten pages to the various ways in which the Washburn-Crosby contradicted Gropius' claims about it.[43] The *Jahrbuch* picture shows a total of three interconnected but very different groups of cylindrical grain tanks: the first was built out of tile by the Barnett-Record

---

[42] Henri Lefebvre, *The Production of Space*, p. 403.
[43] Reyner Banham, *A Concrete Atlantis*, pp. 143-154.

Company in 1903; the second and third were built out of reinforced concrete by the James Stewart Engineering Company (both in 1909). Unlike the other two, which are surmounted by a very long horizontal gantry, the third group of tanks is attached to a workhouse that is fully *three times the size* of the first group (the gantry coming from it "hits" this colossal workhouse at mid-section). A fourth group of grain tanks and a very unusual marine tower were added by James Stewart's company in 1912, the year before that Gropius' *Jahrbuch* essay was published.[44] There were more additions at Washburn-Crosby in 1922 (a new flour mill that nearly hid the old tile bins from sight, and a second marine tower that could be moved along the dock between the new mill and the very tall workhouse that had been built in 1909) and again in 1925 (an extension of the grain tanks built in 1913).

Banham concludes: "The result of all this activity, as complex and as additive/subtractive as the work on a Gothic cathedral, is a structure that is conspicuously deficient in the kind of classical or functional 'clarity' that appealed to a Gropius or a Le Corbusier [...] Most long-standing complexes that have survived changes of function, trading patterns, or productive technology will obviously present a similarly disorderly appearance to Gropius' hypothetical

---

[44] "James Stewart and Company recently erected a marine tower for the Washburn-Crosby Company of Buffalo, New York [...], cylindrical in form and 160 feet in height, equipped with a marine leg and by far the fastest on the great lakes [*sic*], being able to unload grain at an average speed of 22,000 bushels per hour. The tower also contains automatic scales and delivers the grain direct to the company elevators by means of a conveyor belt running through a tunnel." Barney I. Weller, "Concrete Elevators," *Proceedings of the Ninth Annual Convention, held at Pittsburg, Pennsylvania, December 10-14, 1912*, Vol. IX (National Association of Cement Users, 1917), p. 343.

passerby, though they usually make perfectly good sense to those who manage and work in them."[45]

Walter Gropius didn't need to know anything about grain elevators to accomplish his purpose, which was simply to cause a sensation. Which he did. After the publication of "The Development of Modern Industrial Building," his own career as an architect and designer took off. In 1918, Gropius became the director of the Weimar School of Art and later the founder and director of the Bauhaus. His text from 1913 quickly found a wide audience among other European modernist architects, including Erich Mendelsohn, Charles-Edouard Jeanneret, and Moisei Ginzburg, among others. The images that accompanied the *Jahrbuch* essay were reprinted again and again in the 1910s and 1920s. Even if Gropius' readers or the people who looked at these images had never seen a grain elevator in person, didn't know how one worked, or couldn't clearly see what one looked like from the reprinted photos, they could still imagine a general and purely mythological resemblance between this modern American colossus (a simple but huge box or cylinder, it hardly mattered) and its reputed ancient Egyptian predecessor (a simple but huge pyramid). And that was enough.

Here's the myth of the early Gropius in the words of Siegfried Giedion: "One of the [*Deutscher Werkbund*] yearbooks bore the title 'Art in Industry and Trade' (1913) and displayed pictures of the American grain silos and factories, which up till then no one had considered anything other than mere containers of grain or places of work. Walter Gropius was the first to proclaim their 'unacknowledged majesty' far superior to anything of the kind in Germany. For a whole year he wrote to Canada and the United States for materials which, in the 1913 yearbook, he presented together with an article on 'The development of modern industrial architecture' where he openly stated that the 'monumental

---

[45] Reyner Banham, *A Concrete Atlantis*, p. 154.

power' of the grain silos of North America 'can stand comparison with the constructions of ancient Egypt.' "[46]

Erich Mendelsohn was the first European architect to share Walter Gropius' enthusiasm for American grain elevators, but he often isn't given his due. For example, Reyner Banham's *A Concrete Atlantis* offers no sustained discussion of his writings, though it carefully examines those of Gropius, "Le Corbusier" (Charles-Edouard Jeanneret), and even Moisei Ginzurg, whom Banham describes as a man with a "fundamentally ordinary mind."[47] Perhaps Banham shared the aesthetic prejudices of Philip Johnson and Henry-Russell Hitchcock, who excluded Mendelsohn from the exhibition called "The International Style: Architecture Since 1922" (organized by the Museum of Modern Art in New York in 1932) on the grounds that he was an expressionist, not a functionalist.

Other factors contributed to Mendelsohn's marginalization. Born in 1887 in East Prussia (Olsztyn, Poland), he settled in Berlin after World War I, but didn't teach at the Bauhaus and wasn't part of Gropius' circles until 1924, when the two of them (plus Mies van der Rohe) co-founded a progressive architectural group called *Der Ring*. Though inspired by American industrial buildings, which he too found to be "primeval," Mendelsohn felt no need to associate them with ancient Egyptian architecture, nor did he imagine himself to be some sort of neo-primitive. Mendelsohn wasn't interested in preventing what Gropius had called "social catastrophe," nor did he seek to escape from the ruins of European society pre- or post-World War I: "The simultaneous occurrence of revolutionary political events and fundamental changes in human relations, economics, the sciences, religion, and the arts is evidence of

---

[46] *Walter Gropius: Work and Teamwork*, Reinhold, New York, 1954, p. 22.

[47] Reyner Banham, *A Concrete Atlantis*, p. 231.

an always-present belief in a new order," he states in "The Problem of a New Architecture," which was presented as a lecture to the *Arbeitsrat fur Kunst* (Labor Council for Art) in Berlin in 1919. "They all testify to the possibility of a new birth within the misery of world-shaking catastrophes [...] From the unique perspective of architecture, this is precisely what social upheaval means: necessary changes in the management of traffic, economics, culture, and new possibilities of construction using the new materials of glass, steel, and concrete."[48]

During his military service, Mendelsohn – obviously inspired by the illustrations, if not the arguments, of Gropius' *Jahrbuch* essay – made about a dozen sketches of imaginary "grain silos." Banham reproduces one of these sketches;[49] several others are included in Bruno Zevi's *Erich Mendelsohn: The Complete Works*[50]; but somehow not a single one is in *Erich Mendelsohn: Complete Works of the Architect: Sketches, Designs, Buildings* (Princeton Architectural Press, 1992). These often overlooked sketches are significant in that they only depict the "male" form of the grain elevator (rows of freestanding cylindrical tanks); no "female" forms are sketched out. Gropius, of course, had impartially displayed examples of both genders.

Like Gropius, Mendelsohn had a favorite *Getreidesilo*. His was the Washburn-Crosby elevator complex in Buffalo. Gropius' reprinted photograph of it was part of Mendelsohn's lecture on "The Problem of a New Architecture," as was a picture of the Wayss und Freytag grain elevator in Wurms,

[48] *Erich Mendelsohn: Complete Works of the Architect: Sketches, Designs, Buildings*, Princeton Architectural Press, 1992, pp. 7-8.
[49] Reyner Banham, *A Concrete Atlantis*, p. 10.
[50] Birkhauser, 1999, pp. 17, 24 and 40.

then under construction.[51] In this lecture, Mendelsohn says the following of the Washburn-Crosby: "An obvious mastery of the mass, however, is the aim of the architectural will-to-form of the new age. The group of grain silos [*sic*] in Buffalo masters its spatial components by deploying within its spaces modern construction techniques and technical assemblages of large massings, which seem the result of mathematical pragmatism. But our horror at the colossal dimensions of such built spatial geometry testifies to its expressive effect, a successful design of purely functional basics created by the intuition of the artist-engineer."[52] It is certainly gratifying to hear *someone* in the early 20th century acknowledge that the "colossal" size of American grain elevators evokes negative emotions ("horror") as well as positive ones. But it is difficult to overlook the obvious contradiction between "mathematical pragmatism," on the one hand, and "the intuition of the artist-engineer," on the other. By definition, pragmatists do not trust or put faith in "intuition," and "intuitive" builders – professionals who use the "rule of thumb" method, possess extensive experience in the field, and draw upon knowledge of the building site – do not need to know mathematics.[53]

In 1923, Mendelsohn gave a lecture on "The International Consensus on the New Architectural Concept, or Dynamics and Function" at the *Architectura et Amicitia* conference in Amsterdam. Once again, he used Gropius' reprint of the Washburn-Crosby to illustrate his remarks, and yet he did so in a context that was explicitly critical of "those

---

[51] *Erich Mendelsohn: Complete Works of the Architect*, pp. 9 and 10.

[52] *Erich Mendelsohn: Complete Works of the Architect*, p. 16.

[53] At least this was the claim of Charles-Francois Viel's *De l'Impuissance des mathematiques pour assurer la solidite des batiments* [*The Powerlessness of Mathematics to Assure the Solidity of Buildings*], published in Paris in 1805.

who seem to have found their dogma in the slogan 'function.'"[54] Unlike the machine, which "always carries out work and enforces or overcomes power, architecture is only the expression of powers whose effect is achieved through the static gravity of its construction," Mendelsohn declared. "Architecture is only the spatial expression for the game of forces that annul the effect of one another." Therefore, it is "a complete misjudgment of architecture's nature to attempt to transfer these laws of motion onto architecture."[55] Indeed, "it seems impossible [...] to somehow want to transfer the purposeful function of machines to the space, or the technical organization to the organism of architecture." Mechanical functionality is certainly of "great importance," as is "the clarity of its technical potential," but "this component alone does not create architecture."[56]

According to Mendelsohn, "this silo in Buffalo is proof of that fact." Despite Gropius' claims about American industrial buildings, the Washburn-Crosby Elevator possesses only one of the two necessary components "for [it to be] architecture"; it is missing "the ability to find an architectural expression for the basic assumptions." Mendelsohn explains:

> In the first component – intellect, brain, the organizing machine – spatial possibilities of expression strike with lightning force, as in a vision, in the activity of the subconscious; the second, drawn from the completed organization, is that of the creative impulses, the blood, the

---

[54] *Erich Mendelsohn: Complete Works of the Architect*, p. 29.

[55] *Erich Mendelsohn: Complete Works of the Architect*, p. 26.

[56] *Erich Mendelsohn: Complete Works of the Architect*, p. 31.

> temper, the senses, and organic feeling. Only the
> union of the two components leads to the mastery
> of spatial elements.[57]

In other words, the Washburn-Crosby Elevator – striking
though it was – just wasn't *self-conscious* enough to be either
"modern[ist]" or "architecture." It was still asleep, still
dreaming and unaware of itself, still in need of a proper
architect (a kind of psychoanalyst) who would discover and
reveal to the world what the Washburn-Crosby really is and
really means.

Drawing upon Siegfried Giedion's remark in *Bauen in
Frankreich* (1928) that, "In the nineteenth century, [mere]
construction plays the role of the subconscious,"[58] Walter
Benjamin's *Arcades Project* makes several strong
connections between the building arts and dreams: "Not
architecture alone but all technology is, at certain stages,
evidence of a collective dream";[59] "Dream houses of the
collective: arcades, winter gardens, panoramas, factories,
wax museums, casinos, railroad stations";[60] and "The
hallucinatory function of architecture: dream images that rise
up into the walking world."[61] But Benjamin does not imagine
that an individual dream-interpreting architect, or even an
international team of such architects, would be able to wake
human society from its slumbers. Humanity can only awaken
from capitalism – "capitalism was a natural phenomenon
with which a new dream-filled sleep came over Europe, and,
through it, a reactivation of mythic forces"[62] – when the real

---

[57] *Ibid.*

[58] Walter Benjamin, *The Arcades Project*, p. 3.

[59] Walter Benjamin, *The Arcades Project*, p. 152.

[60] Walter Benjamin, *The Arcades Project*, p. 404.

[61] Walter Benjamin, *The Arcades Project*, p. 908.

[62] Walter Benjamin, *The Arcades Project*, p. 391.

forces of the proletariat, the class of revolutionary consciousness, have been brought back to life.

In 1924, Mendelsohn did something that Gropius didn't think to do: come to America and visit the grain elevators of Buffalo, New York, in person. In a letter to his wife dated Pittsburgh, 22 October 1924, Mendelsohn reported seeing

> Mountainous silos, incredibly space-conscious, but creating space. A random confusion amidst the chaos of loading and unloading corn ships, of railways and bridges, crane monsters with live gestures, hordes of silo cells in concrete, stone and glazed brick. Then suddenly a silo with administrative buildings, closed horizontal fronts against the stupendous verticals of fifty to a hundred cylinders, and all this in the sharp evening light. I took photographs like mad. Everything else seemed to have been shaped interim to my silo dreams. Everything else was merely a beginning.[63]

It is clear that Mendelsohn was describing the Washburn-Crosby complex, which faced west and thus the setting sun. His references to "glazed brick" and "enamel" (see below) can only be to the tile bins that the Barnett-Record Company erected in 1903. It seems that he went on a brief walking tour, self-guided,[64] without any experts in the grain-elevator

---

[63] *Letters of An Architect*, edited by Oskar Beyer, translated by Geoffrey Strachan, London: Abelard-Schumann, 1967, page 69.

[64] Had *I* been Mendelsohn's guide in Buffalo, I would have hired a boat and started out in the center of the harbor. The tour would've begun with the last remaining wood-binned elevators from the 19th century (the Exchange, the Marine and the Evans), continued with the steel, tile and

or grain-trade business: thus his "random confusion amidst the chaos" and his failure to visit or even mention the Concrete-Central, one of the biggest reinforced-concrete grain elevators in the world. Once again, Mendelsohn was honest enough to report that he was a little afraid to be in the presence of such colossal structures ("crane monsters with live gestures").

Back in Europe, Mendelsohn published *Amerika: Bilderbuch eines Architeckten* [America: Picture Book of an Architect] (1926), and then *Russland Amerika Europa: Ein architektonischer Querschnitt* [Russia America Europe: An Architectonic Cross-Section] (1929), both of which were photo-books with captions. As Reyner Banham points out, in "neither [...] is his captioning very helpful – the name of the elevator was not given, and in one case it [the Washburn-Crosby] was identified as being in Chicago!"[65] Mendelsohn filled his captions with poetic evocations, not basic information, perhaps echoing or following through on his call to "create symbols, not forms."[66] Underneath his photos of grain elevators in Buffalo (the American, the Washburn-Crosby, and the Kellogg), we read these embellishments of his letter to his wife.

> Elevator fortresses in the transshipment port at the northeastern end of Lake Erie where the Niagara flows into it. Unplanned confusion, in the chaos

---

concrete elevators along the City Ship Canal (the Great Eastern, Dakota, the Washburn-Crosby, and the Great Northern), and concluded with the steel-binned Electric and the colossal reinforced concrete elevators along the Buffalo River (the American, the Superior, the Dellwood, and the Concrete-Central).

[65] Reyner Banham, *A Concrete Atlantis*, p. 144.

[66] *Erich Mendelsohn: Complete Works of the Architect*, p. 9.

of the loading and unloading grain ships, railroads and bridges. Monster cranes with gestures of living creatures, crowds of silo compartments of concrete, stone and *enamel*. Suddenly an elevator with managed, uniform layered facades against the stupendous verticality of a hundred cylinders [...] Childhood forms, clumsy, full of primeval power, dedicated to purely practical needs. Primitive in their functions of ingesting and spewing out again. Surprised by the coinciding needs, to some extent a preliminary stage in a future world that is just beginning to achieve order [...] If the will to organize becomes clear in this way, then the delirium is transformed into boldness and the confusion into harmony.[67]

The incredible thing about Mendelsohn's photographs is that, on the one hand, they added to and thus enriched Walter Gropius' collection of images of American grain elevators, which had become "public property" with the publication of the *Jahrbuch* essay; and, on the other hand, they completely *contradicted* the assertions made about these elevators by both Gropius (a "functionalist") and Mendelsohn (an "expressionist").

For example, in the photograph of the American Elevator,[68] we might think we are seeing two separate grain elevators, each equipped with a tall marine tower and a series of cylindrical grain bins. But we are in fact seeing a single grain elevator with two marine towers, between which there is a wide, almost "obscene" space: the tower on the right is a stationary or "stiff" leg, while the one on the left is a "loose"

[67] *Amerika*, Dover Books, New York, 1993, pp. 44-47, emphasis added.

[68] Erich Mendelsohn, *Amerika*, p. 44 and Reyner Banham, *A Concrete Atlantis*, p. 162.

leg that has been moved to its extreme position (so far away it looks like it is a part of Perot Malting, when it is not).

In the photograph of the Kellogg Elevator,[69] we see another loose leg, but as before Mendelsohn gives no indication that he knows that this is *a building on motorized wheels*. Too bad: its very existence disproves his assertion that it is "impossible" to "somehow want to transfer the purposeful function of machines to the space, or the technical organization to the organism of architecture." It is quite possible to do so if, as in this case, *automobility* blurs or erases the neat line that Mendelsohn drew between machine (movement) and building (stasis).

Finally, in the photographs of the Washburn-Crosby,[70] we are confronted with an embarrassment of riches. First and foremost, this complex of buildings looks nothing like it did in 1909, when it was photographed by Gropius' sources in America. If we use the towering workhouse in the center of Gropius' picture as our reference point, we can see that the bins that were on the right are now almost completely obscured by a tall, narrow structure (yet another loose leg!) and a four-story flourmill. (The tops of the reinforced-concrete bins of 1909 and the tile bins of 1903 are still visible in Mendelsohn's photo: look above the flourmill's roof.) On the left side of our reference point there have also been a major change: the addition of an entire bin-structure made out of reinforced concrete. In 1925, just a year after *Amerika* was published, yet another series of reinforced-concrete bins (surmounted by a rooftop tower) would be added to this part of the complex.

Given all these changes, it is understandable that Mendelsohn might have overlooked a single, spectacular

---

[69] Erich Mendelsohn, *Amerika*, p. 45 and Reyner Banham, *A Concrete Atlantis*, p. 161.

[70] Erich Mendelsohn, *Amerika*, p. 46-47 and Reyner Banham, *A Concrete Atlantis*, p. 150.

"detail": the windowless cylindrical form, evidently made out of reinforced concrete, that stood on its own, directly in front of the reinforced concrete bins that were constructed in 1912,[71] and that was almost as tall as the colossal workhouse built in 1909. (See figures 3 and 4.) If Mendelsohn saw that cylinder or, rather, if an adherent to the form-follows-function credo saw it, he/she/they might reasonably think that it was just another grain silo. After all, *grain silos are cylindrical because the cylinder is the best form for containing grain, which is a grain silo's function; this thing is cylindrical, just like the grain silos right behind it; therefore this thing must also be a grain silo.* But the informed observer can discern that this cylinder is in fact the only cylindrical marine tower ever built in Buffalo. It is full of the machinery that elevates the grain, but no grain is stored inside it.

"Whoever did that leg," Banham writes, "the conceptual leap is striking; and the idea that the concrete cylinder might simply be a constructional device that could be used to support or contain matters other than grain was to be widely exploited."[72] It was in fact exploited to the maximum at the Annex to the Electric Elevator, built in Buffalo in 1942, that is, at the very end of the line begun by Joseph Dart and Robert Dunbar in 1843. "All this, of course, has a curious effect on one of the persistent themes of the

---

[71] A photograph of the cylindrical marine tower appears over the caption "The Frontier Elevator and Mill, Buffalo, N.Y." in Barney I. Weller, "Concrete Elevators," *Proceedings of the Ninth Annual Convention, held at Pittsburg, Pennsylvania, December 10-14, 1912*, Vol. IX (National Association of Cement Users, 1917), p. 342. In this photograph, the cylindrical tower stands alone, without any bins immediately behind it, which suggests that the bins were added after the tower was completed and operational.

[72] Reyner Banham, *A Concrete Atlantis*, p. 153.

present study – the common notions of 'functionalism,' "
Banham writes. "It is no longer so immediately clear to the
passerby what the various parts of the structure mean [...]
since a cylinder might be a bin or a leg, might contain grain,
machinery or men. [...] At Washburn-Crosby and its
progeny, engineers [...] were making nonsense of that
treasured concept."[73]

But this just scratches the surface. A visitor to the site
in question and yet completely ignorant of what he saw there,
Erich Mendelsohn had spoken of the Washburn-Crosby in
the most condescending terms: "Childhood forms, clumsy,
full of primeval power, dedicated to purely practical needs.
Primitive in their functions of ingesting and spewing out
again. Surprised by the coinciding needs, to some extent a
preliminary stage in a future world that is just beginning to
achieve order." What could he have possibly said if someone
had told him that the cylindrical marine tower at the
Washburn-Crosby was in fact an instance of form following
aesthetics, not function? How could he admit that he had
failed to recognize a deliberate, sophisticated and witty
attempt to make a pun on visual resemblances?

Though Erich Mendelsohn was the first, Charles-
Edouard Jeanneret is certainly the best known of the
European modernists who, inspired by the images reprinted
by Gropius, reprinted them again, added a couple of new
ones, and made a few odd comments about what "the grain
elevator" can teach other architects. Born in a French-
speaking part of Switzerland in 1887, Jeanneret often
traveled to Paris as a young man. In 1907, he found work at
the firm run by August Perret, one of the pioneers of the use
of reinforced concrete in France. In 1910, Jeanneret moved to
Berlin and began learning German so as to work at the firm
of Peter Behrens, where he met Walter Gropius and Mies van
der Rohe, among others. During World War I, Jeanneret

---

[73] Reyner Banham, *A Concrete Atlantis*, p. 153.

returned to Switzerland, where he worked on models for the "Domino House," which was to be built out of reinforced concrete. Back in Paris in 1918, Jeanneret met and started collaborating with the painter, Amédée Ozenfant, with whom he wrote a manifesto, *Après le Cubisme*, and started a new movement, *Purisme*.

In 1920, Ozenfant and Jeanneret (adopting the name "Le Corbusier," which means "the Builder" in French and was a pun on his maternal grandfather's name, Lecorbésier) founded a Purist journal called *L'Esprit Nouveau*. It was in the first issue of this journal that Le Corbusier published his "Three Reminders to Architects," which was illustrated by reprinted photographs of grain elevators. The last issue of *L'Esprit Nouveau* came out in 1922. The next year, Le Corbusier published his "theoretical" writings in a famous collection called *Vers une architecture*.[74]

Unlike Erich Mendelsohn's writings of the late 1910s and early 1920s, which embraced and were inspired by the social upheavals of those tumultuous years (essentially the Russian Revolution of 1917 and the Spartakist uprising in Germany in 1919), Le Corbusier's *Towards a New Architecture* was a throwback to the concerns of the *Deutscher Werkbund* in 1913. In the summary of the chapter entitled "Architecture or Revolution," Le Corbusier wrote,

> The machinery of Society, profoundly *out of gear,* oscillates between amelioration, of historical importance, and a catastrophe.
> The primordial instinct of every human being is to assure himself of a shelter. The various classes of workers in society to-day *no longer*

---

[74] Translated into English by Frederick Etchells as *Towards a New Architecture* (London, Rodker, 1931); reprinted by Praeger in 1960 and by Dover in 1986.

have dwellings adapted to their needs; neither the artizan [sic] *nor the intellectual.*

It is a question of building which is at the root of the social unrest of to-day: architecture or revolution.[75]

And so, for Le Corbusier, "architecture" wasn't a revolutionary demand or the furtherance of "the revolution" into the built environment, but a spatial practice that would prevent revolution from breaking out (again).

Unlike Gropius, who had been primarily concerned with the design and construction of public buildings (factories and offices), Le Corbusier was exclusively concerned with building "houses" (private residences). "We are to be pitied for living in unworthy houses, since they ruin our health and our *morale*," he wrote. "Our houses disgust us; we fly from them to frequent restaurants and night clubs; or we gather together in our houses gloomily and secretly like wretched animals; we are becoming demoralized."[76] But something else might have been causing this widespread demoralization. In "*Bauen Wohnen Denken*," an essay from 1951, Martin Heidegger asserts that,

> However hard and bitter, however hampering and threatening the lack of housing remains, *the real plight of dwelling* does not lie merely in a lack of houses. The real plight of dwelling is indeed older than the world wars with their destruction, older also than the increase of the earth's population and the condition of the industrial workers. The real plight of dwelling lies in this, that mortals ever search anew for the essence of dwelling, that

---

[75] Le Corbusier, *Towards a New Architecture*, Dover Books, 1986, p. 8.

[76] Le Corbusier, *Towards a New Architecture*, p. 14.

they *must ever learn to dwell.*[77]

One need not be a mystic, enamored of the "fourfold" (earth, sky, divinities and mortals), as Heidegger had been, to see that in the 1920s Le Corbusier was attempting to disguise or dissimulate society's real problems with a superficial solution. In the terms used by Walter Benjamin,[78] Le Corbusier was arguing that "the interior" (the refuge of the private individual, in which he or she builds and maintains a unique personal identity) had been shattered by modern society and now had to be artificially re-constituted.

Of course, Le Corbusier knew that not all "private individuals" are the same. He writes: "On the one hand the mass of people look for a decent dwelling, and this question is of burning importance," and "On the other hand the man of initiative, of action, of thought, the LEADER, demands a shelter for his meditations in a quiet and sure spot; a problem which is indispensable to the health of specialized people."[79] And so, modern architects, if they wish to get the patronage of "these same business men, bankers and merchants,"[80] must devise a single architecture that can accomplish two closely related tasks: keep the mass of workers in line ("happy") and provide adequate rewards for their bosses.

It is in this context that we should understand Le Corbusier's resuscitation of Gropius' call that the neo-classicist architects (those historicizing bastards!) should step aside and let the industrial engineers have their turn. "Our engineers are healthy and virile, active and useful, balanced and happy in their work," Le Corbusier proclaims. "Our

---

[77] Translated by Albert Hofstadter as "Building Dwelling Thinking," in Marin Heidegger, *Poetry, Language, Thought,* New York, 1971, p. 161.

[78] Walter Benjamin, *The Arcades Project*, pp. 8-9.

[79] Le Corbusier, *Towards a New Architecture*, p. 20.

[80] Le Corbusier, *Towards a New Architecture*, p. 18

architects are disillusioned and unemployed, boastful or peevish. This is because there will soon be nothing more for them to do. *We no longer have the money* to erect historical monuments. At the same time, we have got to wash! Our engineers provide for these things and they will be our builders [...] Now, to-day, it is the engineer who *knows*, who knows the best way to construct, to heat, to ventilate, to light. Is it not true?"[81] Le Corbusier isn't simply making a psycho-aesthetic judgment about the relative merits of industrial engineers. He is also suggesting that capitalism itself can be saved if more workers are encouraged to become engineers. Build him a truly modern house – "the house is a machine for living in," Le Corbusier claims[82] – and the modern worker will both behave like a good machine *and* take an interest in how (other) machines work. "In handling a mathematical problem," he writes, "a man is regarding it from a purely abstract point of view, and in such a state, his taste must follow a sure and certain path."[83]

What should modern architects do in the meantime? Well, they could read Le Corbusier's "three reminders," which were reprinted in *Vers une architecture*. In Frederick Etchells' translation, they were: "MASS which is the element by which our senses perceive and measure and are most fully affected," "SURFACE which is the envelope of the mass and which can diminish or enlarge the sensation the latter gives us," and "PLAN which is the generator both of mass and surface and is that by which the whole is irrevocably fixed."[84] The decision to translate *volume* as "mass" was most unfortunate. "Mass" mistakenly suggests that Le Corbusier was referring to quantities of matter, not volumes of spaces,

---

[81] Le Corbusier, *Towards a New Architecture*, pp. 14-15.

[82] Le Corbusier, *Towards a New Architecture*, p. 4.

[83] Le Corbusier, *Towards a New Architecture*, p. 15.

[84] Le Corbusier, *Towards a New Architecture*, p. 17.

when, following the Gropius/Worringer line, he spoke of "abstraction" in the first "Reminder": "Architecture has graver ends [than styles]; capable of the sublime, it impresses the most brutal instincts by its objectivity; it calls into play the highest faculties by its very abstraction."[85] But Etchells' mistranslation has the merit of reminding us that – despite their apparently liberal embrace of the values, "economic laws" and building materials of mass society – Le Corbusier's ideas were actually quite elitist and conservative. Like Erich Mendelsohn, Le Corbusier didn't really like grain elevators: he simply found them to be *irreplaceable as examples*. "Finally, it will be a delight to talk of ARCHITECTURE after so many grain-stores, workshops, machines and sky-scrapers," he confesses,[86] speaking about the second half of his book.

The structure of Le Corbusier's first "Reminder" is somewhat similar to that of Gropius' lecture on "The Development of Modern Industrial Building." The *clincher*, that is to say, the single emphatic reference to American grain elevators, is delivered at the end of the spiel.

> *Not in pursuit of an architectural idea, but simply guided by the results of calculation (derived from the principles which govern our universe) and the conception of A LIVING ORGANISM, the ENGINEERS of to-day make use of the primary elements and, by co-ordinating them in accordance with the rules, provoke in us architectural emotions and thus make the work of man ring in unison with universal order.*
>
> *Thus we have the American grain elevators and factories, the magnificent FIRST-FRUITS of the new age. THE AMERICAN ENGINEERS*

---

[85] Le Corbusier, *Towards a New Architecture*, p. 26.
[86] Le Corbusier, *Towards a New Architecture*, p. 19.

OVERWHELM   WITH   THEIR
CALCULATIONS   OUR   EXPIRING
ARCHITECTURE.[87]

As with Gropius's finale, this exclamation sends the reader's eyes in search of illustrations. What do these grain elevators *look* like? Of course Le Corbusier anticipated this curiosity, and planned in advance: he distributed a total of nine reprinted photographs of grain elevators throughout the text of the first "Reminder." The reader had already seen them, identified by a total of three, very inadequate captions: "Grain elevator"; "Canadian grain stores and elevators"; and "American grain stores and elevators."

And so these pictures would be viewed twice: first as concurrent sources for or proofs of Le Corbusier's general assertions – made at the start of the first "Reminder" – that "cubes, cones, spheres, cylinders or pyramids are the great primary forms which light reveals to advantage [...] These are *beautiful forms, the most beautiful forms*. Everybody is agreed as to that, the child, the savage and the metaphysician"[88] – and then retrospectively as particular examples of what the allegedly unself-conscious calculations of American industrial engineers can produce. In both instances, grain elevators could easily have been replaced by other examples. On the one hand, "Egyptian, Greek or Roman architecture is [also] an architecture of prisms, cubes and cylinders, pyramids or spheres: the Pyramids, the Temple of Luxor, the Parthenon, the Coliseum, Hadrian's Villa."[89] On the other hand, grain elevators are not discussed at length, unlike ocean liners, airplanes and automobiles, each of which merit their own section in the chapter of *Vers une Architecture* entitled "Eyes Which Do Not See."

---

[87] Le Corbusier, *Towards a New Architecture*, p. 31.
[88] Le Corbusier, *Towards a New Architecture*, p. 29.
[89] Le Corbusier, *Towards a New Architecture*, p. 29.

Though Le Corbusier does not say so – indeed, his acknowledgements only mention Anglo-American construction companies and "the architects whose names appear below the plates"[90] – Walter Gropius was the primary source for his pictures of American grain elevators. In fact, four of Le Corbusier's nine photos came from the 1913 *Jahrbuch* essay: namely, the photos of the Grand Trunk Pacific Elevator in Fort William, the Bunge y Born Elevator in Buenos Aires (incorrectly identified by Le Corbusier as "Canadian"), the Dakota and Great Eastern Elevators in Buffalo, and Walter Gropius' personal favorite, the Grand Trunk Pacific Elevator in Montreal (incorrectly identified by Le Corbusier as "American"). The remaining five photos came from Le Corbusier's other sources. Except for the shot of an elongated "lake and rail" transshipment elevator that could be located in Duluth, Milwaukee or Chicago and Harry Pollard's uncredited photograph of the Dominion Government Elevator in Calgary, Alberta, these photos depict small-scale operations: a small flour and feed mill; Wilkins Flour, a small mill on the Patapsco River in Baltimore, Maryland; a wood country-style elevator with a small reinforced-concrete annex.[91]

Like Gropius and Mendelsohn, Le Corbusier had a preference for photographs ("forms in light") and no interest at all in blueprints or measured field drawings; he was seriously confused about the grain elevators' geographical locations (not just wrong about cities or states, but whole continents); he was apparently unable to distinguish the "grain stores" (*les entrepots*) from the grain elevators (*les Élévateurs À Grains*); and he had no inkling about the existence of "loose legs" nor knowledge of the mega-

---

[90] Le Corbusier, *Towards a New Architecture*, p. xviii.

[91] Le Corbusier, *Towards a New Architecture*, pp. 29, 30, 21, 25, and 26, respectively.

elevators built in the 1910s, such as Buffalo's Concrete-Central.

At their best, Le Corbusier's images were an adequate representation of American elevator-design as it had been between 1906 and 1912: six of them show silos made out of reinforced concrete; two show silos made out of steel (the elevators in Montreal and Buffalo); and one shows a silo-building made out of tile (the Bunge y Born). Both "male" and "female" forms are represented. But these images had nothing fresh or interesting to say about the state of elevator design in the early 1920s, when *all* new grain elevators in America were built out of reinforced concrete, in freestanding cylindrical forms, and on a very large scale.

Perhaps this is why Le Corbusier felt that he had to *cheat*, that is, alter a few details in a couple of the images he'd borrowed from Gropius, but without saying that such alterations had been made. He was *embarrassed* by these details, small though they were, because they weren't really "modern" (purely functional forms). The particulars: in the picture of the Bunge y Born Elevator,[92] Le Corbusier used what is today called "liquid paper" to remove from sight a total of three elements: the ten undulating triangular pediments along the front edge of the roof (five pediments on each side of the centrally positioned workhouse); the triangular pediment atop the workhouse itself; and a tree and the corner of something (an awning?) in the lower-right-hand corner. There are other, less egregious but still reprehensible alterations in the picture of the elevator in Fort William,[93] from which Le Corbusier removed the small shed at the lower left and the crane at the lower right (which has the effect of isolating the elevator from its surroundings), and in the picture of the elevator in Montreal,[94] from which he

[92] Le Corbusier, *Towards a New Architecture*, p. 27.

[93] Le Corbusier, *Towards a New Architecture*, p. 27.

[94] Le Corbusier, *Towards a New Architecture*, p. 28.

removed the entire Bonsecours Public Market Building (designed by William Footner and built between 1844 and 1847), presumably because of its "ugly" neo-classical cupola.

Note well that the deletion of Bonsecours was faithfully repeated in Adrien Hébert's *Le Port De Montreal* (1924, currently in the collection of the Musee national des beaux-arts du Quebec). This oil painting uses the Grand Trunk #2 Elevator as the background for a properly "spectacular" scene in which a mere handful of workers and idyll strollers (!) walk along or stand upon the gangplanks of a very large ocean liner. This canvas was obviously inspired by and based upon Le Corbusier's photo, *not* on a personal inspection of the site. Hébert even gives Elevator #2 a horizontal gantry that it *lacks* in both the Gropius or Le Corbusier versions! Perhaps he did so because Elevator #2 was in fact connected to a neighboring building and nearly ringed on its other side by such elevated structures, as other photographs from this era show (cf. the ones that appear on the official website of the City of Montreal).

As long as I am discussing gullibility and/or bad scholarship, I must once again bring up poor Wilhelm Worringer. Inspired by Walter Gropius' 1913 reference to the "abstract" art of ancient Egypt (which had in turn been inspired by a close reading of Worringer's book *Abstraction and Empathy*) and by Howard Carter's highly publicized discovery of the undisturbed tomb of the Egyptian Pharaoh Tutankhamen in 1922, Worringer wrote and published his .own book on *ägyptische Kunst* (Egyptian Art) in 1927. Without knowing that it had already been altered, Worringer reprinted Le Corbusier's version of the photograph of the Bunge y Born elevator, and repeated Le Corbusier's mistaken caption that the Argentinean structure was a "Grain Elevator in Canada." To make matters worse, Worringer matched this unfortunate image with a drawing of an ancient Egyptian temple (the Egyptian Gate Building of the Temple of the

Dead of King Sahu-Ra), as if the two structures had something in common.[95]

It may have been nonsense, but it worked for the American historian Lewis Mumford, among others. Alongside a photograph of a grain elevator in Chicago, reprinted from Erich Mendelsohn's *Amerika*, he wrote: "Modern grain elevator. Esthetic effect derived from simplicity, essentiality, repetition of elementary forms; heightened by colossal scale. See Worringer's suggestive essay on Egypt and America."[96] Note well that Mumford's bibliography doesn't list either *Egyptian Art* or *Abstraction and Empathy*, but does cite Worringer's *Form in Gothic* (1927), which Mumford describes as "interesting, if not always substantiated."[97]

One of the most enthusiastic readers of Le Corbusier's texts outside of France and Germany was the Russian architect Moisei Ginzburg. Born in Minsk in 1892, Ginzburg studied and received degrees in architecture from the Accademia di Belli Arti in Milan in 1914 and the Polytechnic in Riga, Latvia, in 1917. While visiting the Ecole des Beaux-Arts in Paris in 1920, he came across copies of *L'Esprit Nouveau*. Greatly inspired by them, Ginzburg attempted to apply Le Corbusier's *purisme* to architecture in Russia after he moved to Moscow in 1921. In 1924, when copies of *Vers une Architecture* were beginning to turn up in Moscow, Ginzburg published *Stil'I epokha: problemy sovremennoi arkhitektory* [Style and Epoch: The Problems of Contemporary Architecture] under the aegis of Gosizdat, the official press of the Russian/Soviet government. *Stil'I epokha* quickly exerted a profound influence on Russian

---

[95] See Wilhelm Worringer, *Egyptian Art*, translated by Bernard Rackham, London 1928, plates 21-22, page vi.

[96] Lewis Mumford, *Technics and Civilization*, Harcourt Brace, New York, 1934, p. 340.

[97] Lewis Mumford, *Technics and Civilization*, p. 473.

"constructivism," especially its architectural formulations. Unfortunately for readers in England and the United States, it took more than fifty years before Ginzburg's book was published in English.[98]

Perhaps it is surprising that Ginzburg, an avid supporter of the Russian Revolution, was also a partisan of American industry and American industrial buildings (and thus square in line with his German and French predecessors). He writes:

> If Europe, with its vast size, presents a picture of complete decline, America, primarily the United States of North America, offers a more instructive view [...] An American tempo of life is emerging, utterly different from that of Europe – businesslike, dynamic, sober, mechanized, devoid of any Romanticism [...] When the crude and sober but nonetheless potentially vigorous spirit of the new pioneers manifested itself, brilliant structures teeming with unexpected poignancy and force were created spontaneously in an absolutely organic manner. I have in mind the industrial structures of America.[99]

> In the industrial structures of the last decade in the largest cities of Europe and America, we see already realized not only the foundations of a modern aesthetic, but even individual elements of architecture, systems of supports, joints, spans, openings, terminations, flashes of compositional schemes and flashes of new forms, which can already be transferred to domestic architecture, can already serve as the concrete and profoundly

---

[98] Moisei Ginzburg, *Style and Epoch*, translated by Anatole Senekevitch, Jr., MIT Press, 1982.

[99] Moisei Ginzburg, *Style and Epoch*, p. 70.

practical material that will be able to help the architect find a true course for creative work and help transform the language of abstract aesthetics into a precise lexicon of architecture.[100]

But we shouldn't be surprised. Like many other revolutionaries of the period, Ginzburg was a committed internationalist. He writes, "Local and national characteristics in the present instance [modern architecture] appear to be insignificant when compared with the equalizing force of modern technology and economics."[101] Furthermore, it is easy to confuse the Bolshevik government that ruled Russia during and immediately after the Civil War (1917-1922) with the Soviet Union, which only became belligerently anti-American in the 1940s. As late as 1932, Russia was still commissioning American industrialists such as Henry Ford and Albert Kahn to build tractor plants for Stalin's collectivized farms.

Perhaps the huge American-style grain elevator in Stalingrad, now called Novograd, was built in this period (between 1922 and 1932). An exhibition catalogue called *The Great Utopia: the Russian and Soviet Avant-Garde 1915-1932* includes a student project for a "grain elevator" dated 1922; it is credited to the painter Ivan Lamtsov.[102] This project suggests that the government had been soliciting designs for such a building. "We are reconstructing industry, we are reconstructing agriculture," El Lissitzky announced in "The Reconstruction of Architecture in the Soviet Union."[103]

---

[100] Moisei Ginzburg, *Style and Epoch*, p. 108.

[101] Moisei Ginzburg, *Style and Epoch*, p. 83.

[102] *The Great Utopia: the Russian and Soviet Avant-Garde 1915-1932* (Guggenheim Museum, 1992), plate 647.

[103] Original 1930, translation in *The Tradition of Constructivism*, edited by Stephen Bann, New York, 1974, p. 140.

"A wide road must be opened for this architecture in the Land of the Soviets – the land where socialist culture is being built, where mighty plants and factories, grandiose power stations, giant state farms, the citadels of agricultural industry, are being created," proclaimed Erik Fedorovich Gollerbakh in "The Problems of Constructivism in Their Relation to Art."[104]

Like Le Corbusier, Ginzburg was narrowly focused on housing. He says, "Thus moving to the forefront as the basic task confronting modernity is the development of solutions for all the architectural organisms associated with the concept of labor – *workers' housing and the house of work* – and for the innumerable problems generated by them."[105] "It is from industrial architecture rather than from anywhere else that we can expect realistic indications concerning how and in what way these paths can be found. What we are talking about here is adding to the existing landscape of modernity – the machine, the engineering and industrial structures – the latest link in the architectural chain: residential and public buildings equal to these structures."[106]

I am not sure who came up with the metaphor ("the latest link in the architectural chain"), Ginzburg or his translator, but it is very telling. It suggests that "modernity" is a chain composed of several heavy links forged out of steel, with each link marking another transformation wrought by industrialization: first, the tool used at work (the machine); then, the design and construction of the workplace itself; and now, government buildings and the workers' own residences. Will humanity end up enslaved to industry when the last link in the chain of architecture is forged?

---

[104] Original 1931, translation in *The Tradition of Constructivism*, pp. 151-153.

[105] Moisei Ginzburg, *Style and Epoch*, p. 78.

[106] Moisei Ginzburg, *Style and Epoch*, p. 109.

A good person to ask would be Henri Lefebvre. In *The Production of Space*, Lefebvre observes:

> At that time, around 1920, just after the First World War, a link was discovered in the advanced countries (France, Germany, Russia, the United States), a link which had already been dealt with on the practical plane but which had not yet been rationally articulated: that between industrialization and urbanization, between workplaces and dwelling-places. No sooner had this link been incorporated into theoretical thought than it turned into a project, even into a programme. The curious thing is that this 'programmatic' stance was looked upon at the time as both rational and revolutionary, although in reality it was tailor-made for the state – whether of the state-capitalist or the state-socialist variety [...] When it comes to the question of what the Bauhaus's audacity produced in the long run, one is obliged to answer: the worldwide, homogeneous and monotonous architecture of the state, whether capitalist or socialist [...] Whereas they [the constructivists] were characterized as reactionaries in their country, their Bauhaus contemporaries were dubbed subversives. This confusion has already persisted for half a century and is still far from having been dispelled [...] In the realm of nature rediscovered, with its sun and light, beneath the banner of life, metal and glass still rise above the street, above the reality of the city. Along with the cult of rectitude, in the sense of right angles and straight lines. The order of

power, the order of the male – in short, the moral order – is thus naturalized.[107]

Perhaps this longstanding "confusion" explains why Reyner Banham said such strange things about Moisei Ginzburg. Was this Russian constructivist a reactionary or a subversive? "His built work is always extremely competent, without ever approximating genius, and this thinking seems to match. A complete professional, he may properly stand as an *architecte moyen sensuel* of the modern persuasion."[108] This is very obscure stuff: the italicized phrase is a "détournement" of an expression that was already difficult to translate into English: *l'homme moyen sensuel*, which can be rendered as "the average stud." And so *architecte moyen sensuel*, if it means anything at all, means something like "the average studly architect."

Banham certainly joked about Ginzburg's potency because he felt threatened by what the Russian represented, that is to say, the uncanny ease and speed with which he mastered the main ideas of his counterparts in Germany and France. Banham writes: "Perhaps because [Ginzburg's commentary on American industrial structures] is so largely derivative, as well as informed and intelligent, it gives as clear and compact a picture as we are likely to get of the modern architect's America, a bright prospect of the Concrete Atlantis far across the sea and thus ultimately beyond the reach of an old and decrepit Europe."[109]

I think this "clear and compact [...] picture" shows something else: the simple but ironic or embarrassing fact that modernist architecture didn't become "the International

---

[107] Henri Lefebvre, *The Production of Space*, translated by Donald Nicholson-Smith, Blackwell Publishers, 1981, pp. 124, 126, and 304-305, respectively.

[108] Reyner Banham, *A Concrete Atlantis*, p. 232.

[109] Reyner Banham, *A Concrete Atlantis*, p. 234-235.

Style" because it was theorized and practiced by architects who happened to live in different countries and speak different languages. The mere existence of different languages did not and still does not necessarily imply or involve a difference in basic social structure. Modernist architecture finally became "international" after World War II because its "style" (its spatial practice) answered and further stimulated the need for what Henri Lefebvre called "abstract space." And in the 1920s and 1930s, in countries as apparently different as France, Germany, Russia and the United States – that is to say, those countries in which a bureaucratic form of capitalism was establishing itself – abstract space was in great demand.

Lefebvre defines the phrase in the following way. "Abstract space functions 'objectally', as a set of things/signs and their formal relationships: glass and stone, concrete and steel, angles and curves, full and empty. Formal and quantitative, it erases distinctions, as much those which derive from nature and (historical) time as those which originate in the body (age, sex, ethnicity). The signification of this ensemble refers back to a sort of super-signification which escapes meaning's net: the functioning of capitalism, which contrives to be blatant and covert at one and the same time. The dominant form of space, that of the centres of wealth and power, endeavours to mould the spaces it dominates (i.e. peripheral spaces), and it seeks, often by violent means, to reduce the obstacles and resistance it encounters there [...] Abstract space is not defined only by the disappearance of trees, or by the receding of nature; not merely by the great empty spaces of the state and the military – plazas resemble parade grounds; nor even by commercial centres packed tight with commodities, money and cars. It is not in fact defined on the basis of what is perceived [...] It operates *negatively*. Abstract space relates negatively to that which perceives and underpins it – namely the historical and religio-political spheres [...] What we seem to have, then, is an apparent subject, an impersonal pseudo-subject, the abstract 'one' of modern social space, and – hidden within it, concealed by its illusory transparency – the real 'subject', namely state (political) power. Within this space, and on the subject of this space, everything is openly declared: everything is said or written. Save for the fact that there is very little to be said – and even less to be 'lived', for lived experience is crushed, vanquished by what is 'conceived of'."[110]

This "crushing" of lived experience in/by abstract space is accomplished by several different means. First, very tall buildings (typically with transparent glass surfaces, but not always) rise to miraculous heights, and thus make the people standing on the ground next to them feel very small, powerless and insignificant in comparison (emotionally "crushed"), which is both an individual and a collective ("social") response. Second, very tall buildings induce the quite reasonable fear that, if something, indeed, *anything* (especially the building itself!) should fall from such a height, it would literally crush the bodies of the people standing on the ground. Third, and most significantly: in abstract spatial practices, very tall buildings are surrounded by perimeters that have been flattened ("crushed" in the physical sense of the word), emptied out, and thus rendered completely submissive to the visual, emotional, physical and ultimately political powers that such buildings symbolize, embody, make use of, and transmit.

Here we have a possible explanation for why Le Corbusier and Ginzburg were fascinated by ocean liners, airplanes and automobiles, none of which were architectural creations. Indeed, though these sleek, high-speed vehicles were indeed designed by function-conscious engineers, none

---

[110] Henri Lefebvre, *The Production of Space*, pp. 49 and 51.

of them were even "buildings" in any sense of the word. But Le Corbusier and Ginzburg cited them because they evoked the "industrial prestige of America," which means that *the spatial practices of American capitalism*. Far from being isolated "objects," these vehicles presupposed and depended upon *American space*, that is to say, abstract space(s) big, open and empty enough to drive ocean liners, no matter how big; airplanes, no matter how fast; and automobiles, no matter how numerous.

Elsewhere in *The Production of Space*, Lefebvre says "These forces [of abstraction] seem to grind down and *crush* everything before them, with space performing the function of a plane, a bulldozer or a tank."[111] Unlike Le Corbusier and Ginzburg, who were writing during the "peaceful" years between the two World Wars, Lefebvre chose examples whose common theme is warfare: planes deliver bombs and transport troops; bulldozers knock down buildings (as well as frighten, intimidate and bully those confronted by them); and tanks assault enemy positions and fortifications. For Lefebvre, abstract space isn't the freedom to travel or built as one wishes. It is the crushing "victory" of the abstract mind *over* matter. Lefebvre doesn't simply condemn destructive objects *in* space, but a space/spatial practice that is itself destructive, *before* anything is placed "inside" it.

Even Reyner Banham praises Ginzburg's *Style and Epoch* for its pictures of American grain elevators. "When Ginzburg illustrates a grain elevator, it is not one of the Gropius-Corbusier set that were to become canonical images. His illustrations are strictly his own, and throughout the book they strike a note of independent originality, even when they illustrate mechanistic themes that were becoming commonplace, such as aircraft, ships, bridges, cooling towers, and the like. His factories and aircraft as Italian

---

[111] Henri Lefebvre, *The Production of Space*, p. 285, emphasis added.

(Ansaldo, Fiat, Caproni), his locomotives and earth-moving equipment are German (Kraus). His grain elevators are all in Buffalo, but even when they are examples that appear in other literature (Washburn-Crosby, Kellog [*sic*]), they are seen in unfamiliar views, while one, the Electric, is unknown in the rest of the modernist literature."[112]

Undetected by Banham, who reprinted none of Ginzburg's grain-elevator pictures, the presentation of *Style and Epoch* strikes several wrong notes. Its translator refers to Ginzburg's interest in "the grain elevators of rural America,"[113] as if *Buffalo* were a small rural town, not a major port city! Ginzburg himself tells us "the illustrations included in the present book are not directly related to the text"[114] – which was also the case in Gropius' essay in the *Jahrbuch*, Mendelsohn's *Amerika: Bilderbuch eines Architeckten*, and Le Corbusier's "Three Reminders to Architects," unfortunately – but Ginzburg doesn't make clear whether he is talking about the six photographs of grain elevators that precede his remarks or the dozens of constructivist sketches that follow them. Indeed, the very page on which Ginzburg discusses his illustrations – "the author consciously resisted the tempting opportunity afforded by the illustrative material to venture into a formal analysis and criticism of it [...] the author could not quite suppress the desire to illustrate his ideas with architectural material that, while perhaps still incomplete, is nonetheless already sufficiently revealing even in that state"[115] – he reprints a photograph of an "Elevator in Buffalo."

To make matters worse, such an elevator was never built in Buffalo. At the very least, I have never seen a picture

---

[112] Reyner Banham, *A Concrete Atlantis*, p. 232-233.
[113] Moisei Ginzburg, *Style and Epoch*, p. 17.
[114] Moisei Ginzburg, *Style and Epoch*, p. 121.
[115] Moisei Ginzburg, *Style and Epoch*, p. 121.

of it before.[116] *Wherever* it was built (possibly another port city on the Great Lakes: it has a marine tower, a stationary one), this particular grain elevator was designed and constructed before the widespread availability of electricity (circa 1897). The small, one-story building adjacent to the marine tower was obviously the location of a steam-powered engine: its smokestack rose almost as high as the marine tower itself. The placement of the engine room in line with and not next to the grain elevator, which is arrayed alongside the waterfront, suggests an abundance of space that didn't exist in Buffalo at the time (the 19th century). In another anomaly, this "anonymous" grain elevator is the only one of the six depicted in *Style and Epoch* that enclosed its bins within a house (looks like ironclad wood, in this instance) and didn't display them as freestanding tanks.

The five other photographs (each of them captioned "Elevator in Buffalo") are not grouped together under one of the book's seven chapters, several of which would have been suitable for such illustrations: "Construction and Form in Architecture" (chapter 5); "Industrial and Engineering Organisms" (chapter 6); or "The Characteristic Aspects of the New Style" (chapter 7). Instead, these photographs are scattered throughout these three chapters, none of which contain passages that directly refer to grain elevators. In order of appearance: on page 96, the Electric Elevator, seen on its "unfamiliar" side, which looks just as awkward as the

---

[116] In the following pages, I note that the mismatching of captions and photographs occurs again and again. So the reader does not incorrectly deduce that such mistakes were only made by European publications, I note that the photograph captioned "A Modern Grain Elevator, Buffalo (Courtesy of Buffalo Chamber of Commerce)" in Thurman Van Metre's *An Economic History of the United States* (H. Holt & Co., 1921), p. 571, shows an elevator that to my knowledge was never built in Buffalo.

other (a small cupola is perched atop the horizontal galleries that are themselves suspended above an array of large steel tanks); on page 108, the Kellogg Elevator, also seen on its "unfamiliar" side, from which one can easily see its pair of automotive marine towers; on page 112, the Washburn-Crosby Elevator complex, photographed before 1921, that is to say, before the additions of the flour mill and the rectangular marine tower that are visible in Erich Mendelsohn's photographs; and page 116, which presents us with two mysteries.

The first mystery is the photograph on the top of the page, which seems to show another "marine" (waterside) grain elevator that wasn't built in Buffalo: its elevating tower has an unfamiliar shape (unless the photograph was altered, the tower has a flat roof) and its reinforced-concrete bins are surmounted by a short and thus atypical gallery. The second mystery is the photo on the bottom of the page, which shows a close-up of an elevator in Buffalo (it has both a Buffalo-style "loose leg" and bins that are raised above the ground to create a "basement" below the bottoms of the bins): it could be and probably is the Superior "A" Elevator (built in 1915). I can't be sure.

Between 1927 and 1930, several European architects published major works that that weren't so much polemics *in favor of* modernist architecture – as were the various texts by Gropius (1913), Mendelsohn (1919), Le Corbusier (1923) and Ginzburg (1924) – but *histories* of what modernist architecture had accomplished since 1900. Not surprisingly, American grain elevators featured prominently in each of these accounts.[117]

---

[117] The second edition (1930) of Gustav Adolph Platz's *Die Baukunst der Neuesten Zeit* [*The Building-Art of the New Times*], first published in Berlin in 1927, contained two fresh pictures of North American grain elevators: "*Getreidesilos*, Fort William (Ontario, Canada), 1914," which showed a

The German architect Walter Curt Behrendt (born in 1884) provided the first and fullest expression of this retrospective turn.

> To do justice, it is necessary to say, and this will probably surprise the reader, that it was the example of America that gave the impulse to the German architects when they first tried to clarify the problem of structure. To be sure, this impulse did not originate in the skyscraper [...] but in the simple structures of industrial building such as the grain elevators and big silos to be found in the great ports all over South America [*sic*]. These examples of modern engineering, designed for practical use only, and obviously without any decorative assistance from an architect, made a deep impression by their simple structures reduced to basic forms of geometry such as cubes and cylinders. They were conceived as patterns exemplifying once more the essence of the pure use of form, gaining its impressive effect from its bare structure. The influence spreading from this pattern was soon apparent, and indeed was sometimes so strong as to lead to mere imitation.[118]

---

typically "American" array of cylindrical, freestanding tanks made out of reinforced concrete (p. 524), and "*Silos und Elevatoren, Buffalo,*" which showed the Lake & Rail Elevator in the foreground (both "loose legs" in operation) and the Marine A in the background (both of *its* loose legs are shown).

[118] *Der Sieg des Neuen Baustils* [The Victory of the New Building Styles], 1927, translated into English in 1937 as *Modern Building: Its Nature, Problems and Forms*, New York, p. 99.

According to the Ukrainian architect Louis Lozowick (born in 1892): "the skyscrapers of New York, the grain elevators of Minneapolis [*sic*], the steel mills of Pittsburgh, the oil wells of Oklahoma, the copper mines of Butte, [and] the lumbers yards of Seattle give the American cultural epic in its diaspora" ("The Americanization of Art," 1927).

As if he were competing with Behrendt for the most dramatic re-telling of what Reyner Banham called "the official myth" of German modernism,[119] the German architect Bruno Taut (born in Konigsberg, East Prussia, in 1880) declared:

> At the turn of the century, men were certainly confronted by the monumental task of extricating themselves from the labyrinth of crumbling ruins and forging for themselves a way out to the New Land. They themselves were still befogged by moldering dust, and yet they were hardly prepared to forsake their dilapidated old refuges without more ado, while the storm howled without and they still had to seek some new shelter. Or to make another comparison: they had need of all their energy to fight their way with crowbars through the refuse of the ruins, until, breathless and exhausted, they found themselves in the open. And as sometimes happens with highly gifted people, they fared as did Christopher Columbus when, seeking for India in the West, he incidentally discovered America unawares.[120]

---

[119] Reyner Banham, *A Concrete Atlantis*, p. 230.

[120] Bruno Taut, *Die Neue Baukunst in Europa und Amerika* [The New Building-Arts in Europe and America], bi-lingual edition, translated as *Modern Architecture* [London, the Studio, 1929], pp. 39-40.

In these four sentences, the worst qualities of the Worringer-Gropius line on "primitive" people and their "abstract" art (ignorance, ethnocentrism and racism) were brought to their logical conclusion. As always, the analysis was inverted: Columbus didn't "discover" the North American continent (it had been done before). He was in fact discovered by *the people* who already lived there. Consequently, Taut forgets the obvious: the encounter between the Native Americans and the European explorers, settlers, colonizers and other "highly gifted people" who starting arriving in "the New World" after 1492 resulted in the deaths of more than 50 million indigenous people, the worst of the slaughter being committed in the 19th century. The putative "primitives" who built America's grain elevators in the first decades of the 20th century weren't real "natives," but transplanted Europeans who could possess nothing of the original "savage" spirit of the place.

Significantly or, rather, typically, Taut wasn't knowledgeable about or even much interested in American grain elevators. First, he forgets to mention them: "In pre-war Europe, illustrations of American architectural styles invariably created a profound impression on artists and the artistically inclined public. The general impression gained is ascribable to overwhelming feats of engineering, such as the bridges over the Hudson, some of the factories, the railway stations with their technical installation, and finally, the construction an technical detail of the skyscrapers."[121] Then Taut sees "silo buildings" [*silogebaude*] everywhere he looks!

> It would be unfair were one to look at these silo buildings aesthetically, and judge them from the

---

[121] Bruno Taut, *Die Neue Baukunst in Europa und Amerika*, p. 65.

aesthetic standpoint. Their creators might possibly have preferred to deck them out with Doric, Ionic, or Corinthian pillars, complete with Pallas Athene, Zeus, Hermes and other figures. But they did not happen to be Central Stations or City Halls or such like institutions, where it was of the greatest importance to impress the world with their erudition and refinement. If good architecture has actually been achieved in such silo buildings, it is without their creators either knowing or intending it – possibly even they were ashamed of their stark utility [...] – this contention is but further confirmation of our argument. For architecture is so one with its purpose in all its fundamentals, that nowadays it is already beginning to be good where the architect is from the start debarred from the slightest deviation from the end in view. It is to this circumstance that the nameless American silo buildings owe their great influence on the development of modern architecture – a circumstance that has not lost its effect even to-day.[122]

Such condescension to people one claims to be praising! Of course "good architecture" had been achieved by, say, the unique cylindrical marine tower at the Washburn-Crosby, which was both a fully functional element and a clever pun on visual resemblances that everyone concerned could enjoy and be proud of.

It is clear that Bruno Taut – just like Gropius, Mendelsohn, Le Corbusier and Ginzburg before him – was only interested in grain elevators to the extent that *they*

---

[122] Bruno Taut, *Die Neue Baukunst in Europa und Amerika*, pp. 65-66.

photographed exceedingly well. Like his predecessors, Taut made sure to add a few "new" entries to the canon. There were four such photographs in *Modern Architecture*, all of them of excellent quality and great interest. Three depicted grain elevators in Montreal, and each one was captioned as follows: "Grain elevators, Montreal, Canada. (Photo by courtesy of Harbour Commissioners and Mr. Jacobs, K.C.)." The first photo showed a large transshipping elevator equipped with two marine towers (one stationary, with a pitched roof, the other automotive, with a flat roof) and two types of grain bins (exposed cylinders and enclosed tanks).[123] The second photo showed a large transshipping elevator adjoining a long dock, made of reinforced concrete, upon which there had been erected a long and narrow single-story building, also made of reinforced concrete, which in turn supported a huge steel gallery of horizontal conveyor-belts and downward-pointing iron spouts.[124] (Though this structure was "marine" in both location and function, nothing like it was ever built in Buffalo!) And the third photo showed the opposite or "unfamiliar" side of Elevator #2, built by John S. Metcalf and so favored by both Walter Gropius and Le Corbusier. Once again we see an incredible "marine" structure, the likes of which were never built in Buffalo: a large stationary tower made out of steel and corrugated iron, erected upon its own reinforced-concrete dock, far from the main house, and yet connected to it by a pair of long horizontal gantries. One of these gantries entered the tower, went through it and continued well beyond.[125]

---

[123] Bruno Taut, *Die Neue Baukunst in Europa und Amerika*, p 13.
[124] Bruno Taut, *Die Neue Baukunst in Europa und Amerika*, p 14.
[125] Bruno Taut, *Die Neue Baukunst in Europa und Amerika*, p 15.

The fourth and final photograph, which was captioned "Grain elevators at Buffalo, New York," shows the Concrete-Central.[126] Among other things, Reyner Banham claims, this mega-elevator "has the distinction of appearing for the first time in what seems to be a book – possibly the first book – specifically intended to illustrate modern architecture to a well-informed, art-loving, English-speaking audience. However Taut came to choose [the] Concrete Central, it provided a fitting conclusion to what had been a stirring period of elevator building in the United States and of elevator rhetoric in Europe" (p. 164). Though it was indeed a welcome addition to the European canon – its inclusion had been expected as early as 1924, when Erich Mendelsohn visited Buffalo – the Concrete Central cannot be said to provide a fitting "conclusion" to much of anything. Built in five stages between 1914 and 1917, it was a unique but essentially transitional structure that pointed the way to the "classic" grain elevators built in Buffalo in the 1920s: the Marine A (1925), the Lake & Rail (1927) and the Standard (1928), among them. Indeed, the appearance of the Concrete-Central in Taut's *Modern Architecture* showed that, in 1929, Germany's elevator-enthusiasts (not to mention the elevator-designers and builders) were still 10 to 15 years behind their American counter-parts.

What's striking about Taut's uncredited photo of the Concrete-Central (not reprinted in *A Concrete Atlantis* for some reason) isn't so much the grain elevator itself, but the fact that the entire, thousand-foot-long complex – everything from the freestanding transfer tower on the far right to the last of the three "loose legs" on the far left – was captured by it. No "fish eye" or other specialized lenses were apparently used. The photographer had to be positioned in just the right place for such a shot to be taken. (See figure 7.) It is telling

---

[126] Bruno Taut, *Die Neue Baukunst in Europa und Amerika*, p 13.

that Patricia Bazelon, who provided excellent "present condition" photographs for Reyner Banham, wasn't able to find such a position for *her* photograph of the Concrete Central, in which everything except for the transfer tower is captured.[127]

The problem of properly positioning yourself with respect to a colossal building was familiar to the German philosopher Immanuel Kant. Calling upon Claude-Etienne Savary's *Lettres sur l'Égypte*, first published in 1785, Kant notes:

> We must keep from going very near the Pyramids just as much as we keep from going too far from them, in order to get the full emotional effect from their size. For if we are too far away, the parts to be apprehended (the stones lying one over the other) are only obscurely represented, and the representation of them produces no effect upon the aesthetical judgment of the subject. But if we are very near, the eye requires some time to complete the apprehension of the tiers from the bottom up to the apex; and then the first tiers are always partly forgotten before the Imagination has taken in the last, and so the comprehension of them is never complete.[128]

But this section of the *Critique*, entitled "The estimation of the magnitude of natural things requisite for the idea of the sublime," wasn't intended as practical advice to aspiring photographers, whom of course did not yet exist. It was in fact intended to illustrate the difference between the two

---

[127] Reyner Banham, *A Concrete Atlantis*, p. 167.

[128] Immanuel Kant, *The Critique of Judgment*, German original 1790, translated by Werner S. Pluhar, Indianapolis, Hackett, 1990.

different forms of human imagination: intellectual apprehension (*Auffassung*) and aesthetic comprehension (*Zusammenfassung*). Jacques Derrida writes: "The former can go to infinity, the latter has difficulty following and becomes harder and harder according as the apprehension progresses. It quickly attains its maximum: the fundamental aesthetic measure for the evaluation of magnitudes [...] The mathematical evaluation of size never reaches its maximum. The aesthetic evaluation, the primary and fundamental one, does reach it; and this subjective maximum constitutes the absolute reference which arouses the feeling of the sublime."[129]

And so, unlike the beautiful, the sublime arouses what Kant calls the "negative pleasure" of feeling oneself overwhelmed or being "too close" to the colossal (Section I, Book II, SS 23). It calls for a step backwards. In Derrida's words: "So one has to find a middle place, a correct distance for uniting the maximum of comprehension to the maximum of apprehension, to take sight of the maximum of what one cannot take and to imagine the maximum of what one cannot see. And when the imagination attains its maximum and experiences the feeling of its impotence, its inadequacy to present the idea of the whole, it falls back, it sinks; it founders into itself." But this fall from the elevated heights of the sublime is not without its own pleasure: it "does not leave [the imagination] without a certain positive emotion: a certain transference gives it the wherewithal to feel pleased at this collapse which makes it come back to itself."[130]

Should one fear stepping back too quickly or not quickly enough, one can simply let one's foot on the

---

[129] Jacques Derrida, *The Truth in Painting*, translated by Geoff Bennington and Ian McLeod, University of Chicago Press, 1987, p. 126).

[130] Jacques Derrida, *The Truth in Painting*, p. 142.

accelerator set the pace. Frank Gohlke, a photographer of grain elevators, writes,

> For me, the essential grain elevator view is obtained through the windshield of a car or truck while traveling on a highway in Kansas or Oklahoma or the Texas Panhandle. It is not a static view, but one that begins just as the elevator becomes visible above the center line, above five miles out of town, and continues until it disappears in the vibration in the rearview mirror. In the minutes that pass as the speck grows to colossal size and then shrinks to rejoin the horizon, many contradictory messages are created: we are powerful, we build for centuries, our monuments rival those of other heroic ages; we are insignificant, our hold on this landscape is tenuous, nature and time erode our greatest creations as if they were dust. What lingers is the memory, though, is the image of a solitary, upright form in *the middle distance* of an endless plain.[131]

---

[131] "Measures of Emptiness," preface to *Measure of Emptiness: Grain Elevators in the American Landscape* (Johns Hopkins University Press, 1992), p. 23, emphasis added.

.

Chapter 7
Reyner Banham

Despite the strong and consistent interest in American grain elevators among many European modernist architects before World War II, the subject hadn't been given much serious attention before Reyner Banham came on the scene in 1986. Though they were big, even colossal, grain elevators had somehow managed to "slip through the cracks" of history. No doubt the unclassifiability of the elevators themselves was a big factor. If they were machines (grain *elevators*), then they should have been discussed under the rubrics of applied mechanics or mechanical engineering. And if they were buildings (grain *silos*), they should have been discussed under the general heading of architecture. But if they were actually machine-buildings (even *buildings on wheels*, in the case of Buffalo-style mobile marine towers), then grain elevators . . . seemed to leave almost everyone with nothing to say.

Obviously there were problems created by the way that architecture had traditionally distinguished itself from mere building. "A bicycle shed is a building. Lincoln Cathedral is a piece of architecture [...] The term architecture applies only to buildings designed with a view to aesthetic appeal," Nikolaus Pevsner famously proclaimed in his *Outline of European Architecture*.[1] If this is true, then a grain elevator is virtually impossible to characterize. It certainly isn't a bicycle shed, a simple frame that doesn't have to contend with the complex lateral pressures of a semi-liquid such as grain in bulk, nor is a grain elevator completely unadorned

---

[1]   Nikolaus Pevsner, *An Outline of European Architecture*, 1943; fifth edition, 1957, p. 23.

(one might easily say that the cylindrical elevating tower built at the Washburn-Crosby Flour Mills in Buffalo in 1913 is one big piece of sculpture, and certainly an instance of "architecture"). On the other hand, a grain elevator obviously isn't a cathedral, that is to say, a building whose primary function is to attract, elevate and even crush the spirits of those who see and perhaps enter it. The "marine tower" at the Washburn-Crosby was not intended to produce such "beautiful," not to mention "sublime," effects. It was modestly intended to be clever and sophisticated. And yet one can't deny that grain elevators appealed to architects and visionaries, who were capable of experiencing those effects, sometimes simply by looking at *pictures* of grain elevators.

There are in fact so many books on modern architecture that do not mention grain elevators you could fill a small library with them. First, grain elevators were ignored in such classic studies as Henry-Russell Hitchcock and Philip Johnson's *The International Style: Architecture Since 1922* (published in 1932), Nikolaus Pevsner's *Pioneers of the Modern Movement: From William Morris to Walter Gropius* (1936), and Siegfried Giedion's *Space, Time and Architecture: The Growth of a New Tradition* (1941). Then, they were ignored – for how important could grain elevators be? – by the next generation(s) of historians and writers. They aren't mentioned in *Global Architecture Document*'s Special Issue #2 on "Modern Architecture 1851-1919," edited by Kenneth Frampton (Japan, 1981), or in Alan .Phillips' *The Best in Industrial Architecture* (Switzerland, 1992).

Of course, there were exceptions, and they are telling. In "Buildings Types," the last volume of Talbot Hamlin's four-volume set, *Forms and Functions of Twentieth Century Architecture*, grain elevators are mentioned and photographed – *not* under the rubric of "Buildings for Commerce and Industry," as one might reasonably expect –

but under "Seaports and Ship Terminals."[2] The seaports mentioned are Montreal and New Orleans, and the seaport photographed (from the air) is Vancouver.[3] One wonders what happened to Thunder Bay, Duluth,[4] Chicago and Buffalo. Why weren't they mentioned?

Vincent Scully's *American Architecture and Urbanism* and Robert Venturi, Denise Brown and Steven Izenour's *Learning from Las Vegas* reproduce photographs that were reprinted fifty years previously by Charles-Edouard Jeanneret ("Le Corbusier") in *Vers une architecture* (1923). In the former case, the photograph of Elevator #2 in Montreal,

---

[2] Talbot Hamlin, *Forms and Functions of Twentieth Century Architecture*, in four volumes (Columbia University Press, 1952), p. 560.

[3] Talbot Hamlin, *Forms and Functions of Twentieth Century Architecture*, p. 562.

[4] Forgotten Duluth is evoked at the end of "Engineers and Mastering Space," written by Louis Bergeron and Maria Teresa Maiullari and published in *La Revue* #19, June 1997:

"The forecast is not good for 'historic' grain silos, particularly those belonging to the category of giant terminal elevators," states a newsletter published by the American Society for Industrial Archeology, in late 1993. In 1994, in the port of Duluth, located on the extreme western side of Lake Superior and symmetrical in its function to that of Buffalo, on the extreme eastern side of the Great Lakes, there were plans to demolish the 1887 Globe Elevator, doubtless the oldest survivor of the generation of silos with a wooden outer envelope, while activity continued at the Great Northern Elevator, a 1901 steel structure designed by the engineer Max Toltz. In fact, Duluth possesses a 'stock' of silos, greater in number, even bigger and . . . even less well-known than those in Buffalo and Minneapolis but, like them, exposed to sale, demolition or vandalism and fire. Among them is the first big silo to feature reinforced concrete cylinders, built by the Peavey Co. in 1900."

Canada is mistakenly captioned "Buffalo, New York. Grain
Elevator. Reproduced by Le Corbusier in *Vers une
Architecture*, 1923."[5] And in the latter case, the photograph
of the Wilkins Four Mill in Baltimore, Maryland, is
surrounded by pictures of "daylight" factories designed by
Albert Kahn in Clearing, Illinois; a picture of the Bauhaus in
Dessau, Germany; and a hand-written set of equations that
conclude that Walter Gropius (the one who introduced grain
elevators to Le Corbusier) was hasty or even cheated when
he assumed that Vitruvius' demand for "delight" could be
achieved by simply adding "firmness" and "commodity"
together.[6] The implication (or proof) is that the grain elevator
in Baltimore is not (necessarily) "delightful."

Were they alive in the 1980s, the European modernists
who had been fascinated by American grain elevators in the
1920s (Gropius, Le Corbusier, Erich Mendelsohn, and
Moisei Ginzburg, among others) might well have wondered:
"What ever happened to those *Amerikanischer
Getreidesilos*?" If they'd wished to hunt the grain elevators
down, where would they have started? Vincent Scully's
mistake (placing Montreal's Elevator #2 in Buffalo) suggests
the difficulties that would have immediately presented
themselves.

Let's say they consulted a classic scholarly work
written from Canada. In Harold Kalman's "The Elevator is
Going Down," they would have read that the grain elevator is

---

[5] Vincent Scully, *American Architecture and Urbanism*
(Praeger, 1969), plate 232, p. 123; compare with Le
Corbusier, p. 28.

[6] Le Corbusier, p. 25, and Robert Venturi, Denise
Brown and Steven Izenour, *Learning from Las Vegas: The
Forgotten Symbolism of Architectural Form* (MIT, 1972;
revised edition 1977), p. 143.

"the most Canadian of architectural forms."[7] It would certainly have been difficult for them to argue that Canada didn't love its grain elevators! In 1930, it printed and circulated a 30-cent postage stamp that depicted the annual harvest with grain elevators in the background. (This stamp was reissued in 1933 with inscription "World's Grain Exhibition and Conference, Regina, 1993.") Other Canadian stamps depicted a Great Lakes ship being loaded at a terminal elevator (1942) and, under the title "Summer Stores," various prairie elevators (1967). A prairie grain elevator even appeared on the Canadian dollar from 1954 to 1967. But by far the greatest expression of Canadian pride in its grain elevators was the country's submission to the "International Exposition of the Arts and Techniques that are Applied to Modern Life," held in Paris in 1937: a model of a grain elevator built in reinforced concrete, which was offered as a symbol of Canada "as the greatest individual exporter of wheat."[8]

Perhaps a bit suspicious of all this nationalistic pride, our friends from the 1920s might have consulted an American source, as well. Perhaps Guy A. Lee's "The Historical Significance of the Chicago Grain Elevator System."[9] In this article, they would have read that "the elevator system" was "first developed at Chicago," and that, "although a few ideas may have been borrowed from the Buffalo model, the development of elevators in Chicago was largely independent and soon far outgrew the older system."

---

[7] Harold Kalman's "The Elevator is Going Down," *Canadian Heritage*, Vol. 11, February/March 1984, p. 19.

[8] Elspeth Cowell, "The Canadian Pavilion at the 1939 New York World's Fair," *Society for the Study of Architecture in Canada Bulletin*, vol. 19, March 1994, p. 23.

[9] Guy A. Lee, "The Historical Significance of the Chicago Grain Elevator System," *Agricultural History*, Vol. II, No. 1, January 1937, pp. 16-32.

Other than Chicago, the only noteworthy grain ports in the United States were "Toledo, St. Louis, Milwaukee and Cincinnati"; Duluth, Superior, Minneapolis and Buffalo were not mentioned.[10]

The ghosts from the 1920s might even have begun to wonder if America still used grain elevators to . . . ah . . . elevate its grain. If they sought answers in the pages of *Patrimoine industriel des Etats-Unis*, written by Louis Bergeron and Maria Teresa Maiullari-Pontois, they would have been told in a caption to a photograph of the Great Northern Elevator (built in Buffalo in 1897) that "a 'marine leg' is thrust into the hold of a ship to *suck out* the grain and transport it to the top of the elevator."[11] Perhaps this vampiric image is simply the result of a bad translation. But "marine legs" – the leg-shaped mechanisms that "step" into grain-laden boats and unload them automatically – do not "suck," that is to say, they do not use pneumatic-suction equipment to move large amounts of grain from one place to another. The marine legs at the Great Northern (depicted on p. 151), the Concrete-Central, built in Buffalo between 1914 and 1917 (p. 152) and the Superior, built in Buffalo in 1915[12] – as well as the elevating devices in use at the wood-framed elevator in Herman, Minnesota, the steel-binned Pioneer Steel Elevator in Minneapolis, and the reinforced-concrete elevator in Herman[13] – all use "Buffalo buckets" attached to high-speed

---

[10] Guy A. Lee, pp. 31, 18, and 17, respectively.

[11] Louis Bergeron and Maria Teresa Maiullari-Pontois, *Patrimoine industriel des Etats-Unis*, translated as *Industry, Architecture and Engineering: American Ingenuity 1750-1950*, Harry N. Adams, New York 2000, p. 151, emphasis added.

[12] Louis Bergeron and Maria Teresa Maiullari-Pontois, pp. 151-152.

[13] Louis Bergeron and Maria Teresa Maiullari-Pontois, pp. 188-189.

conveyor-belts to elevate grain (this is what makes them grain *elevators*, not grain *suckers*).[14]

There *are* grain suckers, of course: they were invented in America in the 1950s. James F. Munce, the author of *Industrial Architecture: An Analysis of International Building Practices*, seems to see them everywhere. He claims that "Modern silos [sic] are basically identical, and there is a high degree of similarity in the mechanical equipment used for receiving and discharging grain [...] In the unloading of vessels, barge elevator and pneumatic-suction equipment are the most usual."[15] And yet, when the reader searches Munce's book for an illustration of a "grain elevator" that uses pneumatic-suction equipment, all she can find is a drawing entitled "Group of Silos," which was based (no acknowledgement) on an obscure photograph of a minor grain elevator built at Barby an der Elbe, Germany in 1922.[16] No pneumatic-suction equipment is in sight.

---

[14] Dan Morgan refers to them as "vacuvators" (*Merchants of Grain*, Viking, 1979, p. 318). They were first used in the 1880s. See "A 'Cyclone' in Buffalo," *New York Times*, October 10, 1887: "Lyman Smith has spent some years in perfecting a pneumatic grain transfer elevator." Built in Cleveland, the Cyclone was towed to Buffalo over Lake Erie. The elevator's transfer capacity (twelve thousand bushels an hour) was "twice as much as the best elevator machinery now in use [...] The 1,700 scoopers now employed on the docks are expected to fight the new contrivance, as it will rob them of their employment if its proves successful." See also J.G. Westbrook, "Compressed Air Grain Shoveling," *Compressed Air*, May 1905.

[15] James F. Munce, *Industrial Architecture: An Analysis of International Building Practices*, F.W. Dodge, New York, 1960, p. 178.

[16] James F. Munce, *Industrial Architecture*, p. 190. The photo was originally published in *Deutsche Baukunst der Gegenwart*, volume I, Leipzig: Langewiesche, 1929, p. 60,

From reading Bergeron and Maiullari-Pontois'
Industry, Architecture and Engineering, our ghosts from the
1920s would know that the grain elevator was in fact
invented by Joseph Dart and Robert Dunbar in Buffalo,
sometime in the early 1840s, but they would also have been
told that, "in reality, the grain elevator was not a product of
port technology, but the result of an organization of long-
distance overland trade that was particular to the mode of
settlement and development in North America."[17] By
"overland trade," Bergeron and Maiullari-Pontois mean "over
the railroads," that is to say, not over the Great Lakes and/or
the many canals opened or begun in New York,
Pennsylvania, Ohio and Indiana in the 1820s, *forty years
before* the railroads became a major factor in the grain trade
in North America.

Technically speaking, the year 1986 didn't mark the
moment that Reyner Banham "came on the scene." A very
well-known English architectural historian and critic, Peter
Reyner Banham (his friends called him Peter) had been "on
the scene," that is, both present and at the cutting-edge, ever
since the mid-1950s, when he first started publishing essays
about modern design, technology, architecture and urban
planning. His first book, *Theory and Design in the First
Machine Age* (Cambridge: MIT Press) was published in 1960
and became a classic. His book about American daylight
factories and grain elevators – *A Concrete Atlantis: U.S.
Industrial Building and European Architectural Modernism,*

---

and reprinted in Reyner Banham, *A Concrete Atlantis*, 1986,
p. 213.
[17] Louis Bergeron and Maria Teresa Maiullari-Pontois,
Industry, Architecture and Engineering: American Ingenuity,
p. 159.

1900-1925[18] – would turn out to be his last. He died of cancer just two years later, at the age of 66. In honor of his passing, MIT published *A Concrete Atlantis* in a soft-cover edition in 1989. It was this edition that circulated among and made a very strong impression on people living in Buffalo at the time.

As far as rediscovering the majesty of America's grain elevators, Banham was in fact the first. *A Concrete Atlantis* was directly inspired and informed by the four years that he spent teaching at and chairing the School of Architecture and Environmental Design at the State University of New York at Buffalo in the late 1970s. (In 1980, he left Buffalo to teach at the University of California at Santa Cruz, where he remained until 1988.) His acknowledgements give us some idea of how and when *A Concrete Atlantis* was written.

> A study such as this, which has taken me into many parts of the United States and some in Europe, leaves me deeply indebted to innumerable helpful persons and organizations, libraries, and other seats of learning: my prime debts to organizations are to the University of California, for a grant in aid of European travel and a timely sabbatical leave of absence; to the various libraries at the University of California at Berkeley and the HcHenry Library at Santa Cruz; to the State University of New York at Buffalo and the students in the summer fieldwork sessions of 1977, 1978 and 1979; to Columbia University, students in the summer session of 1982, and the Avery Library; to the staff and library of the Historic American Engineering Record,

---

[18] *A Concrete Atlantis*, MIT Press, 1986. References will hereafter appear in the text as ACA, followed by the page number.

Washington, D.C.; to the Library of the Royal
Institute of British Architects; and to the Bartlett
School of Architecture and Planning at University
College London. (ACA, p. viii)

And so it seems that the conceptual bases of the book
(including field drawings made by Banham's students, and
photographs taken by Patricia Bazelon and the author
himself) were worked out in Buffalo between 1977 and 1979,
and that the images of grain elevators reprinted by Gropius,
Mendelsohn and Le Corbusier in the 1920s were collected in
1982. It is likely that the bulk of the book was written
between 1983 and 1985. In "Chapter 2: The Grain Elevator,"
Banham says of Buffalo's long-abandoned Electric Elevator,
which was demolished soon after the permits were granted on
27 March 1984: "By the time this chapter was completed, all
the steel parts had been torched and removed, leaving a wide
hole in what had become for me a familiar riverside scene"
(ACA, p. 173).

The demolition of the Electric was in fact a "perfect"
illustration of Banham's main arguments, namely, that the
grain elevators of Buffalo:

> were as good [as architecture] as their European
> admirers had supposed [...] They do have an
> almost Egyptian monumentality in many cases,
> and in abandonment and death they evoke the
> majesties of a departed civilization [...] Outside
> of the modernists' polemics of the twenties, they
> have practically no part in the records of
> architectural history and have yet to draw a critic
> worthy of their austere virtues. That is regrettable,
> for they deserve a better fate than to be left to the
> industrial archeologists and prettifying
> rehabilitators who seem at present to be the only
> parties with any interest in them. They need to be

brought back among 'the canons of giant architecture,' and they deserve far more respect and honor than they commonly receive in America, for – as much as the work of a Richardson or a Wright – they represent the triumph of what is American in American building art [...] The factories and grain elevators [...] seem to have been influential precisely because they were thought to derive from some subculture that did not normally connect to the high culture of architects and other artists. And, insofar as these supposedly nonarchitectural buildings may have helped to fix the forms and usages of what we now call 'The International Style,' which has so far been the dominant style of twentieth-century architecture, Americans owe them the same degree of respect they award other native arts that have affected the rest of the world, such as the Hollywood film, dance theater, and jazz (ACA, pp. 19-21).

Given the urgency of Banham's project, I am not sure why it took two years for MIT Press to publish *A Concrete Atlantis*, but it was worth the wait. Both the hard- and soft-cover editions of the book were full of high-quality black-and-white reproductions of dozens of photographs and drawings, which were all placed in close proximity to the passages that referred to them, as one would hope and expect from a book that in part examines the role *bad reproduction* played in the reception of pictures of grain elevators that were reprinted over and over in the 1910s and 1920s. Most unfortunately, the undated "Classic" edition of the book that MIT is currently selling is a disgrace. Way too many illustrations have become either illegible (ACA, pp. 112, 120, 162, 238, and 241) or completely invisible (ACA, pp. 128, 220, and 221). One entire page has slipped out of position, pushing one illustration (an important one) right off the edge (ACA, p. 172).

Because he had a great gift for language (both spoken and written), and because he loved to give and go on guided tours of unusual places – see the very engaging documentary *Reyner Banham Loves Los Angeles*, which he made with BBC Television in 1972 – *A Concrete Atlantis* is in part the autobiographical account of an urban explorer. He doesn't use a map as his guide; he uses old photographs. The most dramatic moments concern Banham's encounters with Buffalo's exotic Concrete Central.

> [Bruno] Taut's illustration shows it flat on, squatting enigmatically low on the far side of an almost equally enigmatic flat landscape [...] Although it is still possible, at some risk to life and limb, by climbing across railroad bridges and the like, to see Concrete Central from the other side, that is the less interesting and less familiar side of the complex, offering nothing to the view but hundreds of bins and interstitials. The more familiar and more rewarding view is the one shown in Taut of its wharf side and its three loose legs [...] Closer views are not normally to be had, unless one goes up river to it or is prepared to undertake an adventurous and circuitous safari on foot – it is completely inaccessible by wheeled vehicles these days – through thickets of red sumac bushes and along rusting rail tracks. That journey is worth it, however. In lonely but not yet totally ruinous abandonment, this huge rippled cliff of concrete dominates a quarter-mile reach of the river [...] Because it consists almost entirely of closed storage volumes to which there is no casual access, it remains impermeable, secret, and aloof. There are some elevators where one can

> penetrate into gigantic storage volumes – the
> Electric extensions of 1940, for instance – and
> marvel at their sheer dimensions, but at Concrete
> Central the storage volumes remain as
> inaccessible as the interior of an Egyptian
> pyramid [...] The first time I reached Concrete
> Central by land, a series of incidents emphasized
> its abandonment and isolation [...] Yet the sense
> of distance from help and civilization was
> exhilarating rather than depressing; the presence
> of the huge abandoned structure produced a mood
> more elegiac than otherwise (ACA, pp. 165-166).

This is pretty corny stuff. Banham wants his readers to believe that he risked "life and limb" to see the Concrete Central up close and personal: "my foot crashed through a rotten plywood cover that had been laid over an open culvert [...] Had I sustained an incapacitating injury, rather than mere scratches, in that fall, even those who knew approximately where I was would have no idea how to reach me, after they had finally decided that they waited too long for their return" (ACA, p. 166). As a matter of fact, the elevator district in Buffalo is an unpleasant, forbidding and unsafe place. It is isolated and filled with illegally dumped garbage and other wastes. The elevators themselves are in substantial disrepair, especially Concrete Central, which sits upon an exposed and increasingly damaged wooden dock. And yet Reyner Banham wants us to believe that *he* wasn't scared or depressed; no, *he* was positively exhilarated! And the presence of Concrete Central wasn't menacing or even evil, but merely sad and mournful.

I wholeheartedly agree that these conceits have been strong or "evocative" enough to get people to actually go out and visit places such as the Concrete Central (they certainly worked on me), and that Banham should be applauded for his efforts. But it must be pointed out that once you do go out and visit the Concrete Central, you quickly realize two things: first, there are dozens of children in the area who have no fear whatsoever about climbing across (or even diving into the water from) railroad bridges and the like; second, Banham was in *his fifties* when he first came to Buffalo and – no matter how young or macho you think you are – fifty is old compared to teenagers who aren't afraid to jump 100 feet or climb a building twice that height.

The last ten pages of "Chapter 2: The Grain Elevator" are devoted to Banham's "afterthoughts" on "survival and obsolescence." In them, he offers a few suggestions on what places like Buffalo should do with their old factories and grain elevators.

> The elevators, mills, and factories of Buffalo, Minneapolis, Detroit, or even Rockville [Connecticut], are important in themselves, as monuments to the history of the building arts or to the technical innovations [...] that made the invention of new building types necessary. But there is no way – except allusively and [al]most obliquely – that any building at any of the Ford plants could monumentalize Ford's most consequential social innovation, the five-dollar-a-day wage, and *only an ill-informed belief in the imagined 'seamlessness' of the web of modern culture or in the 'totalizing' tyranny of capitalist ideology could make anyone suppose otherwise.* There are better ways to remember social innovations than in preserving the buildings, constructed for a previous regime or social order in which they just happened to take place; and there are more convincing reasons for preserving historic factories and mills – because they are important to the history of building, for instance, or because they are better architecture than the

common expectations of their times required.
(ACA, pp. 171-172, emphasis added)

Though general, these are good recommendations to
preservationists and the National Parks Service, which is in
charge of the national Registry of Historic Places. Choose
your buildings well; do not simply pay heed to their local
significance, but also to also their significance at the national
and international levels; pay attention to "social innovations."
Though Banham himself may have been uncomfortable with
the idea, any good determination of the "social innovations"
of the grain elevator has to include *collective ownership*
(private shipments mixed together and stored in common
bins in public warehouses), which of course is a classic
Marxist theme.[19]

In any event, Banham's efforts as an activist were
successful. Inspired by Banham, who had in turn been
inspired by them, local groups such as the Industrial Heritage
Committee (founded in 1985) and the Preservation Coalition
of Erie County (founded in 1986), took up the cause of
Buffalo's grain elevators with renewed vigor. In 1990, they
managed to convince the National Parks Service to send a

---

[19] I should not fail to note that Banham has a very good
point when he claims (without mentioning vulgar Marxism,
though it is clearly the target of his polemic) that "only an ill-
informed belief in the imagined 'seamlessness' of the web of
modern culture or in the 'totalizing' tyranny of capitalist
ideology could make anyone suppose otherwise." Indeed,
following Banham and yet still remaining a Marxist, I have
been endeavoring to show that – *in addition to* using the
cheapest raw materials, employing the least expensive means,
depending upon inexpensive labor and thus producing a lot of
junk – "modern culture" and "capitalist ideology" have *also*
used substantial resources and skills to produce some truly
top-quality, durable products (certain grain elevators in
Buffalo and elsewhere).

team to Buffalo from the Historic American Engineering Record, which is tasked with documenting "sites of national significance that are in danger of demolition or loss by neglect." Led by Craig Strong, the HAER team was composed of four architects, three industrial historians and a photographer (Jet Lowe). It spent a total of three months weeks photographing, measuring, researching and writing up Buffalo's elevators, with special attention paid to the wood-framed Wollenberg, the brick-boxed Great Northern, and two reinforced-concrete giants, the Standard and Concrete Central. By the time the team completed its work and made it available through the Library of Congress in 1992, local groups had already erected a plaque on the Buffalo waterfront that bore the fairly short-sighted inscription "BIRTHPLACE OF THE GRAIN ELEVATOR: In 1842, the world's first steam powered elevator to transfer and store grain opened on this site. Buffalo merchant, Joseph Dart, and machinist, Robert Dunbar, built the elevator following precedents set by Oliver Evans. Its basic principles are still used in elevators along Buffalo's waterfront." Local groups had also managed to convince the City of Buffalo to award the Great Northern Elevator – threatened with demolition by its then-owner, the Pillsbury Flour Company – with city landmark status. In 2003, these activists convinced the Parks Service Department to place both the Wollenberg and the Concrete Central on the National Registry of Historic Places.

Today, Banham's reputation in Buffalo is mixed. On the one hand, he is the source of a lot of local pride. He was the one who wrote these wonderful lines, possibly in response to people in London who had exclaimed "*Buffalo?! What the bloody hell is in Buffalo?*" when they heard that Banham was moving there in 1976.

> Whatever happened in Paris or Berlin or London
> was perceived to be important, New York also as
> much so, and Chicago could not be gainsaid

because of the manifest genius of Frank Floyd Wright, which made it necessary to bracket into the argument his predecessors like Louis Sullivan. But who ever heard of Cincinnati, Minneapolis, Bayonne, Buffalo, Oakland, Montreal, Duluth . . . even somewhere as conspicuous in the history of modern manufacturing technology as Detroit? (ACA, p. 107).

Banham was the one who put Buffalo back on the map. On the other hand, Banham is an embarrassment, even an outrage. *A Concrete Atlantis* is full of mistakes and, because of that, an intolerable arrogance.

Note Banham's comments about the engineering firm of A.E. Baxter, founded in Buffalo in 1896.

The only architect of title recorded for any part of the [Washburn-Crosby] complex in this period of its development was A.E. Baxter of Buffalo, who was responsible in 1910 for the concrete-framed milling building that lies along the river bank in front of the first and second set of bins. Baxter was to collaborate in the design of many later elevators, but his 'architecty' contributions are easy to recognize by their preoccupations with style rather than function and their generally conservative, not radical, strain [...] The author of this particular architectural contrivance [a long, rectangular "International Style" window inserted into the basement wall of the 1933 extension to Perrot Malting] was A.E. Baxter, who was extensively involved in the design of grain elevators and gave his preferred raised-basement treatment (though not always his decorative details) to a number of elevators in the Buffalo area (ACA, pp. 149 and 156).

But, as a matter of fact, the A.E. Baxter Company had *nothing* to do with either the Washburn-Crosby complex or the 1933 extension to Perrot Malting, no matter what the students whom Banham sent to do research at City Hall told him. Thus Banham's objections to Baxter's "'architecty' contributions" and "preoccupations with style" are completely baseless.

In response to these outrages, A.E. Baxter's son, Henry Baxter (who ran his father's company until 1968) worked up a chart that lists *correct information* concerning which designers and builders constructed which elevators in Buffalo and when. Included in *Reconsidering Concrete Atlantis: Buffalo's Grain Elevators*,[20] this chart doesn't mention Reyner Banham, but he takes a drubbing in it. Out of 15 elevators left standing in Buffalo, Banham only mentioned 10 of them. He offers detailed information about 8 of these 10. In half of these cases (the Washburn-Crosby, Perrot Malting, Concrete Central, and the Kellogg), he is dead wrong. These elevators weren't designed by A.E. Baxter, but by either James Stewart or Harry Wait. One would have thought that any publication that contained such a damning indictment would never refer to the work of such a shoddy scholar in its title, but this testifies to Banham's enduring popularity in Buffalo, at least at SUNY.

I think it's funny that Nigel Whiteley, author of *Reyner Banham: Historian of the Immediate Future*, believes that *A Concrete Atlantis* is about "American industrial buildings such as the daylight factory and the grain *silo*" and commends Banham for his "detailed research" and "the scale

---

[20] Edited by Lynda Schneekloth and published by the School of Architecture and Planning at SUNY at Buffalo, 2006, p. 14.

of the footnotes."[21] But he's certainly not as funny as Romy Golan, who claims in her review of Whiteley's book that *A Concrete Atlantis* was "written in the early 1970s" and "published, posthumously, in 1986."[22]

---

[21] Nigel Whiteley, *Reyner Banham: Historian of the Immediate Future* (MIT Press, 2001), pp. 71-72, emphasis added, and p. 74.

[22] *Art Bulletin*, volume 85, issue 2 (June 1, 2003), p. 404.

Chapter 8
Town and Country

More than twenty years after the publication of Reyner Banham's *A Concrete Atlantis*, grain elevators remain rich objects for aesthetic contemplation. About a dozen books on the subject have been published to date.[1] Significantly, almost all of them focus on the small country elevators that stand in rural areas, and ignore the colossal terminal elevators that stand in major port cities. It is clear that this preference or bias is designed to counter-balance Banham, who ignored country elevators and focused exclusively on terminal elevators in Buffalo and Minneapolis. But no balancing out is possible if either or both "sides" try to separate itself or

---

[1] Mary S. Fielding, *Prairie Sky Scrapers: A Pictorial Record of Grain Elevators in Iroquois County, 1986-1989* (Iroquois County Historical Society, 1989), Frank Gohlke, *Measure of Emptiness: Grain Elevators in the American Landscape* (Baltimore, 1992), Lisa Mahar-Keplinger, *Grain Elevators* (Princeton University Press, 1993), Russell Stubbles, *Skyscrapers of the Prairie: South Dakota's Historic Wooden Grain Elevators* (Brookings, 1997), Greg McDonnell, *Wheat Kings: Vanishing Landmarks of the Canadian Prairies* (Boston Mills, 1998), Brock V. Silversides, *Prairie Sentinel: The Story of the Canadian Grain Elevator* (Fifth House, 1999), Elizabeth McLachlan, *Gone But Not Forgotten: Tales of the Disappearing Grain Elevators* (NeWest, 2004), Jon Volkmer, *The Art of the Country Grain Elevators* (Bottom Dog Press, 2006), Bern and Hilla Becher, *Grain Elevators* (MIT Press, 2006), and John Bower, *After the Harvest: Indiana's Historic Grain Elevators and Feed Mills* (Studio Indiana, 2007).

themselves from the other. Though the terminal elevator came first (thirty years before the country elevator), and though the country elevator comes first in the "stream" that brings grain from the farm to the consumer, the two are indissoluble parts of a single, integrated system.

It seems easy or, rather, it is tempting to separate the country grain elevator from the international grain trade of which it is a part because the country elevator is apparently self-contained and central to the commercial and social lives of the small districts or "territories" in which they operate. Unlike terminal elevators, which are typically erected on the peripheries of the city, along with the other industrial structures, country elevators are typically erected right in the middle of town, where the railroad tracks cross Main Street.

Because they were originally built every six to ten miles in grain-growing regions, country elevators in the United States and Canada needed to have strong connections with their respective territories, which can vary widely in terms of the numbers of acres planted, the productivity of those acres, and the proximity of the next elevator on the line. Unlike terminal elevators, at which grain arrives alone, "impersonally," or at least no longer in the company of the farmer(s) who grew and harvested it, country elevators are places at which farmers congregate and can do a whole variety of things. They can buy essential supplies such as animal feed, fertilizers and seeds. They can catch up on both local gossip and the latest regional/national news concerning the weather, price fluctuations and the availability of rail cars during harvest time. They can pay to have their grain cleaned, dried or ground into animal feed. And, of course, they can have their grain sampled, graded and hopefully purchased by the country elevator's owners, who engage in either cash transactions or contracted exchanges (the most popular of which is the forward cash contract, which allow certain "details" of the exchange to be worked out later). Though most country elevators ship out the grain in their bins as soon as possible, some store grain to maximize the capacities of their buildings and to take advantage of the possibility that prices might be higher at a later time.

In the 19th century, entry into the business of running a country elevator was relatively easy. "Many plants were built years ago when construction costs were lower, margins were wider, and distance from farm to elevator was more important than at present," L.J. Norton recalls from the perspective of the early 1940s. "Grain marketing areas were interlaced with many railroads, each seeking to get its share of the grain tonnage and encouraging the construction of [more] elevators."[2] But with the switch from wood to steel (or even reinforced concrete) in the construction of country elevators, and the use of long-distance trucks instead of railcars to transport grain,[3] country elevators became more expensive to build and they faced increasingly stiff competition, not just from country elevators in neighboring territories, but also from the formerly distant grain terminals.[4]

---

[2] L.J. Norton, "Business Policies of Country Grain Elevators," *Bulletin 477, University of Illinois, Agricultural Experiment Station*, April 1941, p. 295.

[3] "The largest movement of grain by truck in Illinois is to the Illinois and Mississippi Rivers. The savings in transportation costs resulting when grain is moved to terminal markets by truck and river barge instead of rail are sufficient to draw grain in volume to stations on these rivers from distances up to 30 or 40 miles." L.J. Norton, "Business Policies of Country Grain Elevators," *Bulletin 477, University of Illinois, Agricultural Experiment Station*, April 1941, p. 297.

[4] See Shannon Ruckman, "Rural cooperatives evolve with changing times, support communities, *The Prairie Star*, October 10, 2008: "'There were five elevators between here (Winifred) and Lewistown (Mont.),' recalled Bergum. 'Now, the grain goes all the way to Moccasin (Mont.), which is 60 miles away.' Modernized transportation is mostly to blame

Every since then, but especially since the 1960s, when terminal elevators on the Great Lakes began to close down, the country elevator has been in serious decline. More often than not, abandoned country elevators in the United States and Canada have not been left to rot, but have been demolished and stripped for the wood they contain.

Not surprisingly, there is a mournful or melancholy tone to many of the recent books about the country elevator, which is "disappearing" or "vanishing," just as there is a such a tone in Reyner Banham's tribute to the abandoned and ruined terminal elevators of Buffalo and Minneapolis. But unlike Banham, who consistently stresses the *functionality* of the terminal elevator, the authors of these newer books are content with superficiality – with the external surfaces and shapes (the "forms") of small grain elevators – and express or incite no interest in what's inside them (the machines, the people who operate them and, of course, the grain itself). This is more than a matter of differing tastes or preferences. These biases render these books incapable of making the simple but quite essential distinction between granaries (grain silos) and grain elevating and storage warehouses (grain elevators).

Take for example Bernd & Hilda Becher's book *Getreidesilos* [Grain Silos], which was translated into English as *Grain Elevators*.[5] A large collection of photographs taken in the USA, Great Britain, France and

---

for the decreasing number of elevators and agricultural cooperatives throughout Montana, said Bob Taylor, a Denton, Mont., farmer and secretary of the Central Montana Co-op. 'There used to be a bunch of cooperatives and elevators all over central Montana,' he said. 'Transportation pretty much messed that up. Grain now gets hauled up to 100 miles or more when it used to be a lot less.'"

[5] Schirmer/Mosel Verlag, Munich, 2006; MIT Press, 2006. No translator is listed.

Germany between 1961 and 2006, this book begins with an unsigned essay entitled "On Function." But "On Function" is primarily concerned with highlighting the kinds and locations of grain silos in use. Only five of its sentences are devoted to the "silo [sic] system."

> From the ground floor, where the grain is weighed, moisture level checked, and temperature monitored, it is taken vertically or at an acute angle up to the top of the silo to enable it to pass through as many levels as possible moving purely by gravity's pull. The grain is moved upward either by using pneumatic suction tubes, bucket elevators, or screw conveyors (Archimedes' screw). The tower, often the working house, contains the drives and aggregates used to clean and dry the grain and extract the dust. The gallery mainly houses the horizontal conveyors used to fill the silo containers. By virtue of gravity the grain falls down to the very bottom of the containers – whence it can later be removed.[6]

What follows is nothing but photographs of the exteriors of abandoned grain elevators. We see no inner spaces, no machines in operation and no workers. We only see *forms*, a great variety of them, so many in fact that it is easy to lose track of what they share in common.

The captions provided merely locate these forms in space and time (that is, the year that they were photographed). The first one, "Peotone, Illinois, USA 1982," is typical of the rest. *Where in blazes is Peotone, Illinois?* Where is it in relation to the many other places in Illinois that

---

[6] *Grain Elevators*, MIT Press, pp. 5-6.

the Bechers photographed grain elevators?[7] Why are there so
many grain elevators in Illinois? Did they operate
independently of each other or did they form a system?
Connected by rail or by canal? Is the grain elevator in
Peotone still standing or was it demolished sometime after
1982?

As far as I can tell, the Peotone elevator is/was an
unremarkable example of the typical "country" grain elevator
that was built alongside railroad tracks in rural Canada and
the United States between 1880 and 1950. Consequently,
nothing much is lost by wrenching the Peotone from its
context and presenting it in this "spectacular" manner. But
the same cannot be said for *dozens* of other grain elevators,
truly significant ones, that were photographed and summarily
captioned by the Bechers. A single example will suffice: the
Electric Elevator in Buffalo, which appears under the generic
title "Buffalo, New York, USA, 1982" in two instances
(plates 150 and 213).[8] In the first photograph, we are
standing close to the Electric's steel bins (the first
freestanding, cylindrical, unenclosed grain tanks made out of
steel) and, in the second, very close to the remains of the
Electric's two marine towers, one of which (the one on the
left) was the world's first electrically powered "loose leg."
The disconnection from the context is total: we don't know
that we are looking at two sides of the same historic grain
elevator, and we don't know that this unnamed elevator in

---

[7] Buckley, Crescent City, Roberts, Penfield, Rantoul,
Mahonet, Joliet, Clifton, Chebanse, Armstrong, Piper City,
Elliott, Gibson City, Sheldon, Beecher, Onarga, Kankakee,
Grand Park, Gilman, East Chicago, and Calumet.

[8] Other (possibly) significant grain elevators in this
volume that call for contextualization are the ones built out of
reinforced concrete in France (especially plates 109-112, 114,
119-124, 141-146, 151, 152, 163, 165, 166, 221, 222, 229
and 230).

Buffalo, New York was in fact destroyed just two years after
the Bechers photographed it, in 1984.[9]

Significantly, I think, the authors obsessed with the
forms taken by grain elevators cannot completely dispense
with "function," which of course is impossible when the
subject at hand is a machine/building that was assembled
with a very specific set of purposes in mind. But when they
finally speak of the function that the grain elevator provides,
these authors do so indirectly and innocently, as if they were
speaking of something else. Take for example Frank Gohlke,
a photographer and writer who published *Measure of
Emptiness: Grain Elevators in the American Landscape* in
1992. In the essay that accompanies his photographs, Gohlke
says,

> When Le Corbusier called grain elevators the
> "cathedrals of the prairies," he was saying more
> than he knew. A woman in Plainview, Texas, told
> me, "Out here the churches don't need to have tall
> steeples, we have the grain elevators," confirming
> Le Corbusier's intuition and highlighting the
> amalgam, some would say confusion, of the
> spiritual and the material that is so characteristic
> of American public mythology.[10]

I have been unable to find this reference in the published
works of Le Corbusier. It seems unlikely that Le Corbusier
would say such a thing: he *hated* cathedrals, especially

---

[9] The other grain elevator in Buffalo photographed by
the Bechers and captioned "Buffalo, New York, USA, 1982"
– that is to say, the H-O Oats Elevator, built out of steel in
1931 – was demolished in 2006 to make room for a casino.

[10] Frank Gohlke, "Measure of Emptiness," in *Measure
of Emptiness: Grain Elevators in the American Landscape*
(Johns Hopkins University Press, 1992), p. 23.

Gothic ones. In *Vers une architecture* (1923), directly beneath a nice-looking, large-scale, reinforced-concrete grain elevator built in Canada, he declares:

> Gothic architecture is not, fundamentally, based on spheres, cones and cylinders. Only the nave is an expression of a simple form, but of a complex geometry of the second order (intersecting arches). It is for that reason that a cathedral is not very beautiful and that we search in it for compensations of a subjective kind outside plastic art.[11]

Perhaps Gohlke was thinking of Vincent Scully, who swears in *American Architecture and Urbanism* that "the great grain elevators of the wheat-bearing plains out beyond St. Louis are [...] without referential scale, gleaming, farseen American cathedrals, devoid of images and congregations."[12] Or maybe Yousuf Karsh, who said with respect to his photographic essay on the grain elevators in Port Arthur, Canada: "I treat grain elevators just like cathedrals."[13] Or one of the many other no doubt well-intentioned people who have taken liberties with the simple observation that, yes, in small rural towns, the only tall buildings around are the grain elevators and churches.

But churches *aren't* cathedrals: their functions are quite different. Churches are tall but simple buildings, rarely adorned, and designed for public worship. (The word "church" can also refer to a particular denomination or a

---

[11] Translated by Frederick Etchells, *Towards A New Architecture*, Dover Books, 1986, p. 30.

[12] Vincent Scully, *American Architecture and Urbanism*, New York: F.A. Praeger, 1969.

[13] *MacLean's Magazine*, vol. 67, February 15, 1954, p. 17.

congregation of worshippers.) But cathedrals are large, imposing buildings, rather ornate and designed to contain the bishop's throne, otherwise known as the cathedra. Such buildings have little or nothing to do with the concerns of the members of "the public," other than the Church's need to appear to them as rich, powerful, elevated and blessed by God.

Elsewhere in his essay, Gohlke asks, "If grain elevators are secular cathedrals, it is because the spiritual has invaded the domain of the material, transforming dross into gold, or has the material appropriated the spiritual, reducing it to a hypocritical justification for the exploitation of the land and the pursuit of wealth?" Unfortunately, he doesn't answer this pointed question, which he immediately takes back.

> It is not necessary to portray the issue in such judgmental terms to recognize that the vertical reach of the grain elevator proposes a connection between human industry, the land's bounty and divine favor. Whether that claim is advanced in a spirit of thankfulness or self-congratulation is unclear, one of the ambiguities that makes these buildings such rich objects of contemplation.[14]

I'm surprised that Gohlke didn't realize the unfortunate similarity between "the vertical reach of the grain elevator" and the Biblical story of the Tower of Babel, which of course was destroyed by God, who had no difficulty distinguishing thankfulness from self-congratulation. No matter. Grain elevators are not simply symbols of "the land's bounty and divine favor" and "rich objects of contemplation." They are also symbols of misery, poverty and hunger *amidst and despite* abundance.

---

[14] Frank Gohlke, "Measure of Emptiness," p. 23.

There are three pictures of American grain elevators in *Say, Is This The U.S.A.*, the second collaboration between photographer Margaret Bourke-White and author Erskine Caldwell.[15] Each of these grain elevator pictures is gripping. At the base of a long row of cylindrical grain tanks so tall they rise right through the very top of the picture, an all-black steam locomotive comes down the tracks, right in our direction.[16] The caption says: "HUTCHINSON, KANSAS. This America is a jungle of men living in the extremes of good and bad, heat and cold, wealth and poverty. You are born here and you die here, and in the intervening years you take out more than you put back." Behind a dried-out cornfield, there is a line of buildings, neatly arranged in height-order. From left to right, shortest to tallest, we see a long building with a pitched roof (a schoolhouse perhaps), then a church, a country-style grain elevator and a water tower.[17] The caption says "VIRGIL, SOUTH DAKOTA. This is the joy and sorrow of your life. Dry-farming, you live in hope of winter rain and snow, because you know under the blazing sun of summer there is no hope." On one side of the railroad tracks that go right underneath our feet, we see a water tower marked PRETTY PRAIRIE; on the other side, we see three buildings, each one a grain elevator, though the last one in line stands out because it is made of gleaming-white reinforced concrete, not dark wood.[18] The caption says "PRETTY PRAIRIE, KANSAS. Seedings, births, elevators, wheat, larks, combines, marriages, housewarmings, homecomings, yearlings, burials, tornadoes, tumbleweeds, cottonwoods, jackrabbits."

---

[15] Margaret Bourke-White and Erskine Caldwell, *Say, Is This The U.S.A.* Original 1941, reprinted by Da Capo, 1977.

[16] The very first picture in the book (p. 5).

[17] *Say, Is This The U.S.A.*, p. 39.

[18] *Say, Is This The U.S.A.*, p. 49.

But the best caption by far accompanies a photograph that shows a farmer (who looks like the Hollywood actor Robert Mitchum) standing in a wheat field, under very dark skies, breaking open a wheat berry in his hands and looking intently at the results.[19] The caption says "ANNELLY, KANSAS. All these people, all this abundance, all these things, is this America we live in; but none of us knows what to do about it. This is us, this is what we have; but nobody knows what to do next."

If the grain elevator *is* the American (and Canadian) cathedral, this is not because "the spiritual" has "invaded the domain of the material," thus "transforming dross into gold." The grain elevator was not erected to thank God, Ceres, or "the goddess of progress," to quote Walter B. Herbert.[20] Nor has "the material appropriated the spiritual," thus "reducing it to a hypocritical [and self-congratulatory] justification for the exploitation of the land and the pursuit of wealth." All that was done long before the invention of the grain elevator. No, brothers and sisters, the grain elevator is the American (and Canadian) cathedral because North America's god is Money and its religion is Capitalism. And if these "secular cathedrals" are "devoid of images and congregation," as the Rev. Scully observes, this is simply because Money is a false god and Capitalism is a satanic religion.[21]

---

[19] *Say, Is This The U.S.A.*, p. 11.

[20] "Castles of the New World," *The Canadian Geographical Journal*, Vol. 6, No. 5 May 1933, p 255.

[21] "The standard comparison likens an elevator to a sentinel, but I had decided, after thousands of miles and hundreds of grain elevators, that they resemble giant Monopoly hotels and act like medieval churches – dominating, identifying and justifying the villages in their dusty shade." Mark Abbey, *Beyond Forget: Rediscovering the Prairies*, Toronto, 1986, p. 197.

The whole cathedral thing is really beaten to death in Lisa Mahar-Keplinger's *Grain Elevators*, which also happens to be the most misinformed of the recent books on the subject. For example, in the essay that accompanies her photographs, Mahar-Keplinger asserts that Charles Sheeler's *Classic Landscape* (1931) "harmoniously reconciled industry and nature, grain elevator and landscape,"[22] when in fact the building in question is a *coal* elevator at the Ford Motor plant in River Rouge. Is it surprising that the book's publisher, Kevin Lippert, didn't catch this glaring mistake? In his post-face to *Grain Elevators*, Lippert blithely declares that "The evolution of a building type is in some way arbitrary; the function of the building is less interesting than its form, which is quite literally the vessel of meaning [...] The grain elevator is one of the clearest examples of the machine aesthetic of form following function."[23] But a grain elevator – even a small one built out of wood, standing alone way out in the middle of the Great Plains – is *not* an ordinary building, but a unique machine/building hybrid, which means that, in it, the relations between "form" and "function" will be much more complicated than a simple model in which one "follows" the other. In an almost painful instance of misunderstanding, Lippert further declares "The grain elevator developed following the laws of physics, seeking to avoid explosions caused by the internal pressure of grain storage."[24] In point of fact, explosions are not caused by grain pressures, but by sparks that ignite the clouds of grain dust that are an inevitable presence when grain in bulk is handled or stored. The laws of physics are certainly in play, but they concern the height, width and thickness of the grain bins, which have to contend with the lateral pressures that

---

[22] Lisa Mahar-Keplinger, *Grain Elevators* (Princeton University Press, 1993), p. 9.

[23] Lisa Mahar-Keplinger, *Grain Elevators*, p. 83.

[24] *Ibid.*

grain in bulk (a semi-liquid) exerts when stored or even transported by horizontal conveyor-belts.

In her essay, Mahar-Keplinger dutifully notes that in a place like Danville, Kansas "the elevators and the church are the two primary [visual] elements."[25] In his post-face, Kevin Lippert points out: "Although some of the large concrete elevators admired by Le Corbusier and others are still in use, most have fallen into disrepair, taking on a romantic air, not unlike the ruins of a European cathedral. Now graying, walls fissured or crumbling, these massive cathedrals of agriculture have become monuments to the golden age of American farming."[26] And in *his* introduction, which is titled (you guessed it!) "Timeless Cathedrals," the famous Italian architect Aldo Rossi observes: "To those who travel the great highways of the Midwest [*sic*], silos appear like cathedrals, and in fact they are the cathedrals of our times."[27]

Of course, grain elevators have been built in places other than "the Midwest," but you wouldn't know it from the books about grain elevators that have been published since 1989. Perhaps the worst offender in this regard is Gohlke's book. Despite the inclusiveness of its subtitle (*Grain Elevators in the American Landscape*), it doesn't include a single photograph of Buffalo, the city in which the American grain elevator was invented. As a matter of fact, Gohlke's photographs were taken in two dozen rural/agricultural locations, all of them in the Great Plains: Montana (Missoula), Minnesota (Red Wing and Minneapolis), Wisconsin (Bay City), Kansas (Homewood, Kinsley, Copeland, Bellefont, Montezuma and Wellington), Oklahoma (Enid, Hennessey and Woodward) and Texas (Tulia, Happy, Brownfield, Roscoe, Abilene, Ropesville, Dumas, Plainview, Follett, Perrytown, Littlefield, Earth and

---

[25] Lisa Mahar-Keplinger, *Grain Elevators*, p. 9.
[26] Lisa Mahar-Keplinger, *Grain Elevators*, p. 83.
[27] Lisa Mahar-Keplinger, *Grain Elevators*, p. 7.

Lamesa). Big as it is, the area covered by this version of the "American Landscape" (the so-called heartland) is actually a small part of the United States. Missing from it is enough to fill a couple of basic textbooks on American geography and history: the Great Lakes and its inland ports, the eastern seaboard and its deepwater ports (active even when "America" was a British colony), the entire Mississippi water system and the deepwater ports on the Gulf of Mexico, and the Columbia River and the deepwater ports in Portland. Gohlke's vision of America deliberately excludes "the modern city" in favor of a preoccupation with the "hometown." He writes:

> Grain elevators were prominent buildings in my hometown of Wichita Falls, Texas, but the terminal elevators of the Midway [between Minneapolis and St Paul] were different – bigger and more numerous than the ones I was used to. Seen end-on, as they were from the Kasota Avenue overpass on Highway 280, they were like a city: their proportions were similar to those of typical office buildings, while the rhythms of their massing mimicked those of the downtown Minneapolis skyline two miles to the west. The analogy with the modern city broke down, however when the elevators were viewed as closer range. On my frequent detours across the tracks and along the rutted dirt roads that ran between the elevators, I found an area that was rough, unfinished and empty. University Avenue, a major thoroughfare connecting Minneapolis and St. Paul, was only a few blocks away, but it could have been miles, or centuries […] The trip [to New Mexico] was a revelation; it altered my conception of the project in fundamental ways,

372

moving its center of gravity from the city to the country.[28]

There are in fact *two* Americas here: an America of the prairies, which is the America of yesteryear, "rough, unfinished and empty," and an America of modern cities, which is the America of today (presumably polished, complete and full of people and things). The difference between them is completely subjective: Gohlke is personally inspired by the "'space where nobody is,' the emptiness of the prairies,"[29] and he is not inspired by the places where *everybody* is or wants to be (the overcrowded cities). But is this any way to document American history?

Gohlke's interest in grain elevators is in fact secondary. The primary task of his project (undertaken between 1972 and 1977) was measuring the "emptiness" of the landscapes in the prairies and the High Plains. "Grain elevators," he says, "were [merely] the presence against which that emptiness could be measured."[30] Anything that was big and tall enough to be visible from a distance would have been sufficient. "Grain elevators are the product of a culture that favors the sense of sight above others. We need to *see* our presence manifested in the landscape, preferably over great distances. The workaday operations of the grain elevators could cease, and they would still serve a vital function on the prairies simply by being so definitively *visible* [...] By its constant, far-flung visibility, [the grain elevator] symbolizes to the inhabitants the coherence, vitality, and continuity of

---

[28] Frank Gohlke, "Measure of Emptiness," p. 15 and 19.
[29] Frank Gohlke, "Measure of Emptiness," p. 24. Internal quote is from Gertrude Stein, "In the United States there is more space where nobody is than where anybody is," cited by Gohlke earlier in his text.
[30] "Measure of Emptiness," p. 24.

their communities."[31] But the very same things could be said about the skyscrapers in America's cities: they, too, can be seen from a distance and used to "measure the emptiness" of the intervening space.

Not surprisingly, Gohlke doesn't know how grain elevators work: "A grain elevator is in fact a container, a volume to be filled, a shell surrounding more empty space."[32] When he proclaims "the locations of the early elevators had been dictated by the available means of transportation and the suitability of the terrain, soil, and climate for a particular kind of agriculture," I'm not sure he understands that such was the case *in rural areas only* and that, in urban areas – where the *earliest* elevators were constructed – the suitability of the terrain, soil, and climate were not relevant factors at all. But the truly irritating thing about Gohlke is that he claims that he *tried* to understand these things, but failed.

> There is literally a great deal more to a grain elevator than meets the eye. I began asking questions of the workers I encountered on my visits to the Midway. What is stored inside, and what happens to it while it's there? How are the elevators constructed? What are those big, funnel-like structures hanging on the sides? What is your job? [...] I thought that if I could discover others who shared my intuitions or could give them a foundation in fact or theory, then I could proceed more confidently [...] I kept hoping that one of my informants would open a door to the larger dimensions which I was sure the elevators inhabited, but their responses were insistently straight-forward and factual. The features of the

---

[31] "Measure of Emptiness," pp. 22-23, and 23.

[32] "Measure of Emptiness," p. 19. What he is in fact describing is a granary, not a grain elevator.

elevators that I found so visually compelling all had predictably mundane explanations, and the people who had daily contact with them had, also predictably, little inclination to see them in other terms. My enthusiasm for a particularly beautiful surface was received with ironic amusement by a foreman in green coveralls, to whom it was an eyesore, caused by a bad batch of black paint that had weathered quickly to reveal the swirling marks of the concrete workers' trowels [...] As interested as I was in what I was learning [*sic*], I was frustrated by the discrepancy between the ordinariness of the facts surrounding the grain elevators and the intensity of my emotional response to the objects themselves.[33]

Rejected by the salt of the earth (a few grain elevator workers in the American Midwest), Gohlke tries to turn the tables on them: *it is not I who fail to understand what you are doing; it is you who fail to understand what you yourselves are doing!* He writes:

To me, the photographs I was making argued that there are deeper impulses lurking somewhere in the functional surfaces and details of the grain elevators, and that subjective choice as well as objective necessity has a role in determining their form [...] I felt sure that there were aesthetic and symbolic dimensions one could not ignore if one wanted to understand the grain elevators fully, and that these intangible qualities arose from concrete relationships among the buildings, the people, and the land. Were my photographs tuning

---

[33] "Measure of Emptiness," pp. 16, 18 and 17, respectively.

in to a level of intention in the great elevators hidden perhaps even to their makers, or were they purely projections of my own need to see the subject in a certain way?[34]

But this rhetoric is both uninteresting and irrelevant: the subject at hand is American grain elevators, and not Frank Gohlke's "intuitions" about them. I say this with such bluntness because neither his essay nor his photographs answer the very questions that he himself posed: "What is stored inside, and what happens to it while it's there? How are the elevators constructed?" All of his photographs were taken from the outside of these machine-buildings, and so none capture the grain or the machinery inside. Furthermore, only three of the book's thirty-eight photographs have captions that mention the material out of which the grain bins at the grain elevator in question were constructed (it is steel in each instance).[35] And so readers without prior expertise could not know that, over the course of the *other* thirty-five grain elevators, they are seeing grain bins built out of a variety of building materials, including wood, tile, and reinforced concrete.

Seeking better information than he or she has been provided so far, the reader of *Measure of Emptiness: Grain Elevators in the American Landscape* turns to John C. Hudson's essay, "The Grain Elevator: An American Invention," which appears at the end of the volume. Once again, despite the inclusiveness of the subtitle, the focus of the text is very narrow: rural America, which stands in "sharp

---

[34] "Measure of Emptiness," pp. 16 and 17.

[35] "Steel elevator / near Ropesville, Texas 1975" (p. 42), "Steel elevator and feed mill / Abilene, Texas 1975" (p. 43), and "Steel elevator and shed /near Abilene, Texas 1975" (p. 45).

contrast" to urban American.[36] "The sheer size and bulk of a grain elevator is magnified by its surroundings, typically a small town on the open prairie," Hudson writes. "The grain elevator was the link between the farmer and the railroad."[37] The presumably rural location in which this "American Invention" was first put to use goes unmentioned. Buffalo gets mentioned, as does Cleveland, Toledo and Oswego, but not in the right places.

> By 1840, nearly one-third of the American wheat crop was raised in Ohio, Indiana, Illinois, Michigan, and Wisconsin. The Great Lakes and the Erie Canal were the routes by which the product moved east, and cities such as Cleveland and Toledo were the major shipping points. Grain handling was still a fairly primitive affair, with many small warehouses assembling shipments [by hand]. New wheat frontiers in Wisconsin opened in the 1840s, and by the end of the decade more than twenty million bushels were being sent via Great Lakes vessels. Nearly all of it was destined for the port cities of Buffalo and Oswego, New York, where the first large terminal elevators in the American grain trade appeared. Continued

---

[36] "Two visual images of the American grain elevator stand in sharp contrast. One is the weather-beaten country elevator standing above the prairie. The other is of a massive block of concrete silos that make up the terminal elevator located alongside a railyard or wharf in a city. The country elevator evokes the sense of empty loneliness on the plains; the terminal elevator, in contrast, validates our sense of American agricultural productivity." Hughes, "The Grain Elevator: An American Invention," in *Measure of Emptiness*, p. 97.

[37] "The Grain Elevator: An American Invention," pp. 90 and 92.

expansion on the western frontier made Chicago
the principal assembly point for grain by 1850.[38]

In point of fact, grain was shipped from every inland port on
the Great Lakes (Cleveland, Toledo, Chicago, Milwaukee,
Superior and Duluth) to Buffalo, because Buffalo stood at the
link between the Great Lakes and the Erie Canal/the Hudson
River (that is to say, at the link between the Great Lakes and
New York City, the largest grain market in America), and
because Buffalo had mechanized grain elevators that could
transship large amounts of grain in bulk from lake steamers
to canal boats. Sometimes grain got sent to Oswego, but it
was milled into flour, not transferred for shipment to another
market.

Like Gohlke, Hudson doesn't know much about how
grain elevators work. The latter writes:

> The grain elevator has evolved continuously over
> the course of American agricultural history. Its
> function – to store grain between harvest time and
> shipment to market – has changed scarcely at all,
> but its appearance has repeatedly been
> transformed as agriculture has grown in
> productivity and transportation technology has
> evolved in response. The basic structure is known
> as an "elevator" because it typically contains one
> or more vertical conveyors for lifting grain from
> ground level to an overhead system of belts and
> chutes that [after the grain has been garnered into
> batches and weighed] redirects the grain into
> various storage bins. From there, it is lofted once
> again [by a second set of elevators] and then fed
> by gravity or mechanical means into waiting
> railroad cars, trucks, or barges for shipment to

---

[38] "The Grain Elevator: An American Invention," p. 95.

market. Elevating the grain is merely a handy means of transferring it from one bin to another, although grain storage facilities of all kinds are commonly known as elevators whether they contain such an apparatus or not.[39]

In point of fact, it is the presence of elevating machines that distinguish grain elevators from simple granaries. A grain elevator that doesn't have a grain-elevating machine is not an "elevator," just a simple grain bin.

Many of the same mistakes can be found in Mahar-Keplinger's book, *Grain Elevators*. Buffalo is mentioned – or, rather, there are captions that identify "Buffalo, New York" as the location of about a dozen photographs[40] – but neither the name of the city in which the grain elevator was invented nor the date of that presumably relevant event are indicated. And so the author's rather cursory history gives the quite mistaken impression that the grain elevator rather suddenly appeared in the middle of the American Midwest during "the 1910s," when "Le Corbusier, Erich Mendelsohn, and Walter Gropius discovered the elevator in American trade journals."[41] The parallel with Christopher Columbus's infamous "discovery" of America, which presumably didn't exist in any meaningful way until a European explorer arrived on its shores, is striking. Indeed, this parallel had already been drawn – and in the precise context of European modernist architecture – in 1929 by the German architect Bruno Taut:

---

[39] "The Grain Elevator: An American Invention," p. 89. Text between brackets [thus] are my additions.

[40] *Grain Elevators*, pp. 59, 64, 66, 67, 70, 73, 74-75 and 81.

[41] Mahar-Keplinger, *Grain Elevators*, p. 8.

At the turn of the century, men were certainly confronted by the monumental task of extricating themselves from the labyrinth of crumbling ruins and forging for themselves a way out to the New Land. They themselves were still befogged by moldering dust, and yet they were hardly prepared to forsake their dilapidated old refuges without more ado, while the storm howled without and they still had to seek some new shelter. Or to make another comparison: they had need of all their energy to fight their way with crowbars through the refuse of the ruins, until, breathless and exhausted, they found themselves in the open. And as sometimes happens with highly gifted people, they fared as did Christopher Columbus when, seeking for India in the West, he incidentally discovered America unawares.[42]

The parallel is ignorant at best. Just like the Native Americans, who had been living in North America for hundreds, if not thousands, of years before they were "discovered" by the likes of Christopher Columbus, grain elevators had been built in Buffalo for more than fifty years before Gropius, Le Corbusier, *et al.* first laid eyes on pictures of them.

Though Mahar-Keplinger traveled all over America to write her book, she didn't stop in Buffalo to take pictures of the grain elevators there. Instead, she borrowed a batch from Jet Lowe, who was part of the team dispatched to Buffalo in 1990 by the Historic American Engineering Record. Nothing is borrowed from Reyner Banham, but there *is* a very telling

---

[42] *Die Neue Baukunst in Europa und Amerika* [The New Building-Arts in Europe and America], bi-lingual edition, translated as *Modern Architecture* [London, the Studio, 1929], pp. 39-40.

reference to him in the caption to a very exact drawing of Buffalo's grain elevator district: "[This is an] axonometric of Buffalo's elevators (after Reyner Banham)."[43] As if Banham's name has become a curse or a sign of bad scholarship, this plan shows Buffalo in or before 1984, that is, at least nine years before Mahar-Keplinger's *Grain Elevators* was published (the Electric Elevator is still standing!).

Mahar-Keplinger also mentions (by way of captions) Brooklyn, another city that used to be central to America's grain trade. The Port Authority of New York built a large-scale, reinforced concrete grain elevator at the mouth of Brooklyn's Gowanus Canal in 1922. Mahar-Keplinger offers her readers a few horizontal cross-sections of the main building, no photographs, and then moves on.[44] One of these diagrams *happens* to indicate the movements that the elevator's canal spouts were capable of making (interesting, but a mere detail). Other than that, we are given no relevant information about how this particular machine-building actually functioned and what, if anything, made it distinctive, worth mentioning in a book about grain elevators or being built in the first place. This is most unfortunate, because, as it turns out, this particular grain elevator was an extraordinary one that has not been adequately documented in the existing literature on the subject.

Designed to connect the heart of commercial South Brooklyn with the Gowanus Bay, and thus with the very center of the New York City's large and deep "inner" harbor (it feeds into but is shielded from the Atlantic Ocean), the Gowanus Canal was planned as long ago as 1849, and finally built between 1867 and 1869. Though it was only a mile and a half long, the canal quickly became the center of Brooklyn's commercial activities, especially the

---

[43] Mahar-Keplinger, *Grain Elevators*, p. 81.
[44] Mahar-Keplinger, *Grain Elevators*, p. 72.

transshipment of grain in bulk to nearby flourmills and ocean vessels headed for Europe. Like the Erie Canal, the Gowanus Canal fell into decline in the 1890s, when the railroads completely took over the transportation of grain from the American Midwest to the port cities on the Atlantic coast. Activity on the Gowanus Canal resurged in 1920, when the State of New York announced that it was supporting the New York State Barge Canal System (begun in 1905 and finally completed at great expense in 1918) by building two large-scale, state-of-the-art grain elevators: one in Oswego, New York; the other in South Brooklyn.

Oswego was chosen because, unlike Buffalo, it wasn't completely controlled by the railroad companies. In the frank words of Noble E. Whitford, author of *History of the Barge Canal of New York State*, "The logical points for transferring grain cargoes carried by canal were Buffalo and New York [City]. Buffalo was supplied with several elevators, although canal boatmen found difficulty in securing the privilege of using them."[45] Whitford writes:

> At Buffalo the problem did not involve an actual lack of elevators, as at New York, but there seemed to be operating some cause which was working against the canal grain traffic. There were twenty-three elevators at Buffalo. Their storage capacity was 28,250,000 bushels and they were capable of putting 1,871,000 bushels into canal barges in a period of ten hours. But despite all this splendid equipment and although Buffalo was constantly increasing in importance as a grain port, the canal traffic in grain from Buffalo was steadily decreasing year by year. Whether this

---

[45] *Supplement to the Annual Report of the State Engineer and Surveyor for the Year Ended June 30, 1921* (Albany, 1922).

inimical agency was antagonism, discrimination adverse to canal traffic or excessive charges, was not entirely clear. It was generally understood that some if not all of the elevators were dominated by the railroad influence.

Oswego was also a good "move" for the United States to make in its game of chess with the Canadians.

Excellent elevators had been installed at Montreal and in 1918 that port had handled approximately twenty-five per cent of the total wheat exports of the principal Gulf and Atlantic ports. [...] Canada was now enlarging th[e] [Welland] canal so as to accommodate lake vessels of twenty-five feet draft. It was expected that by this means considerable grain would be diverted from Buffalo, the lake boats passing into Lake Ontario and going to Kingston or on down the St. Lawrence to Prescott [...] It was imperative, therefore, that New York should provide a competitive port on Lake Ontario and the logical site for that port was Oswego. [...] It was contended that the State would be negligent in failing to foresee the impending diversion of grain at Buffalo and in not providing at Oswego facilities which would attract that grain after it had entered Lake Ontario. Evidence of the soundness of the reasoning was found in the reported plans of a railroad company to deepen a harbor, erect a coal trestle and construct a grain elevator at a point a few miles west of Oswego.

The Gowanus Elevator was intended to break the railroads' monopoly at *its* end (the terminus) of the New York State Barge System. Whitford reports that, in the 1910s,

New York had almost no elevator facilities, virtually none available for canal use [...] For many years there had been passing through that harbor half the foreign and domestic commerce of the whole United States and yet there existed but five or six grain elevators and only two were situated so that canal boats could reach them. Both of these were owned by railroads and there was not even a shadow of a chance that canal boats would be allowed to use them. As a result of this state of affairs barges laden with grain were obliged to wait the arrival of ships to which their cargoes were to be transferred. This might be one week or two or three or sometimes even longer. During this delay demurrage charges were mounting, the earning power of the barge was being lost and the cost of shipping grain by canal was rising so high as to be prohibitive.

The photograph of the Gowanus Elevator that accompanies Whitford's report shows a complex that looks like it was inspired by elevator design in Montreal, the United States' main competitor for international commerce over the Atlantic Ocean. Perhaps it was modeled after the Grand Trunk Pacific Railroad's Elevator #2, constructed in Montreal in 1906. In any case, the main building faces away from Gowanus Bay. In front is a slip in which there is room for vessels coming from the Great Lakes to be unloaded by the elevator's two stationary marine towers, both of which are made of reinforced concrete. Given the fact that the main building is only 429 feet long (half the length of the Concrete Central), one might have expected that at least one of these towers would be automotive. There were in fact two automotive towers at the elevator built in Oswego, both designed and installed by the James Stewart Engineering Company (Chicago) in 1925.

The workhouse of the Gowanus Canal elevator is also made of reinforced concrete, and it rises to the height of 150 feet. There's a second workhouse, clad with corrugated iron, which is evidently powered by the small brick building (complete with smokestack) that stands between it and the main building. Thanks to this second workhouse, the Gowanus Elevator can discharge grain in two different directions and, mind you, by two different methods. For the smaller vessels docked in the slip in front of it, the elevator uses the "conventional" system, long in use in places like Buffalo and Oswego (spouts that swing out over the boats and use gravity to conduct the grain down into their holds). But for the ocean tankers waiting at an adjacent pier, the elevator uses a system common in Montreal. There are two elevated horizontal gantries that, combined, are 1,221 feet long; that are connected at a right angle by a small transfer tower; and that house conveyor-belts that bring grain from the "back" side of the main building to the tankers, though they are docked hundreds of feet away.

Whitford reports that "Upon a new shorter pier it is planned to install unloaders, possibly of the pneumatic type, for handling flaxseed or other imported grains," but none of it was ever built. The grain terminal was deactivated and abandoned in 1965, just 43 years after it was built. The entire loading pier and conveyor structure remained in place until 1987, when it was finally demolished.[46] As for the grain elevator in Oswego: built in 1925, it was abandoned in 1965 and demolished in 1999.

Neither Brooklyn nor Buffalo are mentioned in Russell Stubbles' *Skyscrapers of the Prairie: South Dakota's*

---

[46] Christopher Gray, "The Columbia Street Grain Elevator; Recycling Red Hook's 1922 Magnificent Mistake," *New York Times*, May 13, 1990.

Historic Wooden Grain Elevators or Greg McDonnell's *Wheat Kings: Vanishing Landmarks of the Canadian Prairies*. I gather that mentioning *any* city would have distracted the reader's thoughts away from the attention-starved provinces in the Dakotas and Canada. But in their well-intentioned desire to preserve and spotlight local history, both books attempt to separate the country elevator from the various regional and national systems of which it is an inextricable part. The grain that is stored in country elevators in the prairies doesn't remain there, of course, but is shipped by railcar to a transshipping elevator, which inevitably means a port city (Vancouver or Montreal; Duluth or Chicago; Portland, Oregon or Portland, Maine). The simple fact is that country elevators, which were first built in the 1870s, wouldn't have existed in the first place without transshipping elevators, which were invented thirty years earlier. Indeed, the primary reason so many country elevators in both Canada and the United States have been closed down, abandoned and demolished over the course of the last fifteen years is the fact that, *thirty* years previously, the same thing happened to the transshipping elevators in "Rust Belt" cities such as Chicago, Toledo, Cleveland, Erie, Philadelphia, Baltimore, Brooklyn and Buffalo.

Why is it that almost everyone forgets Buffalo? Wasn't it just a few years ago that Reyner Banham put Buffalo back on the map? How could it have slipped off again? Of course, it isn't just Buffalo and Buffalo alone that has suffered this double disappearance: so have all the other Rust Belt cities. This fact suggests an answer to our questions. The authors of the books we have been discussing have failed to come to grips with the centrality of the city, the *modern* city, to the development and maturity of American agriculture, that is to say, to the development and maturity of American society itself. To them, American society is originally and fundamentally a rural, agriculture-based society, in which industrialization and urbanization were later developments. William Cronon points out that,

> For cultural reasons that date from this same historical period [the nineteenth century], Americans have long tended to see city and country as separate places, more isolated from each other than connected. We carefully partition our national landscape into urban places, rural places, and wilderness [...] Even professional historians often fall into this trap. Urban historians rarely look beyond the outskirts of cities to the hinterlands beyond, western and frontier and even environmental historians usually concentrate far more attention on rural and wild places than on urban ones.[47]

Thus, the country elevator *must* have come before the transshipping elevator, not the other way around.

Even Dan Morgan's *Merchants of Grain* forgets to mention Buffalo: "A steam-operated system for removing bulk grain from the holds of ships with a bucket lift was invented in *America* in 1843, and rodent-proof and weatherproof concrete storage silos replaced wooden warehouses and elevators at the end of the century."[48] But this is "acceptable" to me because, when it came time to select and caption photographs of grain elevators in America, Morgan chose exceedingly well.[49] Two of the three photographs depict colossal elevators in port cities: "The Farmer's Union 12-million-bushel terminal grain elevator at

---

[47] *Nature's Metropolis: Chicago and the Great West* (WW Norton, 1991), p. xiv.

[48] Dan Morgan's *Merchants of Grain*, p. 35, emphasis added.

[49] Between pages 264 and 265.

Superior, Wisconsin" (two colossal grain elevators are connected to each other via an elevated horizontal transfer gantry); and "Continental's terminal grain facility north of New Orleans" (at which an explosion in December 1977 killed thirty-six people). The third photograph is captioned "A typical grain elevator of the American interior," but actually shows a country-style elevator that standing next to *and being dwarfed by* a truly huge reinforced-concrete elevator that is "typical" of those in America's port cities. The underlying assumption is clear: the grain business is an international affair, and international affairs penetrate into both large cities and small towns.

The *locus classicus* of the notion that American history has unfolded in a logical, orderly and evolutionary direction is Frederick Jackson Turner's analysis of "The Significance of the Frontier in American History." The frontier, Turner declared,

> begins with the Indian and the hunter; it goes on to tell of the disintegration of savagery by the entrance of the trader, the pathfinder of civilization; we read the annals of the pastoral stage in ranch life; the exploitation of the soil by the raising of unrotated crops of corn and wheat in sparsely settled farming communities; the intensive culture of the denser farm settlement; and finally the manufacturing organization with city and factory systems.[50]

According to this highly compressed (or accelerated) chronology – it apparently covers the 350-year-long period between the 1640s and the 1890s – the grain elevator *had to be* invented during the "intensive culture of the denser farm

---

[50] Included in *The Frontier in American History* (1920); quoted in William Cronon, *Nature's Metropolis*, p. 31.

settlement," that is, after the establishment of the "sparsely settled farming communities" (circa the 1830s) and before the establishment of "the manufacturing organization with city and factory systems" (the 1890s). This sequence, which places the hypothetical invention of the grain elevator somewhere in the 1860s (fairly close to the actual date of the first country elevators), makes a certain amount of sense. The intensive agricultural practices of farmers in the American Midwest led to the over-production of grain, which in turn created the need for the mechanization of the systems by which grain was collected, transported and distributed. Because mechanization encouraged sparse farming communities to become more densely settled, the cycle began anew. Those were the days!

And so the grain elevator (here indistinguishable from the country elevator) harkens back to certainly troubled, but much more innocent times. It isn't a modern invention, like the big city, but pre-modern, like a European cathedral. In the words of Robert B. Riley, grain elevators are "symbols of time, place and honest building"[51] in an era of amnesia, rootlessness and dishonesty. Aldo Rossi says of the "Great Plains of America" – the birthplace of the steamship, the airplane, the automobile and the grain elevator – "Secret are its villages turned inward on their religious sects and antique languages, as if time had stood still. These people were not seeking America, but were escaping from Europe, and in these first wooden silos there is a memory of, and an obsession with, architecture from different parts of central Europe."[52] Such comforting thoughts!

But the grain elevator was in fact invented in a bustling city (Buffalo, New York), and it was invented *forty years* before the first skyscrapers were erected in Chicago, Cincinnati, and New York City. In the words of Walter Curt

---

[51] *AIA Journal*, vol. 66, November 1977, pp. 50-57.
[52] Mahar-Keplinger, *Grain Elevators*, p. 7.

Behrendt, speaking of the "impulse" among European modernists in the 1910s and 1920 to build upwards: "To be sure, this impulse did not originate in the skyscraper . . . but in the simple structure of industrial building such as the grain elevators and big silos to be found in the great ports."[53] And American society *did not* develop and mature in the way that Frederick Jackson Turner thought that it did. As William Cronon points out, "the central story of the nineteenth-century West is that of an expanding metropolitan economy creating ever more elaborate and intimate linkages between city and country," even though "the persistent rural bias of western history has often prevented us from acknowledging this fact."[54] The city and the country – rather than constituting spatially and temporally distinct socio-economic zones, with a "frontier" between them that can be opened and closed like a door – "formed a single commercial system, a single process of rural settlement and metropolitan economic growth." According to Cronon, "to speak of one without the other" makes "little sense."[55]

Some observers of our young country were able to see this. For example, in *North America*, the British novelist Anthony Trollope noted that in "this young world" – unlike the "old countries" of Europe, in which "agriculture, following on the heels of pastoral patriarchal life, preceded the birth of cities" – "the cities have come first."

The new Jasons, blessed with the experience of the old world adventurers, have gone forth in

---

[53] *Der Sieg des Neuen Baustils* [The Victory of the New Building Styles], 1927, translated into English in 1937 as *Modern Building: Its Nature, Problems and Forms*, New York, p. 99.
[54] William Cronon, *Nature's Metropolis: Chicago and the Great West*, WW Norton, 1991, p. xiii.
[55] William Cronon, *Nature's Metropolis*, p. 47.

search of their golden fleeces armed with all that science and skill the East had as yet produced, and in setting up their new Colchis have begun the erection of first-class hotels and the fabrication of railroads.[56]

Such an interesting analogy! Young and modern America, in which "the city" and "pastoral patriarchal life" were miraculously born at the same time, is both a return to ancient Greece and a better version of it. The "new Jasons" (the Americans in their cities) will easily and speedily win possession of the Golden Fleece, especially because a couple of the tasks they must accomplish, at least in the ancient Greek myth, concern agriculture (plowing a field using fire-breathing oxen and sowing dragons' teeth).

Forty years after Anthony Trollope, Frank Norris, author of *The Pit: A Story of Chicago*, saw an America in which the cities were directly and constantly connected to the allegedly remote frontier villages of the American West. He wrote:

The Great Gray City, brooking no rival, imposed its dominion upon a reach of country larger than many a kingdom of the Old World. For thousands of miles beyond its confines was its influence felt. Out, far out, far away in the snow and shadow of northern Wisconsin forests, axes and saws bit the bark of century old trees, stimulated by this city's energy. Just as far to the southward pick and drill leaped to the assault of veins of anthracite, moved by her central power. Her force turned the wheels of harvester and seeder a thousand miles distant in

[56] Anthony Trollope, *North America*, edited with notes by Donald Smalley and Bradford Allen Booth, Knopf, New York, 1951.

Iowa and Kansas. Her force spun the screws and propellers of innumerable squadrons of lake steamers crowding the Sault Sainte Marie. For her and because of her all of the Central States, all the Great Northwest roared with traffic and industry.[57]

Norris was writing about Chicago, but the central hub and power-source for the American Machine could just as easily have been Buffalo or New York City.

America was already a modern society in the 1840s. Nearly everything we recognize today as "modern" was already present in rudimentary form in Buffalo and Chicago in, say, 1848: high-speed communications (the telegraph); high-speed travel (the railroads); labor-saving devices and unemployment (the use of steam engines to replace laborers); political subversion (Karl Marx and the Communist Party); abstract value-forms and financial speculation on the market (paper money, elevator receipts and "to arrive" contracts); "decadent" or extremist literature (the works of Edgar Allan Poe);[58] free trade, price normalization, and globalization (the demand for American grain in England after the repeal of the Corn Laws);[59] and buildings so tall they appeared to "scrape

---

[57] Frank Norris, *The Pit: A Story of Chicago* (New York, 1903).

[58] Poe wasn't simply a pioneering figure in modernist art and literature because of his influence on the French poet and translator Charles Baudelaire, but also because of the intensity of his interest in modern cities (especially "The Man of the Crowd" and the Inspector Dupin stories).

[59] "Parliament, with its stroke of repeal, had changed the world. Repeal of the protectionist system had opened England to the wheat of all the world, created incentives for the settlement of vast territories across the oceans, and established the conditions for modern international trade, with new sea routes and modern trading empires." Dan

the sky" (grain elevators). As a result, nothing that took place in the country between the 1840s and the 1890s – in particular, the Civil War, the bungled Reconstruction and the acceleration of the displacement and mass murder of the remaining Native Americans in the 1870s and 1880s – can be minimized or dismissed as "mistakes" or "missteps" made by a precocious, but still immature child. America was old enough to know better.

Morgan, *Merchants of Grain* (Viking, New York, 1979), p. 30.

Chapter 9
On Dwelling

A foreseeable and thus preventable tragedy took place on the night of Sunday, 1 October 2006, when the Wollenberg Grain & Seed Elevator at 133 Goodyear Avenue in Buffalo, New York, caught fire and burned down. Only three years previously, on 25 June 2003, it had been entered into the national and New York State Registries of Historic Places. The Wollenberg merited this rare distinction because it was in fact the last remaining wood-binned grain elevator in Buffalo, the city in which the grain elevator was invented. Built in 1912, the Wollenberg was designed by C.H.A. Wannenwetsch for Louis and John Wollenberg. For sentimental reasons, perhaps, Wannenwetsch incorporated wood that had been salvaged from the old Kellogg "B" elevator – built in 1892 and later demolished make room for an elevator built of reinforced concrete – into the structure of this "new" elevator.

Ever since it closed down in 1987, the Wollenberg was one big firetrap. When he photographed the structure for the Historic American Engineering Record (HAER) in 1990, Jet Lowe feared that his flash would ignite the piles of grain dust that stood four inches thick on all of the buildings' floors. (Or so he told me in 1991. He also reported seeing rats "the size of dogs" there, so it is possible that he was exaggerating slightly.) In the report that they wrote for HAER between 1990 and 1991, the historians Thomas Leary, John Healey and Elizabeth Sholes stated, "the elevator's fate remains uncertain, however, as it survives in an increasingly deteriorating neighborhood that has already been assaulted by arson."[1] And yet the City of Buffalo, the official caretaker of the property, did only the minimum to protect this treasured building: it merely sealed all its doors and windows.

Of course, these seals were broken, and the place was often visited. Two types of people were attracted to the Wollenberg: those who came from other neighborhoods and thought that this abandoned grain elevator was "a cool place to explore," and those who lived in the neighborhood and found the abandoned building a good place to hide, deal drugs, do drugs or sleep. In the aftermath of the fire and the subsequent clearing of the site, several different opinions were "voiced," that is to say, posted to various Internet blogs. One read that the City of Buffalo was negligent in allowing such an important, historic landmark to be destroyed;[2] that the people who are *obsessed* with such buildings should stop their "preservationist" work because it only keeps Buffalo tied to its industrial past;[3] and that unlike the "urban

---

[1] HAER No. NY-242, p. 8.

[2] Mark Sommer, "Fire loss of historic grain elevator is called another case of city neglect," *Buffalo News*, 4 October 2006.

[3] See, for example, this comment by "gaustad," posted March 24, 2008th, in response to a neo-boosterist proposal to reuse Buffalo's grain elevators in the same way that Portland reclaimed its waterfront: "Why do we keep going back to this grain elevator rehab project? The HO complex stood abandoned for years. If someone wanted to preserve and covert it, I think it would have happened. Same with the other grain elevetors [sic]. Although they are an important part of our history, right now they add no value whatsoever to revitalizing downtown. There are no interested parties that want to rehab any of them. In my opinion, they add to the decay and pollution already on the waterfront and inhibit growth....... most sites/grain elevators should be demolished and cleaned up. It's time to move on Buffalo. Clinging to our

explorers," who dwelled *upon* the Wollenberg and were fully aware of its significance, the people from "that side of the tracks" (the "squatters" and "urban campers")[4] actually dwelled *in* it, without really knowing what the building was or what it meant. And if it turns out *they* burned the elevator down, then it would hardly matter if it had been done accidentally or on purpose.

This discussion reminded me of a graffito that I'd seen during an "official" inspection of an abandoned grain elevator in Tonawanda, New York, conducted during the summer of 1992. With the approval and in the presence of a local councilman (whose name I have forgotten), the three of us – Orrin Pava, a photographer, Henry Baxter, a retired engineer and designer of grain elevators, and William J. Brown, who said he was writing a book about Buffalo's grain elevators – were allowed to enter and explore the Eastern States Farmers' Exchange Feed Mill and Grain Elevator on Military Road in Tonawanda. Built by Henry's father's company, A.E. Baxter Engineering, in 1934, and then extended by Henry himself in the 1940s, the Eastern States didn't appear (and still doesn't appear) in the existing literature on the subject because it was built along railroad tracks in Buffalo's industrial suburbs, and not in its harbor, alongside the water. Both the elevator and the flourmill were closed and abandoned in the 1960s.

By the time we encountered it, the grain elevator was a fright. It was set back from the road and partially hidden from sight behind the huge, multi-storey flourmill that ran alongside it (all of the mill's windows had been broken). Normally not unsettled by such isolated places, I detected

---

past only inhibits our progress. Its time to reinvent." http://www.buffalorising.com/story/grain_elevator_reuse_portland accessed 24 August 2008.

[4]   http://fixbuffalo.blogspot.com/2006/05/east-side-grain-silos.html accessed 12 August 2008.

intense "bad vibes" (or maybe that was simply panic induced by reading newspaper accounts about children falling to their deaths and animals being been "sacrificed" there). The councilman informed us we could buy the elevator from the City for exactly one dollar, but that it would probably take millions to insure it.

One of the first things we saw when the councilman opened up the door to the elevator's basement was the graffito "Frankenstein lives here!" I've had some time to think about this remarkable exclamation, and I note the following. First, Frankenstein is *alive*, not dead, and this fact alone is more important than the exact location of his current place of residence. Second, even though he's a monster, Frankenstein needs a dwelling, a place to stay, a house/home, to which he can return after he's run amok and caused mayhem amongst the townspeople. Third, he's chosen an abandoned grain elevator, and not an abandoned church or cathedral, because he recognizes a "kindred spirit" in it: in James Whale's film *The Bride of Frankenstein* (1935), the Monster lives in a ruined mountainous windmill. (It is in this former grain-processing plant that the Monster learns how to speak: "Bread is *good*.") Fourth and last, if Frankenstein lives *here*, in this particular grain elevator, then *you* (the reader of the graffito) should leave without dwelling any further: the danger is great.

Our language contains a value judgment about "dwellers," but not, as one might expect, in favor of those who dwelled upon the Wollenberg and against those who dwelled in it. The verdict is the other way around. In English, "to dwell" is both a physical action (to make one's home, to reside or to live) and an intellectual one (to linger over something in thought or speech). The meanings of the old English words *dwellen*, *dwellan*, *dvelja* and *dhwel* suggest that someone who lingers – or, rather, someone who lingers too long – is hindered, led astray, deceived, dull, obscure or thick. Such a person isn't "at home" in his or her own head;

he or she is so intent upon one idea, person or object that he or she has lost touch with the whole world. Many people suffer from this affliction: some are devotees of "urban exploration," others write books on grain elevators.

"Not every building is a dwelling," Martin Heidegger reminds the readers and auditors of *"Bauen Wohnen Denken*," which he delivered as a lecture to the "Man and Space" Symposium at Darmstadt, Germany, on 5 August 1951. "Bridges and hangars, stadiums and power stations are buildings but not dwellings; railroad stations and highways, dams and market halls are built, but they are not dwelling places."[5] Civilized people don't dwell in such industrial buildings; they only inhabit them temporarily, then they go home. Here we find unexpected echoes of Le Corbusier's proclamation that "an architectural structure is a house, a temple *or* a factory,"[6] and Nikolaus Pevsner's famous distinction between a bicycle shed, which is a mere building (a place that we inhabit on occasion), and Lincoln Cathedral, which is architecture (a place in which our very souls dwell).[7]

But Heidegger wasn't finished speaking. "Even so, these [industrial] buildings are in the domain of our dwelling. That domain extends over these buildings and so is not limited to the dwelling place [...] These buildings house man. He inhabits them and yet does not dwell in them, if to dwell means solely to have our lodgings in them [...] Yet those buildings that are not dwelling places remain in turn determined by dwelling insofar as they serve man's dwelling.

---

[5] Translated by Albert Hofstadter, "Building Dwelling Thinking," in Martin Heidegger, *Poetry, Language, Thought*, New York, 1971, reprinted in *Basic Writings*, 1977.

[6] *Vers une architecture*, 1923, translated by Frederick Etchells, *Towards a New Architecture*, Dover Books, 1986, p. 39, emphasis added.

[7] *Outline of European Architecture*, 1943; Harmonsworth fifth edition, 1957, p. 23.

Thus dwelling would in any case be the end that presides over all building."[8] To explain this reversal of perspective – "we do not dwell because we have built, but we build and have built because we dwell"[9] – Heidegger calls our attention to the various meanings that the word *bauen*, "to build," has in German. "The Old High German word for building, *buan*, means to dwell. This signifies to remain, to stay in a place [...] Where the word *bauen* still speaks in it original sense it also says *how far* the essence of dwelling reaches. That is, *bauen, buan, bhu, beo* are our word *bin* in the versions: *ich bin*, I am, *du bist*, you are, the imperative form *bis*, be. What then does *ich bin* mean? The old word *bauen*, to which the *bin* belongs, answers: *ich bin, du bist* mean I dwell, you dwell. The way in which you are and I am, the manner in which we humans *are* on the earth, is *buan*, dwelling."[10] And how is dwelling (that is, living on earth) accomplished? By building, that is to say, by engaging in "the building that cultivates growing things and the building that erects buildings."[11]

The reader may well find such remarks about language quite interesting, but rather abstract. If it is true that *any* building can be a "dwelling," and *any* building can be "dwelled upon," then why do some people prefer grain elevators? Is it because grain elevators bring together cultivation (grain) and buildings (elevators)? Exactly *how* is a grain elevator such as the Wollenberg a "dwelling" in the

---

[8] Martin Heidegger, "Building Dwelling Thinking," pp. 323-323.

[9] Martin Heidegger, "Building Dwelling Thinking," pp. 326.

[10] Martin Heidegger, "Building Dwelling Thinking," pp. 324-325.

[11] Martin Heidegger, "Building Dwelling Thinking," p. 326.

expanded sense of the word that Heidegger has given it (or has discovered by way of etymological analysis)?

In part II of "Building Dwelling Thinking," Heidegger approaches the question from the other way around. That is to say, he provides a general theory of space. His starting point isn't in fact a "point," but a connection, contact or transition between *two* points: the bridge.

> To be sure, the bridge is a thing of its *own* kind; for it gathers the fourfold [Heidegger's name for the earth, the sky, the divinities and mortals] in such a way that it allows a *site* for it. But only something that is itself a location can make space for a site. The location is not already there before the bridge is. Before the bridge stands, there are of course many spots along the stream that can be occupied by something. One of them proves to be a location, and does so because of the bridge. Thus the bridge does not first come to a location to stand in it; rather a location comes into existence only by virtue of the bridge [...] Only things that are locations in this manner allow for spaces. What the word for space, *Raum*, designates is said by its ancient meaning. *Raum*, *Rum*, means a place cleared or freed for settlement and lodging. A space is something that has been made room for, something that is cleared and free, namely, within a boundary [...] Space is in essence that for which room has been made, that which is let into its bounds. That for which room is made is always granted and hence is joined, that is, gathered, by virtue of a location, that is by such a thing as the bridge. Accordingly, spaces receive their essential being from locations and not from "space" [...] The space provided for in [the traditional] mathematical manner may be called

"space," the "one" space as such. But in this sense "the" space, "space," contains no spaces and no places. We never find in it any locations, that is, things of the kind the bridge is. As against that, however, in the spaces provided for by locations there is always space as interval, and in this interval there is space as pure extension.[12]

In sum, space "itself" doesn't exist: there are only spaces, spaces between spaces, and spaces within spaces, all linked together by "locations." Such spaces do not exist "naturally," nor are they always already "there." And so "the essence of the erecting of buildings" – structures that stand in the locations where space was cleared for them – "cannot be understood adequately in terms either of architecture or of engineering construction, nor in terms of a mere combination of the two." The essence of building is in fact the "production" of spaces.[13]

In *La Production de l'Espace*, the French sociologist and philosopher Henri Lefebvre objects that, in this essay and the ones that are related to it, Heidegger consistently refers to things that are "far from us now precisely inasmuch as they are close to nature: the jug, the peasant house of the Black Forest, the Greek temple."[14] Lefebvre also reminds us that Heidegger focuses on the essential peacefulness of dwelling: "[The Gothic word] *Wunian* means to be at peace, to be

---

[12] Martin Heidegger, "Building Dwelling Thinking," *Basic Writings*, p. 331-333.

[13] Martin Heidegger, "Building Dwelling Thinking," *Basic Writings*, p. 337.

[14] Henri Lefebvre, original 1974, translated by Donald-Nicholson Smith as *The Production of Space*, Blackwell, 1991, p. 121.

brought to peace, to remain in peace."[15] Indeed, what could be more natural and peaceful than a bridge over a stream? From the perspective of the English language, this setting risks being dull (*dhwel*), even deceived (*dvelja*).

And so, let us try to correct or rewrite Heidegger by replacing his example of "the bridge" (connection, contact or transition between two points) with something closer to us in time and space: "the grain elevator" (transfer in bulk between two points). Now the relevance of his theory of space becomes clear! The grain elevator does not simply *occupy* the space that had been cleared and prepared for it; it also *produces* new spaces. Erich Mendelsohn clearly understood this when he described the grain elevators in Buffalo as "incredibly space-conscious, but creating space."[16] But unlike Buffalo's urban explorers and homeless people, Mendelsohn never ventured *inside* a grain elevator; he simply didn't linger long enough to do so. And so he failed to discover that the *appearance* of such buildings (simple "male" forms on a massive scale) in no way prepares you for the "female" forms that you find inside them: a far-from-simple honeycomb or catacomb of big bins, little bins, interstitial bins and outer bins. For any number of different reasons, urban explorers and homeless people enjoy repeating the experience of having (their) space turned inside out. At some level, they all know "the truth": there is no "abstract" or "absolute" space; all space is in fact *interstitial space*.

It is hardly surprising, then, that the most common way to "adaptively reuse" abandoned grain elevators is to convert

---

[15] Martin Heidegger, "Building Dwelling Thinking," *Basic Writings*, p. 326-327.

[16] Letter to his wife dated Pittsburgh, 22 October 1924, *Letters of An Architect*, edited by Oskar Beyer, translated by Geoffrey Strachan, London: Abelard-Schumann, 1967, page 69.

them into houses.[17] Didn't some functioning grain elevators serve as homes to their owners, that is, when they were young and struggling to make ends meet?[18] In 1980, the old Quaker Oats complex in Akron, Ohio, was converted into a hotel. Floors were placed within the silos, and windows were inserted into their sides, thus forming circular rooms. In 1982, the old Cereal Grading Company in Minneapolis, Minnesota, was converted into a condominium complex called Calhoun-Isles. In 2007, the old Baltimore & Ohio Grain Terminal in Baltimore, Maryland – "once the tallest and fastest grain elevator in the world"[19] – was converted into "Silo Point." That same year, the *New York Times* ran a story about a woman named Jill Baumler, who had turned a country-style grain elevator in Bozeman, Montana, into her home.[20] "Just over an hour from Bozeman, in Alder," the *Times* reporter stated, "Ray Smail operates a business, CGB Housing, that converts grain bins into homes." To date, "CGB has created seven grain bin houses, and he [Smail] lives in a 2,400-square-foot four-story home ranch made from two stacked bins." On 1 February 2008, the

---

[17] The same is now being done with the huge steel shipping containers that came into use in the 1980s. See the Associated Press, "Shipping containers could be 'dream' homes for thousands," 24 September 2008. The containers are 40 feet long, eight feet wide and eight and a half feet tall.

[18] Speaking of the founder of Cargill, Inc. (William W. Cargill) Stephen George, author of Enterprising Minnesotans: 150 Years of Business Pioneers, University of Minnesota Press, 2005, writes: "In 1867 two of his brothers joined him. They saved money by living in one of the [grain] warehouses, sleeping on cots in the same room they used as an office" (p. 33).

[19] Karl B. Hille, "Grain elevator reborn as high-end condos," *The Baltimore Examiner*, 2 November 2007.

[20] Jim Robbins, "From Grain Elevator to Dream House," *New York Times*, 14 January 2007.

Philadelphia Business Journal reported that a reinforced concrete elevator built in 1924 (on the site of "a wooden grain elevator" constructed in 1862 and "used during the Civil War") had been converted into a group of condos called The Granary. Finally, as this chapter was being completed (November 2008), the old Bunge y Born Elevator in Minneapolis, Minnesota – or at least part of it – was being converted into the "Van Cleve Court Apartments East," which, when completed, would be the first such reconversion project intended for "public" (low income) housing.

When I visited the *das Getreide Terminal Hamburg* (the Hamburg Grain Terminal) in early 1994, I expected to see what I saw at Eurosilo in Ghent, Belgium: grain elevators built after World War II and in the "classic" American style of the 1920s (rows of gleaming-white cylindrical tanks). I was both surprised and delighted to see a long line of elevators that had instead been built in a variety of styles. There were big windowless brick buildings with flat roofs; big windowless brick buildings with pitched roofs; big windowless towers painted a gleaming white; several buildings with many windows that looked like enormous houses; and even a few freestanding cylindrical tanks made out reinforced concrete, but topped by cupolas that looked air-traffic-control towers.[21] Curious, I asked someone who worked there, and was told that the buildings that looked like enormous houses were in fact grain elevators that were built during the war and intentionally disguised as houses so as to keep them from being bombed.

------

[21] See the following photographs that have been posted on-line: http://commons.wikimedia.org/wiki/Image:Getreide_Terminal_Hamburg_02.jpg, http://commons.wikimedia.org/wiki/Image:Getreideterminal_Hamburg_012.jpg, and http://commons.wikimedia.org/wiki/Image:Getreideterminal_Hamburg_005.jpg all accessed 20 August 2008.

In 1990, when I still lived in Buffalo, a good friend (Mr Orrin Pava) and I would talk about buying a grain elevator and doing "something" with it. We didn't have enough money to buy one and, even if we did get enough, we weren't sure that converting one of Buffalo's abandoned grain elevators into a house (even ours!) would be the best thing to do with it. It had been the ruinous nature of these buildings that attracted us, like so many others, to them in the first place. Why not simply let them remain ruins? What they've lost can never be replaced.

Personally, I can see the value and appropriateness of the current plan, which is to use the American, the Perrot and the Lake & Rail – all of which were decommissioned over the course of the last eight years and yet remain in good working condition – to store the corn out of which ethanol is made,[22] even though I am opposed to the production of ethanol on the grounds that using food to power private automobiles is socially irresponsible. (The current plan also calls for the partial rebuilding of the Marine "A," which was abandoned to dereliction in the 1960s but was fortunate enough not to fall prey to structural damage or permanent flooding.) I would love to see the establishment of a "grain elevator museum," especially if it was housed within a grain elevator (the Standard, the Great Northern and the Electric Annex would be safe and suitable places). But there is

---

[22] On 22 September 2008, the Lake & Rail elevator – now owned by Whitebox Commodities – received and unloaded the *American Fortitude*, an immense freighter that carried a 400,000-bushel shipment of wheat from Owen Sound, Ontario. Just a few days before that, the Lake & Rail received two millions bushels from railcars. See Sharon Linstedt, "Grain elevator returns to life," *Buffalo News*, September 23, 2008. Clearly not part of any ethanol-production plan, these huge shipments of wheat were no doubt designed for one or several of the local flourmills or cereal-production factories.

virtually nothing to be done with the larger elevators upstream, namely, the Superior and the Concrete Central, both of which were abandoned to dereliction and decay over thirty years ago. The basement of the Superior has been continuously flooded for many years, and the Concrete Central rests upon a wooden dock (not a concrete one!) that is very slowly but gradually breaking up at the southern end.

Here I reveal two "items" that Orrin and I discovered, so that these achievements may not become forgotten in time, and may receive their proper glory. But I do not record them in an attempt to also show how *fearless* we were back then (even more fearless than Reyner Banham!). Indeed, the most accurate description of our urban explorations in Buffalo between 1989 and 1992 would not be "we risked life and limb," but "we knew when to stay away."

On the day that we visited Meyer Malting, with the intent of documenting what we'd found during our first visit to this often-ignored but utterly fascinating grain elevator at 1314 Niagara Street,[23] we heard a sound that suggested that

---

[23] Built in 1914 for the George Meyer Malt & Grain Company by H.R. Wait and the Monarch Engineering Company, this elevator was unique in many ways. It was the only one in Buffalo to be build alongside the Erie Canal/New York State Barge Canal after 1900; and it was the first one built in Buffalo to feature a machine workhouse made out of reinforced concrete. By 1920, the elevator (designed to unload barley) was part of a huge complex that included malt houses, flourmills and cereal factories. Thirty years later, Meyer Malting was the biggest malt house "east of Chicago" (HAER Report No. NY-259, p. 3). Because it stood between the Barge Canal and the railroad tracks laid down by the New York Central, Meyer Malting was able to survive the construction of the New York State Thruway, which cut the grain terminal off from the water in the late 1950s. The malt house arranged to get its barley through the Kellogg Elevator, which was located in Buffalo's harbor. Purchased by

someone was already inside. The only way into the building (as far as *we* knew) was a single small window in the reinforced-concrete wall that faced the New York State Thruway: you had to jump up, grab the ledge and pull yourself up to climb inside it. If there was in fact someone living inside the building, and if he or she (or even *they*) were hostile to our apparent invasion of "their" space, and if we wanted to get out of there was fast as possible, that narrow little window was our only way out, and we'd have to find and climb through it in the darkness. It simply wasn't worth the risk, and so we left, never to return.

We did the same thing when we visited the H&O Oats Elevator at 54 Fulton Street. The basement of this steel-binned elevator, built in 1914 by A.E. Baxter, looked to be permanently flooded. Someone had used a series of wooden planks to create a dry route to a staircase that led to the upper levels. There didn't seem to be anyone around, other than ourselves, but we didn't know who or what we might encounter along the way, especially at the top. One of us remembered seeing a then-recent local TV news story about the rescue of a stray dog that had managed to get to the top of the 70-foot-tall structure, but couldn't get back down. And we decided not to climb it.[24]

On one of the walls in the basement of the Marine "A," there is a very detailed, almost gentle, multi-colored chalk portrait of the Standard Elevator, which sits across from the Marine "A" on the Buffalo River. Accurate but not fussy about the details, this careful portrait was made by someone who either had a photograph to work from, or knew the

---

Schaefer Brewing in 1960, the complex was closed down and abandoned in the late 1980s.

[24] Both of these elevators (Meyer Malting and H & O Oats), as well as the one at Kreiner Malting, were demolished by or with the approval of the City of Buffalo between 2005 and 2006.

Standard by heart. Such a portrait could only have been made with adequate lighting, which hasn't existed in the basement of the Marine "A" since 1965, when the elevator was closed down and abandoned. My best guess is that this portrait was sketched by someone who worked at the Marine "A," while it was still in operation and not by someone who entered the building after it had been closed down and abandoned.

On a wall at the bin-floor level of the Superior Elevator, next to a button that caused a horn to sound and thus alert everyone in the area that the "loose leg" (the automotive marine tower) was about to go into operation, we saw the stenciled image of a Native American warrior in silhouette and the word HORNBLOWER. A reference to *Horatio Hornblower*, the swashbuckling hero of C.S. Forester's series of novels, which were published between 1937 and 1962? Seems unlikely. Was Hornblower in fact the name of a Native American warrior? No, apparently not. Perhaps the juxtaposition was a joke. Did the operator of the loose leg like to call himself Hornblower? *Chief* Hornblower? Perhaps the images were added in stages: first HORNBLOWER, then the Native American warrior. The second image could have been put up by a contemporary of the creator of the first one or by a stranger, who came many years later and completely unknown to the first.[25]

Standing in front of such hieroglyphs, Orrin and I would experience what Reyner Banham called "double vision": the apprehension of two images (images of the past

---

[25] For another odd juxtaposition of grain elevators and Native Americans, see the mural entitled "Sainte-Marie among the Hurons," painted by the artist Fred Lenz upon the reinforced-concrete storage tanks at a grain elevator in Midland, Ontario. An inland port on the Georgian Bay, Midland is the home of the Archer-Daniels Midland Milling Company, upon whose elevator Lenz's mural was painted between 1999 and 2001.

and the present) that overlap but do not quite fit together. On our tour of the Standard Elevator in the fall of 1992, one of the men who worked at the elevator, but who wasn't our guide, approached one of us and, indicating the river below, asked, "Do you ever get the feeling that you don't belong here? That the water is drawing you down to it?" Affably phrased, these questions certainly weren't threats or an attempt to "get a rise" out of the person in question (who happened to be afraid of heights), but a kind of confession or taking-into-confidence: *I experience these feelings. Does being up here make you feel them, too?*

It is in the context of his self-mythologizing discussion of his first visit to the Concrete-Central Elevator in Buffalo that Reyner Banham introduces the problematic of the "double vision." Actually, he introduces it twice. First, here:

> Coming out on to the wharf, dominated by the three largest loose legs ever built in Buffalo [...] it was difficult not to see everything through eighteenth-century picturesque visions of ancient sites or even Piranesi's views of the temples of Paestum. Longer study, however, suggested something more like the view that early Christian pilgrims might have taken of Rome: a *double vision* of something that was in itself ancient and therefore to be revered but that was also to be respected for a newer body of meanings laid over it by the beliefs of later peoples. I was looking at one of the great remains of a high and mighty period of constructive art in North America, a historical monument in its own inalienable right. But at a slight cultural remove, I was also – inevitably, given my European and modernist education in architecture – looking at a monument to a different civilization that had been as unknown to its builders as Christianity had been

to the builders of most of the monuments in
Rome: the culture of the European modernist
movement.[26]

I know, I know: it's *preposterous* to claim that American
elevator-designers and European modernist architects lived in
different "civilizations," when they simply lived on different
sides of the Atlantic Ocean, at roughly the same time (the
1910s and 1920s), and yet managed to share a common
interest in reinforced concrete (the *lingua franca* of the
International Style). Bear with me.

> In the presence of the great elevators of
> Minneapolis or Buffalo, I was struck again by the
> cultural width of the Atlantic, by the sheer gulf of
> space and missed understandings that separates
> these structures, admirable and remarkable as they
> are in purely American terms, from those who had
> never stood as close to them as I did and who
> admired their images under quite other lights. The
> difference between the tangible fact and the
> utopian vision of a Concrete Atlantis seemed
> perfectly clear to me, but I wondered if it had also
> struck informed visitors like, say, Erich
> Mendelsohn. Did he never sense another reality
> behind these manifestations of his "silo dreams"?
> Was *the vision double* for him, as it was for me, or
> did he see it with the single eye of faith, in the
> heyday of that idea of modernism, now in decline,
> that we have wished upon these our adoptive
> ancient monuments?[27]

---

[26] Reyner Banham, *A Concrete Atlantis*, pp. 166-168,
my emphasis.

[27] Reyner Banham, *A Concrete Atlantis*, p. 168,
emphasis added.

In both instances, Banham compares his own double visions with those of someone else, thereby producing a doubled-doubling. But he doesn't answer the questions he asks at the end of the second passage, and doesn't return to the theme of the double vision, thereby leaving his readers somewhat at a loss concerning his ultimate meaning.

The answer, I believe, lies in one of Mendelsohn's remarks about the grain elevators that he had seen during his trip Buffalo in 1924: "Childhood forms, clumsy, full of primeval power, dedicated to purely practical needs. Primitive in their functions of ingesting and spewing out again."[28] Mendelsohn certainly didn't believe that he had been looking at the mechanical or architectural equivalents of a human infant. It seems far more likely he believed that America was the literal and figural Child of the Modern Age and that, as a result, she couldn't help but produce forms and functions that harkened back to the childhood of humanity itself. (Had Mendelsohn believed this, he wouldn't have been the only one. At least two other German writers with whom Mendelsohn was no doubt familiar had made the same point with respect to the enduring attraction of ancient Greek art: Karl Marx, in his *Economic and Philosophical Manuscripts of 1844*, and Sigmund Freud, in *The Interpretation of Dreams*.) Putting all the pieces of our puzzle together, we can say that grain elevators symbolize the possibility that the age-old separations between the child and the adult, the ancient and the modern, and the savage and the civilized can one day be dissolved and replaced by the bonds of universal community.

One day in the summer of 1994, in the company of my parents, I traveled by car from our home on Long Island to the family cemetery in New Jersey, a route that took us through Brooklyn, the borough of New York City in which I

---

[28] *Amerika*, Dover Books, New York, 1993, p. 47.

had been born, thirty-five years previously. Though my mother invited everyone in the car to look at the great view of the Manhattan skyline that was presenting itself to our right (we were going south on the Brooklyn Queens Expressway),[29] I didn't feel I needed to interrupt my reading to look at something that I had already seen many times before. But then, just a few minutes later, I experienced a most peculiar sensation: *if I look up right now, I'll see something **really** interesting.* And so I did; and there stood the Gowanus Elevator! I was dumbstruck. I had been reading about, exploring and writing about grain elevators for many years, and had never encountered this grain elevator before; I didn't even know that it existed. I'd presumed that all of the New York's grain elevators had long since been demolished, but I'd been mistaken.

And then it hit me. As a boy, after the family had left Brooklyn for Long Island in 1966, we often traveled along this very route: it was in fact the way to my Grandma Dora's house in Park Slope. No doubt I'd seen this massive, very odd-looking building (not knowing that it was *a grain elevator*, or that it had just recently been closed down, only forty years after its construction), and it made a powerful, even indelible impression on me. The child in me knew exactly where it was and the precise moment to look up and see it (for the first time, again). But prior to that day on the BQE, I'd remembered none of it. For five years I'd believed – we all have our personal mythologies – that I had become interested in grain elevators in Buffalo in 1989, when a fellow student named Seth Tamrowski loaned me his copy of *A Concrete Atlantis*, which was required reading in his architecture class. But I had been wrong: I'd known about the

---

[29] The grain elevators that used to stand on Brooklyn's Atlantic Dock were destroyed in the 1940s and 1950s to "create space" for the construction of this very highway.

Brooklyn grain elevator for thirty years, and I'd been interested, even obsessed, with grain elevators in general ever since I was a child. But it was only then that I realized it.

Appendix
The Grain Elevators of Buffalo

Agway/G.L.F. (concrete), 1936 and 1942, 1.2M

American (concrete), 1906, 2.25M

Arunah B. Nimb (floater), 1866

Bennett (wood), 1864, 800K, taken down 1912

Brown (wood), 1848-1855? 500K

Buffalo (wood), 1846, burned 1870

Buffalo (floater), circa 1865, 125K

Buffalo Lake Shore (transfer tower), 1886, 90K

Buffalo (transfer tower), 1895,

Chicago (transfer tower)

City (wood), 1846, 375K, burned and rebuilt 1859, burned and rebuilt 1863, taken down 1908

City B (wood), 1890, 800K, taken down 1908

C.J. Wells (wood), 1863, 550K, burned 1912

Cloverleaf Mill (steel), 1915 100K, demolished 1934

Coastworth (wood), 1886, burned and rebuilt 1894, 650K, called Kellogg "A," taken down 1909

Coatsworth (transfer tower), 1863, 40K

Coburn, 1861 (wood), burned 1862, rebuilt as the C.J. Wells 1863

Commercial (wood), 1879, burned 1882

Concrete-Central (concrete), 1915-1917, 4.5M

Connecting Terminal (wood), 1882, 950K, burned 1914

Connecting Terminal (concrete), 1914 and 1954, 1.6M

Corn Dock (wood), burned 1865

Cutter & Austin (wood), circa 1863

Cyclone (floater), ca. 1865

Dakota (wood), 1887,
 burned 1900
Dakota (steel), 1901,
 1.25M, demolished 1966
Dart (wood), 1843, 110K,
 burned 1862
Dellwood (concrete), 1914,
 1917 and 1922, +1M,
 demolished 1960s
Dispatch (floater), ca. 1865
Eastern (wood), 1895, 1M
Eastern States (concrete),
 1934 and 1946, 2.5M,
 demolished 2000
Electric (steel), 1897, 1.8M,
 demolished 1984
Electric Annex (concrete),
 1942, 6M
Empire (wood), 1861,
 200K
Empire (floater),
Erie, a.k.a. the New York,
 Lake Erie & Western
 Railroad (wood), 1879,
 700K, burned 1882 and
 rebuilt 1883
Erie Basin (wood), 1854,
 100K, later called the
 Exchange?
Erie Canal (wood),
 originally Clinton Mill
 (Black Rock) 1890

Evans (wood), 1847, 300K,
 burned and rebuilt 1863,
 burned and rebuilt 1864
Evans & Tifft (wood),
 burned 1862, rebuilt
 1863
Excelsior (transfer tower),
 1862, 30K burned 1874
 or 1876
Exchange (wood), 1863,
 200K, burned 1889,
 rebuilt 1890
Export (steel), 1895,
 1,000K
Free Canal (floater)
Free Trade (floater)
Frontier (wood), 1886,
 650K
Fulton (transfer tower),
 1862
George Urban (steel), 1903,
 60K
Grain Dock (wood), burned
 1861
Great Eastern (steel), 1901,
 2.5M, demolished 1948
Great Northern (steel),
 1897, 2.5M
H & O Oats (steel), 1931,
 demolished 2006

Hatch (wood), 1847, 150K,
burned 1847, rebuilt as
the Marine 1848
Hazard (wood), 250K,
burned 1874
Hefford (transfer tower)
Holley & Johnson (wood),
1848-1855, 100K
Hollister (wood), 1847,
burned 1858, rebuilt as
the Ohio Street
Horton (transfer tower),
1866 72,000K
Husted (wood), burned
1899, rebuilt 1907
(concrete), burned 1913
International (wood), 1886
Ira Y. Munn (floater), circa
1865
Iron Elevator (iron), 1902,
600K, demolished 1940
Jan Kan Malting, a.k.a.
John Kam Malting
(steel), 1901, 50K
Kellogg "A" (wood), 1892,
650K, taken down 1912
Kellogg "B" (concrete),
1909, 1M
Kreiner Malting (concrete),
1925 and 1936, 280K
Lake & Rail (concrete),
1927-1930, 4.4M

Lake Shore (wood), 1886
Lyon (wood), circa 1881
Main Street (wood), 1848,
200K, burned 1865,
rebuilt at Hazard, burned
and rebuilt 1881 as the
Lyon
Marine (wood), originally
1848, 200K, burned 1879
and rebuilt 1881, 650K
Marine A (concrete), 1925,
2M
Maritime Milling (tile),
100K
Marquette (floater), circa
1865
Merchants (transfer tower),
30K 1862
Meyer Malting (concrete),
1909, 500K, demolished
2006
Monarch (steel), 1905,
800K, demolished 1950
National and Globe Mills
(wood), 100K, burned
1863
National (transfer tower),
65K (Black Rock?)
New York & Erie (wood),
circa 1865, 200K
Niagara A (wood), 1867,
800K

Niagara B (wood), 1881,
1,200K
Niagara C (wood), 1887,
200K
Niagara (floater)
Northwest (transfer tower)
Ohio Basin (wood), 1863,
burned 1866
Ohio Street (formerly the
Hollister)
Ontario (wood), 1889,
450K, collapsed 1904
Perot Malting (concrete),
1907, 1933, 500K
Plympton (brick), 1868,
later called the Tifft
Queen City (wood), 450K
Ralston Purina (concrete),
1907, 400K
Raymond (floater) 1893,
Raymond (transfer tower),
1893
Raymond (steel), 1897
. Reed (wood), 1847, burned
in 1859, rebuilt 1862,
200K
Richmond (wood), 1863,
250K
Riverside Malting
(concrete), 1907, 200K,
demolished 1965
Ryan (floater), burned 1897

Saskatchewan Pool
(concrete), 1925-1926,
2M
Schreck (transfer tower),
circa 1880
Seymour & Wells (wood),
circa 1865, 125K
Standard (concrete), 1928,
1942, 5M
Sterling (wood), 1847,
Sternberg A (wood), 1847,
burned and rebuilt 1862
Sternberg B (wood), 1861,
burned 1883, 350K
Sturges (wood), 1848-1855,
400K, burned 1866,
rebuild 1867, 350K
Superior (concrete), 1915,
1923, 1925, 4.5M
Swiftsure (wood), 1847,
burned 1862, rebuilt,
150K, demolished after
1889
Tifft (brick), previously
called Plympton, 1868
Union (transfer tower),
circa 1867, 40K
Wadsworth (wood), 1846,
150K, burned 1878
Washburn-Crosby (tile),
1903, 150K

Washburn-Crosby
(concrete), 1909, 1912,
1925
Watson (wood), 1862,
600K, burned 1907
Wells, C.J. (wood), 1861,
renamed Wheeler,
burned 1890, rebuilt
1891
Western (transfer tower)
Wheeler (wood), 1889,
350K, burned 1909

Wheeler (concrete), 1909,
700K
Wilkinson (wood), 1861,
burned 1862, rebuilt
1863,400K
Williams (wood), circa
1865, 150K, later
renamed William Wells
Wollenberg (wood), 1912,
25K, burned 2006

K = one thousand bushels of storage capacity.
M = one million bushels of storage capacity.

Bibliography

Articles and Essays

Brown, Bill [William J.]. "Buffalo's Grain Elevators." *Metropolis*, vol. 12, no. 9, May 1993, pp. 33-36.

Brown, William J. "Walter Gropius and Grain Elevators. Misreading Photographs." *History of Photography*, Autumn 1993, p. 306.

Chang, Andrea. "Chevron reports record profit of $6 billion." *Los Angeles Times*, 2 August 2008.

Cowell, Elspeth. "The Canadian Pavilion at the 1939 New York World's Fair." *Society for the Study of Architecture in Canada Bulletin*, vol. 19, March 1994, p. 23.

Dart, Joseph, Jr. "The Grain Elevators Of Buffalo." *Publications of the Buffalo Historical Society*. 1879.

Fite, Emerson D. "The Canal and the Railroad from 1861 to 1865." *Yale Review*, Volume 15, May 1906 to February 1907. New Haven, 1907, p. 212-213.

Gray, Christopher. "The Columbia Street Grain Elevator: Recycling Red Hook's 1922 Magnificent Mistake." *New York Times*, May 13, 1990.

Gropius, Walter. "Die Entwicklung Moderner Industriebau Kunst." *Industrie und Handel: Jahrbuch des Deutschen Werkbundes.* Jena: Eugen Diederichs, 1913, pp. 17-23.

Gueritte, T.J. "Reinforced Concrete Grain Silos: A General and Historical Survey." *The Structural Engineer*, March 1933, p. 107.

Herbert, Walter B. "Castles of the New World." *The Canadian Geographical Journal*, Vol. 6, No. 5. May 1933, p 255.

Hille, Karl B. "Grain elevator reborn as high-end condos." *The Baltimore Examiner*, 2 November 2007.

Jarzombek, Mark. "The Discourses of a Bourgeois Utopia 1904-1908, and the Founding of the Werkbund." *Rethinking*

German Modernism, National Gallery of Art exhibition catalogue, 1996, p. 131.

Kalman, Harold. "The Elevator is Going Down." *Canadian Heritage*, Vol. 11, No. 1, February/March 1984, pp. 18-24.

Kaplan, Steven Laurence. "Lean Years, Fat Years: the 'Community' Granary System and the Search for Abundance in Eighteenth-Century Paris." *French Historical Studies*, 1977, Vol. 10, Issue 2, page 198.

Krauss, Clifford. "Exxon's Second-Quarter Earnings Set a Record." *New York Times*, August 1, 2008.

Langdale, John. "Impact of the Telegraph on the Buffalo Agriculture Commodity Market: 1846-1848." *The Professional Geographer*, Volume 31, May 1979, Number 2, p. 165.

Marling, Karal Ann. "*My Egypt*: the Irony of the American Dream." *Winterthur Portfolio* 15:1, Spring 1980 p. 34.

McMordie, Michael. "Grain Elevators." *The Canadian Encyclopedia*. Edmonton: Hurtig, 1988.

Overmire, E.P. "Modern Fireproof Grain Elevators." Parts 1 and 2. *Northwestern Miller*: 56, November 18, 25, 1903, pp. 1103-1104, 1155-1156.

Riley, Robert B. "Grain Elevators: Symbols of Time, Place and Honest Building." *AIA Journal*, Vol. 66, No. 2, November 1977, pp. 50-57.

Robbins, Jim. "From Grain Elevator to Dream House." *New York Times*, 14 January 2007.

Rothstein, Morton. "Frank Norris and Popular Perceptions of the Market." *Agricultural History*, volume 56, 1982, p. 58

Sawyer, Tom, *et al.* "Plans Laid for Next Phase As Iraq Rebuild Continues." *Engineering News-Record*, 20 October 2003.

Schmidt, Louis Bernard. "The Grain Trade of the United States, 1860-1890." *Iowa Journal of History and Politics*, State Historical Society of Iowa, 1922, p. 436.

Sommer, Mark. "Fire loss of historic grain elevator is called another case of city neglect." *Buffalo News*, 4 October 2006.

Tunel, George G. "The Diversion of the Flour and Grain Traffic from the Great Lakes to the Railroads." *The Journal of Political Economy*, Vol. 5, No. 3, page 371.

Welch, Jane Meade. "The City Of Buffalo." *Harper's Monthly*, July 1885, p. 197.

Articles and Essays (Author Unknown)

"Buffalo may seek to aid to tear down tragedy elevators." *Courier Express*, 13 April 1976, page 1.

"Famous Inventor: The Death of Mr. Robert Dunbar." *Buffalo Commercial*, September 18, 1890, p. 6.

"Grain-dust explosions." *Engineering News*, Volume 72, 1914, p. 821.

"*Les Mysteres d'un Elevateur a Grains.*" *Album Universel*, 21 October 1905.

"Strikes, Unrest, Bread Riots: Return to the Bad Old Days?" *Middle East & Africa Monitor*, 7 April 2008.

"The Metropolis of the Prairies." *Harper's New Monthly Magazine*, volume 61 1880, p. 726.

"The Tide Water Grain Elevator." *Philadelphia Independent*, April 2004.

"The U.S. Has No Remaining Grain Reserves." *The TriState Observer*. June 10, 2008.

"Traffic On Lake Ontario." *The Rochester Union & Advertiser.* October 21, 1893.

"Ugly But Profitable: The Grain Elevators of Buffalo: Examples of Hideousness in Architecture – A Wonderful Branch of the City's Commerce – Its Inception and Development." *The Buffalo Commercial*, 2 April 1891, page 10.

Books

Abbey, Mark. *Beyond Forget: Rediscovering the Prairies.* Toronto: Douglas & McIntyre, 1986.

Adams, Henry. *Letters. Volumes 4-6: 1892-1918.* Boston: Belknap Press, 1989.

Andreas, A.T. *History of Chicago from the Earliest Period to the Present Time in Three Volumes*. Chicago: A.T. Andreas, 1884.

Atkins, Barton. *Modern Antiquities: Comprising Sketches of Early Buffalo and the Great Lakes*. Buffalo: Courier Company, 1898.

Badger, Daniel. *Illustrations of Iron Architecture*. New York: Baker & Godwin, 1865-1867.

Bakker, Pamela A. *Pondering Four Controversial Sites in Biblical Archaeology: Eden, Noah's Landing, Joseph's Main Granary, the Exodus Crossing Point*. Parker, Colorado: Outskirt Press, 2007.

Banham, Reyner. *A Concrete Atlantis: U.S. Industrial; Building and European Modern Architecture, 1900-1925*. Cambridge, MIT Press, 1986. German translation. *Das gebaute Atlantis: Amerikanische Industrie bauten und die Fruhe Moderne in Europa*, Basel: Birkhauser Verlag, 1990.

Banham, Reyner and Francis R. Kowsky. *Buffalo Architecture: A Guide*. Cambridge: MIT Press, 1981.

Baudelaire, Charles. *Les Fleurs du mal*. 1863, translated by William Aggeler, Fresno, CA: Academy Library Guild, 1954.

Baxter, Henry H. *Grain Elevators*. Buffalo and Erie County Historical Society, 1980.

Becher, Bern and Hilla. *Grain Elevators*. Munich: Schirmer/Mosel Verlag, 2006; Cambridge: MIT Press, 2006.

Behrendt, Walter Curt. *Der Sieg des Neuen Baustils*. 1927, translated as *Modern Building: Its Nature, Problems and Forms*, New York, 1937.

Benjamin, Walter. *Das Passagen-Werk*. Frankfurt am Main: Suhrkamp Verlag, 1982, translated as *The Arcades Project*, Harvard University Press, 1999.

Bergeron, Louis and Maria Teresa Maiullari-Pontois. *Patrimoine industriel des Etats-Unis*. Translated as *Industry, Architecture and Engineering: American Ingenuity 1750-1950*, New York: Harry N. Adams, 2000.

Bower, John. *After the Harvest: Indiana's Historic Grain Elevators and Feed Mills*. Bloomington: Studio Indiana, 2007.

Broehl, Wayne G. *Cargill: Trading the World's Grain*. University Press of New England, 1992.

Brown, Edward J. *Mayakovsky: A Poet in the Revolution*, Princeton: Princeton University Press, 1973.

Caldwell, Erskine and Margaret Bourke-White. *Say, is this the U.S.A.* New York: Da Capo, 1977.

Capote, Truman. *In Cold Blood: A True Account of a Multiple Murder and Its Consequences*. New York: Vintage, 1965.

Cervantes, Miguel de. *Don Quijote*. Translated by Buron Raffel. New York: W.W. Norton, 1999.

Clark, T.J. *The Painting of Modern Life: Paris in the Art of Manet and his Followers*. New York: Knopf, 1986.

Cronon, William. *Nature's Metropolis: Chicago and the Great West*. New York: WW Norton, 1991.

Debord, Guy. *La Societe du Spectacle*. 1967, translated as *The Society of the Spectacle*. Detroit: Black & Red, 1977.

_____. "Abat-Faim." 1985, translated as "Hunger Abatement." New York: NOT BORED! 2004.

_____. *Commentaires sur La Societe du Spectacle*. 1988, translated as *Comments on the Society of the Spectacle*. London: Verso, 1990. NOT BORED! 2004.

Derrida, Jacques. *The Truth in Painting*. 1978, translated by Geoff Bennington and Ian McLeod, University of Chicago, 1987.

Descartes, Rene. *Discourse on the Method of Rightly Conducting the Reason, and Searching for Truth in the Sciences*. London: Thames Newcomb, 1649.

Desnes, Agnes. *The Human Argument: The Writings of Agnes Denes*. Putnam, Connecticut: Spring Publications, Putnam, 2008.

Edgar, William C. *The Story of a Grain of Wheat*. New York: McClure, Phillips & Co., 1903.

Ensminger, Audrey. *The Food and Nutrition Encyclopedia, A to H*. CRC Press, 1994.

Fielding, Mary S. *Prairie Sky Scrapers: A Pictorial Record of Grain Elevators in Iroquois County, 1986-1989*. Iroquois County Historical Society, 1989.

Flaubert, Gustave. *The Letters of Gustave Flaubert, 1857-1880*. Translated by Francis Steegmuller, Harvard University Press, 1982.

Foucault, Michel. *Security, Territory, Population: Lectures at the College de France, 1977-1978*. London: Palgrave, 2007.

Frazer, James George. *The Golden Bough: A Study in Magic and Religion*. London: Palgrave, 1914.

Freud, Sigmund. *Die Traumdeutung*. 1899, translated by Joyce Crick. London: Oxford University Press, 1999.

George, Henry. *Progress and Poverty*. New York, 1879.

Giedion, Siegfried. *Space, Time and Architecture*. German original, 1941; Harvard University Press, 1967.

Ginzburg, Moisei. *Style and Epoch*. Translated by Anatole Senekevitch, Jr. Cambridge: MIT Press, 1982.

Gohlke, Frank. *Measure of Emptiness: Grain Elevators in the American Landscape*. Baltimore: Johns Hopkins University Press, 1992.

Graham, Benjamin. *Storage and Stability: A Modern Ever-normal Granary*. New York: McGraw Hill, 1937.

Hamlin, Talbot. *Forms and Functions of Twentieth Century Architecture*. Four volumes. New York: Columbia University Press, 1952.

Harris, George H. *The Life of Horatio Jones*. Buffalo Historical Society, 1903.

Heidegger, Martin. *Poetry, Language, Thought*. Translated by Albert Hofstadter. New York, 1971.

Hill, Charles S. *Reinforced Concrete: Part Two: Representative Structures*. Second edition. New York: Engineering New Publishing Company, 1906.

Hill, Henry Wayland. *Municipality of Buffalo, New York, A History. 1720-1923*. New York: Lewis Historical Publishing Company, 1923.

Hobbes, Thomas. *Leviathan or the Matter, Forme, & Power of a*

Common-Wealth Ecclesiastic and Civill. London: Andrew
Crooke, 1651.

Holder, Robert. *The Beginnings of Buffalo Industry*. Volume V,
Adventures in Western New York History, Buffalo & Erie
County Historical Society, 1959.

Kant, Immanuel. *The Critique of Judgment*. German original 1790,
translated by Werner S. Pluhar, Indianapolis, Hackett, 1990.

Kesey, Ken. *One Flew Over the Cuckoo's Nest*. Viking, New
York, 1962.

Ketchum, Milo S. *The Design of Walls, Bins and Grain Elevators*.
Engineering News Publishing Company, New York, 1911.
Revised and enlarged. New York: McGraw Hill, 1919.

King, Philip and Lawrence Stager. *Life in Biblical Israel*.
Westminster: John Knox Press, 2002.

Kipling, Rudyard. *The Writings in Prose and Verse of Rudyard
Kipling: Letters of Travel*. vol. 24, New York, 1920.

Lawrence, Felicity. *Eat Your Heart Out: Why the Food Business Is
Bad for the Planet and Your Health*. Penguin Books, London,
2008.

Leacock, Stephen. *My Discovery of the West*. Boston and New
York: Hale, Cushman & Flint, 1937.

Leary, Thomas E. and Elizabeth C. Sholes. *Images of America:
Buffalo's Waterfront*. Buffalo: Arcadia Publishing, 1997.

Le Corbusier. *Vers une architecture*. 1923, translated by Frederick
Etchells, *Towards a New Architecture*. New York: Dover
Books, 1986.

Lefebvre, Henri. *The Production of Space*. 1974, translated by
Donald-Nicholson Smith. London: Blackwell, 1991.

Lucas, Adam. *Wind, Water, Work: Ancient and Medieval Milling
Technology*. Leiden: Brill Publishers, 2006.

Mahar-Keplinger, Lisa. *Grain Elevators*. New York: Princeton
University Press, 1993.

Mansfield, J.B. *History of the Great Lakes, Volume I*. Chicago:
J.H. Beers, 1899.

Marcus, Greil. *The Shape of Things to Come: Prophecy and the
American Voice*. New York: Picador, 2006.

Marx, Karl. *Das Kapital*, vol. 1, orig. 1864; Hamburg reprint, 1922.

McDonnell, Greg. *Wheat Kings: Vanishing Landmarks of the Canadian Prairies*. Erin, Ontario: Boston Mills Press, 1998.

McLachlan, Elizabeth. *Gone But Not Forgotten: Tales of the Disappearing Grain Elevators*. Edmonton: NeWest, 2004.

Mendelsohn, Erich. *Letters of An Architect*. Edited by Oskar Beyer, translated by Geoffrey Strachan, London: Abelard-Schumann, 1967.

_____. *Erich Mendelsohn: Complete Works of the Architect: Sketches, Designs, Buildings*. New York: Princeton Architectural Press, 1992.

_____. *Amerika*. New York: Dover Books, 1993.

Morgan, Dan. *Merchants of Grain*. New York: Viking, 1979.

Muller-Wulckow, Walter. *Deutsche Baukunst der Gegenwart*, volume I. Leipzig: Langewiesche, 1929.

Mumford, Lewis. *Technics and Civilization*. New York: Harcourt, Brace, 1934.

_____. *The Culture of Cities*. New York: Harcourt, Brace, 1938.

_____. *The City in History: Its Origins, Its Transformations, and Its Prospects*. New York: Harcourt, Brace, 1961.

Munce, James F. *Industrial Architecture: An Analysis of International Building Practices*. New York: F.W. Dodge, 1960.

Nerdinger, Winfried. *The Architect Walter Gropius*. Exhibition catalogue, Bauhaus-Archiv, 1985, expanded 1996.

_____. *The Walter Gropius Archive*, Vol. 1. Illustrated catalogue, Harvard University Press, 1990.

Pevsner, Nikolaus. *An Outline of European Architecture*. 1943; Harmonsworth: Penguin, fifth edition, 1957.

Platz, Gustav Adolph. *Die Baukunst der Neuesten Zeit*. Berlin, 1927.

Posener, Julius. *Hans Poelzig: Reflections on His Life and Work*. Cambridge: MIT Press, 1992.

Robinson, Mansel. *Street Wheat*. Regina: Coteau Books, 2003.

Sandburg, Carl. *Cornhuskers*. New York: Henry Holt & Co., 1918.

Schneekloth, Lynda (ed). *Reconsidering Concrete Atlantis: Buffalo Grain Elevators*. Buffalo, Urban Design Project, 2006.

Scully, Vincent. *American Architecture and Urbanism*. New York: Praeger, 1969.

Severance, Frank H. *Historical Sketch of the Board of Trade, the Merchants' Exchange and the Chamber of Commerce of Buffalo*. Buffalo Historical Society, 1909.

Severance, Frank H. *Picture Book of Earlier Buffalo*. Buffalo Historical Society, 1912.

Shakespeare, William. *The Unabridged William Shakespeare*. Running Press, Philadelphia, 1989.

Sharfarevich, Igor. *The Socialist Perspective*. Translated by William Tjalsma. New York: Harper & Row, 1980.

Shell, Marc. *Money, Language, and Thought: Literary and Philosophical Economies from the Medieval to the Modern Era*. Berkeley: University of California Press, 1982.

Shelton, Brenda Kurtz. *Reformers in Search of Yesterday: Buffalo in the 1890s*. Albany: SUNY, 1976.

Silversides, Brock V. *Prairie Sentinel: The Story of the Canadian Grain Elevator*. Calgary: Fifth House, 1999.

Smith, H. Perry. *History of the City of Buffalo and Erie County*. Syracuse: D. Mason, 1884.

Smith, William and Charles Anthon. *A Dictionary of Greek and Roman Antiquities*. New York: Harper & Brothers, 1847.

Stubbles, Russell. *Skyscrapers of the Prairie: South Dakota's Historic Wooden Grain Elevators*. Brookings: Harold's Printing Company, 1997.

Taut, Bruno. *Die Neue Baukunst in Europa und Amerika*. Bilingual edition, translated as *Modern Architecture*. London, the Studio, 1929.

Trollope, Anthony. *North America*. Edited with notes by Donald Smally and Bradford Allen Booth. New York: Knopf, 1951.

Trollope, Frances. *Domestic Manners of the Americans*. Original, 1832, edited by Donald Smalley. New York: Knopf, 1949.

Van Metre, Thurman. *An Economic History of the United States*. New York: H. Holt & Co., 1921.

Van Tielhof, Milja. *The 'Mother of All Trades': The Baltic Grain Trade in Amsterdam from the Late 16th to the Early 19th Century*. Leiden: Brill, 2002.

Venturi, Robert, and Denise Brown and Steven Izenour. *Learning from Las Vegas: The Forgotten Symbolism of Architectural Form*. Cambridge: MIT Press, 1972; revised edition, 1977.

Vernant, Jean-Pierre. *Myth and Thought Among the Greeks*. French original 1965; translated into English, London: 1983.

Viel, Charles-Francois. *De l'Impuissance des mathematiques pour assurer la solidite des batiments*. Paris, 1805.

Virilio, Paul. *The Original Accident*. Cambridge: Polity, 2007.

Vitruvivus. *The Ten Books on Architecture*. Translated by Morris Hicky Morgan, Harvard University Press, 1914.

Volkmer, Jon. *The Art of the Country Grain Elevators*. Huron, Ohio: Bottom Dog Press, 2006.

Wallace, Henry A. *Henry A. Wallace: Democracy Reborn*. New York: Reynal and Atitchcock, 1944.

Weber, Helmut. *Walter Gropius und das Faguswerk*. Munich: G.D.W. Callwey, 1961.

Whiteley, Nigel. *Reyner Banham: Historian of the Immediate Future*. Cambridge: MIT Press, 2001.

Worringer, Wilhelm. *Egyptian Art*. Translated by Bernard Rackham, London: G.P. Putnam's, 1928.

Zevi, Bruno. *Erich Mendelsohn: The Complete Works*. Basel: Birkhauser, 1999.

Dissertations

Lee, Guy A. *History of the Chicago Grain Elevator Industry, 1850-1890*. Harvard University, 1938.

Odle, Thomas D. *The American Grain Trade of the Great Lakes, 1825-1875*. University of Michigan, 1951.

Thrush, Alan J. *Organization and Strategies for Grain Producers and the Grain Industry*. Michigan State University, 2003.

Government Reports, Publications and Submissions
"Grades of Grain, Established by the Committee on Grain of the
New York Produce Exchange." *Report of the New York
Produce Exchange for the Year 1879.* New York: Jones,
1880, pp. 181-182.
*Historical Sketch and Matters Appertaining to the Granary Burial
Ground.* Cemetery Department of the City of Boston, 1902.
Frame, Robert M. "Grain Elevators in Minnesota to 1945."
National Register of Historical Places – Multiple Property
Documentation Form 1990, Section F, Page 7, dated 1989.
Frame, Robert M. and Jeffrey A. Hess, "Northwestern
Consolidated Elevator A: Written Historical and Descriptive
Data," Historic American Engineering Record, HAER No.
MN-16, January 1990.
*Report of the New York Commerce Commission, Volume II,
transmitted to the legislature January 25, 1900.* Albany,
1900, p. 1225.
*Supplement to the Annual Report of the State Engineer and
Surveyor for the Year Ended June 30, 1921.* Albany, 1922.

On-line Resources
Buffalo Architecture and History
http://www.buffaloah.com
Buffalo History Works
http://www.buffalohistoryworks.com
Buffalo Rising
http://www.buffalorising.com
Buffalonian, The
http://www.buffalonian.com
Danzig/Gdansk, Poland
http://sabaoth.infoserve.pl/danzig-online/index.html
Duluth/West Superior railroads
http://duluthsuperior.railfan.net
Fix Buffalo Blog
http://fixbuffalo.blogspot.com

Historic American Engineering Record
http://memory.loc.gov/ammem/collections/habs_haer/
Maine Memory Network
http://www.mainememory.net
Maritime History of the Great Lakes
http://www.hhpl.on.ca/GreatLakes/
Minnesota Historical Society
http://www.mnhs.org
NOT BORED!
http://www.notbored.org
Ogdensburg, New York
http://www.ogdensburg.info
Portland, Oregon waterfront
http://www.portlandwaterfront.org
Wheat Genetic and Genomic Resources Center
https://www.ksu.edu/wgrc/

Postcards

Malderen, Luc Van. *American Architecture: A Vintage Postcard Collection.* Australia: Images Publishing Group, 2000.

Mayer, John. *Workshop of the World*. Philadelphia: Oliver Evans Press, 1990.

Translated Anthologies

Bann, Stephen (ed). *The Tradition of Constructivism*. New York: Da Capo, 1990.

Benton, Tim and Charlotte (ed). *Form and Function: A Source Book for the History of Architecture and Design, 1890-1939.* London: Crosby Lockwood, 1975.

Bowlt, John E. ed.. *Russian Art of the Avant Garde*. London: Thames and Hudson, 1976.

Harrison, Charles and Paul Wood (ed). *Art in Theory, 1900-2000: An Anthology of Changing Ideas*. London: Blackwell Publishing, 2003.

Index

abstract art, 276-277, 279-282, 287, 311, 316-318, 330
abstract grid-plans, 76, 77n
abstract markets, 139, 253n, 391
abstract space, 322-325, 401
adaptive reuse, 401-404
Akron, Ohio, 402
Albany, New York, 69, 88-90, 132, 142, 234
America, discovery of, 282, 330, 378-381
America, the United States of, 54, 76, 83, 87, 184, 252-253, 254, 317, 318, 322, 367, 368, 372, 385ff, 409
American
  agriculture, 2, 27-28, 48, 57, 59-60, 92-93, 101, 149, 243, 376, 377, 385, 388
  architecture, 287, 289, 331, 348, 365
  canals, 70, 83
  capitalism, 227, 273, 283-284, 324, 368
  Ceres, 243, 254
  cities, 71, 94, 144n, 242, 371-372, 376
  Colossus, 184, 236ff, 296, 385, 390
  cultural epic, 329
  empire, 72, 84, 184
  exports, 148
  grain, 11, 20, 21, 48, 49, 57, 175, 181-182, 204, 252, 253, 376, 391
  industrial buildings, 131, 283, 285ff, 297, 300, 312-313, 317-318, 322, 324, 328, 332, 346, 356, 409
  inventors, 104
  foreign policy, 16, 28
  modernity, 390, 391, 410
  mythology, 364
  natives (*see* "Native Americans")
  power, 243
  recolonization, 30
  rural areas, 326-327, 372-373, 375
  spatial practices, 324
  style of elevator design, 44n, 45, 146n, 221, 227, 278, 319, 328, 403
  wars, 73, 228
American Elevator, the, 178, 224-227, 230, 302n, 303, 304, 404, 413
Andre Grain Company, 14, 15

Figure 1. "First Shipment of Grain from Chicago's first dock." Loading grain into the *Osceola of Buffalo* from Newberry & Dole's warehouse in Chicago.
An event from 1830 celebrated in 1884.
Note the "spectacular" absence of crowds of people.

From *History of Chicago from the Earliest Period to the Present Time, in Three Volumes.*
(Chicago: A.T. Andreas, 1884).
Courtesy Maritime History of the Great Lakes.

AN OLD TIMER AT OUR ELEVATOR, BUFFALO, N.Y.

Figure 2. "An Old Timer at C.T.T. elevator, Buffalo, NY." Unloading grain at the Connecting Terminal Elevator, circa 1882. The elevator leg that has been lowered down into the storage compartment of the "old time" steam-powered, wood-hulled vessel owned by the *Lackawanna Green Bay Line* is part of the world's first mobile marine tower. Its height can be suggested by the great height of the internal "lofting" leg (not a marine tower) at the neighboring structure. Note as well the congestion of the harbor and the various sizes of the vessels competing for access to the wharves.

Courtesy the Library of Congress, Prints & Photographs Division, Detroit Publishing Company.

Figure 3. "The Canal Harbor, Buffalo, New York." The entrance to the City Ship Canal, circa 1920. From the left: part of the Great Eastern; all of the Dakota; a wooden marine tower (part of the old Frontier Elevator) that would soon after be demolished and replaced; part of Washburn-Crosby's unique cylindrical marine tower; and (behind the raised bridge) the Great Northern.

Courtesy the Library of Congress, Prints & Photographs Division, Detroit Publishing Company.

Figure 4. "Buffalo, New York. Grain Elevators on the Erie Canal."
Along the City Ship Canal. From the left: part of the Connecting
Terminal; the Dakota; and the Washburn-Crosby Complex (later a
part of General Mills). Note the two marine towers in operation on
the same vessel: one is cylindrical and made of reinforced
concrete; the other is rectangular and made of iron and steel.

Photographed by Marjory Collins, 1943.
Courtesy the Library of Congress, Prints & Photographs Division,
Farm Security Administration, Office of War Information.

Figure 5. "Close-up view of tripper." The Standard Elevator, Buffalo, New York. Located on the bin floor, the tripper (sometimes called a trimmer) sweeps grain from the horizontal conveyor-belt into the top of a grain bin through a chute. Note the great length of that conveyor-belt. Each of those small circles along the left-hand side is the capped opening to a towering grain silo made of reinforced concrete.

Photographed by Jet Low, 1990.
Courtesy the Library of Congress, Prints & Photographs Division, Historic American Engineering Record.

Figure 6. "Detail of concrete bin bottom and conveyor." The
Standard Elevator, Buffalo, New York. Located in the
building's basement, the hopper conducts grain from the bin
above it onto a horizontal conveyor-belt. Note the long
corridor-like crawl-space at the lower right.

Photographed by Jet Low, 1990.
Courtesy the Library of Congress, Prints & Photographs Division,
Historic American Engineering Record.

Figure 7. The Concrete-Central Elevator in Buffalo, New
York. A quarter-mile in length and over 150 feet tall. The
three loose legs are unloading grain from a single lake vessel.
On our right side, other vessels cluster near the elevator's
transfer tower. Note the height the photographer needed to
reach in order to take this photograph.

Photographed by Hare, Buffalo, NY, on 15 January 1919.
Courtesy of the Library of Congress, Prints & Photographs Division.

The author. Photo © 2008 Reid R. Radcliffe.